SUCCEEDING WITH AGILE

Praise for *Succeeding with Agile*

"Understanding the mechanics of an agile process is just not enough. Mike Cohn has compiled a superb and comprehensive collection of advice that will help individuals and teams with the intricate task of adopting and adapting agile processes to fit their specific challenges. This book will become the definitive handbook for agile teams."
—**Colin Bird**, Global Head of Agile, EMC Consulting

"Mike Cohn's experience working with so many different organizations in the adoption of agile methods shines through with practical approaches and valuable insights. If you really want agile methods to stick, this is the book to read."
—**Jeff Honious**, Vice President, Innovation, Reed Elsevier

"Mike Cohn has done it again. *Succeeding with Agile* is based on his experience, and all of our experience, with agile to date. He covers from the earliest days of the project up to maturity and offers advice for the individual, the team, and the enterprise. No matter where you are in the agile cycle, this book has something for you!"
—**Ron Jeffries**, www.XProgramming.com

"If you want to start or take the next step in agile software development, this book is for you. It discusses issues, great solutions, and helpful guidelines when scaling up in agile projects. We used the guidelines from this book extensively when we introduced agile in a large, FDA-regulated department."
—**Christ Vriens**, Department Head of MiPlaza, part of Philips Research

"If making the move to agile has always baffled you, then this book will unlock its mysteries. Mike Cohn gives us all the definitive, no-nonsense guide to transforming your organization into a high-powered, innovative, and competitive success."
—**Steve Greene**, Senior Director, Program Management and Agile Development, www.salesforce.com

"Mike Cohn is a great advisor for transforming your software organization. This book is a distillation of everything Mike has learned over the years working with companies that are trying to become more agile. If you are thinking of going agile, pick up this book."
—**Christopher Fry**, Ph.D., Vice President Development, Platform, www.salesforce.com

"Whether you're just starting out or have some Scrum experience under your belt, in *Succeeding with Agile*, Mike Cohn provides a wealth of information to guide you in your quest toward continuous improvement. Throughout the book, concepts are reinforced with practical everyday advice, including how to handle objections and thought-provoking 'things to try now.' An extensive list of recommended readings round this out to be a must have book."
—**Nikki Rohm**, Studio Director Project and Resource Management, Electronic Arts

"The first steps along the path of improving your software process with Scrum are hard, and every step reveals new challenges. In *Succeeding with Agile*, Mike Cohn shows how other organizations have followed this path, how you can learn from them to have a successful implementation of Scrum, and put your organization on the path of constant improvement and delivery of value."
—**Johanes Brodwall**, Chief Scientist, Steria Norway

"I began to recommend Mike Cohn's new book as soon as I began to review it. It seems that as soon as someone asked me a question about some corner of agile development, I would realize that I had just read something excellent in one of Mike's chapters. I am so glad the book is finally out so I can stop saying, 'Mike Cohn has a great new book coming out soon that will talk about this problem.' Now I can say, 'Mike's book is out! Get it!'"
—**Linda Rising**, Coauthor with Mary Lynn Manns of *Fearless Change: Patterns for Introducing New Ideas*

"The title says it all; this is an astonishingly insightful and pragmatic guide to succeeding with agile software development. If you only read one agile book, this is the one. I want to give it to all my clients now!"
—**Henrik Kniberg**, Agile Coach, Agile Alliance Board Member, Author of *Scrum and XP from the Trenches*

"Mike Cohn blends thorough theoretical knowledge with practical hands-on techniques. This is another great agile book from Mike. It will help your team, your department, or your whole organization *Succeed with Agile*."
—**Matt Truxaw**, Application Delivery Manager, Kaiser Permanente IT, Certified Scrum Master

"Mike Cohn's new book is the definitive guide for companies transitioning to Scrum. Its contents are practical and easily accessible. Get it, read it, and apply it!"
—**Roman Pichler**, Author of *Agile Product Management with Scrum*

"*Succeeding with Agile* is at once enormously practical, deeply insightful, and a pleasure to read. It combines great ideas with stories and examples from around the software industry and will appeal to a wide range of readers, from those looking to adopt a new company-wide agile process to developers who just need to improve the way a team is running a single project."
—**Andrew Stellman**, Developer, Project Manager, and Author of *Head First PMP*, *Beautiful Teams*, *Applied Software Project Management*

"Adopting agile methods is hard enough on a greenfield web app in a small company. Transforming an enterprise is another matter. This book captures challenges like the ones we faced and offers insight and, more importantly, practical approaches."
—**Michael Wollin**, Senior Development Manager, Broadcast Production Systems, CNN

"Mike Cohn has put together a fantastic book of guidelines to not only start the Scrum implementation, but to turn your entire corporation into an agile community. I have already implemented many of the recommendations included in this text and have seen a positive influence on the support for Scrum within our organization."
—**James Tischart**, CSM, CSP, CTFL, Vice President, Product Delivery, Mx Logic, Inc

"In *Succeeding with Agile*, Mike Cohn has scoured and sifted through the collective experience and lessons of not only scores of different projects, teams, and organizations from his own agile experience, but also from the experience of countless others. He provides real-world stories from the trenches, useful data and studies, and invaluable insights into what has and hasn't worked well when adopting, adapting, and scaling Scrum. What I like best about the book is where Mike provides wisdom on several different alternatives and approaches and the circumstances in which each is most suitable."
—**Brad Appleton**, Internal Agile Consultant at a Fortune 100 telecommunications company

"I believe Mike Cohn's book will answer many questions and issues that people and teams struggle with in terms of how to improve collaboration, communication, quality, and team productivity. I especially appreciate and agree with Mike's statement that 'there can be no end state in a process that calls for continuous improvement.' This is hard work and it requires persistence, teamwork, and good people. I plan to make *Succeeding with Agile* mandatory reading within my organization, just like we did with his book on *Agile Estimating and Planning*."
—**Scott Spencer**, Vice President Engineering, First American CoreLogic, Inc.

"Mike Cohn has done it again. This comprehensive study of agile software development provides numerous techniques and methodologies to achieve success. I enthusiastically recommend this book to anyone who wants to start using agile or wants to improve their software development process."
—**Benoit Houle**, Senior Development Manager, BioWare (a Division of Electronic Arts)

"There's no doubt that Mike Cohn's new book will become the reference on how to run software projects with Scrum. The book is very carefully crafted and avoids the trap of giving you the one, simple recipe to all your problems. Though mainly centered on Scrum, Mike draws on various other techniques to produce a handbook that is thorough and complete. This is not a hasty mash-up supported by just an act of faith or a single experience. The examples are credible and are a testimony of Mike's vast personal experience of the topic."
—**Philippe Kruchten**, Professor of Software Engineering at University of British Columbia

"This book is packed with useful advice on how your organization can become agile. It's a practical handbook for coaches and change agents who face real-world challenges, such as scaling agile for distributed teams, and who seek to engage with the wider organization. I love the way that Mike Cohn brings the book to life with stories from situations he's faced in the industry and follows up with data and insights from research. I learned something new from every chapter, and I bet you will too."
—**Rachel Davies**, Coauthor of *Agile Coaching*

SUCCEEDING WITH AGILE

Software Development Using Scrum

MIKE COHN

✦✦Addison-Wesley

Upper Saddle River, NJ • Boston • Indianapolis • San Francisco
New York • Toronto • Montreal • London • Munich • Paris • Madrid
Cape Town • Sydney • Tokyo • Singapore • Mexico City

The publisher offers excellent discounts on this book when ordered in quantity for bulk purchases or special sales, which may include electronic versions and/or custom covers and content particular to your business, training goals, marketing focus, and branding interests. For more information, please contact

    U.S. Corporate and Government Sales
    (800) 382-3419
    corpsales@pearsontechgroup.com

For sales outside the United States, please contact

    International Sales
    international@pearson.com

Visit us on the Web: www.informit.com/aw

The Library of Congress Cataloging-in-Publication data is on file.

ISBN-13: 978-0-321-57936-2
ISBN-10: 0-321-57936-4
Text printed in the United States on recycled paper at Edwards Brothers in Ann Arbor, Michigan.
Fifth Printing February 2011

Editor-in-Chief
Karen Gettman

Executive Editor
Chris Guzikowski

Senior Development Editor
Chris Zahn

Managing Editor
Kristy Hart

Project Editor
Jovana San Nicolas-Shirley

Copy Editor
San Dee Phillips

Indexer
Lisa Stumpf

Proofreader
Karen Gill

Publishing Coordinator
Raina Chrobak

Cover Designer
Alan Clements

Compositors
Jake McFarland
Bumpy Design

To Laura, Savannah, and Delaney
for making me the one who knows.

Contents

Foreword

All the time I hear people talking about software projects as journeys, and I think they are implying that software projects are not just journeys, but they are journeys into the unknown. We start with funding from a sponsor, muster together a stout-hearted crew, head out in what we guess might be a useful direction, and the rest is The Odyssey. We live the tales of the brave Odysseus: tales of Lotus Eaters, the Cyclops, Circe, the Sirens, Scylla, and Calypso. We succeed or fail only with the help or rage of the gods. How wonderfully romantic, and how perfectly silly.

I think that the more appropriate analogy along this line is the project as an expedition. We have a goal or a short list of goals. We have some well-proven maps; we have some vaguer ones, too. We have the advice and journals from those who have been out there and made it back to tell their stories.

We don't walk out the door and face the unknown; but on the other hand, there are some big question marks, and these bring us into a high-risk position. We accept these risks, because if the expedition can succeed there are surely significant rewards. We have skills, but there are uncertainties.

How do we deal with this? I recommend that we look back, oh, about 300 years, to the York Factory on Hudson Bay in Canada. At that time this was the headquarters of the Hudson Bay Company. The Hudson Bay Company's main line of business was to be the supplier of all necessary provisions for fur traders going out on, you guessed it, expeditions, from Hudson Bay. The fur traders developed a great way to start an expedition, and it was called "The Hudson Bay Start." Having done their one-stop shopping at The Company, the fur traders would go out of Hudson Bay only a mile or two and set up camp. Why? Certainly not to set up traps; they wanted to discover what they forgot to bring while they were less than an hour's hike back into town! Being the excellent project person that you are, you know that for the vast majority of time the leather-faced expert fur trader would reappear for another shopping trip.

What the heck does all this have to do with the book in your hands right now? With *Succeeding with Agile,* Mike Cohn has delivered The Hudson Bay Start for agile development. This is it. This is a weather-beaten experienced fur trapper giving you *the* checklist to work through before you begin your expedition. By reading this book, you will find that Mike brings up issues that you never thought of, offers advice on how you might handle situations, and helps you define new roles on your team.

Don't be the only person on your team to read this book; with self-organizing teams anyone can be expedition leader at any given time. This book is going to lead to many very interesting discussions; I guarantee it.

I worry a bit that I am saying that Mike has handed you a book without choices for you. He points out early and often that you must make your choices on individual, team, and organizational issues.

Succeeding with Agile is not about having a single successful project; it is about how agility can transform an organization. I guess in Hudson Bay terms, it's about how to have a great career as Voyageurs.

If you have any lingering doubts about Mike as an experienced expedition leader, notice that his company is Mountain Goat Software.

Tim Lister
Principal, The Atlantic Systems Guild, Inc.
New York City

Acknowledgments

I owe a tremendous debt to my official reviewers: Brad Appleton, Johannes Brodwall, Rachel Davies, Ron Jeffries, Brian Marick, and Linda Rising. They read and commented on the entire manuscript, sometimes multiple times. Each offered tremendously valuable insights that have immeasurably improved the book.

Special thanks also to Tod Golding, Kenny Rubin, Rebecca Traeger, and my wife, Laura, who spent hours discussing the table of contents with me. There were times we thought those conversations would never end.

There's no way to thank Rebecca Traeger enough. She is a miracle worker as an editor, adviser, and sounding board. As she is the former editor for the Agile Alliance and the Scrum Alliance, I contend that she is the best-read person in the agile world. She's also the world's greatest editor. She worked wonders with this book, doing more slicing and dicing than a Veg-O-Matic on a late-night infomercial. This book is significantly better for her involvement in it.

Wow. A foreword by Tim Lister. I'm incredibly honored. I've known Tim for a handful of years, and so I e-mailed him to ask if he'd write the Foreword. I didn't know it, but he was vacationing at the time I e-mailed him and so he replied a week later. I saw the e-mail reply first on my phone, which only displayed the first two lines. Before I tapped the message to see the full e-mail, I had flashbacks of getting college admission letters—would it be good news or bad news? I was ecstatic when he said yes. I was then doubly thrilled when he had such nice things to say in his Foreword. Thank you, Tim.

My assistant, Jennifer Rai, provided invaluable help throughout this project. From tracking down references, to getting permissions, to keeping my research organized, she did it all. I appreciate her dedication, professionalism, and the consistent thoroughness of her work. I couldn't ask for more in an assistant.

For the past two years I have been posting chapters to this book's website at www.SucceedingWithAgile.com. I have been fortunate to have had a wonderful group of people download, review chapters, and provide comments to me. I would like to thank the following individuals for reading draft chapters posted on that site or for providing anecdotes that made their way into the book: Fridtjof Ahlswede, Peter Alfvin, Ole Andersen, Joshua Boelter, Mikael Boman, Rowan Bunning, Butterscotch, Bill Campbell, Mun-Wai Chung, Scott Collins, Jay Conne, John Cornell, Lisa Crispin, Alan Dayley, Ken DeLong, Scott Duncan, Sigfrid Dusci, Mike Dwyer, Pablo Rodriguez Facal, Abby Fichtner, Hillel Glazer, Karen Greaves, Janet Gregory, Ratha Grimes, Geir Hedemark, Fredrik Hedman, Ben Hogan, Matt Holmes, Sue Holstad, Benoit Houle, Eric Jimmink, Quinn Jones,

Martin Kearns, Jeff Langr, Paul Lear, Lowell Lindstrom, Catherine Louis, Rune Mai, Artem Marchenko, Kent McDonald, Susan McIntosh, Alicia McLain, Ulla Merz, Ralph Miner, Brian Lewis Pate, Trond Pedersen, David Peterson, Roman Pichler, Walter Ries, Adam Rogers, René Rosendahl, Kenny Rubin, Mike Russell, Michael Sahota, George Schlitz, Lori Schubring, Raffi Simonian, Jamie Tischart, Ryan Toone, Matt Truxaw, J. F. Unson, Srinivas Vadhri, Stefan van den Oord, Bas Vodde, Bill Wake, Daniel Wildt, Trond Wingård, Rüdiger Wolf, Elizabeth Woodward, Nick Xidis, Alicia Yanik, and Mauricio Zamora.

Thank you to Jeff Schaich who did a wonderful job creating the illustrations for this book. When I was first introduced to Jeff, I was told he might be as much of a perfectionist as I am. He may be, and his drawings show it.

Stephen Wilbers, author of *Keys to Great Writing*, provided some much needed editing and advice early on. I am thankful for his suggestions and encouragement.

As always, the staff at Pearson was wonderful to work with. Chris Guzikowski showed tremendous patience with me, especially early on when I refused to commit to a deadline of any sort. Chris Zahn provided excellent guidance during those early days when I was working to organize what I wanted to say. Jake McFarland designed the interior of the book and did a wonderful job. Jake also showed tremendous patience with my endless barrage of InDesign questions, for which I am extremely thankful. Raina Chrobak was extremely helpful throughout the project, but especially down the home stretch, which is always a frantic period.

Jovana San-Nicolas Shirley was fantastic as this book's project editor. She kept everything moving smoothly, coordinating each of us involved in the final months of the project. I appreciate her willing replies to my e-mails at all hours of the day and night. San Dee Phillips did a top-notch (or is it top notch?) job for the final copy edit. I thank her for going over the manuscript at exactly the right level and for so carefully finding all the last little errors that really polished the text.

Thank you as well to cover designer Alan Clements. What a beautiful cover! Can you judge a book by its cover? I hope so based on the number of people who have already told me they love this one. Lisa Stumpf did a marvelous job with our indexing. She herself should be indexed under thorough and meticulous. Karen Gill did the final proofreading and was fantastic at finding all the little inconsistencies and problems. Kim Scott of Bumpy Design took care of the final page composition. I appreciate her joining at the end to help all of us make the deadline.

I would also like to thank Chris Guzikowski and Karen Gettman of Pearson for offering me the opportunity to edit a Signature Series of books for Addison-Wesley. I can still clearly remember sitting at Ken Kaplan's place in Ben Lomond in the woods of California in 1985 reading *C Primer Plus*. It was written by Stephen Prata but was part of a series by Mitchell Waite. I didn't know what a series editor did, but it sounded important and cool. Now I'm learning what a series editor does and am incredibly honored by their confidence in me.

My thanks also go to Lyssa Adkins, Lisa Crispin, Janet Gregory, Clinton Keith, Roman Pichler, and Kenny Rubin. Each has written or is writing a book that will be part of this series. We have had many discussions about writing, agile, how to make certain points, and more. Through these discussions, each has improved this book.

A special thank you to all of my clients and to everyone who has ever attended one of my classes. I'm not smart enough to sit around, think big thoughts, and come up with great ideas on my own. Everything I know I've learned from working with teams and observing what worked or from talking with participants in classes. This book would be four pages long if not for you. Thank you.

Thank you to Ken Schwaber, Jeff Sutherland, Mike Beedle, Jeff McKenna, Martine Devos, and others who were there in the earliest days of Scrum. Without them writing about Scrum, presenting about it at early conferences, and talking about it, Scrum wouldn't be what it is today. Thank you as well to all of the trainers and coaches in the Scrum community who push so hard to improve how we do Scrum while pushing just as hard to keep Scrum from becoming more than the simple framework it is. My conversations with you so many of you have influenced me in more ways than you know.

There's no way to thank my family enough for all the sacrifices they made while allowing me the time to work on this book. I couldn't ask for a more wonderful and loving wife than I have in Laura. Our daughters, Savannah and Delaney, remain my practically perfect precious princesses. I cherish every moment with them. And with this book finally done, I promise them many more hours and days doing all the things we haven't done enough of lately—now it's my turn to make you the ones who know how far love goes.

About the Author

Mike Cohn is the founder of Mountain Goat Software, through which he provides training and consulting on Scrum and agile software development. Mike specializes in helping companies adopt Scrum and become more agile as a way of building extremely high performance development organizations. In addition to this book, he is the author of *User Stories Applied for Agile Software Development, Agile Estimating and Planning,* and books on Java and C++ programming.

With more than 25 years of experience, Mike has previously been a technology executive in companies of various sizes, from start-up to Fortune 40. He has also written articles for *Better Software, IEEE Computer, Cutter IT Journal, Software Test and Quality Engineering, Agile Times,* and the *C/C++ Users Journal.* Mike is a frequent speaker at industry conferences and is a founding member of the Agile Alliance and Scrum Alliance. He is also a Certified Scrum Trainer, having co-taught the first Certified ScrumMaster class with Ken Schwaber in May 2003.

For more information, visit www.mountaingoatsoftware.com. Mike maintains a popular blog at blog.mountaingoatsoftware.com. He can also be found on Twitter as mikewcohn and by e-mail at mike@mountaingoatsoftware.com.

Introduction

This is not a book for those who are completely new to Scrum or agile. There are other books, classes, and even websites for that. If you are completely new to Scrum, start with one of those.[1] Nor is this a book for purists. They can find many blogs that will argue the one, true way of agile or Scrum. This is a book for pragmatists. It is for those who have started with Scrum and then encountered problems or for those who have not yet started with Scrum but who know they want to. They don't need to read again about how to draw a burndown chart or what three answers each person gives at the daily scrum. They need advice on the harder stuff—how to introduce and spread Scrum, how to get people to let go of doing a big design at the start of the project, how to deliver software that works by the end of each sprint, what managers do, and more. If these concerns sound familiar, this is a book for you.

To answer these questions, this book draws on my experience with Scrum over the past 15 years, but especially over the last 4. For the last 4 years, every evening after I spent the day with one of my clients, I would go back to my hotel room and make notes about the problems they were facing, the questions they asked, and the advice I gave. I then followed up, either with return visits or e-mails. I wanted to know for sure what advice was working to solve which problems.

As I collected the questions, problems, and advice, I was able to look for common themes. Some obstacles were completely unique to one client or one team. Others were more prevalent and repeated across many teams and organizations. It is these more universal problems—and my advice on overcoming them—that form the basis of this book. This advice is particularly evident in two ways: First, most chapters include boxes labeled *Things to Try Now*. These re-create the advice I found myself giving most often or that was most helpful in particular situations. Second, most chapters also include boxes labeled *Objection*. I have tried in these boxes to reproduce a typical conversation in which someone disagreed with the point I was making at the time. As you read these objections, try to hear the voice of some of your coworkers. I suspect you have heard many of the same objections. In these boxes, you will see how I've sought to overcome them.

---

1   A good starting point is www.mountaingoatsoftware.com/scrum.

What Else I've Assumed About You

Beyond assuming that you understand the basics of Scrum and now want to either introduce it into your organization or get good at it, I assume that you have some influence within the organization. That doesn't mean I have aimed this book at directors, vice presidents, and the CEO. The type of influence I am assuming is just as likely to come from your personality and individual credibility with your coworkers as it is to come from whatever job title is on your business card. Sure, having a fancy title can help. But as we'll see, the type of influence needed to succeed with Scrum more often comes from opinion leaders.

How This Book Is Organized

When I began this book four years ago, my working subtitle was *Getting Started and Getting Good,* as those were the two things I really wanted to help with. In collecting anecdotes and giving advice, I realized that getting started and getting good at Scrum are the same thing. There are not separate techniques we apply to start and then different techniques we use to get good at it.

Part I is about getting started—it includes advice on whether to start small or convert everyone at once, how to help people move from being aware that a new process is needed to desiring change to having the ability to do it, and how to select initial projects and teams. You will use the basic mechanisms introduced in this section not only to get started but also to get good. Among these are the improvement communities and improvement backlogs of Chapter 4, "Iterating Toward Agility."

In Part II, I focus on individuals and the changes each needs to make as part of the process of adopting Scrum. Chapter 6, "Overcoming Resistance," describes the type of resistance some individuals may exhibit. In it, I offer advice for thinking about why someone is resistant and then provide guidance on how to help the person get past the resistance. Chapters 7 and 8 describe the new roles that exist on a Scrum project and the changes necessary in the traditional roles, such as programmer, tester, project manager, and so on. Chapter 9, "Technical Practices," describes some of the technical practices (continuous integration, pair programming, test-driven development, and so on) that should be used or at least experimented with and that can change much of how individuals approach their day-to-day work.

In Part III, we expand outward from individuals to teams. We look first at how to structure teams to best achieve the benefits of Scrum. Next, in Chapter 11, "Teamwork," I cover the nature of teamwork on a Scrum project. In Chapter 12, "Leading a Self-Organizing Team," we look at what it means to lead a self-organizing Scrum team. In that chapter, I provide specific advice for what ScrumMasters, functional managers, and other leaders can do to help a team self-organize for success. Chapters 13–15 round out Part Three with a discussion of sprints, planning, and quality.

Part IV expands our focus outward once more, this time to the organization. In Chapter 17, "Scaling Scrum," we take an extended look at what is necessary to scale Scrum up to work on large, multi-team projects. In Chapter 18, "Distributed Teams," we consider the additional complexities of distributed teams. Then, in Chapter 19, "Coexisting with Other Approaches," we add yet more complexity by discussing how to make Scrum work when part of the project uses a sequential process or when there are compliance or governance requirements. Part IV concludes with Chapter 20, "Human Resources, Facilities, and the PMO," focusing on special considerations of the impact of Scrum on an organization's human resources, facilities, and project management office groups.

Part V contains two chapters. Chapter 21, "Seeing How Far You've Come," summarizes various approaches to measuring how far an organization has progressed in becoming agile. Chapter 22, "You're Not Done Yet," concludes the book with the reminder that being agile requires continuous improvement. It doesn't matter how good you are today; to be agile you must be better next month.

A Note on Some Terms

As with most things, writing about Scrum is harder than talking about it. It is too easy to misinterpret a sentence or take one sentence out of context. To avoid these problems, I have tried to be careful and precise in my use of certain terms. I use the word *developer*, for example, to refer to anyone on the development side of the project. This includes programmers, testers, analysts, user experience designers, database administrators, and so on.

The word *team* poses its own challenges. It, of course, includes the developers, but does *team* include the ScrumMaster and product owner? Naturally, this depends on the context. When I have wanted to be especially clear, I use *whole team* to refer to everyone: developers, product owner, and ScrumMaster. However, slavish use of *whole team* would have reduced the readability of the book. So you will encounter *team* as well, but usually in places where the context makes it sufficiently clear which group I'm referring to.

In referring to Scrum and agile teams, I have also needed a term to refer to those teams that are neither. In various places, I have used *sequential, traditional,* and even *non-agile*. Each conveys a slightly different meaning and is used appropriately.

How to Use This Book

Many books have a heading like the one above this sentence. But those headings usually say How to *Read* This Book. The best way to read this book is to use it. Don't just read it. When you encounter a *Things to Try Now* section, try some of them. Or note them and try them at your next retrospective or planning meeting, if that is what I recommended.

It is not necessary to read the book in order. In fact, there could well be entire chapters you do not need to read. If in your organization's quest to become good at Scrum, you have no significant problems with planning and no distributed teams, then skip or skim those chapters. I do, however, recommend that everyone read at least the first four chapters and read them in order. They lay the foundation for much of what follows.

In Chapter 4 you will be introduced to the idea of improvement communities and improvement backlogs. An improvement community is a group of like-minded individuals who are passionate about driving improvements in a particular area. One improvement community could form when three people passionate about the product backlog decide to collect best practices and advice to share across teams. Another improvement community could include hundreds of people interested in improving how your organization tests its applications. An improvement backlog is exactly what it sounds like—a prioritized list of things that an improvement community would like to help the organization get better at.

One of my hopes is that improvement communities—including the Enterprise Transition Community that guides and energizes the transition effort—will use this book to load their improvement backlogs. In fact, many of the top-level section headings have been deliberately worded so that those headings can go right onto an improvement backlog. As examples, consider "Shift from Documents to Discussions" in Chapter 13, "Prepare in This Sprint for the Next" in Chapter 14, and "Automate at Different Levels" in Chapter 16.

As a long-time Scrum trainer and consultant, I have worked with hundreds of teams and organizations, and I've come to believe that success with Scrum is possible for every organization. Some will have a harder time than others. Some will be challenged by a rigid corporate culture. Others will confront entrenched, difficult personalities facing personal loss. The lucky ones will have supportive leadership and passionately engaged employees. What each of these organizations will have in common, though, is the need for pragmatic and proven advice. I have written this book with the hope of providing it.

PART I

Getting Started

Willingness to change is a strength
even if it means plunging part of the company
into total confusion for a while.

—Jack Welch

Chapter 1

Why Becoming Agile Is Hard (But Worth It)

Many software development organizations are striving to become more agile. And who can blame them? Successful agile teams are producing higher-quality software that better meets user needs more quickly and at a lower cost than are traditional teams. Besides, who wouldn't want to be more agile? It just plain sounds good, doesn't it? It is almost as though one cannot be too thin, too rich, or too agile. But beyond the buzzword and hype, organizations that take becoming agile seriously by adopting a process such as Scrum are seeing dramatic benefits.

They are seeing significant gains in productivity with corresponding decreases in cost. They are able to bring products to market much faster and with a greater degree of customer satisfaction. They are experiencing greater visibility into the development process, leading to greater predictability. And for them, out-of-control, will-it-ever-be-done projects have become a thing of the past.

One company to realize these benefits by adopting Scrum is Salesforce.com. Founded in 1999 in a San Francisco apartment, Salesforce.com is one of the true, lasting dot-com-era success stories. With revenue of more than $450 million and 2,000 employees in 2006, Salesforce.com had noticed the frequency of its releases had dwindled from four a year to one a year. Customers were getting less and waiting longer to get it; something needed to be done. The company decided to transition to Scrum. During the first year of making the switch, Salesforce.com released 94% more features, delivered 38% more features per developer, and delivered over 500% more value to its customers compared to the previous year (Greene and Fry 2008). In the ensuing two years, revenue more than doubled to more than $1 billion. With results like these, it is not surprising that so many organizations have transitioned to Scrum. Or at least tried to.

I say "tried to" because transitioning to Scrum and other agile methods is hard—much harder than many companies anticipate. The changes required to reap all of the rewards being agile can bring are far reaching. These changes demand a great deal from not only the developers but the rest of the organization as well. Changing practices is one thing; changing minds is quite another. It is my aim in this book to show not only how to transition well but also how to succeed long term.

I've personally witnessed several failed agile adoptions that could have been prevented. The first was in a company that had spent more than a million dollars on its transition effort. Executives brought in outside trainers and coaches and hired five people into an "Agile Office" to which new Scrum teams could turn for advice. The company's failure was the result of thinking that the implications of adopting Scrum would be restricted to only the development organization. The executives who initiated this transition thought that educating and supporting developers would be sufficient. They failed to consider how Scrum would touch the work of salespeople, the marketing group, and even the finance department. Without changes to these areas, organizational gravity pulled the company back where it had started.

For completely different reasons, Josef ultimately failed at introducing Scrum to his company. A newly promoted and first-time project manager, Josef was instantly attracted to Scrum because it fit his natural management style. Josef easily convinced his team—who had all been his peers as little as one month before—to try Scrum on their new project. The project was wildly successful, earning accolades for the team and winning Josef the chance at a much larger project. Josef introduced the new project team to Scrum, and most members were willing to try the new approach. Although those working on the project were happy to use Scrum, some of the functional managers to whom they reported got nervous about what Scrum might mean to their careers. Josef's luck ran out. The functional managers—in particular the directors of quality assurance and database development—banded together and convinced the vice president of engineering that Scrum was inappropriate for projects of the complexity and importance being done in their company.

Caroline fared a little better. A vice president of development in a large data management company, Caroline had more than 200 developers in her organization. After seeing the benefits of Scrum on one project, she excitedly launched an initiative to introduce Scrum across her division. All employees were provided with training or coaching. Within a few months nearly all teams were producing working software at the end of each two-week sprint. This was great progress. When I visited this company a year later, though, the employees had failed to make any additional headway. To be sure, teams were producing higher-quality software and doing it a bit faster than they had before starting with Scrum, but her company's gains were only a fraction of what they could have been. Caroline's company had forgotten that continuous improvement is part of Scrum.

Frightening, isn't it? Each of these failures was a well-intentioned effort to transition to Scrum. Yet all the good intentions in the world could not keep them from failing. Don't worry, though. Transitioning to Scrum may be hard, but it's entirely possible with the right approach. In this chapter we examine why transitioning to any agile development process, including Scrum, is especially difficult.

We detail some of the challenges that derailed the companies I've mentioned. Most important, though, we look at the reasons why the benefits of becoming an agile organization are more than worth the effort.

Why Transitioning Is Hard

All change is hard. I've seen employees in an uproar over something so small as a change in their company's healthcare plan. Larger changes can be even more painful. But there are certain attributes of transitioning to Scrum that make it more difficult than most other changes. They are as follows:

- Successful change is not entirely top-down or bottom-up.
- The end state is unpredictable.
- Scrum is pervasive.
- Scrum is dramatically different.
- Change is coming more quickly than ever before.
- Best practices are dangerous.

Successful Change Is Not Entirely Top-Down or Bottom-Up

Successful organizational change cannot be fully top-down or bottom-up. In a top-down change, a powerful leader shares a vision of the future and the organization follows the leader toward that vision. Imagine a charismatic, respected, and powerful leader such as Steve Jobs telling his Apple employees that they are moving beyond computer hardware and software to dominate digital music. His reputation and style might have pointed the company in a new direction, but that alone would not have been enough to pull off such a monumental feat. Change management expert John Kotter agrees.

> No one individual, even a monarch-like CEO, is ever able to develop the right vision, communicate it to large numbers of people, eliminate all the key obstacles, generate short-term wins, lead and manage dozens of change projects, and anchor new approaches deep in the organization's culture. (1996, 51–52)

By contrast, in a bottom-up change, a team or some individuals decide that a change is needed and they set about making it happen. Some teams undertake a bottom-up change with an "ask for forgiveness later" attitude. Others flaunt that they are breaking the rules. Still others attempt to fly under the corporate radar as long as possible.

Most successful changes, and especially a change to an agile process like Scrum, must include elements of both top-down and bottom-up change. Mary

Lynn Manns and Linda Rising agree, writing in *Fearless Change*, "We believe that change is best introduced bottom-up with support at appropriate points from management—both local and at a higher level" (2004, 7). An organization attempting to transition to Scrum without support from the top will encounter resistance that cannot be overcome from below. This usually occurs as soon as the new Scrum process begins to affect how areas outside the original team do their work. In response, middle managers protect their departments by striking out against changes created by Scrum. Top-down support will be needed to remove these kinds of impediments and obstacles.

Similarly, without bottom-up engagement, the transition will feel like sitting under a ceiling fan in an open-air restaurant in Mexico: just a bunch of hot air blowing down from above. When this happens, individuals resist being told what to do. Bottom-up participation will be needed because it will be the individual team members who work through the issues of discovering how Scrum will work best within their organization.

Key to any successful adoption of Scrum will be combining elements of both bottom-up and top-down change.

The End State Is Unpredictable

Perhaps you've read a book on Extreme Programming and have decided that is the right approach for your company. Or maybe you attended a Certified Scrum-Master training course and think Scrum sounds good. Or maybe you read a book on a different agile process, and it sounds perfect for your organization.

In all likelihood, you're wrong.

None of these processes as described by their originators is perfect for your organization. Any may be a good starting point, but you will need to tailor the process to more precisely fit the unique circumstances of your organization, individuals, and industry. Alistair Cockburn concurs: "Having a chance to change or personalize a process to fit themselves seems to be a critical success factor for a team to adopt a process. It's the act of creation that seems to bind teams to 'their own' process."[1]

You may have a clear vision of what "doing Scrum" means to you, and you may get others to buy into exactly that same vision, but where the organization ends up is likely to be somewhat different. In fact, to even refer to end states in a Scrum transition is incorrect; there can be no end state in a process that calls for continuous improvement.

This creates a problem for an organization that wants to transition to Scrum through a traditional change approach that relies on gap analysis and then on closing the identified gaps. If we cannot anticipate the end state of a Scrum

---

1   This and all other uncited references are personal communications between the speaker and me.

transition, we cannot identify all of the gaps between there and the current state. So, a gap analysis–driven change approach will not work. The closest we can come is to identify gaps between where we are now and an improved, intermediate state.

After identifying these smaller gaps, though, we are still left with the problem of how to close them. It is difficult (and often impossible) to predict exactly how people will respond to the many small changes that will be needed on the way to becoming agile. Teamwork expert Christopher Avery views organizations as living systems.

> We can never direct a living system, only disturb it and wait to see the response....We can't know all the forces shaping an organization we wish to change, so all we can do is provoke the system in some way by experimenting with a force we think might have some impact, then watch to see what happens. (2005, 22–23)

So, a transition to Scrum cannot be a process that "articulates and defines the entire change process required to bridge the gap between 'as is' and 'to be' and creates tactical plans," as I read in a traditional change management book (Carr, Hard, and Trahant 1996, 144–5). Creating such a plan would require leaping two impossible hurdles: first, knowing exactly where we'll want to end up; and second, knowing exactly the steps to get there. Because we cannot overcome these impossibilities, the best we can do is adopt a "provoke and observe" approach (Avery 2005, 23) in which we try something, see if it moves us closer to an intermediate, improved state, and if so do more of it. These pokings and proddings of the organization are not random. They are carefully selected based on experience, wisdom, and intuition to drive a successful transition to Scrum.

SEE ALSO

Chapter 4, "Iterating Toward Agility," will describe the overall process I recommend when adopting Scrum.

Scrum Is Pervasive

When a change is isolated, when it doesn't affect everything a person does, that change is often easier to introduce into an organization. Consider the case of an organization using a non-agile process that decides to introduce a mandatory operational readiness review before an application is deployed onto the company's web servers. This is a relatively isolated change. Sure, there will be some developers who will hate the new procedure and will complain, perhaps loudly. But, when it comes down to it, this is not a pervasive change. Even if they don't like this change, they can still continue doing the majority of their work unscathed.

Consider now the case of a developer transitioning to Scrum. This developer has to work on smaller pieces of work at a time to complete something by the end of each timeboxed sprint. The developer might have to write automated tests to go with each new bit of code. She might even alternate short bouts of testing and coding in something called test-driven development. And she might need to do all this with her headphones off while pair programming. These are fundamental changes. They aren't something relegated to a few hours a day or week, as code inspections might be. This type of fundamental change is difficult because it pervades everything about a developer's workday. Resistance will be greater because the impact is greater.

Adopting Scrum is pervasive in a second way as well. Being agile will have implications to the organization that reach far outside the software development department. Introducing the operational readiness review would almost certainly not impact finance, sales, or other departments. But each of those departments can be impacted by Scrum. Finance groups will have to reconcile company policies on capitalizing or expensing with the way Scrum projects run. Sales will want to consider altering how they communicate date and scope commitments and may change how they structure contracts. With more groups affected by a move to Scrum, there is more chance for resistance and certainly more chance for misunderstandings. These add up to make transitioning to Scrum harder than other changes.

SEE ALSO

The impact of Scrum on other groups, such as finance, operations, human resources, and others is discussed in Chapter 20, "Human Resources, Facilities, and the PMO."

Scrum Is Dramatically Different

Not only do the changes created by adopting Scrum pervade everything development team members do, but also many of the changes go against much of their past training. Many testers, for example, have learned that their job is testing for compliance to a specification. Programmers have been trained that a problem is to be analyzed in depth and a perfect solution designed before any coding begins. On a Scrum project, testers and programmers need to unlearn these behaviors. Testers learn that testing is also about conformance with user needs. Programmers learn that a fully considered design is not always necessary (and sometimes not even desirable) before coding begins. Abby Fichtner, who shares her thoughts on her Hacker Chick blog, has told me she agrees with how hard this adjustment can be for programmers.

> Getting used to emergent design is hard because it feels like you're going to be just hacking! And if you've prided yourself on being a very good developer and always doing well-thought-out designs, it turns your whole world upside down and says "no, all those things you thought made you great, now those same things actually make you a bad developer." Very world-rocking stuff.

SEE ALSO

Emergent design and test-driven development are discussed in Chapter 9, "Technical Practices."

Because transitioning to Scrum involves asking people to work in ways that are unfamiliar and run counter to training and experience, people are often hesitant, if not outright resistant, to the change. Consider, for example, the case of Terry, a senior and respected programmer in his company. Terry had participated in a hands-on full-day class on test-driven development and was convinced of its benefits. An enthusiastic Terry returned to the office expecting to stop doing big, up-front designs and allow design to emerge through the use of test-driven development. It didn't go as smoothly as he thought it would. He wrote me an e-mail describing his deflating experience.

> Getting the other programmers to even try test-driven development was much harder than I thought. I tried pushing it as a way to skip the long up-front design phases we'd become accustomed to, but failed miserably. After a few months I got the other developers to start writing tests first, but only because it was a good idea on its own. They still wouldn't abandon the lengthy up-front design phase. It took me another year to make much progress shortening that, and we could still go much shorter.

Change Is Coming More Quickly Than Ever Before

Back in 1970 Alvin Toffler coined the term *future shock*, saying that it is the disorientation people feel when confronted with "too much change in too short a period of time" (1970, 4). Human, and therefore organizational, capacity to change is limited—ask people to change too many things at the same time and they shut down; the shattering stress and disorientation of future shock kicks in.

In many organizations, employees have been suffering from future shock for years. Teams are asked to do more with fewer people. Outsourcing and distributed teams have become increasingly common. These adjustments were preceded by the rush to move applications to a client/server model, then onto the web, and then into services. Add to these the constant, and constantly accelerating, rate of change in technology itself—new languages, new tools, new platforms—and future shock is now. It should not be surprising that transitioning to Scrum can often be the change that pushes people into future shock. The pervasive nature of adopting Scrum and the fundamental changes it causes in how people work and interact have a higher risk of triggering the future shock effect.

Best Practices Are Dangerous

With most organizational change, after someone figures out the right or best way to do something, that way of doing it is captured as a "best practice" and shared with everyone else. For some types of work, collecting and reusing best practices is a tremendous aid to the change effort. An organization that is selling a product to a new type of customer may, for example, capture best practices for overcoming objections from potential customers. When transitioning to Scrum, however, collecting best practices can be dangerous.

Like sirens singing to us from the rocks, best practices tempt us to relax and stop the effort of continuous improvement that is essential to Scrum. Taiichi Ohno, originator of the Toyota Production System, has written that "there is something called standard work, but standards should be changed constantly. Instead, if you think of the standard as the best you can do, it's all over." Ohno goes on to say that if we establish something as the "best possible way, the motivation for kaizen [continuous incremental improvement] will be gone" (1982).

Although team members should always look to share with one another their newly discovered good ways of working, they should resist the urge to codify them into a set of best practices. One example of a best practice gone awry is the company that decided that all daily scrums needed to be held no later than 10:00 a.m. I found this an extremely unnecessary dictate. I'm not entirely sure what purpose the dictate served. But many employees took the rule to be further proof that "Scrum is all about micro-management."

THINGS TO TRY NOW

❑ Think about your current transition to Scrum. Are you just getting started, in the middle, or feeling like you're nearing the end of the transition push? No matter where you are, identify the primary obstacle you think may be holding you back from the next level of success.

Why It's Worth the Effort

Despite all the reasons why transitioning to Scrum can be particularly difficult, stakeholders in companies that have made the transition are happy they've done so. One reason stakeholders are so satisfied is that time-to-market is reduced when using an agile process like Scrum. This faster time-to-market is enabled by the higher productivity of agile teams, which is in turn the result of the higher quality seen on agile projects. Because employees are freed up to do high-quality work and because they see their work delivered sooner into the hands of waiting users, job satisfaction goes up. With higher job satisfaction comes more engaged employees, which leads to more productivity gains, initiating a virtuous cycle of continued improvement.

The rest of this chapter looks in more depth at these claims. In doing so I present evidence in support of each. Some of the evidence is anecdotal and drawn from my experience, experiences of my clients and colleagues, or experiences reported in magazines or at conferences. Additionally, though, the claims are supported by data from the following sources:

- A rigorous comparison of 26 agile projects against a baseline database of 7,500 primarily traditional development projects. This study was conducted by Michael Mah, managing partner of QSM Associates (QSMA), which has been collecting productivity, quality, and other metrics on projects for more than 15 years. The agile projects Mah studied ranged in size from 60 to 1,000 people (Mah 2008).

- Various academic and research papers, including aggregate research by David Rico, Ph.D., who surveyed 51 published studies of agile projects (2008).

- An online survey of more than 3,000 people conducted by agile tool vendor, VersionOne (2008), and another of 642 people conducted by *Dr. Dobb's Journal* (Ambler 2008a), a popular development magazine. Each survey was conducted in 2008. Industry surveys such as these cannot, of course, be taken as definitive. Individuals opting to take such surveys are probably predisposed toward favorable views of agile. Results from these surveys are presented because they are more representative than conclusive. These surveys will be referenced as VersionOne and DDJ in the sections that follow.

SEE ALSO

Data from this chapter is summarized in Microsoft PowerPoint and Apple Keynote presentations available at www.succeeding-withagile.com.

In the following sections we look at these reasons why transitioning to an agile process like Scrum is worthwhile:

- Higher productivity and lower costs
- Improved employee engagement and job satisfaction
- Faster time to market
- Higher quality
- Improved stakeholder satisfaction
- What we've been doing no longer works

Higher Productivity and Lower Costs

There is unfortunately no universally agreed-upon measure of productivity. Martin Fowler has gone so far as to say that measuring productivity of developers is impossible (2003). And although I agree with Fowler, I do think it is possible to measure proxies or stand-ins for productivity. Some teams use the number of lines of code as a proxy for productivity. Others use as a proxy the number of function points delivered or simply the number of features delivered, ignoring that not all features are the same size. Are there problems with these proxies? Absolutely. But I think the usefulness of proxy productivity measures is justified if we can reasonably make the assumption that data has not been gamed by teams fabricating lines of code or function points by duplicating code, failing to take advantage of reuse, or so on. In many cases, especially those involving large data sets as the QSMA study does, I think this is a reasonable assumption.

QSMA calculates a productivity index for the projects in its database. This index takes into consideration effort, schedule, technical difficulty, and more and is an attempt to help make cross-team comparisons more meaningful. In his comparison between agile and traditional projects, Mah found agile projects to be 16%

more productive, an increase that he found to be statistically significant. Figure 1.1 shows the agile projects (as dots) compared to the average productivity and one standard deviation around it in the QSMA database. As you can see, most of the dots are above the industry average line, with a handful of projects more than one standard deviation more productive than the industry average.

FIGURE 1.1

Agile teams are significantly more productive than the industry average. Source: Mah 2008.

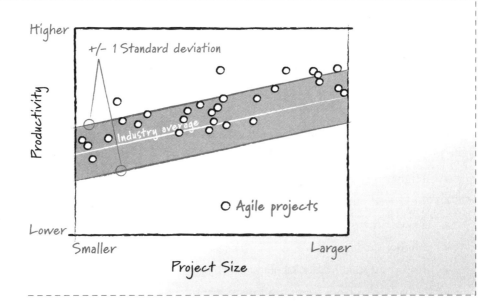

The QSMA results are corroborated by both the DDJ and VersionOne surveys. Eighty-two percent of participants in the DDJ survey felt that productivity was somewhat or much higher when using agile methods like Scrum than it was before. Only 5% felt productivity was somewhat or much lower. Seventy-three percent of the VersionOne respondents believed that being agile had significantly improved (23%) or improved (50%) productivity.

It stands to reason that if people are productive, costs will be lower. The VersionOne and DDJ studies both bear this out, as can be seen in Table 1.1.[2]

David Rico's survey of case studies of agile teams published through 2008 is shown in Table 1.2. Rico found that the median reported productivity increase was 88% and the median cost savings was 26%. These indicate solid evidence that agile teams are more productive, which leads to cost savings to their projects.

---

2   The VersionOne survey asked respondents to answer on a scale that included Significantly Improved, Improved, No Benefit, Worse, and Much Worse. The DDJ survey used a similar scale but used Much Higher, Somewhat Higher, No Change, Somewhat Lower, and Much Lower. For improved readability, all tables in this chapter use the labels from the VersionOne survey.

Development Cost	DDJ	VersionOne
Improved	32%	30%
Significantly Improved	5%	8%

TABLE 1.1

A significant number of survey respondents report that agile improved development costs.

As encouraging as these numbers are, they tell only part of the story. A significant benefit to being agile—but one not reflected here—is that agile teams are less likely to build functionality that is no longer needed. A common criticism of a sequential development process is that by the time the software is delivered, the users no longer need the functionality being provided. Because of the frequent feedback, timeboxed sprints, and ability to reprioritize each sprint, a Scrum team is more likely to work only on features users really need. Were we to include this in our measurement of productivity, we would see even more dramatic results.

Category	Lowest Reported Improvement	Median Improvement	Highest Reported Improvement
Productivity	14%	88%	384%
Cost	10%	26%	70%

TABLE 1.2

Impact of agile on productivity and cost. Source: Rico 2008.

Improved Employee Engagement and Job Satisfaction

One factor contributing to the higher productivity and lower costs on agile projects may be that employees enjoy their jobs more. Fifteen months after adopting Scrum, Salesforce.com surveyed its employees and found that 86% were having a "good time" or the "best time" working at the company. Prior to adopting Scrum, only 40% said the same thing. Further, 92% of employees said they would recommend an agile approach to others. Results such as these are common; many of my clients have done employee satisfaction surveys and always with similar results. In its industrywide survey, VersionOne found that 74% of those surveyed reported morale was improved (44%) or significantly improved (30%).

One reason why employees may enjoy their jobs more is because of the sustainable pace promoted by agile processes. Chris Mann and Frank Maurer of the University of Calgary studied the amount of overtime worked by one team for the year before becoming agile and the first year after (2005). They found that before implementing agile practices, team members worked an average of 19% overtime. After adopting an agile process, that dropped by nearly two-thirds to an average of 7% overtime. Further, even though overtime was occasionally needed even after adopting agile practices, there was less variability in the amount required, as measured by the standard deviations of the team before and after moving to agile. Johannes Brodwall, an agile software architect, says, "Overtime seems to be much less common after we started with agile. Testers are especially noticing the effect. They used to have extremely chunky workloads."

A lack of overtime is likely just one factor contributing to higher job satisfaction among people working on agile teams. There are also the benefits of having more control over your day-to-day work, seeing the results of your work get used sooner, working more closely with coworkers, creating products that are more likely to meet customer and user expectations, and so on. Employees who are happier with their jobs and with their employers will be more engaged in the work they do. Greater employee engagement will result in numerous benefits to the organization.

Faster Time to Market

Agile teams tend to release their products more quickly than do traditional teams. According to the VersionOne study, 64% of participants report that time to market has been improved (41%) or significantly improved (23%). The QSMA study comparing 26 agile projects to a database of 7,500 mostly traditional projects found that agile projects have a 37% faster time to market, as shown in Figure 1.2.

Agile teams have faster times to market for two reasons. First, the higher productivity of an agile team allows them to produce functionality more quickly. Second, agile teams are more likely to release incrementally. When stakeholders realize that a team can produce valuable functionality every sprint, they often decide that they do not need to wait for one big-bang delivery of all functionality.

FIGURE 1.2

Agile projects have a 37% faster time to market compared to the industry average. Source: Mah 2008.

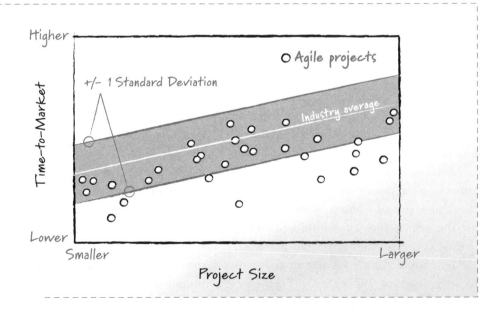

Salesforce.com noticed the benefit of this immediately after its rapid transition to Scrum (Greene and Fry 2008). Figure 1.3 shows the cumulative number of features delivered to customers in 2006 (before adopting Scrum) and 2007 (after initiating the transition around the start of the year). This figure shows a simple metric: the raw number of features delivered and when they were delivered and a powerful view of the additional value provided to customers in the first year of using Scrum.

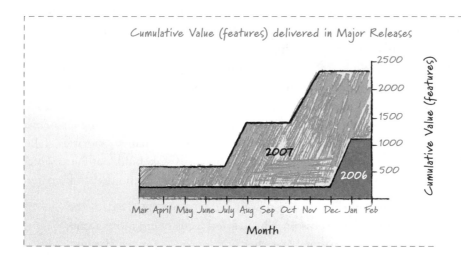

FIGURE 1.3

The cumulative value of features delivered by Salesforce.com in 2006 (pre-Scrum) and 2007 (Scrum).

Higher Quality

If you ask a Scrum team what enables them to be more productive than in their pre-Scrum days, most will say that at least part of their success is that they are consistently producing higher-quality work. Without bugs left behind to drag the team down, they can move quickly and consistently forward. Quality is improved because working at a sustainable pace prevents sloppiness. Quality is also improved through many of the engineering practices such as pair programming, refactoring, and a strong emphasis on early and automated testing.

David Rico's research bears out the claim that agile teams produce higher-quality products. In his survey of 51 published studies of agile projects, he found a minimum quality improvement of 10% and a median improvement of 63%. Rico's research matches my experience at clients where I've been able to measure and report on quality. For example, ePlanServices provides retirement plans to medium-sized businesses. The service is provided largely through a powerful web application. In the first nine months after initiating a Scrum transition, their defect rate per thousand lines of code dropped by 70%.

The VersionOne survey also bears out the claim for higher quality with agile processes such as Scrum. Sixty-eight percent of participants answered that agile had improved (44%) or significantly improved (24%) software quality. Further,

84% of respondents felt that agile had reduced the number of software defects by 10% or more; 30% felt agile had reduced the number of defects by 25% or more. The DDJ survey reported similar results, with 48% saying quality was somewhat higher and 29% saying it was much higher.

Improved Stakeholder Satisfaction

Given all of the benefits of agile processes thus far, it is not surprising that they lead to improved stakeholder satisfaction. The DDJ survey found that 78% of survey participants believe that using an agile process has led to somewhat higher (47%) or much higher (31%) stakeholder satisfaction.

One reason stakeholders are more satisfied by agile processes is because their practices are more friendly toward the shifting priorities that are a fact of life in today's fast-paced, competitive organizations. In the VersionOne study, 92% of participants felt that agile improved the ability to manage changing priorities. Additionally, along with gaining the ability to more easily change priorities, stakeholders on agile projects learn the impact of change. A stakeholder at PetroSleuth, a small development company in the oil and gas industry, found that to be true.

> The Scrum process has led to our being more involved in the daily review and discussion. This has led to us being more aware, and being held accountable earlier in the process for any changes. (Mann and Maurer 2005, 77)

The VersionOne survey looked deeper into additional factors leading to stakeholder satisfaction. Table 1.3 shows the high percentages of survey participants who reported that agile leads to better alignment between the technology and business groups, reduced project risk, better ability to manage changing priorities, and improved project visibility. Steve Fisher, a senior vice president at Salesforce.com and stakeholder to many of the agile teams there, says adopting Scrum has "delivered total visibility, total transparency, and unbelievable productivity...a complete win" (Greene 2008).

TABLE 1.3
Some of the reasons stakeholders are satisfied with agile.

	Improved	Significantly Improved
Enhanced ability to manage changing priorities	41%	51%
Improved project visibility	42%	41%
Improved alignment between IT and business goals	39%	27%
Reduced project risk	48%	17%

What We've Been Doing No Longer Works

One final reason to consider changing to Scrum is if your current development process is no longer working. When a process that has worked in the past stops working, a common tendency is to do more of it. This was certainly the case at Yahoo!, where chief product officer Pete Deemer was one of the first to recognize the need for change.

> Originally, Yahoo! tried Scrum purely out of desperation—the waterfall approach was clearly not working—and a year-long attempt to do the waterfall "better" through more thorough planning and analysis, more in-depth documents, more sign-offs, and so on was making things worse, not better. For the teams that saw benefits, which were most of the teams that tried Scrum, the benefits were visible almost immediately.

Clinton Keith, former chief technology officer at High Moon Studios, developer of console-based video games, tells a similar story.

> As successful project managers at a well-funded startup, we felt we could "apply more waterfall" to our ambitious new projects. This had the opposite effect of what we hoped for and the projects spiraled out of control. Our assumptions were wrong and forced us to rethink how we were managing projects.

❑ Identify the benefits you have gained from using Scrum so far.
❑ If you have not yet gathered metrics on quality, employee morale, stakeholder satisfaction, or so on, select a few factors of interest and measure a baseline you can compare against later.
❑ If you gathered baseline measurements earlier and have been doing Scrum for at least three or six months, remeasure and see what progress has been made. Create your own "why Scrum is worth it" charts that you can share with other teams as they begin to transition to Scrum or with existing teams who are having difficulty sticking with it.

THINGS TO TRY NOW

Looking Forward

Becoming agile is hard. It is harder than most other organizational change efforts I've witnessed or been part of. I started this chapter by laying out some of the reasons why this is so, including the need to change from the top-down and bottom-up simultaneously, the impossibility of knowing exactly what the end state will look like, the dramatic and pervasive changes caused by Scrum, the difficulty of adding more change on top of all that is already occurring, and the need to avoid turning Scrum into a list of best practices.

Because you're still reading, I can assume that this list of challenges didn't send you away. That's fortunate because there are tremendous advantages to be had by the organization that overcomes the challenges. These include more productive teams, lower costs, happier employees, reduced time to market, better quality, and improved stakeholder satisfaction.

In the next chapter we look more closely at what is involved in moving you, your team, and your organization from the stage where you know change is necessary and you believe that Scrum is the answer to a point where you can begin making real progress and continuous improvements.

Additional Reading

Ambler, Scott. 2008. Agile adoption rate survey, February. http://www.ambysoft.com/surveys/agileFebruary2008.html.

> This article presents the results of a survey conducted in February 2008 and goes beyond the results presented here.

Greene, Steve, and Chris Fry. 2008. Year of living dangerously: How Salesforce.com delivered extraordinary results through a "big bang" enterprise agile revolution. Session presented at Scrum Gathering, Stockholm. http://www.slideshare.net/sgreene/scrum-gathering-2008-stockholm-salesforcecom-presentation.

> Greene and Fry led the rollout of Scrum at Salesforce.com. They have shared this entertaining slide deck that covers how they did it, what they learned, and what they'd do differently.

Mah, Michael. 2008. How agile projects measure up, and what this means to you. *Cutter Consortium Agile Product & Project Management Executive Report* 9 (9).

> This is Mah's comparison of 26 agile projects to his baseline database of productivity data on over 7,500 mostly traditional projects.

Rico, David F. 2008. What is the ROI of agile vs. traditional methods? An analysis of extreme programming, test-driven development, pair programming, and Scrum (using real options). A downloadable spreadsheet from David Rico's personal website. http://davidfrico.com/agile-benefits.xls.

> An extensive survey of the available literature on agile projects that summarizes key percentage improvements in productivity, cost, quality, schedule, customer satisfaction, and return on investment.

VersionOne. 2008. The state of agile development: Third annual survey. Posted as a downloadable PDF in the Library of White Papers on the VersionOne website. http://www.versionone.com/pdf/3rdAnnualStateOfAgile_FullDataReport.pdf.

Every year, agile tool developer VersionOne conducts the largest survey of the state of agile adoption. The survey is international in scope and is the broadest view into the use of agile practices.

Chapter 2

ADAPTing to Scrum

Lori Schubring was among the first to realize that things had to change. An application development manager for a large manufacturing company, Lori realized that its development process had become "so formalized that we hindered our ability to remain flexible for the business. It got to the point where we weren't turning around project requests fast enough" (2006, 27). Aware of the need to change, Lori attended a free, half-day seminar introducing Scrum. What she saw there was a better way to develop software, a framework she thought might help her organization. As such, Lori developed the desire to change to Scrum. Next, she acquired the ability to do it by participating in a ScrumMaster class, attending an agile conference, and visiting a company that had already adopted Scrum. Lori then promoted Scrum to her boss and team, convincing them of its benefits. Finally, Lori transferred some of the implications of her team using Scrum to the rest of her company so that organizational gravity would not pull the team back to where it had started.

Lori's story encapsulates the five common activities necessary for a successful and lasting Scrum adoption:

- **Awareness** that the current process is not delivering acceptable results
- **Desire** to adopt Scrum as a way to address current problems
- **Ability** to succeed with Scrum
- **Promotion** of Scrum through sharing experiences so that we remember and others can see our successes
- **Transfer** of the implications of using Scrum throughout the company

Conveniently, these five activities—Awareness, Desire, Ability, Promotion, and Transfer—can be remembered by the acronym ADAPT.[1] These activities are also

---

1   The five activities of ADAPT are based on ADKAR (Hiatt 2006), a general model of change that includes the steps of Awareness, Desire, Knowledge, Ability, and Reinforcement. In practice, I have found separating Knowledge and Ability to be unnecessary. In a field such as software development, knowledge without ability is meaningless. Additionally, the Reinforcement step of ADKAR is replaced in ADAPT with separate Promotion and Transfer steps, emphasizing the importance of these activities to a successful transition.

summarized in Figure 2.1, which shows Awareness, Desire, and Ability as overlapping, whereas Promotion and Transfer repeat and occur throughout the transition effort. After you have transitioned, this cycle will continue as you continuously improve.

FIGURE 2.1

The five activities of adapting to Scrum.

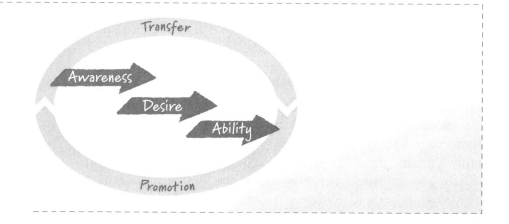

An organization that successfully adopts Scrum can be thought of as engaging in these activities at multiple levels:

- **Organizationally.** The organization as a whole will engage in these activities. No matter how aware one person or group is, there must be a critical mass of people with a similar awareness before the organization will be able to collectively move forward. In thinking of the ADAPT model at this level, we may speak of a company with an organizational desire to adopt Scrum. Or we may say that our organization currently lacks the ability to do Scrum.

- **As individuals.** Because organizations are made up of individuals, it is important to acknowledge that individuals will progress through the overall transition at different rates. For example, you personally may already have acquired the ability to do Scrum; you've learned some new skills and some new ways of thinking about software development. A colleague, on the other hand, is only starting to become aware that the current approach isn't working.

- **As teams.** Individuals can be aided or hindered in the transition to Scrum by their teams. Teams tend to progress through the ADAPT cycle more or less together. In the same way that studies have shown individuals are more likely to be overweight if their friends are overweight (Thaler and Sunstein 2009), you are more likely to have a desire to do Scrum if the rest of your team does as well.

- **Per practice.** The ADAPT model can also be applied to each new skill that is acquired as part of adopting Scrum. Consider the increased reliance on automated unit testing that is common on Scrum teams. The team and its members must first become aware that the current approach to testing isn't working. They must then develop the desire to automate more tests and to do so earlier in the process. To do this will require that some team members learn new skills. Promoting the team's success with automated testing will encourage other development teams to emulate them. Finally, transferring the implications of the team doing more automated testing to other groups ensures that forces external to the team do not prevent it from continuing with the new practice.

One of the first things you'll need to do, whether you are currently using Scrum or just starting your adoption, is to decide where your individuals, teams, and organization are in their ADAPT sequence. It could be that you are acquiring the *ability* to do test-driven development on a team that is *promoting* its success inside a department that *desires* to implement Scrum. The overall organization, however, may be *aware* of only a general need to change. This chapter will discuss not only the five ADAPT activities but also the tools you will need to encourage and develop awareness, desire, ability, promotion, and transfer throughout all levels of the organization.

Awareness

Change begins with an awareness that the status quo is no longer desirable. However, becoming aware that what worked in the past is no longer working can be extremely difficult. The most dramatic example of this I personally experienced was when I was a development director for a healthcare software company back in the mid-1990s. Our company founder recognized that the company's sole product—the one that had led to an extremely successful public offering and tremendous growth in the company—had at most one year of sales left because of the fundamental shift occurring at the time in the United States healthcare industry. Our company would need to develop a new product that could capitalize on the shift toward managed care. In a meeting of the entire company, our founder presented a slide with the chart shown in Figure 2.2.

While most employees had been congratulating ourselves on our success, which we anticipated would last forever, our founder realized we were entering what he called the "Valley of Death." While in the Valley of Death, revenue from the current product would quickly decline well in advance of increases in revenue from the new product we hadn't started developing yet.

FIGURE 2.2

The "Valley of Death" shows declining revenue from the current product in advance of the release of a new product.

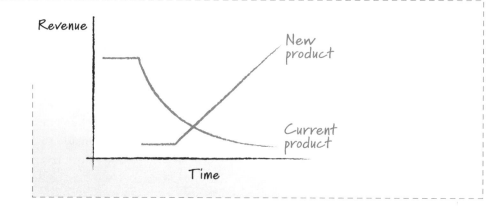

FIGURE 2.2

The "Valley of Death" shows declining revenue from the current product in advance of the release of a new product.

Few of us can be as prescient as this company founder was. There is almost always a lag between when the need to change first arises and when we become aware of it. The lag can be particularly long if the company is doing well. Other common reasons why individuals can be slow to develop an awareness of the need to change include the following:

- **A lack of exposure to the big picture.** The need to adopt Scrum may be the result of a confluence of factors not visible to everyone. The need for a change may be apparent only to those who have seen the decline in sales to new customers, heard the rumors of a strong competitor entering the company's space, and anticipate the need to do more without adding staff.
- **A refusal to see what's right in front of us.** Even when the need to change is clear, we sometimes deny it. We may think the problems are temporary and often fear what change may have in store. The "if it ain't broke, don't fix it" mentality is about as far as can be from an agile "if it ain't perfect (and it never will be), keep improving" mindset.
- **Confusing motion with progress.** Every day we see a flurry of activity. Meetings are being held, status reports are being circulated, documents are being written, and code is being checked in. It is easy to confuse all of this motion with progress. When a lot is happening, it can be hard to admit that all that activity is not leading us any closer to the desired products.
- **Listening to our own propaganda.** The company newsletter is full of rah-rah articles predicting the boundless future. The glass case in the lobby proudly displays past Product of the Year trophies. Hallways are full of gleeful, self-congratulatory chatter. Yet customers ask, "What have you done for me lately?" Listening to our own cheerleading and propaganda causes complacency. By all means, celebrate success but remember the hard work that earned it.

Tools for Developing Awareness

Team members will become aware of the need to change at different times. Those who have come to this realization quickly have the opportunity to assist in bringing others along to the same conclusion. In this section we will look at tools you can use to help develop awareness of the need to change.

Communicate that there's a problem. BioWare is one of the world's leading developers of story-driven video games, with more than 400 employees and well-known games such as *Mass Effect*, *Jade Empire*, *Dragon Age*, *Knights of the Old Republic*, *Neverwinter Nights*, and *Baldur's Gate*. Although BioWare's products had been successful, the projects to deliver them were not very efficient. Projects were afflicted by the usual symptoms of overtime, communication issues, and deliverables that occasionally failed to meet expectations.

Because of its strong track record of successful products, it wasn't obvious to all involved that the projects themselves could be more successful. Fortunately, producer Trent Oster's search for a better way to develop games led him to Scrum, and he was able to hire several project managers with Scrum experience. But this nucleus of early Scrum proponents could not make much progress until they helped others become aware of the need to improve. They did this by communicating a goal that would be shared by all projects.

> High-quality games at a lower cost that are as fun to develop as
> they are to play

This goal was wonderful for a couple of reasons. First, it is very hard to argue with. I can't imagine a team member arguing that it was as fun working all those long nights as it was playing the game that resulted. Second, it neither preached nor proposed the solution. Consider the likely impact if BioWare's early Scrum advocates had instead chosen "High-quality games built with an agile approach." This would have convinced no one of the need to change except for those already in favor of it. William Bridges, author of *Managing Transitions*, stresses the importance of selling the problem, not a specific solution to it (2003, 16).

Use metrics. As part of an overall communication strategy, metrics provide great reinforcement of the core reasons for change. I have seen companies use employee turnover, results from job satisfaction surveys, revenue per employee, and other simple metrics to convey the message that change is necessary.

Provide exposure to new people and experiences. Encourage people to attend conferences or training so that they hear about new techniques and practices. Or send people to a trade show for your industry. Let them see what products competitors are releasing. Or arrange meetings between team members and customers so they can hear firsthand about what features are needed and in what time frame. A good long-term strategy for providing exposure to new people and ideas is to value diversity in new hires. Intentionally seeking people from different backgrounds helps not only bring new ideas into the organization when they're hired, but it also helps the organization with exposure to future new ideas.

Run a pilot project. A successful pilot project demonstrates that things can be better. It is hard to argue with success. When those who aren't yet aware of the need to change see a highly successful project run in a different way, they must either discount the results on that project or become a bit more aware that a change could be appropriate.

Focus attention on the most important reasons to change. If your organization is like most others, you could probably create a lengthy list of reasons why the current development process is broken: Products do not meet user expectations, products take too long to develop, quality is poor, developer morale is low, overtime is excessive, schedules are unpredictable, the cost of development is high, and so on. In helping people become aware of the need to change, it is often best to replace such a laundry list with one that is much shorter. What two or three reasons are causing most of the problems? These reasons alone should be sufficient to justify adopting Scrum. By narrowing the full list of reasons down to just the critical ones, we focus more attention on the most compelling reasons.

One of my clients decided to adopt Scrum because its products had lost their best-in-class status. Customers were continuing to use the products but mostly out of years of loyalty and familiarity. To focus attention on this problem, I asked them to remove all plaques, trophies, and industry awards from the lobby except those earned within the past year. By removing old Product of the Year awards from the lobby, we reinforced the fact that customers were asking "but what have you done for me lately?" After the old mementos had been removed, the lobby still showcased a decent number of awards. But the contrast with what employees had become accustomed to was startling and helped increase the awareness that the company's glory days were behind it unless changes were made.

Desire

Beyond being aware of the need to change, one must also have the desire to change. I am aware that I should eat more vegetables; I don't yet desire to make that change in my diet. Until my awareness turns to desire, my diet will remain the same. Scrum trainer and consultant Michele Sliger tells of a company whose transition was stalled by a similar lack of desire. A few weeks after a training class, Sliger called the company to see how people were doing.

SEE ALSO
Chapter 3, "Patterns for Adopting Scrum," contrasts the merits of starting with a pilot project or transitioning everyone at once. Chapter 5, "Your First Projects," describes how to select an initial or pilot project.

Due to the politics at their company, they decided that agile really wouldn't work there. That's the only group I know that took the time to learn about agile (from an experienced agile consultant and not just a book), really examined their culture and politics, and then said "No." Were they being practical? realistic? or were they being fearful? pessimistic? I don't know. But no other company I've worked with has ever said no like that. Perhaps more should. I really respected the fact that these people decided that they weren't ready, for whatever reason, rather than making some half-hearted attempt.

Because they'd gone to the expense of bringing a Scrum trainer into the company, at least some employees must have been aware of the need to do things differently. But from Sliger's story we can conclude that there was insufficient desire to take the change effort further.

Moving from an awareness that the current development process isn't working to the desire to use a different one can be very hard for many people. After all, we've been educated to prefer a sequential approach, both through our schooling and years of experience. Additionally, although we may be dissatisfied with elements of our projects, we've worked hard to get the right boss and the right team. Scrum would change all that. Finally, as simple as it may seem, sometimes the timing may just not be right.

Twenty years ago a friend of mine recommended I read one of the Travis McGee novels by John D. MacDonald. I bought *The Girl in the Plain Brown Wrapper* that evening and started reading it. I hated it and stopped halfway through. About a year later I saw the book on my shelf and decided to give it another try. I loved it and went on to read all 20 of the other books featuring McGee. Something about my mindset, where I physically was, or such, was wrong when I first read the book. The same can be true when team members hear messages about the benefits of Scrum. If the time isn't right for people, you will not be able to convince them. The good news is that the same message delivered the same way but at a different time will often be enough to move someone along from awareness to desire.

Tools for Increasing Desire

Increasing the desire to adopt Scrum is often much harder than creating an awareness that the status quo must change. Fortunately, there are many tools for moving people from awareness to desire.

Communicate that there's a better way. When building awareness, communication centers on the key problems facing the organization or team adopting Scrum. After we shift from building awareness to increasing desire, communication then focuses on how Scrum can help address those problems. Mixing the two messages (that the current approach isn't working well enough and that Scrum can help) can cause some people to shut down and become unreceptive to either message. However, as more employees become aware of the need to change, the change agent's message can shift to one of evangelism. Lori Schubring, whose story started this chapter, writes of the contagious nature of desire.

> I was convinced agile could help us. I put a plan together, got support from our director, and became the internal evangelist. Because I believed so strongly, it was tough for anyone to ignore. If people challenged the idea, I challenged them right back. My desire caught on to some, others came along a little less willing. A few key people took interest, and that really helped the rest of the group open up to the possibilities of Scrum.

Create a sense of urgency. One way to turn awareness into desire is to turn up the heat. By creating a sense of urgency, we make it clear to others that the status quo cannot continue as such for long. Remember my awareness that I need to eat more vegetables? Suppose my doctor called tomorrow and said that I would die in six months if I didn't start eating broccoli, asparagus, cauliflower, and the like. I would likely respond by figuring out how to like them.

Build momentum. Rather than focus on those who are reluctant or opposed to Scrum, spend your time and effort helping those who are already enthusiastic. Rather than argue what can or can't be done, do it with those who are willing. The goal is to build an unstoppable momentum with each success leading to another. When Steve Greene and Chris Fry of Salesforce.com look back on their company's successful transition, they advise others to "focus on getting several teams to excellence" (2008). Rather than spread support too thinly across all teams, strive to make the adoption of Scrum look inevitable through these early successes. Then others will desire to be part of it.

Get the team to take Scrum for a test drive. Rather than allow team members to argue about Scrum in the abstract, have them get some quick experience with it. Then they can discuss it and argue about specifics. A good approach is to agree to a three-month trial. This will give the team ample opportunity to get past the first one or two sprints, which are likely to still feel very uncomfortable. Hold a thorough retrospective with the entire team at the end of the three months and collectively decide how to move forward. The decision does not need to be "Scrum" or "not Scrum." If the test drive was inconclusive or the team is divided, another option is to continue the test drive for a few more months. Or perhaps the team decides that it is not ready for a particular practice and chooses to temporarily shelve it but will otherwise continue to work with Scrum.

Align incentives (or at least remove disincentives). There are many incentive programs, financial and otherwise, in organizations that can work against the adoption of Scrum. Many organizations have bonus programs to reward one employee for significant contributions to the team or department. Although such a program may appear beneficial at first glance, it works against the "we're all in this together" teamwork mentality we want of Scrum team members. Bonus programs that reward testers based on the number of defects found (and logged in a defect tracking system) have a similarly debilitating effect.

One organization I worked with revised its annual review form, removing the individual-oriented criteria, such as job knowledge, time management, and ability to balance multiple priorities. It replaced them with team-oriented criteria, such as makes others better at their jobs, contributes to shared knowledge, willingness to work beyond job title, and met team deliverable and quality goals.

In another company, I got the product owner and functional managers to promise a unique nonmonetary bonus to the team if the product would be released on schedule with an agreed-upon set of features. Although the product owner and managers trusted the team to continue to do high-quality work, I asked the team members to propose a quality metric. I didn't want them to receive their bonus by sacrificing quality. They proposed that quality would be measured by the number of defects reported in the 30 days following release. Their goal was to have fewer reported defects than two prior releases of a similar size. Four months later the team delivered slightly more functionality than promised on the planned date. When quality was measured a month later, the team members were given their bonus—a four-week sprint during which they would be their own product owners and could work on whatever they wanted. They took the opportunity to do some refactoring that had been bothering them. One tester took time to explore a new testing tool. Two developers added a scripting interface to a part of the application. This type of bonus was a win all around and avoided the problems that tend to arise with cash or similar bonuses.

Focus on addressing fear. How we behave is often influenced by what we fear. Because of bad past experiences, a product owner may fear an out-of-control development organization that builds only what it wants. This leads the product owner to prefer a development process with a detailed, up-front requirements gathering phase, as this will prevent the developers from building only what they want.

On the other hand, executive management may fear excessive schedule delays. This leads them to favor a development process that provides early, precise

SEE ALSO

Many fears are the result of waterfallacies and agile phobias. These are discussed in Chapter 6, "Overcoming Resistance." Many other fears are addressed in the objection sidebars throughout this book.

estimates of delivery dates. Managers almost always know they won't get the product by the date promised. But, they reason, by getting the team to commit to an early date and by keeping the pressure on them, they will get it earlier than they would otherwise and can avoid large schedule slips.

An architect may favor doing a detailed up-front system design because she excels at this. She fears that if the project's design phase is removed, then she will look no more brilliant than her coworkers. When communicating with individuals whose desire may be impeded by a fear, look for opportunities to address why the fears are likely unfounded.

Help people let go. People will not desire a new future until they can let go of the past. Every transition brings with it the possibility of loss, and with loss comes grief. Allow people time to grieve. Listen and accept their losses without arguing. Loss is personal and subjective. You will never convince people who are grieving that they are overreacting and that what was lost wasn't "that important." So don't try.

Don't discredit the past. In describing the transition and the brave, new agile world you are moving to, do not downplay or discredit the past. Whatever development process existed until now helped the organization succeed to the extent it has. It deserves our sincere appreciation and respect. It couldn't have been all bad. William Bridges, author of *Managing Transitions*, describes the consequences of building support for new initiatives at the expense of past efforts.

> Many managers, in their enthusiasm for a future that is going to be better than the past, ridicule or talk slightingly of the old way of doing things. In doing so they consolidate the resistance against the transition because people identify with the way things used to be and thus feel that their self-worth is at stake whenever the past is attacked. (2003, 34)

SEE ALSO

Chapter 4, "Iterating Toward Agility," describes the use of improvement communities as a way of engaging employees in the transition to Scrum.

Engage employees in the effort. Enlist as many allies at this stage as possible. An ideal ally is an opinion leader who has earned the respect of a large part of the audience you are targeting. The infectious enthusiasm of a few opinion leaders can rapidly spread to others in the organization. Benoit Houle, a ScrumMaster with BioWare, experienced this firsthand.

> I was very fortunate to establish a great working relationship with one of the senior programmers on the team who was very respected. He was the ScrumMaster of our initial "pilot" Scrum team for several sprints. He got extremely excited about the process and bought numerous books about Scrum and Extreme

Programming. He did a great job as a ScrumMaster, and his enthusiasm was echoing in every corner of the office.

Get skeptics involved as well. Ask employees what they would need to see, experience, or know before wanting to try Scrum; then find ways to give it to them.

Ability

All of the awareness and desire in the world won't get a team anywhere if it does not also acquire the ability to be agile. As we touched on briefly in Chapter 1, "Why Becoming Agile Is Hard (But Worth It)," succeeding with Scrum requires team members not only to learn new skills but also to unlearn old ones. Some of the larger challenges Scrum teams will face include the following:

- **Learning new technical skills.** It is common for developers new to Scrum to discover that while they are still good at their jobs, they aren't yet good at being agile. They will have to develop skills they didn't require previously (or could justify ignoring). For example, programmers will need to learn how to evolve the design of a system. Testers often must learn how to test a system without as much reliance on documentation. Both usually need to learn new ways of automating tests.
- **Learning to think and work as a team.** Many of us have enjoyed years of working silently in a cubicle, headphones securely on, with as little team interaction as possible. "You develop your part; I'll develop mine. We'll talk if we find any problems when we integrate." Scrum teams are encouraged not to think in terms of *my tasks* and *your tasks* but of *our tasks.* This forces collaboration among team members to new highs. Working in this way also creates a mindset of shared responsibility that will be new to many team members.
- **Learning how to create working software within short timeboxes.** Scrum's short, focused, timeboxed sprints present significant challenges to most teams who are new to working that way. Scrum teams strive to avoid unnecessary handoffs from one specialist team member to another. Developing working software by the end of each sprint will challenge team members to find ways to eliminate wasteful handoffs and to work more closely with each other.

Tools for Developing Ability

In most organizations, developing the ability to become agile (and then becoming good at it) will take longer than building awareness or creating desire. Fortunately, there are many good tools for developing ability, including the following:

Provide coaching and training. Scrum is sufficiently different from traditional software development in that training along with on-site coaching or mentoring is usually required. Lori Schubring, who led a successful Scrum adoption, says, "Our ability to be successful with agile started with an educational process. In my opinion, that was key. If we didn't understand something, we couldn't possibly welcome it with open arms." Elizabeth Woodward, one of the leaders of IBM's agile adoption, concurs.

> We initiated our agile transformation by setting a goal to conduct instructor-led two-day Disciplined Agile Development classes at every major site world wide within the first quarter. Within the first three quarters, we had taught over 4,400 software engineers world wide. This was important for getting everyone on the same page, for sharing the vision, and for building a sense of urgency. We found that there was misinformation about agile that needed to be addressed in order for teams to more willingly embrace agile.

What seems to work best for most companies is some initial training, oriented at creating a willingness to try Scrum and to understanding its core principles. This general training is usually then followed up with practice-specific training or coaching, such as bringing a test-driven development expert on-site to work hands-on with teams in their code.

Shortly after initiating its Scrum adoption, Salesforce.com had me do an on-site training course for more than 30 ScrumMasters, including some individuals who would not be in that role on projects. Two months later it had me do a formal, two-day training session for 35 product owners. Additional on-site coaches were also brought in to work with the teams during this period. In hindsight, even with this early and strong commitment to training and coaching, Chris Fry and Steve Greene wish they had "trained product owners earlier and with more intensity" and that they had gotten "outside coaching earlier." They offer the following advice to companies transitioning to Scrum: "Get professional help" (2008).

Hold individuals accountable. Along with providing coaching and training, employees need to know they will be held accountable for applying the new skills the organization is paying them to acquire.

Share information. While developing the ability to be agile, team members will be awash with new information and challenges. Provide opportunities for them to share information and problems. One way to do this is by cross-pollinating teams: Encourage team members to occasionally attend another team's daily scrum meeting or sprint review. Another option is to make use of the departmental intranet, Wikis, communities of practice, and reading groups to disseminate information. Yet another avenue for sharing is to ask those who have learned a new skill to present a short training session on it to others. Or, if your group is large enough, go further and have a day-long miniature agile conference. This is exactly what Yahoo! did in its California headquarters. J. F. Unson, a Scrum coach with Yahoo! at the time, describes the approach.

SEE ALSO
Communities of practice will be described in Chapter 17, "Scaling Scrum."

> At Yahoo! we had a full-day internal open space conference, where anyone could come in and propose topics. We had a number of good sessions, especially ones dealing with enterprise adoption, distributed agile, and so on. We had folks as far as the UK schedule meetings around the open space and participate. It really helps to build community within your company and get people to come up with and own their solutions. Of course, it helped that as a company we had critical mass to generate enough participation. (2008)

IBM takes a similar approach, conducting two four-day meetings each year that include technical leaders and managers from around the world plus the technical staff at the local site. Elizabeth Woodward describes how the company conducts a number of smaller "mini-conferences" around the world for IBM employees adopting agile.

> Each of those meetings has focused on agile, with presentations, education, experience reports, and community working sessions on agile topics. The working sessions were particularly productive because we were able to address key challenges such as using Scrum in a distributed environment, with face-to-face debate and discussion from a diverse, experienced group of people.

Set reasonable targets. Presented with a goal such as "be agile now," many teams freeze, not knowing how to start. A successful Scrum transition needs to be split into smaller pieces. So rather than asking a team to "start doing test-driven development," the ScrumMaster should ask the team to develop one feature that way in the next sprint. Similarly, organizations must balance a push for rapid progress against the risk of pushing for too much too quickly. By encouraging teams to select realistic, actionable targets, you can help them avoid the hesitation that can occur before initiating any immense undertaking.

Just do it. Don't stall, waiting to know all the answers before you start. The best way to develop the ability to do something is to start doing it. As Greene and Fry advise, "Experiment, be patient, and expect to make mistakes" (2008).

Promotion

There are three goals during promotion. The first is to lay the groundwork for the next pass through the ADAPT cycle. By promoting current successes you will have a jump start on creating awareness for the next round of improvements. The second goal is to reinforce agile behavior on existing teams by spreading the news of the good things those teams have achieved. Finally, the third goal is to create awareness and interest among those outside the groups directly involved in adopting Scrum. Many of those groups (such as human resources, sales, marketing, operations, and facilities) can have a dramatic influence on the success of your transition. In the transfer phase, you will actively pursue making sure that such groups will not pull the development organization back away from an agile mindset.

In seeking to promote Scrum, avoid turning your efforts into a marketing campaign. Many employees have been through countless change initiatives. The endless parade of such initiatives has left them jaded. Employees in many organizations have learned that if they don't like one change initiative, wait; another will soon follow to replace it. An announcement that "we're going agile" is likely to result in derisive comments and skepticism.

A good way to counter this cynicism is to avoid naming the transition effort. Teams that have lived through the "Quality 2000" initiative that was followed by "Better, Faster, Cheaper" and then "Customers First!" will not respond well to the "Scrum and Proud of It" campaign. Organizational development expert Glenn Allen-Meyer says that organizations name and brand their change initiatives because this type of marketing is what most organizations do.

> When people at work hear the marketed messages of change, they know they must either commit, comply, or leave. When they do not see the value-adding features of the change, and they feel they must comply in order to keep their jobs, then the difference between their true feelings and their compliance creates a detachment—a schism—between themselves and their place of work. (2000c, 24)

Getting coworkers to commit to a Scrum transition effort rather than merely comply with it (perhaps waiting for it to blow over) is what we would like to achieve with a successful promotion. One of Allen-Meyer's recommendations is to keep the change process nameless (2000a). My experience from the transitions I've directly managed, participated in, or observed confirms this.

One benefit to pursuing a nameless transition process is that it is harder to resist what you can't name. Thomas, a team leader at a very large commercial software developer, experienced this. After reading some of the early books and articles on Scrum, Thomas thought it would be a good fit for his 40-person project. Without any training or access to people with experience, he introduced

Scrum to the team. Employees were receptive and agreed to try. The team openly promoted the fact that it was doing Scrum as there was no reason to hide it. Unfortunately, it misunderstood a few key elements of Scrum and failed miserably.

When I met Thomas, he was still interested in Scrum and had continued reading about it and learning more. Since his failed project, he'd attended a conference and a two-day training class. Eighteen months had passed since the team's failed attempt at Scrum, and Thomas felt ready to give it another go. So did his team. Despite failing earlier, team members had gotten enough of a glimpse of the benefits that they were willing to try again. Unfortunately, the unique vocabulary of Scrum—*ScrumMaster*, *sprint*, *product backlog*, *daily scrum*, and even *Scrum* itself—had taken on negative connotations within the organization. Thomas knew he would not be able to tell his boss they were going to use Scrum again. He told his boss that they would instead use "agile." (Note the lowercase *a* rather than the capital *A*, which would have again implied a brand.) Thomas and his team went on to successfully apply their version of "agile," which was Scrum without the giveaway vocabulary.

Tools for Promoting Scrum

Having established that coming up with an effective naming strategy and matching T-shirts is one tool we won't use to promote the change process, let's turn our attention to some tools we can use.

Publicize the success stories. As always, communication plays a key role during the promotion activity of the ADAPT cycle. It is especially important to broadcast the successes of the early adopters of Scrum within the organization. A study by McKinsey & Company found that in successful change efforts, the emphasis was on encouraging employees to build on successes rather than on having them fix problems (2008). Promotional activities help shift employees' energy away from all the problems they uncovered during awareness and focus them instead on the successes they have been able to achieve.

A great way to communicate success is through internal experience report presentations from teams that have already adopted Scrum. Nothing beats hearing from someone who is already doing it. These experience reports can be combined with a general "Introduction to Scrum" presentation so that those unfamiliar with Scrum can learn not only what Scrum is but also hear one team's story of using it. If teams have begun collecting metrics, those can be included in the presentations as well. Early metrics may be nothing more than a survey showing the percentage of people who enjoy using Scrum, the percentage who think it has made them more productive, and the percentage who think quality is higher. Later you can add more rigorous metrics.

SEE ALSO

An editable, redistributable presentation for introducing Scrum is available at www.mountaingoatsoftware.com/scrum-a-presentation.

SEE ALSO

Some metrics are presented in Chapter 21, "Seeing How Far You've Come."

Fortunately, the best way to promote the transition to Scrum requires no effort on your part. As Benoit Houle, ScrumMaster at BioWare, puts it: "Like viral marketing, the best vehicle was word of mouth. The staff who worked on an agile team praised the process—greater team ownership, more predictability, less wasted effort and crunch time. Others heard and wanted to be part of it."

Matt Truxaw, a development manager and agile advocate at First American CoreLogic, had a similar experience.

> I liken the agile process to a whirlpool that builds over time, sucking in new people and groups as it builds. We started with limited buy-in from the developers themselves. By regularly talking about it and helping to promote the successes, we got more developers excited about the process. Working both from within the teams and providing coaching and guidance to the project management group, we gained acceptance across most of that team.

Host an agile safari. One of my favorite ways to promote Scrum comes from Google. Team members who are curious about agile but who haven't had the opportunity to work on an agile team are allowed to go on an "Agile Safari." When employees go on safari, they join an agile team for a couple of weeks to get a feel for what agile is like and how it works. They experience agile "in the wild" rather than merely reading about it. I really like this idea because it addresses a concern Machiavelli identified 500 years ago when he wrote that people "do not truly believe in new things unless they have actually had personal experience of them" (2005, 22).

Attract attention and interest. Shamelessly seek attention. The more often people hear about Scrum (or better, see it or experience it), the better you will be doing at the goal of making its ultimate adoption seem inevitable. A few months into her department's transition, Lori Schubring attracted attention to the effort in a novel way.

> We also held an "Open House" on Halloween for the business to come visit our department and see what we were doing with Scrum. We created a Scrum-themed crossword puzzle and gave away prizes. We put up posters explaining the different aspects of Scrum such as the Scrum Board, Burndown Chart, Product Backlog, and ScrumMaster. We gave away prizes and provided food and beverages. The internal information services staff helped make the food and decorate the building, and the event was a huge success.

In their book *Fearless Change*, Mary Lynn Manns and Linda Rising point out that providing food is always a good idea. Not only will you get more attendees, they are likely to be in a better mood (2004). Benoit Houle brought food to sprint reviews at BioWare to encourage broad attendance at those meetings, which he says were "a great way to promote the successes. Everyone in the company was invited to attend." Houle also successfully used team rooms and walls full of index cards detailing the work of the sprint to attract attention and interest.

> Our war rooms full of 4" × 6" cards, team composition pictures, and burndown charts were also quite communicative of our team progress and accomplishments. Because of limited wall space in team rooms, we started to spread miles of corkboards within our corridors for our task boards and to show team progress and achievements.

Transfer

After three years of pushing, attending literally thousands of daily scrums himself, and running dozens of one-day "Intro to Scrum" classes for more than 500 team members, Gino had much to be proud of. Much of the development department was now using Scrum. Gino had started the company's shift to Scrum when he was one of its many development managers. Through early results by his teams, he gained a promotion to director of a new group in the company called the "Scrum Office." The Scrum Office provided support and services to any team that wanted help. It was similar to the project management office (PMO) of a company doing traditional software development. Gino was good in his new role and soon had more than half of the company's development staff working on projects that were to some extent agile. Before the transition was fully realized, Gino accepted a bigger, better position at a company with bigger, harder challenges in transitioning to Scrum. Back at his old company, the Scrum adoption eventually failed—not because Gino was no longer there, but because no one (not even Gino) ever transferred the implications of Scrum outside the development organization.

I visualize Scrum as a rocket. Pushing that rocket forward is the power of its engines. But pulling it back are the forces of gravity. If the rocket is able to push far enough, it can enter into orbit. But if it cannot, it will inevitably get pulled back to earth, right where it started. The implications of Scrum must be pushed far enough into other parts of the organization so that the entire transition is not pulled back by organizational gravity.

Gino did a wonderful job of gaining acceptance for Scrum among programmers, testers, project managers, database developers, user experience designers, analysts, and so on. But the use of Scrum by more than 500 developers never led to changes in human resources, sales, marketing, or other groups. The same individual-oriented bonus and annual review programs existed. Salespeople could still promise one-off enhancements to customers without first discussing such promises with teams.

It is impossible for a development team to remain agile on its own permanently. If the implications of using Scrum are not transferred to other departments, organizational gravity from those departments will eventually stall and kill the transition effort. By this, I do not mean that the rest of the organization needs to start using Scrum. What I mean is that the rest of the organization must become at least compatible with Scrum.

Sources of Organizational Gravity

Previous sections in this chapter provided a list of tools you could use to help move your organization forward in ADAPTing to Scrum. There is really only one tool for transferring agile to other departments: communicating with those departments. So, rather than provide a list of tools, let's look instead at the departments or groups most likely to possess a lot of organizational gravity. These are the groups that deserve attention during the transfer part of the ADAPT cycle. In working with these groups, maintain a goal of educating, not evangelizing. You want other groups to understand how the development organization benefits from Scrum. You do not need to convert them into staunch supporters of your process. Rather, you want them to understand some of its unique principles and how those might lead to friction between your group and theirs.

The following is a list of groups to whom you must transfer the implications of using Scrum. Notice that I have not included testing and product management. These groups are fundamental participants in Scrum rather than groups to which the effects of Scrum are transferred. Involvement of product owners and testers in Scrum is critical and needs to be established at the beginning of the transition effort.

SEE ALSO

The new role of product owner is described in Chapter 7, "New Roles." Changes to the role of tester are described in Chapter 8, "Changed Roles."

SEE ALSO

Implications of Scrum on the human resources group are discussed further in Chapter 20, "Human Resources, Facilities, and the PMO."

Human resources. A development organization using Scrum and the human resources (HR) group are likely to clash in a number of ways. Many organizations have human resources policies that work against the successful adoption of Scrum. A periodic review process that forces managers to rank employees from most to least valuable will undermine efforts to encourage teamwork. Equally damaging is a review process that values individual contributions while ignoring teamwork.

SEE ALSO

Implications of Scrum on the facilities group are discussed further in Chapter 20.

Facilities. Tales of meddling from the "Furniture Police" are common (DeMarco and Lister 1999). Many teams are told they cannot hang index cards, burndown charts, or others signs of progress or work on the walls. Few teams are allowed to adjust their own cubicles; many have learned that the best way around this is to tear down or move cubicles over the weekend in the vein of "it's better to ask forgiveness than permission." Benoit Houle of BioWare has a more encouraging story of successfully transferring the implications of Scrum to his facilities group.

> Facilities redesigned our floors to support agile team rooms. They built us bigger rooms to support teams of six to eight people. Our facilities team has a web application that catalogues everyone's location and allows us to easily submit a move through our intranet. We all have the same desks, so most of the time the only items we are moving are the computer and accessories. It is quick and painless.

Marketing. In many organizations, development groups are so bad at projecting ship dates that the marketing group stops asking and just makes them up. This also happens in organizations where the marketing group is much more powerful than the development group and can therefore dictate desired dates. In transferring the effects of Scrum to the marketing group, a key focus should be on educating them about the transparency provided by Scrum.

Most marketing groups don't like having to lock down plans a year in advance any more than development teams do. The marketing group may need to schedule an ad campaign nine months in advance. But, just like development teams, they usually prefer to have a little flexibility. Rather than specify the exact contents of the ad now, they'd prefer to commit today to running an ad but specify the exact contents of the ad closer to publication date. A Scrum team's progressive refinement of plans combined with its strict adherence to dates should prove beneficial to marketing groups that are open to it.

Finance. The finance group often intersects with Scrum projects in two areas. First is the forecasting of project schedules and budgets. It will be important to get the finance group to understand that—regardless of the development process employed—a team cannot create an estimate that is accurate within 5% from a new product description written on a napkin. Such unrealistic requests usually come from a finance department that has been burned in the past by bad estimates from development teams. It will take time to restore the finance group's confidence and trust in developers.

After a few Scrum teams have started to demonstrate success with the new approach, it is usually helpful to meet with your finance department. In that meeting, acknowledge past project-planning sins, but also show that while Scrum still cannot guarantee on-time delivery, it can provide early exposure to possible schedule slips.

The second area in which development and finance often intersect is in the tracking or reporting of hours. Although Scrum does not require a team to track hours worked, the team should be willing to do so if the finance department needs this information. This would be the case, for example, in a contract development company that bills customers by the hour.

Related to the tracking of hours can be a finance department's desire to capitalize the cost of the project. Capitalizing a project refers to spreading the development cost over the projected useful life of the project rather than accounting for those costs in the month they occurred. Capitalization guidelines vary from country to country, and many of them are based on outdated concepts, including that a project cannot be capitalized until technical feasibility has been demonstrated. From past exposure to development processes, we've trained finance departments to think that technical feasibility is achieved after analysis and design are done. Without distinct analysis and design phases on a Scrum project, the finance group may find it hard to determine when technical feasibility has been achieved.

I've discussed this with many finance departments and have always been able to make the case that technical feasibility is achieved after no more than a few sprints. After all, if the team has produced working software that includes one feature from the finished product, then it must be technically feasible. While I can understand the counterarguments to this position, those arguments could also be applied to considering something technically feasible after analysis and design are done but when nothing has been coded.

There are groups beyond these to whom you will need to eventually also transfer the implications of Scrum. For example, you may work with a project management office, sales, information technology, operations, hardware development, and other groups with organizational gravity. Transferring the implications of Scrum to them will be important to your long-term success.

THINGS TO TRY NOW

❑ Identify the ADAPT activity that most closely describes you. Do this for your team, your department, and your organization. Identify three things you could do to move one of these to the next level of adaptation. Choose one (or work with your team to narrow down the list, if applicable) and begin to implement it.

❑ If you have already begun to adopt Scrum, think about promotion. Identify ways to promote your early successes so that others become intrigued by the process.

Putting It All Together

Like Scrum itself, ADAPTing to Scrum is iterative. It begins when some in the organization develop an awareness that the current way of working is no longer producing acceptable results. As awareness spreads, some individuals develop the desire to try Scrum in an attempt to improve the situation. Through trial-and-error, these early adopters within the organization develop the ability to be successful with Scrum. A new status quo may emerge with a small number of teams successfully using Scrum within a broader organization that does not.

As these initial Scrum teams continue to improve their use of Scrum, they begin to promote their successes—sometimes informally as might occur over lunch with friends on another team, other times more formally as in a department-wide presentation. This helps individuals on other teams begin their own progressions from awareness to desire to ability. And then soon these other teams begin to promote their successes as well.

All of this early success is nice, but it is jeopardized if adopting Scrum is viewed as something that occurs entirely within the development organization. For continued long-term success, it will be necessary to transfer the implications of using Scrum to other departments that will be affected, including sales, marketing, operations, human resources, and facilities. These groups do not need to use Scrum—we don't need salespeople drawing burndown charts or facilities doing daily scrums. But, unless these groups make small but important changes in how they interact with the development group, they will affect the development group's ability to be agile.

In the next chapter, we'll explore choices among patterns you can emulate as you become able to transition to Scrum. We'll consider whether it's best to start small or go all in and how much promotion should occur at the beginning of the transition effort. We'll also discuss several ways to spread Scrum beyond your initial project or projects. Understanding the ADAPT process laid out in this chapter will inform the decisions you will be asked to make in the next.

Additional Reading

Derby, Esther. 2006. A manager's guide to supporting organizational change. *Crosstalk*, January, 17–19.

> In this article, Esther Derby, coauthor with Diana Larsen of *Agile Retrospectives* (2006), presents ten insights on what a manager can do to support a change initiative. Most of the insights are focused on the awareness and desire phases.

Hiatt, Jeffrey. 2006. *ADKAR: A model for change in business, government and our community.* Prosci Research.

> ADKAR, which is an acronym for Awareness, Desire, Knowledge, Ability, and Reinforcement, is a generic model for personal and organizational change. It served as an inspiration in creating the ADAPT model. This book offers excellent, although general, advice on awareness, desire, and ability.

Chapter 3

Patterns for Adopting Scrum

There are many different routes an organization can take to adopt Scrum. Fortunately, from looking at companies that have already transitioned, we are able to identify some common patterns of how to do it successfully. In this chapter, we look at the strengths and weaknesses of four patterns, as well as when each may be appropriate. The four patterns form a pair of questions that must be addressed at the start of any Scrum adoption effort. These questions are as follows:

- Should we start with one or two teams, or should we convert all teams at the same time?
- Should we announce our intent (perhaps just to others in the company but perhaps publicly as well), or should we keep the change quiet for now?

In addition to providing guidance for answering those two questions, we explore three options for spreading Scrum after the initial effort is underway. Finally, the chapter concludes by considering how soon a new Scrum team should begin focusing on adopting agile technical practices.

Start Small or Go All In

Conventional, long-standing advice regarding transitioning to Scrum or any agile process has been to start with a pilot project, learn from it, and then spread agile throughout the organization. This approach is the frequently used *start-small* pattern in which an organization selects typically one to three teams (of five to nine people each), gets them successful, and then expands Scrum from there. As Scrum spreads through the organization, new teams benefit from the lessons learned by the teams that have gone before. There are many variations of start small, depending on how many people the organization wants to transition and how quickly they want to do it. Start small can also be applied differently based on how risk-averse or uncertain about the transition the organization is. For example, in some cases the first team or teams will finish their projects before a second set of teams even begins. Other organizations will take an overlapping approach, where the second set of teams starts only one or two sprints after the first.

The start-small pattern, while popular, is not for everyone. Salesforce.com, for example, followed the opposite pattern (Fry and Greene 2006). I remember answering my phone on October 3, 2006, and hearing Chris and Steve from Salesforce.com tell me that they had just converted 35 teams to Scrum overnight. They asked if I'd like to help. My initial thought was that they needed a psychiatrist more than a Scrum consultant. Not one to shrink from a challenge, though, I agreed to help, packed a copy of Freud alongside my laptop, and set off for their office in San Francisco. Part of what I saw there wasn't entirely unexpected—teams and individuals in an uproar over such a sudden, far-reaching change—but I also saw other things that helped this large-scale, rapid adoption succeed.

Salesforce.com was pursuing the *all-in* pattern, which draws its name from a poker player who bets all of his chips on one hand. Salesforce.com has a hard-driving, aggressive, achievement-driven culture that would not have been a good fit for a cautious start-small approach. When key executives were presented with a proposal to adopt Scrum, they were convinced. They felt that if Scrum was worth doing for one team, it was worth doing for all teams, so they chose to go all in.

Surprisingly, the all-in and start-small patterns can be combined. An increasingly common approach is a one- to three-team pilot project followed immediately by going all in. The pilot in this case serves the typical purpose of allowing the organization to learn about Scrum and how it will function there. However, the pilot in this scenario also serves the more important purpose of increasing organizational awareness about Scrum. If you're going to transition 200 or more people all at once, it is extremely helpful to be able to point to one team who has already done it and say, "We're all going to do what they did."

Reasons to Prefer Starting Small

The start-small approach offers several advantages.

- **Starting small is less expensive.** An all-in transition will almost certainly cost more than starting small. Because of the greater number of people learning a new way of working all at the same time, all-in transitions generally rely more heavily on outside coaches, ScrumMasters, and trainers. The slower pace of a start-small adoption allows the organization to build internal expertise and then use that to help the teams that start later. Starting small also saves money because early mistakes affect only a subset of the organization. Tom Gilb, who was perhaps the original agilist, has written, "If you don't know what you're doing, don't do it on a large scale" (1988, 11).

- **Early success is almost guaranteed.** By carefully selecting the initial project and team members, you can almost guarantee the success of your first

Scrum project. You may consider this cheating; I don't. When starting small, a goal of the first few projects is to generate the knowledge that will enable the successful rollout of Scrum. There may be value in starting with a project and team that make success easy and then learning from its experiences. Additionally, an early success can be vital to gaining buy-in from skeptics or fence-sitters.

- **Starting small avoids the big risk of going all in.** An all-at-once transition can be very risky. Small mistakes will be magnified across the entire transition effort. Perhaps the most significant risk to an all-in approach is that you will be unlikely to get a second chance. If you start to transition the entire organization, make a mistake that increases resistance, and then revert to your pre-Scrum process while figuring out how to overcome the newly discovered issues, it is unlikely that team members will give you a second chance to start the transition. Resistance by that point will likely be so entrenched that the transition effort will have failed. By contrast, if you start small and find a fatal flaw in how you've started, you can keep the next round the same size as the current one, rather than expanding, effectively restarting the transition process.

- **Starting small is less stressful.** Twenty-first century organizations and their employees are under constant stress. An announcement that the whole development organization is adopting Scrum, which affects so many aspects of everyday work, could be the proverbial straw that breaks the camel's back. The stress of transitioning is reduced by starting small because early adopters become coaches and ambassadors. They encourage other groups to make the transition with stories of their successes and honest discussions of the challenges they faced and overcame.

- **Starting small can be done without reorganizing.** Most organizations that fully adopt Scrum will eventually undergo some degree of reorganizing. This can create further stress and can increase resistance from some individuals. By starting small, the need to reorganize can be put off longer, ideally until valuable experience with Scrum has been gained.

Reasons to Prefer Going All In

Just as there are reasons to prefer starting small, there are reasons to prefer an all-in transition:

- **Going all in can reduce resistance.** In anything less than an all-at-once transition, there will always be some skeptics who will hold out hope that the whole effort is a pilot that will soon be abandoned. Like Cortez burning his boats at Vera Cruz to prove his resolve to his soldiers, an organization that goes all in is demonstrating both its commitment to the new process and also that it will not turn back. This level of visible commitment to the change can be beneficial in helping the change succeed.

SEE ALSO

Advice on how a Scrum team can best work in conjunction with a traditional team is offered in Chapter 19, "Coexisting with Other Approaches."

- **It avoids problems created by having Scrum and traditional teams work together.** If you transition anything short of the entire company all at once, you run the risk of having some teams using Scrum and others not. This means there will be times when a Scrum team needs to coordinate work with a traditional team, which creates challenges because of the different attitudes Scrum and traditional teams bring to things like planning, deadlines, and communication. These problems go away when the entire organization adopts Scrum at the same time. Chris Fry and Steve Greene of Salesforce.com report that "the key factor driving us toward a big-bang rollout was to avoid organizational dissonance and a desire for decisive action. Everyone would be doing the same thing at the same time" (2007, 137).

- **An all-in transition will be over more quickly.** One of the central tenets of this book is that an organization is never "done" becoming agile; there are always improvements to be made. However, there is definitely a time when employees can look back and say of the transition that the worst is over. An organization that goes all in can reach this point more quickly.

Choosing Between Going All In and Starting Small

As I mentioned at the start of this chapter, starting small has been the default approach recommended by most agile authors and used in most agile adoptions. The combination of this approach's low risk and high likelihood of success make it hard to find fault with. Always choose to start small when there is a reluctance by leaders in the organization to fully commit to Scrum. Success, even on a small scale, can be the best way to convince the skeptics. Always start small when there is a high cost associated with failure. If the cost of failure is too high for those leading the transition, starting small is the way to go, even if it may not be best for the organization as a whole. Start small is probably not the best approach when your organization urgently needs the benefits of Scrum. (But if you do choose to start small, scale quickly.) Starting small is safe, but it's slow.

SEE ALSO

We explore ways to spread Scrum to other teams later in this chapter.

Going all in should be used in limited cases. Consider going all in if time is critical. Although an all-in approach may cost more money, it will cost less time. If time is your primary concern, all in may be the best solution. Consider going all in if you, like Salesforce.com, want to send a clear message to a small number of critics and stakeholders that Scrum is here to stay. Never go all in without enough experienced ScrumMasters to serve each team. It doesn't matter in the short term whether these ScrumMasters are internal or external; but remember that eventually you'll want all of your ScrumMasters to be internal employees. Finally, size matters. If there are only ten of you, you might as well go all in. But for teams of more than perhaps 400, going all in may not be logistically possible.

Whichever route you choose for adopting Scrum, remember that choosing this pattern is only the first of the many decisions you'll need to make when transitioning. You will next need to decide whether to make your transition public.

Public Display of Agility or Stealth

The next choice to make is whether or not to publicize your transition. One option is to make a *public display of agility*. In this approach, the team or organization announces with great fanfare that it is adopting Scrum. Depending on the scope and significance of the transition, the announcements may range from lunchroom comments to other teams all the way up to press releases in the national media. No matter the extent of the publicity, with a public display of agility, teams make an effort to inform others that something agile is going on.

In contrast to a public display of agility is a *stealth transition*. In a stealth transition, only the team members know they are using Scrum until the project is complete. I found a group doing a stealth transition at one of my clients. On my first visit to this client, I spoke with Sarah, the director of the company's project management office. She told me that the transition to Scrum was well underway. It had begun shortly after I delivered a two-day training class to many developers in its headquarters office. Sarah shared with me a well-thought-out plan she had outlined to introduce Scrum across her company's more than 200 developers.

Sarah's plan showed four initial pilot teams, each of which had been selected for specific reasons. One team was chosen for its willingness to relocate into a shared team space very different from the dedicated cubicle environment in use at the time. Another team was chosen because it would be one of the first to use a new technology in which the company was making a significant investment. The other two teams were selected to be part of the pilot for equally good reasons. Sarah's plan was great because it would enable teams to maximize the learning right from the outset of this transition effort.

I left Sarah's office planning to visit each of the four teams so that I could get their perspective on how things were going. Strangely, though, I didn't find four teams—I found five. When I figured out which of the five wasn't one that Sarah had told me about, I went back and talked with that team some more. I discovered that it was not an officially sanctioned part of Sarah's pilot effort. The members had noticed the goings on of one of the official teams, liked what they had seen, and decided to try it themselves. They had a vague sense that they probably shouldn't be doing what they were doing and had placed their wall-hanging task board and burndown chart well inside a labyrinth of cube walls. I had only stumbled across it because I was unfamiliar with the building and had gotten lost looking for one of the official teams.

This team was doing a stealth transition. Members were using Scrum but were keeping their activities to themselves until the project was complete. There are varying degrees of stealth—some teams may actively try to keep what they're doing quiet while others merely don't publicize the change.

Reasons to Favor a Public Display of Agility

There are many good reasons for making a public display of agility. Among them are the following:

- **Everyone knows you're doing it, so you're more likely to stick with it.** Standard advice to anyone attempting to adopt or abandon a habit is to solicit the help of your friends. Whether you are starting a diet, quitting smoking, or starting an exercise program, telling your friends about the change is a good idea. You'll likely feel an unspoken pressure to succeed because you've announced your intentions; your friends will also be able to support and encourage you. The same is true when transitioning to Scrum.

- **A public display establishes a vision to work toward.** Publicly proclaiming your intent provides an opportunity to create thought and discussion around the goal. With the intent out in the open, team members will feel comfortable talking about the transition with those outside the team. They'll be able to share successes and failures. Those interested in the transition (perhaps wishing they could be part of it) will offer advice; those opposed will offer resistance. A public display can provide the opportunity to engage both groups, providing the opportunities to encourage the former group and to overcome the objections of the latter.

- **Operating in the open is a firm statement of your commitment.** A stealth transition can be perceived as a bit wishy-washy. It is as though the team or organization is saying, "We believe in this but we want to hedge our bets by having the chance to back away if it doesn't go well." There's no backing away from a public display. It makes a powerful statement that not only does the organization plan to initiate the transition, but it also plans to be successful at it.

- **You can solicit organizational support.** If you're trying to keep the use of Scrum quiet, you'll have limited ability to reach outside the team for assistance. There are many obstacles you may encounter as you transition; before abandoning the assistance of possible allies in overcoming them, make sure the advantages to stealth are compelling.

- **Stating your goal and then achieving it sends a powerful message.** Announcing at the end of a project that the project was successful because it secretly used Scrum is much less compelling to skeptics than telling them up front. Baseball player Babe Ruth's most famous home run was the 1932 "called shot." With a count of two balls and two strikes, Ruth pointed to the centerfield fence and hit the next pitch into the centerfield bleachers. Saying what you'll do and then doing it is more powerful than announcing your goal after it has been achieved.

Reasons to Favor a Stealth Transition

Stealth transitions may seem a bit sneaky, but there are actually quite a few advantages to keeping a low profile. These include

- **You have a chance to make progress before resistance starts.** A public announcement about the transition will bring resistors and naysayers out of the woodwork. Their best chance to avert the change is before it gains much momentum, and so they will argue strongly against it after it is announced.
- **A stealth transition keeps additional pressure off.** If adopting Scrum is a high-publicity affair with proclamations in company newsletters, the intranet, and so on, the team can feel a great deal of pressure to succeed—both at the project and at the transition. For teams that thrive under pressure this might be good. However, when the project is finished you won't know if it had been successful because of Scrum or because of the additional pressure the team was under. Bob Schatz and Ibrahim Abdelshafi did not announce a grand change of process when they led Primavera's successful transition to Scrum.

    > One of the first things we didn't do was start telling everyone that we planned to use a new process. We didn't want to make people apprehensive, and we wanted to give them time to adjust to the changes. Plus, when you run around announcing your new process and all its benefits, you can quickly set unrealistic expectations. (2005, 37–38)

- **No one knows about it until you tell them.** When operating in stealth mode, you can wait until the project is successful before indicating that the project was run in a different way. Or, if the project fails, you can adjust how you are doing Scrum, try again, and only tell people after you've figured out the nuances of doing so that lead to success in your environment.
- **If no one knows you're doing Scrum, no one can tell you to stop.** If you start so quietly that no one but the individuals involved know, there's no one who can tell you to stop. I've seen individual teams choose the stealth approach under the premise of it being easier to ask forgiveness than permission. I've also seen vice presidents of development or project

management offices choose to introduce Scrum in stealth mode so that they could prove tangible benefits before having to debate the merits of Scrum with groups they knew would resist.

Choosing Between a Public Display and Stealth

I find that organizations willing to make a public display of agility are more likely to enjoy a successful transition than those that try a stealth approach. Always choose to make the transition publicly known when you are confident in Scrum and committed to the transition. Similarly, strongly consider a public display if you expect there will be stiff resistance to the change but want to overcome it quickly.

In contrast, choose a quieter approach when you want to experiment either with all of Scrum or just parts of it. For example, maybe you introduce daily meetings—don't call them daily *scrums* in this case—and see how that works. Then introduce the idea of working in timeboxed sprints. If these go well, maybe start calling what you're doing *agile* or *Scrum* and proceed from there. Additionally, always choose a stealth approach when it is your only option. If you don't have the political clout to say, "We're doing Scrum," or if doing so will create too much resistance, start quietly.

Patterns for Spreading Scrum

Getting started with Scrum is one thing; spreading it across the organization is another. Unless you have chosen an all-in transition, you will need to build upon the successes of the first few teams as you move Scrum into other teams. There are three general patterns you can use for spreading Scrum beyond the initial teams. The first two patterns involve taking a team that has begun to be successful with Scrum and then using its members to seed new teams. The third pattern takes a different approach and involves spreading Scrum using internal coaches.

Split and Seed

The *split-and-seed* pattern is typically put into use after the first couple of teams have adopted Scrum and run at least a handful of sprints. By that point, team members are beginning to understand what it is like to work on a Scrum team. They certainly won't have figured everything out, but sprints should be ending with working software, and team members should be working together well. In short, the team probably has a long way to go to get good, but Scrum is starting to feel natural.

It is at this unlikely point that we split the team up.

In the split-and-seed pattern, one functioning Scrum team is split in two, with each half of the original team forming the basis of a new team. New people are then added to these splinter teams to form new Scrum teams. This pattern is shown in Figure 3.1, which shows the creation of two teams from one original team. A large initial team could be used to seed as many as four new teams, especially if the initial team included some members with previous Scrum experience or a natural aptitude for it.

FIGURE 3.1

The split-and-seed pattern applied to two initial teams.

The new team members can be either newly hired employees or existing employees moving onto their first Scrum projects. The idea behind the split-and-seed pattern is that newly formed, second-generation Scrum teams will have an easier time learning the mechanics and practices of Scrum because they will have guidance from the experienced members of the team. The new teams are left together for a few sprints until that team begins to jell and its new members have developed a feel for Scrum. Then, again, the functioning teams are broken up into smaller teams and new members are added to fill out the teams. This cycle is repeated until Scrum has been fully introduced.

In a large, enterprise rollout of Scrum, you do not need to leave each generation of teams together for the same number of sprints. You can instead split each team whenever it's ready.

Grow and Split

The *grow-and-split* pattern is a variation of the split-and-seed approach. It involves adding team members until the team is large enough that it can be comfortably split in two, as shown in Figure 3.2. Immediately after splitting, each of the new teams will probably be on the small end of the desirable size range of five to nine members. After allowing the new teams one sprint at this reduced size, new members are added until each team becomes large enough that it can also be split. This pattern repeats until the entire project or organization has transitioned.

FIGURE 3.2

The grow-and-split pattern used to create two teams.

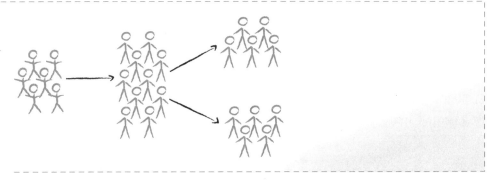

Internal Coaching

Philips Research's Scrum adoption is an example of the third pattern for spreading Scrum: *internal coaching*. Philips had begun adopting Scrum and was facing a problem. Like many organizations, it had some teams that were excelling with their new agile approach and others that were struggling. Philips' Christ Vriens solved the problem by using internal coaching. On each team that was doing well, he identified one person who truly understood what it meant to be agile and designated that person as a coach to another team that had not yet progressed as far in its understanding and use of Scrum.

Coaches were given specific responsibilities, such as attend sprint planning, review, and retrospective meetings; attend one daily scrum each week; and be available for two hours each week to provide other assistance to the mentored team as needed. Coaches were not excused from their responsibilities on their original teams, but it was acknowledged that each coach would have fewer hours to contribute to those teams.

Reasons to Prefer Split and Seed

The split-and-seed pattern's advantages are rooted in its quick-spreading nature.

- **You can add teams more quickly than with most other approaches.** Each new team should ideally include at least 2 members of the previous team. This means that possibly as soon as after 2 or 3 sprints, a team of 8 people could conceivably be split into four 2-person groups used to seed a second set of teams. If each of those 4 teams had 8 people you would have 32 Scrum team members. A few sprints later these 32 people could be used to seed 16 more teams, each with 8 team members for a total of over 100 Scrum-experienced people after only 5 or 6 sprints.
- **Each team has someone with Scrum experience to help guide them.** Only the very first teams to transition will be forced to do so without someone

on the team with Scrum experience. All subsequent teams will benefit from having at least two (and hopefully three or four) team members with at least a couple of sprints of experience under their belts. This can help reduce the discomfort some people will feel about transitioning to something new and unfamiliar.

Reasons to Prefer Grow and Split

The grow-and-split pattern spreads Scrum a bit more slowly than does the split-and-seed approach but comes with some key advantages.

- **You don't have to destroy any existing teams.** The primary problem with the split-and-seed strategy is that teams who are just starting to jell and get a handle on Scrum are demolished to form the basis of new teams. Breaking up a good team is always something that should be done with caution. Growing the team before splitting it overcomes this shortcoming because the team is kept together until it is large enough to form two complete teams, each with agile experience.
- **Team members feel more continuity from sprint to sprint.** When using the split-and-seed pattern, teams are constantly being split and reformed before a true sense of team camaraderie is established. Because the grow-and-split approach divides a team only when it has gotten too big, members can stay together longer, and there is less feeling of disruption.

Reasons to Prefer Internal Coaching

The internal coaching approach is generally my preferred approach. Not surprisingly, there are a strong set of advantages to it, including the following:

- **Well-running teams do not need to be split.** A drawback to the prior patterns is that functioning teams are split to form the foundations of new teams. When using internal coaches, teams stay intact with only the minor disruption of an occasional outsider (the coach) joining the team.
- **Coaches can be hand-selected for new teams.** An approach like the split-and-seed pattern takes a whole-team approach to coaching: The new team is coached collectively by the seeding team members. Some of those individuals will be good in that role; some will not. With internal coaching, the most appropriate coach can be selected for each new team.
- **Coaches can be moved from team to team.** After awhile a team and its coach become stale. A fresh pair of eyes can be helpful in identifying new ways to improve. When internal coaches move from team to team they act like bees, pollinating each team with new ideas.

Choosing Your Approach

There are two driving factors in choosing among these three patterns for spreading Scrum: How quickly do we need to spread Scrum to additional teams, and do we have good internal coaches who can assist the new teams? The answers to these questions will be key to helping you choose the pattern that best fits your organization.

In general, consider using split and seed when you are in hurry. The split-and-seed approach can be one of the fastest ways to spread Scrum through an organization. The approach can be accelerated in a couple of different ways: First, you can split teams a bit earlier than might be ideal. Second, you can split teams into more new teams than might be ideal, perhaps four new teams instead of two, even if this means that some new teams get some less-than-ideal coaches from the earlier teams.

Be cautious, though, about using split and seed if the technology and domain cannot support moving people among teams. Changing team membership is always detrimental to productivity. That loss can be offset, however, by the benefits of quickly spreading Scrum through a large project or organization. However, in some cases, it is just not practical to move people between teams. For example, seeding a .NET team with Java programmers just because they have three sprints of Scrum experience would not be a good idea.

The grow-and-split pattern is perhaps the most natural approach, as it mirrors what would probably happen if no one intervened to help the spread of Scrum. In most organizations, people move between projects, carrying good practices with them. The grow-and-split approach is simply a more directed approach than letting this happen naturally, which would take much, much longer.

Consider using grow and split when there is not enough urgency to push you to the split-and-seed approach. Because growing and splitting a team is a less aggressive (and less risky) approach than splitting and seeding a team, it is often used in similar situations but when there is a bit less urgency. Also consider using grow and split when the team size is growing anyway. True to its name, the grow-and-split approach works best when teams are expanding.

Internal coaching can be used as a spreading strategy on its own, or it can be used to augment either of the other approaches. This approach works best under certain conditions:

- **When the group is large enough that good practices won't fully spread on their own.** One of the strengths of this pattern is that coaches can move from one team to another, spreading good practices as they do so. If your organization is small enough that sharing good practices won't be a problem, then you may not need this approach.
- **When splitting teams is not practical for your projects.** If any of the drawbacks to splitting teams concern you, the internal coaching approach is a good antidote.

- **When you have enough internal coaches or can bring in outside help.** An ideal coach is someone who fundamentally understands Scrum and has probably worked in an agile way for years before even hearing the word. These individuals can be hard to identify in advance; they aren't necessarily the most experienced team members. If you don't have enough good coaches, consider using one of the other patterns initially. After enough teams have run a few sprints, you can begin to augment a seeding approach with internal coaches. You can also spread the coaches you do have out a bit more by having each coach assist more than one team. If budget allows, you can also bring in outside consultants until you have built up your internal coaching corps.

Introducing New Technical Practices

One final decision facing change agents, ScrumMasters, and new Scrum team members themselves is how soon the team should adopt new technical practices. One school of thought is that everything should start with the technical practices. If a team is using the right technical practices—simple design, automated testing, pair programming, refactoring, and so on—then agility will be the natural result.

The alternative view is that a team should be left alone longer and given time to discover the technical practices that work best in its environment. ScrumMasters, managers, and coaches may eventually nudge a team toward trying different practices. "Would this have happened if we had more automated tests?" a ScrumMaster might ask the team. But in general, the team is given longer at the start to work without pressure to adopt or even try specific new technical practices.

In this section, we'll consider both the reasons to encourage an early start at trying new technical practices and the reasons why delaying might be a better choice.

Reasons to Start Soon

There are three very good reasons for putting an early emphasis on adopting new technical practices:

- **Very rapid improvements are possible.** Many of the technical practices can provide some quick wins to the team and organization. Pair programming, for example, can help cross-train programmers across more areas of the system. Introducing a continuous build process can reduce integration hassles to near zero. Other practices—test-driven development, for example—have steeper learning curves, but even these are measured in days and weeks rather than months and years.

- **If the team doesn't try new technical practices early, it might never try them.** Too many Scrum teams adopt the bare minimum of Scrum and stop there, deciding that the improvements already achieved through their new iterative and incremental work style are sufficient. By not considering or trying new or improved technical practices, these teams forgo much of the improvement they could have made. I tend to think of such teams as having learned to work iteratively but having not become agile. Gabrielle Benefield reports having witnessed this problem at Yahoo! while she was the company's director of agile product development.

> The most visible symptoms of dysfunction in Yahoo! product development were at the project and team layer (centered around issues of planning, project management, release management, and team interactions), rather than at the technical practices or tools layer. As a result, Yahoo!'s initial focus was on the adoption of Scrum. There was active debate about whether agile engineering practices should also be adopted in parallel; in hindsight, it would have accelerated the benefits had they been. (2008, 461)

- **It may address the project's most pressing issues.** Introducing a team to the agile technical practices can solve an array of typical project problems, including poor quality, over-engineered solutions, long delivery cycles, and so on. There are other problems, though, that are not addressed by introducing these practices. For example, a project with a disengaged product owner will experience slow or incorrect decision making. This problem will not be remedied solely by introducing new technical practices. The same is true for a project with multiple product owners, each with a competing agenda, or for a project with strong personality clashes among team members. If your project's most pressing issues are ones addressed by one or more of the common agile engineering practices, consider emphasizing those practices early in the transition.

Reasons to Delay

Just as there are strong reasons for encouraging a team to adopt new engineering practices early, there are also reasons why it may be better to wait:

- **There may be strong resistance to some practices.** Introducing certain technical practices can be one of the most difficult challenges you face when transitioning. Many individuals are extremely reluctant to try new things, such as simple design, pair programming, and test-driven development. Although you may have good reasons to push the team to try new practices close to the outset, they will need to be weighed against the risk of increased resistance.

- **Team members may already have their hands full.** Just learning the fundamentals of working on a Scrum team can be challenging in many organizations. The added stress of also learning new technical practices may simply be too much for some teams, causing them to shut down and not try. Given enough time, the pressure of delivering working software within Scrum's strictly timeboxed sprints may bring these same teams to the realization that they need to try new technical practices.

One Final Consideration

This chapter presented two questions that will confront any organization transitioning to Scrum: Start small or go all in? Public display of agility or stealth? Answers do not need to be binary—there is a great deal of middle ground between starting small and going all in for most organizations. The patterns for spreading are similar. They can be used on their own or combined as needed to fit your particular circumstances. Perhaps, for instance, you first decide to split and seed, but as time passes, and enough teams exist, you can slow down and let teams grow before splitting them, while also speeding learning through the use of internal coaching. In addition, no matter what pattern you choose, leaders of the transition effort (and those participating in it) must address how much to change at any one time for the team or teams transitioning. Attempt to change too much and teams are disoriented; change too little and you risk exhausting people through a marathon of small changes.

Joshua Kerievsky, a senior consultant with the Cutter Consortium, is in favor of enacting all changes at once. He is opposed to what he calls "piecemeal transitions" because he says they

- Are more painful because the change process is protracted
- Fail to address root problems
- Rarely lead to complete transitions
- Produce changes too slowly for the business to benefit from
- Tend to be done without expert help, resulting in making easily avoided, costly mistakes (2005)

Although Kerievsky raises some good points, they ultimately derive from thinking of the transition to agile as a one-time thing that can be completed. On the contrary, adopting an agile approach such as Scrum is a process of continuous improvement. There is no predefined end state. Because of this, it is incorrect to talk about a "complete transition" or a change process that takes too long. Change is no longer something organizations "go through." Change is now a perpetual, ongoing occurrence.

Writing in the *Agile Journal*, Liz Barnett presents a different view than Kerievsky's.

> Starting slow is the way to go. For the vast majority of companies interested in agile practices, incremental adoption represents the most pragmatic way to improve their software development organizations while managing risk. As they implement organizational, process, and technology changes, teams can continually reassess their progress and determine the most pragmatic next steps. It's the agile way to become agile. (2008)

Kent Beck and Cynthia Andres, authors of *Extreme Programming Explained*, agree, acknowledging the near necessity of starting with a subset of practices and new ways of working and then improving one thing at a time.

> It's easy to start by changing one thing at a time. I think it's hard to jump in and do all the practices, embrace all the values, and apply all the principles in novel circumstances by reading this book and deciding to do it. The technical skills in XP and the attitudes behind them take a while to learn. XP works best when it is done all together, but you need a starting place. (2004, 55)

This brings us to our next chapter. After you've decided to transition to Scrum, understood the ramifications of change, and made your decisions regarding the pattern you are most likely to emulate, it's time to begin making the changes Scrum requires. As Beck and Andres so aptly point out, the best way to do that is iteratively. We explore how to use the Scrum framework, along with specialized communities of practice called improvement communities, to adopt and spread Scrum, bring about continuous improvement, and transfer agile ideas throughout the organization.

Additional Reading

Beck, Kent, and Cynthia Andres. 2005. Getting started with XP: Toe dipping, racing dives, and cannonballs. PDF file at Three Rivers Institute website. www. threeriversinstitute.org/Toe%20Dipping.pdf.

> Beck and Andres use entering a pool to describe three different approaches for adopting Extreme Programming. Toe dippers enter slowly, adopting one practice at a time. Cannonballers make a big splash and deal with the sudden chaos it creates but transition quickly. They describe a racing dive as an "assisted cannonball," referring to doing a lot of changes quickly but with guidance from an experienced coach.

Benefield, Gabrielle. 2008. Rolling out agile in a large enterprise. In *Proceedings of the 41st Annual Hawaii International Conference on System Sciences*, 461–470. IEEE Computer Society.

> This paper provides detailed information on Yahoo!'s large Scrum adoption effort. Details on both what was done right and what could have been improved are included.

Elssamadisy, Amr. 2007. *Patterns of agile practice adoption: The technical cluster.* C4Media.

> This book, which is available as a PDF through www.infoq.com, focuses on the technical practices that should be adopted by agile teams. As such, it is complementary to the patterns presented in this chapter.

Hodgetts, Paul. 2004. Refactoring the development process: Experiences with the incremental adoption of agile practices. In *Proceedings of the Agile Development Conference*, 106–113. IEEE Computer Society.

> This paper summarizes Scrum trainer Paul Hodgetts' experiences from transitioning a handful of teams to agile. He contrasts the advantages and disadvantages of incrementally adopting agile with adopting it all at once based on experiences with those projects.

Striebeck, Mark. 2006. Ssh! We are adding a process…. In *Proceedings of the Agile 2006 conference*, ed. Joseph Chao, Mike Cohn, Frank Maurer, Helen Sharp, and James Shore, 185–193. IEEE Computer Society.

> Mark Striebeck describes how agile was introduced to the AdWords front-end application at Google. He describes the combination of a start-small and stealth approach, with new practices added incrementally.

Chapter 4

Iterating Toward Agility

Historically, when an organization needed to change, it undertook a "change program." The change was designed, had an identifiable beginning and ending, and was imposed from above. This worked well in an era when change was necessary only once every few years. Christopher Avery has written, "I think in the 1960s and 1970s this approach was probably more frequently successful than it has been in the 1990s and today because the frequency of change has intensified as competition has become global, and the model has broken down" (2005, 18). Avery continues by saying that "if the changes are coming so fast and furious that programmed change won't work, perhaps we have to arrange ourselves (organizationally speaking) to digest many more smaller changes on a continual basis" (20).

Whether you are just starting to adopt Scrum or you are at the point where you are ready to fine-tune your use of Scrum, you should manage the effort in an agile way. Following an iterative transition process—making small changes on a continual basis—is a logical way to adopt a development process that is itself iterative. Doing so will be much more likely to result in a successful and sustainable transition. This is why I believe that the effort of adopting Scrum is best managed using Scrum itself. With its iterative nature, fixed timeboxes, and emphasis on teamwork and action, it seems best suited to manage the enormous project of becoming and then growing agile with Scrum.

In 2004, the leaders of Shamrock Foods realized that change was coming too quickly in their industry. As one of the ten largest food distributors in the United States, Shamrock had for 20 years used a conventional, top-down strategic planning process, dedicating months each year to creating a 5-year plan that was out of date before the ink dried. To address this problem, CEO Kent McClelland abandoned the company's 20-year-old approach and began to apply a Scrum-based iterative strategic planning process.

> Shamrock's process revolved around quarterly strategic "scrums" [sprints]: Team members met at an offsite location for a day to evaluate the company's performance against the action plans from the previous quarter. We asked them to identify the most important things they had learned about the company's strategy

since the previous meeting and to suggest how those insights should be integrated in the strategy going forward. The group created new action plans for the upcoming period. In addition to the quarterly scrums [sprints], the participants met every year for three days, during which time people were asked to step further back and revisit the company's strategic assumptions. (McFarland 2008, 71)

Forty-five managers and employees participated in these sprints and were chosen to represent each division and functional area. At the start of each quarterly sprint, this group selected up to a handful of key areas in which they agreed the company should improve. These were referred to as themes. Because Shamrock was applying Scrum to an organizational improvement effort rather than software development, the themes represented broad business goals. Examples included increasing revenue on Shamrock's house brands, improving how it serviced large customers like Burger King, and improving the company's ability to recruit, retain, and develop good talent.

Many corporate improvement initiatives fail because plans are not made specific and actionable. Because they were using Scrum, Shamrock employees went beyond just identifying themes for improvement: "Planning participants created and prioritized a handful of specific and measurable strategic initiatives that would advance each strategic theme. Then they built detailed action plans and set measurable outcomes they thought could be achieved within 90 days" (McFarland 2008, 71).

Not only does the Shamrock story illustrate the broad applicability of Scrum, it serves as an example of how Scrum can be used to manage an organizational improvement effort. In this chapter, we look at how to use Scrum first to adopt Scrum and then to continuously improve by engaging communities of like-minded employees, such as the 45 people who guided Shamrock's improvement effort.

The Improvement Backlog

Just as Scrum development projects use product backlogs, you should use an *improvement backlog* to track the effort of adopting Scrum in your organization. An improvement backlog lists everything that the organization could do better in its use of Scrum. When IBM began to adopt Scrum, its improvement backlog included the following items:

- Increase the number of teams using Scrum.
- Increase adoption of test automation.
- Enable teams to implement continuous integration.

- Figure out how to make sure each team has a product owner.
- Determine how we're going to measure the impact of adopting Scrum.
- Increase the use of unit testing and test-driven development.

Improvement backlogs, such as the one shown in Table 4.1, are dynamic, with items coming and going as they are thought of, completed, found unnecessary, and so on. Much of what we discussed in Chapter 2, "ADAPTing to Scrum," will find its way onto an improvement backlog. If you're just starting with Scrum, your improvement backlog will emphasize creating awareness and desire. If the transition is already well underway, your improvement backlog may contain more items around developing the ability to do Scrum well, to promote successes, or to transfer it to other groups. Similarly, decisions about which patterns to use, as described in Chapter 3, "Patterns for Adopting Scrum," can create items on an improvement backlog.

A small department or single-project transition may involve a single improvement backlog. But when Scrum is being adopted across a large site, department, or organization, the transition effort becomes large enough that multiple improvement backlogs are used, each of which is created by a community of individuals who are passionate about improving the organization in a particular way. There may be, for example, a community and associated improvement backlog for figuring out how best to do automated testing on Scrum projects, another for developing and becoming great ScrumMasters, and so on.

Additionally, in a large transition effort, there is what might be considered a master improvement backlog, which is maintained by the group that guides the organization's overall transition. It is to that group that we turn our attention next.

The Enterprise Transition Community

The small group that initiates, encourages, and supports an organization's effort to introduce and improve at Scrum is known as the Enterprise Transition Community, or ETC.[1] The Enterprise Transition Community exists to create a culture and environment where change can be released by those who are passionate about the success of the organization and where success leads to more passion from more people. The ETC does this not by imposing changes on the organization but by guiding groups who are implementing changes, by removing obstacles to doing Scrum well, and by creating energy and excitement for the change.

The members of the ETC, who usually number no more than a dozen, come from the highest level involved in the transition to Scrum. If a company is adopting Scrum organization-wide, the ETC should include senior people from

---

1   The acronym ETC is consistent with Ken Schwaber's in *The Enterprise in Scrum*, although he refers to it as the "Enterprise Transition team" (2007).

engineering or development plus vice presidents of groups such as product management, marketing, sales, operations, human resources, and so on. For a departmental adoption of Scrum, the ETC may include the vice president of engineering along with the heads of QA, development, architecture, interaction design, database, and so on. The key here is that the ETC is made up of the most senior people for the level at which the transition is occurring.

TABLE 4.1

An improvement backlog is a list of capabilities to be developed, work to be performed, or issues to be ad-dressed within the organization.

Item	Responsible	Note
Create a Scrum Office (like a Project Management Office) where teams can get help.		Jim (CTO) to talk this up at monthly development meet-ing. Let's see if there's any interest.
Establish an internal program for developing ScrumMasters.		How do we identify good internal candidates? How do we develop them?
Collect and disseminate Scrum suc-cess stories in our company.	SC	Savannah has expressed inter-est in this.
Develop a continuing education program internally.		Consider quarterly open space meetings. Identify and contact industry experts for one-hour lunch meetings.
Start doing lots of automated unit testing (even if it's not test-first) and using FitNesse.		The Scrum team that makes the most progress on this (as voted on by everyone in the department) can have all members attend next summer's Agile conference.
Help a community form to decide how much up-front architecture is enough.	TG	Tod to start soliciting volun-teers but says he can't commit to any goals for it until next quarter.
Resolve dispute with facilities over rearranging second floor cubicles.	JS	Jim to talk to Ursula in facili-ties about budget for this.
Craft message on why we're adopt-ing Scrum; have Jim discuss it at his monthly meeting.	JS	Next meeting is 25 March.

Sometimes Scrum is introduced into an organization in a grassroots manner. One team tries Scrum and successfully completes a project, others become inter-ested, and Scrum spreads from there. In this situation, an ETC is usually formed spontaneously by some of these early Scrum advocates who ask their boss to be allowed time to help other teams learn Scrum. At some point, impediments arise that need the help of that boss, who then joins the ETC. Alternatively, in an enterprise-wide Scrum adoption, the ETC is usually formed more deliberately when the decision is made to widely adopt Scrum.

As an example of an ETC, consider the case of Farm Credit Services of America, a lending and financial services cooperative that works with farmers in the American Midwest. As part of adopting Scrum, Farm Credit formed an Enterprise Transition Community it calls the Agile Champions Team (ACT). The 16 or so individuals on the ACT participate on the team for between 6 to 24 months depending on their role in the organization and ability to commit time to the team. Because the transition at Farm Credit covers the organization's entire information services and business departments, ACT members are chosen to equally represent all functions involved. The Farm Credit ACT meets every other week for two hours and augments those meetings with occasional longer offsite meetings.

Comprising both formal and informal leaders, the ACT often works on issues that arise between the information services department and the broader business. It has resolved issues related to a lack of stakeholder involvement in projects, the proper use and meaning of deadlines, and executive leadership misperceptions of what agile is and can do for the company. Quinn Jones is a software developer at Farm Credit who served what he calls a six-month "tour of duty" on the ACT. He says, "One of the best things to come out of the Agile Champions Team is the wide-open, smack-down brown bag sessions where all are welcome to ask questions and share knowledge. These meetings have also helped uncover root challenges in agile, which could then be addressed by the ACT."

❑ Write a preliminary improvement backlog by convening a 30- or 60-minute meeting. Invite either your team members, a few people you know will be interested, or the whole department. Brainstorm things that you'd like to see improved. Conclude the meeting by asking if there is sufficient passion to pursue just one or two of the items, and then start with those.

THINGS TO
TRY NOW

ETC Sprints

Because the ETC uses Scrum, it makes progress in sprints, exactly like a Scrum development team would. Each ETC sprint begins with a planning meeting and ends with a review and retrospective. These meetings are completely analogous to those held by Scrum development teams and often have the same problems. Thomas Seffernick, of KeyCorp, a large U.S. financial institution, participated in the first sprint review of his organization's ETC, which it called an Agile Enablement Team. He recalls how that team made a mistake common to many new

Scrum development teams—talking about its plans rather than demonstrating its progress.

> That first Agile Enablement [ETC] sprint review was painful as leaders stood up and described their plans to remove the impediments they volunteered to address. The message was clear—plans are good, but results count. The dynamic of those reviews changed from that point, and results became the focus. (2007, 202)

Some ETCs hold daily scrums, and I think that is a good practice. But, I am not as insistent upon this as I am with a Scrum development team. The work being done by members of an ETC is not as tightly interwoven as the work of a development team, making a daily scrum a great thing to do but not essential. Similarly, ETC members are rarely full-time. Most have demanding jobs already, and in many cases it is beneficial for them to remain in their jobs. A development director who stays in that position, for example, can likely remove more organizational impediments than a development director who steps out of that position to serve on the ETC.

The length of an ETC sprint is up to its members. However, in my experience two-week sprints work best. This is also the sprint length recommended by Ken Schwaber (2007, 10). Elizabeth Woodward, a member of the ETC that is guiding the large-scale adoption of agile at IBM, describes the company's sprint length experience.

> We've used both two-week and four-week sprints. And, so far, the greatest success we've seen is with those on two-week sprints. I believe the reason is that the "deliverables" demonstrate momentum and visible progress. We capture the efforts from each community in a brief digest—a nice e-mail message that people can read in about fifteen minutes.

The Sponsor and Product Owner

Most successful Scrum adoptions have been initiated or driven by an identifiable sponsor, who is a senior person in the organization responsible for the success of the transition. Salesforce.com's highly successful large-scale transition was sponsored by company cofounder Parker Harris. As the executive vice president of technology, Harris was well positioned to champion a change that would dramatically alter how everyone in the Salesforce.com development organization worked.

The transition's sponsor should come from the same level in the organization at which the transition is being planned. Salesforce.com needed an executive as its sponsor because it was doing an enterprise-wide transition. If you are involved in a departmental transition, a department-level leader is an appropriate choice.

The sponsor is also the product owner for the ETC. This means that sometimes an ETC will have a product owner with little direct experience with Scrum. That's OK. Like all product owners, the sponsor of the ETC can fulfill the role by calling on other ETC members for help. As the ETC's most senior member, the sponsor will play a significant role in communicating about the transition effort, but this person does not need to be the sole source of the vision.

Primavera learned the importance of a strong sponsor when it adopted Scrum. Bob Schatz and Ibrahim Abdelshafi, technology executives within Primavera at the time, write about the importance of a sponsor's support.

> Adopting agile, or implementing any significant change, requires
> an executive's sincere support. It can be a bumpy ride until things
> settle down, and having executive support lets the learning take
> hold despite any problems or failures. (2005, 38)

It is critical that the sponsor demonstrate commitment to the transition effort by participating on the ETC. Good sponsors do not initiate a transition, proclaim support for Scrum, and then remove themselves from the effort of getting there. If a sponsor is not committed, others will not be either. Scrum coach and author of *Collaboration Explained*, Jean Tabaka considers a checkbook-only commitment from a sponsor to be one of the most likely reasons a Scrum adoption might fail: "Agile adoption requires a passionately engaged sponsor willing to make tough organizational changes that serve agile teams and their success" (2007).

Although it would be fair to characterize ETC members as leaders of the Scrum adoption effort, theirs is not what we think of as conventional leadership. Writing in *Harvard Business Review*, internationally respected management author Henry Mintzberg describes the necessary type of leader.

> Communityship requires a more modest form of leadership that
> might be called *engaged* and *distributed* management. A commu-
> nity leader is personally engaged in order to engage others, so
> that anyone and everyone can exercise initiative. (2009, 141; em-
> phasis his)

Mintzberg goes on to say that during an organizational change like adopting Scrum, "we need *just enough leadership*—leadership that intervenes when appropriate while encouraging people in the organization to get on with things."

> **OBJECTION**

> **"The sponsor of our transition project says he's committed, but he's unable to come to any meetings or to put any time into the effort. He gives us anything else we need, but we can't get any of his time."**

You probably have the wrong sponsor. Although his willingness to support the transition in other ways is admirable, a successful Scrum transition requires some of the sponsor's time. You don't want to lose this powerful ally, but you may need to look for a different sponsor. Alternatively, you may want to negotiate with your sponsor for a small amount of his time. The ETC can then prioritize how that time should be spent. It could perhaps be in meetings or as a public supporter of the transition in other forums.

Responsibilities of the ETC

An ETC is a working group. It is not a steering committee. During sprint planning, the ETC commits to completing some amount of work and demonstrating it at the end of the sprint. However, even more important than the tangible things the ETC accomplishes is that it ignites the interest of others. Members of the ETC can only achieve so much themselves. They will need to rely on others in the company to do most of the work of adopting Scrum and becoming agile. Change management experts Edwin Olson and Glenda Eoyang concur.

> In a self-organizing system, the leader has an important role to play, but creative and long-lasting change depends on the work of many individuals at many different levels and places in the organization. (2001, 5)

One of the most important jobs of the ETC is creating energy around the adoption of Scrum. Not everyone will be excited by the change, of course. But the ETC needs to ignite the passion of those who will work to make adopting Scrum successful. ETC members do this by showing their own enthusiasm and by participating in constructive dialogue about the changes occurring. To ignite the passion of others in the organization so that they become involved in the type of creative and long-lasting change needed to adopt Scrum, the ETC is responsible for the following:

- **Articulate the context.** Beyond conveying a vision of the organization's agile future, the ETC must also help employees both understand the need to change and develop a desire to change. They do this by articulating the context of the change: Why? Why now? Why Scrum? Members of the ETC use their seniority, personal credibility, and more to get others to understand the answers to these questions.

- **Stimulate conversation.** All sorts of good things happen when people talk. Debating the merits of various technical practices, sharing success stories, probing reasons for failure, and other discussions will generate ideas.

- **Provide resources.** Adopting Scrum will take time, effort, and money. For example, individuals who are trying to figure out how to be more agile (say, learning how to write automated unit tests on a complicated code base) may need to be granted time away from their development projects. Because the ETC includes the most senior people involved in the transition, the ETC is in a position to ensure that both time and money are available.

- **Set appropriate aspirations.** Change efforts with clearly defined and truly transformational goals are ten times more likely to succeed (McKinsey & Company 2008). The ETC is responsible for setting and communicating appropriate goals for the transition, which may (and probably should) change over time as the organization improves. The ETC may establish goals such as moving from one annual release to quarterly releases, a 50% decrease in post-release defect rate, or so on.

SEE ALSO
Advice on appropriate metrics for measuring your progress is offered in Chapter 21, "Seeing How Far You've Come."

- **Engage everyone.** Scrum has long tentacles and will reach into many areas of the organization. The ETC makes sure that the transition effort does not become narrowly focused on just one group. Within the groups that are affected, broad participation is encouraged.

Additional Responsibilities

Beyond encouraging people to engage in the transition, the ETC has the following additional responsibilities:

- **Anticipate and address people issues.** The ETC should try to anticipate which groups or individuals are going to struggle the most with the changes brought about by Scrum and proactively work with them. The cross-functional makeup of the ETC helps in this regard as it allows the group to see problems from multiple perspectives.

- **Anticipate and remove impediments.** Members of the ETC are responsible for removing any organizational impediments to adopting Scrum or doing it well. Beyond merely removing impediments it is informed of, the ETC should try to anticipate obstacles and remove them before they cause problems.

- **Encourage a simultaneous focus on practices and principles.** Adopting Scrum involves incorporating new practices and valuing new principles. An organization cannot adopt the practices without the underlying principles, nor can it adopt the principles without the practices. An effective ETC looks for imbalances in how each is being adopted. If one is being accepted faster than the other, the ETC can bring them back in line by directing conversation, attention, and resources toward the laggard.

If an ETC performs these tasks well, not only will it be moving the organization forward on its own, but it also will have generated interest and excitement among others in the organization. To harness that passion, individuals with a common interest in improving the organization in a particular way (perhaps its adoption of automated testing) come together, form a community of their own focused on that improvement, and then run their own sprints. These communities are known as *improvement communities* and are the topic of the next section.

OBJECTION

"I can't get the organizational backing to create an ETC. Can I still transition to Scrum?"

Yes. Start with whatever sphere of influence you do have. Get your team to do Scrum. If it is successful, people will notice. Perhaps another team will want to do Scrum and ask for advice. Or a manager will get interested. As people get interested, start the community informally as just a few people who get together occasionally to talk about how Scrum is going and what could be done better. A grassroots approach is very feasible but will take longer to spread.

THINGS TO TRY NOW

❏   If you don't already have an ETC or equivalent group, identify several people who ought to be on the ETC. If you are one of them, begin forming this group. If you are not, share the idea of an ETC and improvement communities with others in your organization who can help form these groups.

Improvement Communities

An improvement community (IC) is a group of individuals who join together to work collaboratively to improve the organization's use of Scrum. An IC may form when individuals notice an item on the ETC's improvement backlog and decide to work together to achieve that goal. Or an IC may form because individuals see and are passionate about an improvement opportunity that hasn't made the ETC's radar yet. IBM, for example, has five ICs, which are focused on test automation, continuous integration, test-driven development, the role of the product owner, and the general use of Scrum itself.

The Enterprise Transition Community and improvement communities I am referring to are specialized types of what are known as *communities of practice* (Wenger, McDermott, and Synder 2002). A community of practice is a group of like-minded or like-skilled individuals who voluntarily come together because of their passion and commitment around a technology, approach, or vision. We will see other types of communities of practice throughout this book. They will be thoroughly discussed in Chapter 17, "Scaling Scrum."

Graphically, the relationship between an organization's one ETC and its multiple ICs can be seen in Figure 4.1. The ETC guides the transition process; it does not direct or manage it. A big part of its role is fostering an environment in which ICs form and dissolve organically in pursuit of improving how the organization builds products.

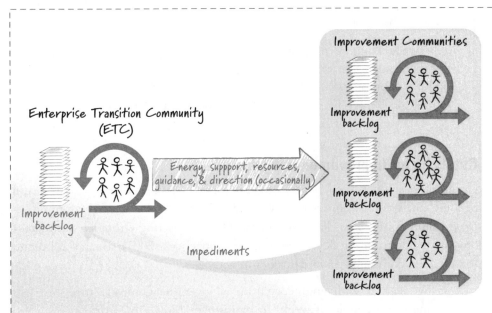

FIGURE 4.1

An Enterprise Transition Community guides the adoption of Scrum, but most of the work is done by multiple improvement communities.

This approach should be scaled up or down depending on the size of the organization undertaking the transition. A software development department of 30 people may have an ETC of 5 people and nothing more. A company-wide transition for a department of 200 developers may have a 10-person ETC (including representatives from groups outside development) plus a handful of improvement communities at any time. Things can scale from there as needed; IBM, for example, has over 800 people in some of its improvement communities.

Most participants in an IC spend only a small part of their time engaged with the community. They may read postings to its discussion list, add a comment on a wiki, and nothing more. The amount of time an IC member spends on the community is determined by each individual, the person's boss, or organizational culture.

OBJECTION

"Scrum teams are supposed to be self-organizing. Doesn't an ETC conflict with this? Shouldn't teams get to decide what they want to improve at?"

Self-organization occurs in response to a challenge taken on by a group of individuals. For a development project, the company may tell a team, "Develop this software to run faster and take less memory than the current version and do it two months faster than we've done in the past." Individuals then organize themselves around how to achieve that goal. It is no different with the ETC. An ETC states what it would like to see improved but not necessarily how to achieve that improvement. The how is left up to the improvement communities or Scrum teams.

Additionally, keep in mind that an ETC's biggest goal is to create an environment such that improvement communities identify their own goals and form spontaneously to address them. We will look at self-organization in detail in Chapter 12, "Leading a Self-Organizing Team."

Catalysts for Improvement

Communities, when used as part of the effort to adopt and get good at Scrum, become catalysts for improvement. Consider the case of Google, where improvement communities are called "grouplets." Google's Testing Grouplet was formed "to drive adoption of developer testing" (Striebeck 2007). Bharat Mediratta founded the community and describes its activities.

> We started with engineers from all over the company meeting every couple of weeks to brainstorm. Slowly, over time, we started turning into activists, planning to actually start improving things. We started building better tools and giving informal talks to different technical groups. (2007)

Notice that although this community met initially to brainstorm, they soon found themselves as activists with plans for actual improvements. Improvement communities act. This is why they aren't called task forces, work groups, committees, or any of the other terms that too often bring to mind ineffective groups. If the Google Testing Grouplet had merely created presentations on the benefits of developer testing, or if it had chosen to convince a powerful vice president to mandate developer testing, its efforts would have been fruitless.

What the testing community at Google did instead was find direct and immediate ways to help teams. Mediratta recalls how, in addition to building tools, the community found a unique way of providing concrete, short examples and advice about testing.

> One day, toward the end of a long brainstorming meeting, we came up with the idea of putting up little one-page stories, called episodes, in bathroom stalls discussing new and interesting testing techniques. Somebody immediately called it "Testing on the Toilet," and the idea stuck. (2007)

The most effective communities are usually those that form not in response to management dictate but because company culture or the ETC has created an environment in which communities can naturally emerge. J. F. Unson, a coach at Yahoo! during its large-scale Scrum rollout, says this is exactly what happened at one of Yahoo!'s remote facilities.

> At Yahoo!, in our Santa Monica campus, all the entertainment agilistas started a monthly ScrumMaster lunch. This happened organically as Scrum started to grow in the organization, without having the agile group [ETC] pushing it. (2008)

Not all communities will form in such an organic manner, of course. Especially during the early weeks or months of adopting Scrum, the ETC will need to encourage an improvement community to form by highlighting the importance of a goal and then hoping a community forms around that goal. Occasionally, an ETC may need to go so far as to ask someone to form a community around a specific goal.

Two Metrics for Effectiveness

Professor Jeffrey Goldstein has written, "Change does not need to be imposed; it simply needs to be released" (1994, 32). You can gauge how well the ETC is doing at releasing change in two ways:

1. The number of improvement communities that have formed without a direct request from the ETC

2. The percentage of such improvement communities to the total number of improvement communities

If the number of spontaneously formed improvement communities is high, and especially if these represent a majority of the total number of communities, this indicates strong interest in Scrum and the changes it is creating. If these metrics are increasing or remain high over time, the organization is well on its way to becoming agile. You should, of course, look at other metrics. These are just two that I like.

An Improvement Community Sprint

As you might suspect, ICs perform their work in sprints as well. As with the ETC, each IC can select its own sprint length, but two weeks is the recommended length. An IC that was formed spontaneously will usually serve as its own product owner, with members of the community electing to devote their time to the improvements they are the most passionate about. An IC that was formed in response to an ETC-identified goal, on the other hand, will usually work with a member of the ETC as its product owner to plan a sprint.

That being said, an improvement community does not exist to serve the ETC. It exists to serve its customers: the Scrum development teams who are building products or systems. Although an ETC member will act as product owner for some improvement communities and will serve as the official product owner for the sprint reviews, you should expect members of interested development teams to be active participants as well. Additionally, the wise ETC understands that the best results will be achieved when improvement communities are given broad latitude in achieving their goals. In practice, this means an IC, even one formed in response to ETC-identified goals, will be responsible for prioritizing its own work, while balancing the needs of the organization to improve in particular ways and its members' passion for working on those issues.

During its sprint planning meeting, each improvement community selects one or more things it can commit to completing during the sprint. If an improvement community has formed in response to a specific goal of the ETC, sprint planning begins by taking an item from the ETC's backlog and breaking it down into smaller items that will be placed on the improvement community's improvement backlog. The best way to see this is with an example.

The ETC improvement backlog shown in Table 4.1 on page 64 includes the item, "Establish an internal program for developing ScrumMasters." An improvement community formed a month after the ETC put that on the improvement backlog and made it known to the rest of the company that creating such a program would be valuable. There were three people in the community initially, but that was plenty to make progress toward this goal. In their first sprint planning meeting, they discussed the ETC's goal ("Establish an internal program for developing ScrumMasters") and created their own improvement backlog of what they would do to achieve this goal, which is shown in Table 4.2.

Also during sprint planning, the community members took some of the items in Table 4.2 and identified the tasks necessary to complete each. For example, for the final item in Table 4.2 (working with local groups to share the expense of bringing in speakers), the community identified the following tasks:

- Search web to see what user groups are in our area.
- Create budget of expenses.

- Send e-mail to internal distribution lists to see if anyone here is connected to these groups.
- Set up phone calls to introduce ourselves and what we're doing.
- Conduct phone calls. See if any groups have previously split the cost of bringing a speaker into town with another company. See if any will work with us on this.
- Meet with Susan to go over budget and get approval.

What	Note
Figure out how to identify good candidates to become ScrumMasters (in addition to those who ask to participate in this program).	
Establish an internal mentoring program.	
Develop some internal classroom training. Which courses? Who can teach them? Develop our material, or can we license it?	
Determine which classes we can teach internally.	
Get budget for next year for external coaching. How many days? At what expected daily rate?	James has already asked for rates from three coaches.
See what we can do with local user groups to share the expense of bringing in speakers.	Savannah has contact in local Scrum lunch meetup group.

TABLE 4.2

An improvement community's backlog for establishing an internal program to develop ScrumMasters.

As in a development team's sprint planning meeting, the community then estimated each item and decided they could commit to completing these tasks during the sprint. Two weeks later at its sprint review, this team showed its product owner, a member of the ETC, a list of local user groups and a plan to work with one of them twice a year, sharing the expenses of bringing nationally known speakers into the area.

- ❏ Add to your improvement backlog by looking at the section headings of the chapters in this book. Many of them were written with this possibility specifically in mind.
- ❏ Review any notes available from recent sprint retrospectives. These are often an excellent source of improvement backlog items.

THINGS TO
TRY NOW

Focus on Goals with Practical Relevance

For an improvement community to have the most impact, its members must focus on goals of immediate and practical relevance to the development teams using or attempting to get started with Scrum. The best way to do this is for improvement community members to work side by side with development team members on something important to the development team. This is what Google's "test mercenaries" do. Test mercenaries are members of the testing community who are experienced engineers with a passion for and expertise in testing. They spend up to 20% of their time for three months on a project other than their own. During this time they add tests and refactor code as a direct help to the development team.

I suppose that test mercenaries could instead spend this time creating presentations and spreading the gospel of developer testing. Something tells me, though, they are better able to achieve their goals by working with a team rather than preaching to it. A development team that has had the help of a test mercenary ends up with improved code and more tests. It also witnesses the benefits of an additional focus on developer testing. This works wonders in motivating those on the Scrum development team to continue the effort after the mercenary moves on to another team.

Focusing on providing practical assistance to development teams also helps keep improvement community members from falling into the habit of preaching to the development teams. A common problem when adopting Scrum is that the early adopters often become zealots anxious to convert everyone else. What zealots often forget is that it took them time to get comfortable with the idea of Scrum and the changes it requires. When others fail to convert instantly, zealots often perceive the delay as resistance. Because zealotry and pushing others to rapidly adopt new ideas can cause more harm than good, it is important for improvement community members to understand that their role is to consult rather than preach (Allen-Meyer 2000c, 25).

Improvement Community Members

Organizational change expert Glenn Allen-Meyer says that change should be done "with, not to, the people expected to change" (2000b). Because of this, it is important that anyone with a passion for an improvement opportunity be encouraged to participate in its community. Membership should not, for example, be restricted to only the organization's most senior employees. Broad participation in improvement communities helps everyone in the organization feel that change is occurring with them rather than to them. There should be no limit on the number of people participating in an improvement community. Communities often include well over 100 members, with individual participation levels going up and down over time based on the other demands of each person's job.

Participating in a community is not meant to be a full-time job; it is something someone takes on in addition to regular work. Improvement community leaders at IBM are asked to contribute two hours per week, although many contribute more based on a desire to see more rapid progress. A participant's manager, product owner, and ScrumMaster, though, are responsible for ensuring that those passionate enough about a change to work toward it are given sufficient time to do so. Google accomplishes this by telling each employee to spend 20% of each week on something of interest. The time could be spent, for example, exploring a new product idea or participating in a community.

Successful Scrum adopter Salesforce.com has a similarly innovative approach it calls PTON, pronounced pee-tee-on and meaning "paid time on." Patterned after the common PTO ("pee-tee-oh") policy for paid time *off* in many companies, Salesforce.com's PTON program gives employees dedicated time at work to pursue initiatives of their own choosing. Each employee is given one week of PTON for each year with the company. Salesforce.com employees can use the PTON time to work on a community initiative, explore new product ideas, or do just about anything they want.

Google's 20% policy and Salesforce.com's PTON programs were not created specifically to allow people to work in an improvement community. And organizations do not need to make such dramatic changes just to get started adopting Scrum. An easy starting point is simply for managers to commit to freeing up some number of hours each week for those who want to work on an improvement community.

"We've been working on this new product for a year. We ship it in four weeks and, as the product owner, I need the team's full time and attention for the next four weeks."

OBJECTION

Absolutely. Team members probably already know this and have plans to scale back participation in any communities to the minimum possible over that period. A team member who generally feels valued and allowed to devote time to the longer-term initiatives of a community will willingly minimize community participation during a true crunch period because she knows she can devote more time to it later.

"These improvement communities seem just like the Software Engineering Process Groups (SEPGs) our company created to push CMMI. Isn't this just a new name for an old idea?"

Not really, but I can understand why you might think so. Both ICs and SEPGs are focused on helping the organization improve how people develop software. However, while their goals are the same, an SEPG and an IC differ in a few subtle but important ways:

- An SEPG looks at the process and answers the question, "What could we improve?" Members of an improvement community look at their own projects and ask, "What could we improve?" and "What are we doing well that others should know about?"
- Some SEPGs force compliance with a process; an improvement community has no authority from which to force compliance.
- Some SEPGs are chartered to look only at portions of the overall development process. ICs are encouraged to look beyond the product development process to find improvement opportunities.
- Improvement communities are self-motivated and self-organizing. In general, no one is told to join an improvement community. (Although this may occasionally be done to start a new community.)
- Members of an IC are more likely to take an experimental, try-it-and-see approach to process improvement.
- Improvement communities are ad hoc and organic, formed whenever passion for a topic brings people together. SEPGs are formally created and often discouraged from functioning in an ad hoc manner.

Disbanding a Community

Most communities will eventually disband. A community formed to promote automated testing, for example, may exist with members coming and going for years as long as that is an area in which the organization needs to improve. Eventually (at least we'd like to think), the organization becomes good enough at automated testing that those community members can contribute more by devoting time to other improvement communities and the opportunities they represent.

Regarding the ETC specifically: It should disband once the organization has realized its transition to Scrum and has entered a phase of continuous improvement. The ETC exists only during the transition period, which may be multiple years for a large transition.

❑ Identify an improvement you are passionate about. Ask two or three coworkers to help you. Create an improvement backlog and plan a first sprint. Even if you can manage only an hour a week on it, start. As you begin to make progress, incorporate your improvement in the work of your team or offer it to another team. Generate interest by telling (or, even better, showing) others what you've accomplished.

THINGS TO TRY NOW

One Size Does Not Fit All

In this chapter, I've presented a community-driven approach to Scrum adoption. A guiding community—the Enterprise Transition Community—does some of the work of the transition, but most important it creates an environment that encourages other communities to form. These communities—called improvement communities—are formed when a group of employees choose to work together to improve the organization's use of Scrum. Both types of communitites use Scrum to drive the organization toward becoming agile.

But one size clearly does not fit all. The approach I am describing in this chapter works well when transitioning a medium or large department to Scrum. Scale it down as appropriate. A software department of 20 professionals, for example, may benefit from having one group of passionately agile individuals who help drive change and improvement. They are both an ETC and an IC in that case.

Looking Forward

So far, in the chapters that make up the initial section of the book, we've discussed why transitioning to Scrum is hard, but worth it. We've talked about the activities that accompany change and some tools you can use to help people make the switch to Scrum. We've discussed patterns for adoption that can guide our general approach to transitioning to Scrum. Finally, we've looked at how to combine all of that information, and the Scrum process itself, and use it to manage a Scrum adoption, on any scale. Throughout the first four chapters, I've made a point of saying that, unlike other change initiatives, with Scrum there is no end state. There is no point when you're done. Instead, Scrum requires continuous improvement, which can be managed through improvement communities, using Scrum itself.

In our next chapter, we discuss how to pick your first project, your first team, and get started with the business of becoming agile with Scrum.

Additional Reading

Conner, Daryl R. 1993. *Managing at the speed of change: How resilient managers succeed and prosper where others fail.* Random House.

> In this book, Conner describes eight key patterns of how people behave during organizational change. One of the goals of his process for change management is to foster resilience in people and organizations. His view of resilience is compatible with this book's presentation of change as continuous and agility as something to be iterated toward.

Katzenbach, Jon. R. 1997. *Real change leaders: How you can create growth and high performance at your company.* Three Rivers Press.

> Katzenbach's book is based on extensive interviews with individuals who he found to be the true source of change in organizations. These are the "real change leaders" of the book's title. The book contains many engaging stories about individuals who would make good improvement community members.

Kotter, John P. 1996. *Leading change.* Harvard Business School Press.

> Kotter's highly respected book is a classic on organizational change. In it, he lays out an eight-step process for creating change. In his second step, Kotter advocates the creation of a guiding coalition, which has some similarities to an ETC. Additionally, his article in *Harvard Business Review* (1995) offers a concise summary of this book.

Schwaber, Ken. 2007. *The enterprise and scrum.* Microsoft Press.

> In this book, Schwaber, the coinventor of Scrum, describes what is necessary to transition an entire organization to Scrum. Included is advice on the improvement backlog and on the Enterprise Transition team, which is similar to the Enterprise Transition Community as I have presented it.

Wenger, Etienne, Richard McDermott, and William M. Snyder. 2002. *Cultivating communities of practice.* Harvard Business School Press.

> Wenger is recognized as the authority on communities of practice. This highly readable book describes everything you need to know to begin cultivating communities within your organization, including a chapter dedicated to advice to community coordinators.

Woodward, E.V., R. Bowers, V. Thio, K. Johnson, M. Srihari, and C. J. Bracht. Forthcoming. Agile methods for software practice transformation. *IBM Journal of Research and Development* 54 (2).

> Members of IBM's Quality Software Engineering organization are using an approach very similar to the one described in this chapter to spread agile throughout IBM. This excellent paper describes how they function as an Enterprise Transition Community, ways in which they encourage improvement communities to form, and how they use the Scrum framework to drive improvements in how they use Scrum.

Chapter 5

Your First Projects

Unless you are operating in stealth mode, all eyes will be on the first project to try Scrum, especially during the first sprints. Selecting the right project and team is critical. Your initial Scrum project should be one that is considered important and significant, so that the results are not discounted, yet not so large that it is ungainly. Team members should be selected with an eye toward not only their compatibility but also their willingness to try something new.

As the first sprint starts, expectations about the advantages Scrum will bring may be sky high. Sometimes this is the result of general optimism; other times it is the result of zealotry by an organization's early agilists, whose exuberance leads others to think Scrum will cure all ills. You must correctly set and manage these expectations; otherwise an initial project that should be viewed as wildly successful will instead be considered a dismal failure when it does not live up to oversized expectations.

In this chapter we consider the critical topics of selecting the right first project and assembling the ideal team, and the subtle art of setting realistic expectations.

SEE ALSO

Transitioning in stealth mode was introduced in Chapter 3, "Patterns for Adopting Scrum."

Selecting a Pilot Project

I was about to start this section with something like, "Scrum pilot projects have become more and more rare over the past four years. The benefits of Scrum have become so recognized that companies are now forgoing pilot projects and jumping right in." And then I decided that perhaps I should look up the definition of *pilot project*. Perhaps, like *inconceivable* to Vizzini in *The Princess Bride*, it did not mean what I thought it meant. What I found was that there are indeed two slightly different meanings. One is that a pilot project is a test, with the results used to determine if more of whatever is being tested will be done. This is the type of pilot project that most companies now bypass—they know they want to use Scrum; they don't need to "pilot it" to verify that.

The other definition I found is that a pilot project is undertaken to provide guidance to subsequent projects; it pilots the way in doing something new. It is this second meaning that I'm interested in—the pilot that leads the way rather than the one that is conducted as a test. As an industry we have enough evidence that Scrum works; what individual organizations need to learn is how to make Scrum work inside their organizations. So, they often conduct one or more pilots as learning projects.

Four Attributes of the Ideal Pilot Project

Selecting the right project as a pilot can be challenging. Jeff Honious, vice president in charge of innovation at Reed Elsevier, led his company's transition to Scrum. He and colleague Jonathan Clark wrote of their struggle to select the right pilot.

> Finding the right project was the most critical and challenging task. We needed a meaty project that people would not dismiss as being a special case, yet we did not want a project to fill every possible challenge—too much was riding on its success. (2004)

Not every project is equally suited to be your first. The ideal pilot project sits at the confluence of project size, project duration, project importance, and the engagement of the business sponsor, as shown in Figure 5.1. You may find it impossible to identify the "perfect" pilot project. That's OK. Consider the projects you do have and make appropriate trade-offs between the four factors presented in Figure 5.1. It is far better to pick a project that is close enough and get started than it is to delay six or more months waiting for the perfect pilot to present itself.

FIGURE 5.1

The four attributes of the ideal pilot project.

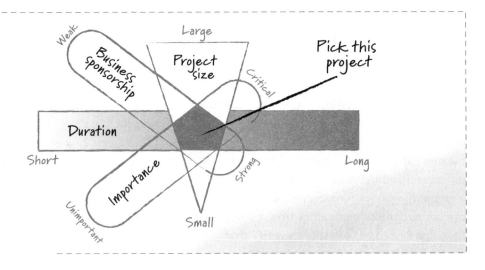

Duration. If you select a project that is too short, skeptics will claim that Scrum works only on short projects. At the same time, if you select a project that is too long, you risk not being able to claim success until the project is over. Many traditionally managed projects claim to be on track 9 months in to a 12-month schedule, yet in the end are over budget and late, so a Scrum project proclaiming the same may not be very convincing.

What I find best is to select a project whose length is near the middle of what is normal for an organization. Ideally and frequently this is around three or four months. This gives a team plenty of time to start getting good at working within sprints, to enjoy it, and to see the benefits for the team and for the product. A three- or four-month project is also usually sufficient for claiming that Scrum will lead to similar success on longer projects.

Size. Select a project that can be started with one team whose members are all collocated, if at all possible. Start with one team, even if the pilot project will grow to include more teams. Try to select a pilot project that will not grow to more than five or so teams, even if such projects will be common in your organization. Not only is coordinating work among that many Scrum teams more than you want to bite off initially, but you also probably wouldn't have time to grow from one team to more than five anyway if you are also looking for a project that can be completed in three or four months.

Importance. It can be tempting to select a low-importance, low-risk project. If things go badly, not much will be lost. And people may not even notice a failure on a low-importance project. Don't give in to this temptation. Instead, pick an important project. An unimportant project will not get the necessary attention from the rest of the organization. Additionally, some of the things required of a team transitioning to Scrum are difficult; if the project isn't important, people may not do all that is required of them. Early agilist and inventor of the Adaptive Software Development process Jim Highsmith advises, "Don't start with an initial 'learning project' that is of marginal importance. Start on a project that is absolutely critical to your company; otherwise it will be too difficult to implement all the hard things Scrum will ask of you" (2002, 250).

Business sponsor engagement. Adopting Scrum requires changes on the business side of the development equation, not just the technical side. Having someone on the business side who has the time and inclination to work with the team is critical. An engaged business sponsor can help the team if it needs to push against entrenched business processes, departments, or individuals. Similarly, there is no one more useful in promoting the success of the project afterward than a sponsor who got what was expected. One sponsor commenting to another that a recent

NOTE
Scrum projects work with a product owner, who is described in detail in Chapter 7, "New Roles." The sponsor referred to here may or may not be the product owner. Minimally, it is someone on the business side of the project who will recognize the project as successful.

project tried Scrum and delivered more than past projects did will do wonders in getting other sponsors to ask their teams to also try the new approach.

Choosing the Right Time to Start

That so many new exercise programs and diets begin on New Year's Day is testament to the human desire to align change with outside factors, such as the calendar. Just as we may feel that exercise programs should begin on the first day of the year, we may think that a new software development process should be introduced on the first day of a new project. Choosing a new project (or restarting a failed one) for your pilot lets you make a fresh start. Teams who have chosen to start fresh begin by focusing on the product backlog. Such a team will usually wait to begin its first sprint until it has created a product backlog that contains all of the features that are known at the time. Trond Wingård, an agile project manager, has been successful with this approach.

> In one of my first agile projects, our client had already spent one year and approximately $150,000 to have another contractor write a classic requirements document. I was able to convince our client that we should replace this requirements document with user stories. So the 150-page document was replaced with a product backlog with 93 user stories. We would not have been able to do agile if we hadn't done this.

Making a fresh start has only one major disadvantage: Waiting for a new project to appear—and then hoping you think it is a suitable first Scrum project—needlessly delays the benefits Scrum brings.

Resurrecting a failed project can also bring a fresh start feeling to your pilot. Spending a few days creating its product backlog can help restore focus to the project team, reengage stakeholders, and create buy-in throughout the organization. Remember when starting fresh that you don't want to spend weeks (or months!) bogged down in creating your preliminary product backlog. Consider the irony of starting your Scrum transition with a two-month requirements-gathering phase. When starting fresh, have the discipline to write the backlog quickly and in as lightweight a manner as possible.

Impending Doom

Sometimes starting fresh is either not possible or not the right choice. If a project is in midstream and could benefit from Scrum, I see no reason not to switch. My personal favorite pilot projects are ones that are currently headed toward impending doom yet still have enough time to recover and succeed. Although this can be a risky approach, a struggling project has nowhere to go but up. Delivering at all is often viewed as a success; delivering on time is often viewed as an amazing success. Because of the focus and intensity created through working in short sprints and because of the emphasis on creating at least some forward progress, Scrum is often ideally suited to these types of projects, especially when an experienced Scrum-Master or consultant is available to the team.

As the chief technology officer of Sammy Studios (now High Moon Studios), Clinton Keith knew something drastic was needed. His team was developing what was to be a Triple-A video game for the Sony PlayStation and Microsoft Xbox. Teams were working hard, but the game was not coming together as quickly as the development studio's off-site owners had hoped. Without a change the project would fail.

Fortunately, at about this time Keith learned about Scrum and decided to introduce it to his teams. Employees of game studios are distinguished by a fierce amount of individualism, so introducing a process that would require lots of talking, collaboration, daily scrums, and other similar hallmarks of Scrum was difficult. Wisely, Keith chose to introduce Scrum at a time when team members were becoming aware that the current process and approach was not likely to lead to the finished product that all desired.

Another common time when you might want to stress the risk of impending doom is when the company will go out of business, or (in a more diversified company) cancel the project, if development continues at its current pace. Anytime a continuation of the status quo has serious repercussions, demonstrating the impending doom of inaction can help fuel Scrum adoption. After all, if doing things the "old way" will only lead to failure, it's easier to convince team members to try something new, experiment with different practices, and make a leap to Scrum they would otherwise resist.

Forecasting impending doom can be powerful but is also dangerous. For it to work, the peril faced by the project or organization must be real. In one company where I worked, our CEO was notorious for announcing that the fate of the company rested on every project we undertook. Cry wolf enough times and people stop believing. You, too, may be tempted to exaggerate the peril; don't. However, if a project is on its way to failure unless dramatic action is taken, point it out. Team members probably know already but are reluctant to acknowledge it. Additionally, if team members have become apathetic about their project and their work, I will sometimes point out a likely doom that may occur if things don't change. I used this recently with a team who knew its company was in merger talks with a competitor. "So," I asked members, "when this merger finishes and the big bosses of the combined company are trying to figure out which projects are redundant and which teams should get the best new projects, how would you like this project and team to be viewed?" This jolt of awareness is just what some teams need.

Selecting a Pilot Team

The intersection of the four factors of Figure 5.1 and the discussion of timing leave out probably the most important factor in the success of a pilot project—the individuals involved. I deliberately chose to leave people out of the discussion of selecting the right pilot project under the assumption that we can select the project and team independently. That is, we can select the best project as our Scrum pilot and can then look around and assemble the right team for that project. I understand this is an uncommon luxury in many organizations—the project and the team often come as a package, just like the ham and eggs in a Scrum team's favorite breakfast. If you cannot separate the decisions of the ideal pilot project and the ideal pilot team, simply consider all factors together in selecting the best available pilot.

Put initial teams together with an eye toward compatibility, constructive dissension among team members, willingness and ability to learn and adapt, technical skills, communication skills, and so on. Of these, the most important consideration in selecting a pilot team is the willingness of the individuals to try something different. Ideally, all will have moved through the awareness and desire steps of the ADAPT acronym presented in Chapter 2, "ADAPTing to Scrum." When presented the opportunity to influence who will be on the pilot team, I look to create a combination of the following types of individuals:

- **Scrum lobbyists.** The project may not be big enough to include everyone who has been lobbying to adopt Scrum, but I want to be biased toward including as many of these individuals on the project as I can. It would be painful for them to have to be on the sidelines even though they'd still be hopeful for the project's success.
- **Willing optimists.** These individuals understand that a new development approach is needed but didn't go so far as to actively argue for a change to Scrum in the past. Knowing what they now do about Scrum, they believe it sounds promising and want to see it succeed.
- **Fair skeptics.** I don't want someone on the project who will work to sabotage the pilot or the teamwork necessary to become a Scrum team, but this does not mean I want to avoid all skeptics. It can be very beneficial to include a well-respected, vocal skeptic as long as the skeptic has demonstrated a past willingness to admit being wrong or change an opinion. These individuals can become some of the transition's strongest supporters when convinced of the benefits through hands-on experience.

Of course, all of this must be mixed with an eye toward combining the right set of skills for the project. If your pilot project's goal is to develop a video game, you had better put an animator on the team. I also look for individuals who have a track record of working together successfully. Sometimes you find an existing entire team that can become the pilot team. Other times, you can think back over the past few years and put together people who worked together well on past projects.

"All this effort toward selecting the right team is stacking the deck in your favor. Of course, a team like this will succeed. But once we adopt Scrum, not every project will be able to be staffed with willing people who have worked well together in the past."

Of course, this is stacking the deck in your favor. I said earlier that a pilot isn't undertaken as a test of "will Scrum work or not." We know Scrum works. There is plenty of anecdotal evidence (and even some hard data) to prove this. What we don't know is, how will Scrum work best here? The pilot is not some clinical, double-blind trial. It is an attempt to use a new approach to deliver an important project. So, we stack the deck in favor of doing so and see what we can learn.

What if a Pilot Isn't a Success?

What if, after all your decision making, planning, and hard work, the pilot project fails anyway? First, you would be wise to avoid pinning all your hopes on one big pilot project. Instead, run multiple pilots and keep in mind that the purpose of a pilot project is to illuminate the way for the Scrum projects that follow. The most successful pilot projects will be able to create advice of two forms: *do this* and *don't do that*. As long as the teams involved in the pilot learn about what is likely to work or not work, which aspects of Scrum will be easily brought into the organization, the types and sources of organization-specific resistance, or any other similar information, then I am reluctant to call the pilot a failure.

But, what if the pilot project fails to deliver the expected results?

In these cases I start by assessing whether the expectations placed on the project were realistic. Perhaps before starting the project we agreed they were, but by the end we've learned otherwise. If that's the case, clearly communicate this to all stakeholders. Don't do so as an excuse for failing to deliver what was expected. Stakeholders need to know that the team accepts responsibility for any part it played in setting or agreeing to overly optimistic plans. But do make sure that stakeholders understand that although the pilot failed to meet all expectations, it may, in hindsight, have done as well or better than should have been expected.

At the end of a Scrum pilot, I find that the pilot project is often compared to the unrealistic assumptions of a perfectly run sequential ("waterfall") project. There may be an old Gantt chart around showing a project plan that allows for two months of analysis, a month of design, two months of coding, then concludes with a month of testing. This very idealized six months is then compared to the reality of a first-ever Scrum project that, let's say, also took six months. The opponents of Scrum will say, "See, there are no advantages. It takes the same amount of time each way. And the old process has better design and is more maintainable over the long run." The unfair comparison here is between the reality of a Scrum project that took six months and a plan showing a waterfall project delivering in the same schedule. Do not allow (or make) comparisons between the reality of one project and the myth of another.

Setting and Managing Expectations

That brings us to our next topic: setting and managing expectations. In 1994 I managed a team that delivered a project that any outsider or any project team member would have considered a success. The product represented a great leap forward for the company. It included far more features than the product that was being replaced, was built using new state-of-the-art technologies with which the company had no prior experience, and included the development of three data centers that went on to provide 99.99999% uptime over the next six years. However, the project was almost considered a failure.

The project was to be delivered into multiple call centers with more than 300 nurses on the phones. It was to replace a quirky but familiar system that the company was rapidly outgrowing. The nurses' expectations of what the new system would deliver were sky high. In monthly sprint reviews with the nurses, I was routinely shocked by what they'd come to expect, some of which wasn't even technically feasible. With about three months left on the year-long project, I realized my focus had to change. From then on, I spent almost all of my time on expectations management. I met with nurses in each of the call centers and described exactly what would and would not be in the delivered system. I toned down their expectations about the system's impact on world peace, global warming, and personal weight loss. Without this effort, the product would have been perceived as a failure.

Since that project, I have been acutely aware of the importance of expectations management to the overall success of any project. Setting and managing expectations is perhaps even more important at the start of a major shift such as adopting Scrum. In initiating a transition to Scrum, I find it helpful to set and manage expectations about four things: progress, predictability, attitudes, and involvement.

Expectations About Progress

If peripherally involved stakeholders and outsiders have heard one thing about Scrum, it is probably that teams will be faster. I witnessed this when I was invited to speak at a large Silicon Valley company that had been previously visited by a Scrum consultant who oversold company executives on the benefits of Scrum. When I presented to the same group, I started by asking what they knew about Scrum already. All they could recall from the prior session was, "Teams will go faster, and we can change our minds whenever we want." After recovering from my stunned silence, I told them that those two things could be true but a lot of hard work would be required to get there, and there would be a productivity cost to changing their minds too often.

As for expectations that a team will go faster, Jim Highsmith's advice is much more conservative and realistic.

> In a six-month project, the goal might be to match historic productivity levels (down in the beginning, up at the end) while improving quality and better matching with customer expectations. Putting too much pressure on early will cause teams to abandon their newly minted practices and revert to the older ones in which they still have more confidence. (2005)

Whether a team is more productive or not will largely be a function of how well the team was doing before adopting Scrum. A team that is already doing reasonably well (having learned to work around the inefficiencies and impediments of the current organization and process) will likely, as Highsmith says, slow down at first. In contrast, a team that is really struggling could indeed be faster right from the start.

There are two things, though, that I have observed to be nearly universally true of teams right from the start:

- **Most teams will overestimate how much they will achieve in the first sprint.** Unless a team has significant prior experience working in truly timeboxed iterations, team members will probably think they can get more done in a few weeks than will be realistic. A team, for example, may collectively commit to completing 850 hours of planned work in the coming four-week sprint. In the end, the team finds that due to interruptions, unplanned work, corporate overhead and other factors, they complete only 725 hours of that planned work. They worked just as hard as they had planned to; they were able to complete less planned work, though, because they underestimated all other demands on their time.
- **Most teams will be more useful.** I'm using the term "useful" here for what we probably mean by "productive." But "productive" carries with it connotations of how much product was produced; and usually in a

software project it isn't far from that connotation to measuring lines of code. While I'm not completely opposed to measuring lines of code (and do it myself for some purposes), I don't want to say that Scrum teams start out writing more code per period of time, especially because more code may or may not be a good thing. What I do want to claim is that right from the start, most teams begin to do more useful work shortly after adopting Scrum. This is because sprints focus their attention on "what can we do in the next such-and-such weeks." Many traditional projects stall trying to find "the best" or "the right" or "the complete" solution. A Scrum team will be more likely to find a good-enough solution, try it, learn, and change as needed.

Expectations About Predictability

When I was running development organizations, rather than consulting to them as I do today, keeping my teams productive was not my only concern. I was equally concerned with whether I could make predictions about how long a team would take to finish a project. In many ways, I preferred a team that went at a reasonably consistent (and therefore predictable) pace to a team that sometimes went amazingly fast but that also sometimes went very slow. When piloting an organization's first Scrum projects, you should be clear with stakeholders that the pace will initially be less predictable than with the organization's prior approach to software development.

Scrum teams measure progress using a metric known as *velocity*, which is a measure of the work completed (or planned to be completed) in a given sprint. It is expressed in units such as story points or ideal days. Velocity is particularly volatile during a team's or an organization's first few sprints. After all, the team is learning to work in a new way, and many of the team members may be learning to work with each other for the first time.

SEE ALSO

Velocity is described in more detail in Chapter 15, "Planning."

It is important to communicate to stakeholders that early calculations using velocity will be particularly suspect. For example, after a team has established some historical data, it will be useful to say things like, "This team has an average velocity of 20, with a likely range of 15 to 25." These numbers can then be compared to a total estimate of project size to arrive at a likely duration range for a project. A project comprising a total of 150 story points, for example, may be thought of as taking from 6 to 10 sprints if velocity historically ranges from 15 to 25.

Until a team has sufficient historical data, though, projections like this can be very risky. This means that a high-risk contract with large penalties for late delivery is probably not an ideal Scrum pilot. (Nor is it an ideal pilot for any process change.) So how much data do you need before you can make projections like this? The easy answer is the more, the better. You can start making predictions after a team has completed its first sprint, but you should do so with a wide margin of assumed error around that first observed velocity. Perhaps more helpfully, I'll say that the velocity of most teams will stabilize sufficiently after the third or fourth sprint. Don't take this as a rule; if there are a lot of other things changing in a project's environment (such as new technologies, team members coming and going, and so on), velocity may very well bounce around longer.

Expectations About Attitudes Toward Scrum

After having been given time to adjust to working in a new way, most developers prefer Scrum. A survey at Yahoo! found, for example, that 85% of all team members would continue using the Scrum approach they'd adopted if the decision were left solely to them (Deemer et al. 2008, 16). But this usually won't be where attitudes start. Those initiating the transition need to be prepared for lots of objections and complaining at first. Common complaints include the following:

- All the time wasted in daily scrums
- The time wasted in making sure the product is well tested at the end of each sprint, even though it won't ship that often
- Managers not being able to assess me well enough to write my annual review because they can't tell which work is mine
- The system falling apart six months after release because we're not producing adequate maintenance and support documentation

At the first sign of trouble, there will be a temptation to give in and fall back to the old way of doing things. As Daryl Conner, author of *Managing at the Speed of Change*, has written, "It is relatively easy to get your people to acknowledge that a change is to be made and to get started on it. The really tough job is to get them to stick with it when the going gets tough" (1993, 116). One of the best ways to head off a slide back to old habits is to anticipate it and talk about it in advance and for team members to agree that when obstacles arise, they will stick to Scrum despite the discomfort and worry.

Expectations About Involvement

One of the most important expectations to set early on is about involvement in the process. Many project stakeholders accustomed to traditional-style development view their role in a software development project as akin to dropping a car off for service: You tell someone what you need done and come back at an appointed time to pick up the finished work. Stakeholders, especially anyone in a product owner role, will need to understand that this is not the right way to build software-intensive products.

Be sure to discuss expectations with the product owner and with other stakeholders whose input and feedback you will solicit either during the sprints or during sprint reviews. Make sure that each stakeholder knows what level of commitment the team expects and needs.

Scrum is not a silver bullet that will eliminate a development organization's problems. You should work right from the start to make sure that expectations do not rise to unrealistic levels. Managing expectations will be perhaps one of the most important things you can do early on. If you don't, you run the risk of an otherwise successful Scrum transition being viewed as a failure.

It's Just a Pilot

Pete Deemer, an independent Scrum consultant, was the chief product officer at Yahoo! when he initiated a program there to pilot Scrum. He recognized that a pilot project is an experiment, and the purpose of that experiment is to gain knowledge that will help later projects succeed. Deemer also recognized that by calling them pilot projects, he was acknowledging that he knew things would not always go smoothly. He said his hope was that "when difficulties cropped up, people would be more likely to just roll up their sleeves and try to find a solution." Deemer was using the label *pilot* to create some safety around the execution of the process.

Deemer recognized this safety as the valuable thing it was. It created the comfort zone teams needed in which to experiment so that they could be successful in finding the right ways to do Scrum. A year into the company's transition effort, though, and with well over one hundred Scrum teams, Deemer was still calling every project a pilot. I asked him when he would stop calling them pilots. He told me that until every project at Yahoo! had adopted Scrum and until they knew everything there was to know, he would continue to call them pilots.

Whether you view every project as a perpetual pilot, the first few sprints will be tremendously important. You can help ensure these initial sprints start your teams on the right path by carefully selecting the right first project and team members and by accurately setting and managing expectations.

Additional Reading

Karten, Naomi. 1994. *Managing expectations*. Dorset House.
> A good, easy-to-read book with solid advice. The book is focused on customer communication but almost all of its advice is applicable to other workplace relationships. Advice is provided on topics such as listening, clarifying perceptions, avoiding conflicting messages, and creating win/win solutions.

Little, Todd. 2005. Context-adaptive agility: Managing complexity and uncertainty. *IEEE Software*, May–June, 28–35.

Author Todd Little, a board member of the Agile Alliance and cofounder of the Agile Project Leadership Network, presents a framework for categorizing projects as Bulls, Colts, Cows, or Skunks based on the amount of uncertainty and complexity inherent in the project. The framework could be applied to choosing an initial Scrum project, where you avoid selecting the type of projects that Little calls Bulls (high-uncertainty, high-complexity projects).

PART II

Individuals

We have come to value…
Individuals and Interactions
over Process and Tools.

—The Agile Manifesto

Chapter 6

Overcoming Resistance

In a 1969 article in the *Harvard Business Review*, Paul Lawrence noted that change "has both a technical and a social aspect. The technical aspect of the change is the making of a measurable modification in the physical routines of a job. The social aspect of the change refers to the way those affected by it think it will alter their established relationships in the organization." When facing resistance, there is a tendency to emphasize the benefits of the technical aspect of change. After all, *we* are already convinced ourselves, so it's easy to assume that all we need to do now is to convince others. Lay out the perfect intellectual argument in favor of the change, we think, and people's resistance will vanish. Lawrence argues against that flawed logic: "We may sometimes wish that the validity of the technical aspect of the change were the sole determinant of its acceptability. But the fact remains that the social aspect is what determines the presence or absence of resistance" (1969, 7).

Although it is the social aspect of change that can create resistance, all resistance comes from specific individuals. Teams or departments do not resist changing to Scrum; individuals do. This chapter, therefore, focuses on effective techniques for overcoming individual resistance. We look first at how to anticipate their resistance and take preemptive measures against it. Next, we look at how to communicate about the change and why different messages are best delivered by different messengers. Finally, in this chapter we look at how and why individuals resist and then use that information to identify appropriate responses to overcoming their resistance.

Anticipating Resistance

It should not be surprising that some people will resist the change to Scrum. Some people resist all change. I suspect you could walk into a company, announce that everyone will be getting a 20–50% raise, and there still will be resistance. Some will suspect the boss's ulterior motives—What do you bet there are strings attached? Others will consider the raises unfair—I work harder than he does, why did he get a bigger percentage raise?

A transition such as the one to Scrum brings great upheaval to the organization. Responsibilities broaden, reporting relationships are altered, organizational power shifts, and expectations change. Some individuals stand to gain personally or professionally from such changes; others stand to lose. Understanding how these shifts will affect your organization is vital to anticipating where resistance will occur.

This is confirmed by a 2007 study of why people resist change, which revealed that managers' number one reason for resistance was a fear of losing control and authority (Creasey and Hiatt). The top reasons given by employees and managers for resisting change are shown in Table 6.1.

TABLE 6.1

The top reasons for resisting change, as given by employees and managers.

Number	Employees	Managers
1	Lack of awareness	Fear of losing control and authority
2	Fear of the unknown	Lack of time
3	Lack of job security	Comfort with the status quo
4	Lack of sponsorship	No answer to "What's in it for me?"
5		No involvement in solution design

Who Will Resist?

In attempting to anticipate where resistance will arise, it can be helpful to consider the answers to questions such as these:

- Who will lose something (power, prestige, clout, or so on) if the transition to Scrum is successful?

- What coalitions are likely to form to oppose the transition?

By identifying individuals who will lose from the change and coalitions that will form to oppose it, you will know where to target initial efforts at reducing resistance.

Although some individuals resist change, others enjoy it. Musselwhite and Ingram categorize individuals based on their disposition to change as shown in Figure 6.1 (Luecke 2003). At one end are conservers, who enjoy predictability; focus on details and routines; are deliberate, disciplined, and organized; and who prefer change that maintains the current structure of the organization. Conservers are estimated to be about 25% of the population.

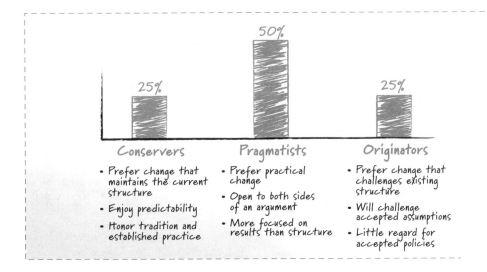

FIGURE 6.1
Individual disposition to change.

At the other end of the range are originators, who also represent about 25% of the population. Originators may appear disorganized and undisciplined, enjoy taking risks, have little regard for policies, and prefer change that challenges the current structure. In between conservers and originators are pragmatists, who represent the remaining 50% of the population. Pragmatists are usually practical, agreeable, and flexible; are more focused on results than structure; usually appear more team-oriented than conservers or originators; are open to both sides of an argument; and usually make great mediators between conservers and originators.

I've found that being aware of these three dispositions to change is helpful in identifying who will be likely to resist. Clearly, conservers will resist the transition to Scrum. The types of changes that Scrum brings to ways of working, team member interactions, and expectations are the type of changes that go against the nature of a conserver.

Categorizing people as conservers, pragmatists, and originators presents an incomplete and overly simplistic picture. Of course, each person needs to be considered and treated as a unique individual. Understanding these categories, however, can help you to formulate strategies for overcoming resistance. An individual's role in the organization can offer additional insights into why someone is resistant. Many of these causes of resistance are described in Chapter 7, "New Roles," and Chapter 8, "Changed Roles."

NOTE

Conservers will not be alone, however, in resisting Scrum. Some of the pragmatists will also resist. Because pragmatists are much more open to seeing both sides of an argument for themselves and then adding their support to the right side, laying an early groundwork for success can help turn pragmatists into Scrum advocates. Consider the following activities to help bring pragmatists around to Scrum:

- Run a pilot project and include pragmatists on the team.
- Make sure pragmatists who aren't on the pilot team see the results of it.
- Provide training to pragmatists.
- Expose pragmatists to the successes of other companies through conferences, regional agile interest groups, and so on.
- Be open to the drawbacks and challenges of Scrum rather than overselling it as a silver bullet.
- Involve pragmatists on the improvement communities that were described in Chapter 4, "Iterating Toward Agility."

Waterfallacies and Agile Phobias

Many of the specific arguments you'll hear against Scrum are predictable and common across many organizations. Others, of course, will be unique to your organization. You can often anticipate the arguments you'll hear by thinking through the challenges presented by your organization, domain, technologies, products, culture, and people. In doing so, you'll find that many of the objections (both the universal and the specific ones) can be categorized as either *waterfallacies* or *agile phobias*. A waterfallacy is a mistaken belief or idea about agile or Scrum created from working too long on waterfall projects. Examples include

- Scrum teams don't plan, so we're unable to make commitments to customers.
- Scrum requires everyone to be a generalist.
- Our team is spread around the world. Self-organization clashes with some cultures, so we can't be agile.
- Our team is spread around the world, and Scrum requires face-to-face communication.
- Scrum ignores architecture, which would be disastrous for the type of system we build.
- Scrum is OK for simple websites, but our system is too complicated.

An agile phobia is a strong fear or dislike of agile practices, usually due to the uncertainty of change. Some of the agile phobias you are likely to encounter include the following:

- I'm afraid I'll have nothing to do.
- I'm afraid I'll be fired if the decisions we make don't work out.
- I'm afraid of conflict and of trying to reach consensus.
- I'm afraid people will see how little I really do.
- It's so much easier and safer when someone tells me exactly what to do.
- It's so much easier and safer when I can tell people exactly what to do.

Although a waterfallacy can often be countered with rational arguments, anecdotes, and evidence, an agile phobia is usually much more personal and emotional. Sometimes people just need to know that their objections have been heard.

Throughout this book I have tried to preempt as many waterfallacies and agile phobias as possible. Many chapters include "Objection" sidebars, which provide my advice on how to address common questions and misunderstandings about Scrum.

Communicating About the Change

If you look back at Table 6.1, you'll notice that the number-one reason employees gave for resisting change was a lack of awareness. I'm confident, though, that if we searched the deleted e-mail folders of all who participated in that study, we would find at least one message explaining the reason for the change. However, having been told the reason and understanding the reason are not the same. Most of us need to be given a message multiple times, and usually in multiple ways, before it finally sinks in and we understand it. In addition to hearing a message multiple times, there are some messages we hear better when they come from leaders and others we hear better when they come from our peers.

Hearing from Leaders

Not surprisingly, research has shown that employees prefer to receive different types of information from different people (Hiatt 2006, 12). Employees prefer to hear messages about why a change is needed from someone high up in the organization. The same employees prefer to hear about how the change will affect them personally from their immediate supervisor. This means that while the president of the company or the general manager of the division may be best at communicating the reason for switching to Scrum, individuals need the opportunity to meet with their own managers to discuss the implications for them personally. Still other messages are best communicated by peers.

If you are a formal leader in your organization or are informally recognized as one, you will likely find yourself in a position to communicate about the transition. When communicating about an uncertain future, there is a good chance you will be asked questions you do not know how to answer: Will there be layoffs? Who will I report to? Who will write my annual review? If you don't know the answer to a question, don't guess. And always be honest. A single lie will destroy all previously established credibility.

Additionally, when communicating about the transition, be sure to listen. As a formal or informal leader, your role is not only to communicate what needs to be passed along but also to listen and hear the objections that are being stated (and the ones that are implied). Look once more at the list of common reasons for resisting shown in Table 6.1. Notice that none of the reasons was "I don't think this change is a good idea." Yes, of course, there will be some in the organization who think shifting to Scrum is a bad idea, but there will be more who resist for other, more personal reasons—the social aspects of change mentioned at the start of this chapter. In every conversation with others, spend more time listening than talking. For each person who resists the transition, see if you can complete this sentence for them: "I can't do Scrum because it means I…." There are an infinite number of ways to complete that sentence. After a recent client engagement, I was able to finish the sentence this way for some employees I met that day:

- I would have to work harder than I want to right now.
- I would have to stop doing the part of my job I enjoy most.
- I would have to travel more often to work more closely with my remote team.
- I would not be able hide that I am no longer a good hands-on programmer.
- I would not have as many people reporting to me.

None of these statements was uttered by the people I met with that day. But, each was there to be heard when I listened carefully enough. Understanding why individuals are resisting will be the first step in helping them overcome their resistance.

Hearing from Peers

Any successful communication plan will include plenty of opportunities for unconvinced employees to hear from their peers. An article in the *MIT Sloan Management Report* conveys a similar message.

Particularly during a period of uncertainty, the best route to influence others can be from the side rather than from above. For leaders, this means allowing employees who have yet to accept a change to hear from those who have, perhaps through team meetings. Even just one exposure to the favorable position of a peer can have a greater impact than multiple exposures to the similar position of a supervisor. (Griskevicius, Cialdini, and Goldstein 2008, 86)

An interesting anecdote concerning the power of peer influence involves Sylvan Goldman, who invented the shopping cart in 1937 after noticing that shoppers at his market stopped shopping when their hand-carried baskets became heavy. Surprisingly, Goldman's carts were not immediately popular. The carts sat unused until Goldman hired male and female actors to push the carts around the store, pretending to shop. After shoppers saw people they perceived as peers using the carts, usage took off. Shopping carts are now a ubiquitous part of the grocery shopping experience.

To make this more personal: Consider a time when you were at a conference or trade show and saw a throng crowded into one vendor's booth to hear the pitch. Admit it: You moved closer to hear what had everyone so interested. Or recall a time you walked through an area with street performers, perhaps a mime, musician, or juggler. You may have noticed that after a small crowd started to form around one performer, the crowd got bigger and bigger.

These examples show the power of peer influence. If one's peers proclaim the benefits, people listen. An effective transition effort will include many opportunities for peer-to-peer discussion. Many will be informal and spontaneous—coworkers talking at lunch, for example. But, effective leaders of a transition to Scrum should also seek to create additional opportunities. This can be done by encouraging participation in communities of practice or even by occasionally scheduling more formal peer-to-peer lunchtime presentations. To the extent possible, try to match the messenger to the audience. Consider this advice from a study on the impact of peer influence.

When working to ensure that the voices of supportive employees will be heard, managers often select those who are the most articulate when they should instead favor those who are the most similar in circumstances to the individuals who are still unconvinced. So if resistance to an initiative is strongest among employees with the longest tenures, then a fellow old-timer who has genuinely embraced the change could be a better advocate than someone who might be more eloquent but has only recently come on board. (Griskevicius, Cialdini, and Goldstein 2008, 86)

The Hows and Whys of Individual Resistance

People resist changing to Scrum for many different reasons. Some may resist because they are comfortable with their current work and colleagues. It has taken years to get to their current levels in the organization, to be on this team, to work for that manager, or to know exactly how to do their jobs each day. Others may resist changing to Scrum because of a fear of the unknown. "Better the devil you know than the devil you don't" is their mantra. Still others may resist due to a genuine dislike or distrust of the Scrum approach. They may be convinced that building complex products iteratively without significant up-front design will lead to disaster.

Just as there are many reasons why some people will resist Scrum, there are many *ways* someone might resist. One person may resist with well-reasoned logic and fierce arguments. Another may resist by quietly sabotaging the change effort. "You think no documentation is a good idea? I'll show you no documentation," the passive resistor may think, proceeding to write nothing down, even bug reports the team has agreed should continue to be stored in the defect tracking system. Another may resist by quietly ignoring the change, working the old way as much as possible, and waiting for the next change du jour to come along and sweep Scrum away.

Each act of resistance carries with it information about how people feel about adopting Scrum. As a change agent or leader in the organization, your goal should be to understand the root cause of an individual's resistance, learn from it, and then help the person overcome it. There are many techniques you can use for doing this. But unless the technique is carefully chosen, it is unlikely to have the desired effect. To help select the right technique, I find it useful to think about *how* and *why* someone is resisting. We can group the reasons why someone is resisting Scrum into two general categories:

- They like the status quo.
- They don't like Scrum.

Reasons for resistance fall into the first category if they are actually a defense of the current approach. This type of resistance to changing to Scrum would likely result no matter what type of change was being contemplated. Reasons fall into the second category if they are arguments against the specific implications of beginning to work in an agile manner. Tables 6.2 and 6.3 provide some examples of different reasons for resistance and how each would be categorized.

Categorizing *how* individuals resist is even simpler: Is the resistance active or passive? Active resistance occurs when someone takes a specific action intended to impede or derail the transition to Scrum. Passive resistance occurs when someone fails to take a specific action, usually after saying he will. Combining the two general reasons people may resist Scrum with the two ways in which they will do it leads to the standard two-by-two matrix, as shown in Figure 6.2.

Examples of Liking the Status Quo
I like who I work with.
I like the power or prestige that comes with my current role.
This is the way I was trained to do it and the only way I know how.
I don't like change of any sort.
I don't want to start another change initiative because they always fail anyway.

TABLE 6.2

People may resist Scrum because they like how things are today.

Examples of Not Liking Scrum
I think Scrum is a fad and we'll just have to switch back in three years.
Scrum is a bad idea for our products.
I got into this field so that I could put headphones on and not talk to people.
Scrum doesn't work with distributed teams like ours.

TABLE 6.3

People may resist because they don't like Scrum.

Each quadrant of Figure 6.2 is given a name descriptive of the person who resists in the way indicated by the labels on the axes. A skeptic is someone who does not agree with the principles or practices of Scrum but who only passively resists the transition. Skeptics are the ones who politely argue against Scrum, forget to attend the daily scrum a little too often, and so on. I am referring here to individuals who are truly trying to stop the transition, not people with the healthy attitude of "this sounds different from anything I've done before but I'm intrigued. Let's give it a try and see if it works."

Above the skeptics in Figure 6.2 are the saboteurs. Like skeptics, saboteurs resist the transition more from a dislike of Scrum than support for whatever software development process exists currently. Unlike a skeptic, a saboteur provides active resistance by trying to undermine the transition effort, perhaps by continuing to write lengthy up-front design documents, and so on.

On the left side of Figure 6.2 are those who resist because they like the status quo. They are comfortable with their current activities, prestige, and coworkers. In principle, these individuals may not be opposed to Scrum; they are, however, opposed to any change that puts their current situation at risk. Those who like the status quo and who actively resist changing from it are known as diehards. They often attempt to prevent the transition by rallying others to their cause.

The bottom left of Figure 6.2 shows the followers, who like the status quo and resist changing from it passively. Followers are usually not enraged by the prospect of change, so they do little more than hope it passes like a fad. They need to be shown that Scrum has become the new status quo.

FIGURE 6.2

Four different types of resistors based on why and how they resist.

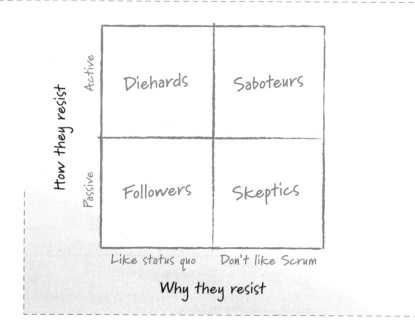

Skeptics

Thad had no choice but to adopt Scrum. His company had been acquired and was being told by the new owners to begin using Scrum immediately. This wasn't a direction Thad would have chosen himself, and he had serious concerns about it. Would the daily scrums add value, especially with a product owner who worked from her home 600 miles away? How could a new product as complicated, large, and novel as theirs be done without a lengthy up-front design phase? He could see the value of iterating through the construction phase, but surely an up-front design was still needed.

Thad was a skeptic. I knew this from his willingness to admit that Scrum was fine for other domains, technologies, or environments—just not his. Thad openly acknowledged the appropriateness of Scrum for web development but questioned it for his company's scientific applications.

As the most experienced member on his team and one of the longest-tenured developers in the organization, Thad was an opinion leader. Others looked to him to see how he would behave under the mandate to adopt Scrum. Thad exhibited a healthy amount of doubt; people should not be expected to change how they work without the opportunity to ask hard questions or be expected to fully embrace Scrum until they've worked on a Scrum team and experienced the benefits for themselves. Thad's uncertainty, however, went beyond doubt to the point where he was resisting the transition in small but important ways.

Because he didn't see the benefit of daily scrums, Thad consistently pushed to skip them. At the end of one meeting he said, "It sounds like we're all on stuff that will take at least today to finish. So let's skip tomorrow's daily scrum and just meet again the day after. Every other day is probably good enough anyway." Sometimes his ScrumMaster could successfully counter these arguments, but not always. After all, the ScrumMaster was new to Scrum, too.

Additionally, like many skeptics, Thad would sometimes claim to support a Scrum practice but would then continue to work as he always had. For instance, he said that he supported working iteratively and claimed to understand the value of having a potentially shippable product at the end of each sprint. In truth, though, Thad didn't believe that all parts of their product could be designed, coded, and tested within a single sprint. Consequently, he habitually pushed the team to bring more work than it could handle into each sprint. Overcommitting was his way of making sure that some features were worked on over at least two sprints.

Some of the tools that are useful in overcoming the resistance presented by skeptics include

- **Let time run its course.** If you can keep the transition effort moving forward, evidence of the benefits of Scrum will start to accumulate. Even if this evidence is merely anecdotal, it lessens the amount of resistance a skeptic can put up.

- **Provide training.** Some of a skeptic's resistance is a result of not having done something or not having seen it done before. Training—whether formal classroom training or as provided by an external coach brought in to work with the team—helps by giving the skeptic the experience of seeing firsthand how it can work.

- **Solicit peer anecdotes.** If you've never experienced something yourself but your friends or those you relate to have, their personal stories will resonate with you. If there are Scrum success stories from other teams in your organization, make sure the skeptics hear them. If Scrum is new to your organization, invite experienced agile outsiders in. Inviting a local software architect to speak at lunch about her company's success with Scrum will do wonders in persuading your own skeptical architects.

- **Appoint a champion skeptic.** In their book *Fearless Change*, Mary Lynn Manns and Linda Rising suggest designating someone as the company's "champion skeptic" (2004). The champion skeptic should be influential, respected, and well connected but should not be openly hostile to the change. The champion skeptic is invited to all meetings and is given a chance to point out problems. Use this information to sincerely address the concerns the champion skeptic brings up. Doing so demonstrates open-mindedness and prevents any one concern from escalating into a crisis.

- **Push the issue.** Put the skeptic in charge of some part of the transition. Suppose you are struggling with a skeptical tester who does not believe testing can be done in the same sprint as the design and programming of a feature. Challenge that tester to identify five ways to help bring the team closer to the goal of testing within the same sprint. The tester won't be able to come up empty for fear that the next person who takes on the task successfully identifies five items. Then, ask the team to either try all five things or to select the one or two ideas that seem most promising initially.

- **Build awareness.** Presumably you have chosen to do something as difficult as introduce Scrum because there is a compelling need to do so. Perhaps a new competitor has entered your space, perhaps your last product took a year too long to release, or perhaps you have any of a number of similar reasons. Make sure that those involved in the transition are aware of the better future that will follow a successful transition.

> **NOTE**
>
> More tools for overcoming resistance will be described in the sections that follow on saboteurs, diehards, and followers. Although it is possible that any tool may work on any type of resistor, I have listed the tools along with the type of resistor for whom I have found the tool most useful.

In Thad's case, we were able to overcome his skepticism by pushing the issue. We put a stop to his passive resistance to iterating by switching to shorter sprints. The team had been using four-week sprints but was bringing in about six weeks worth of work in each sprint planning meeting. I told them we were going to try two-week sprints until they got a handle on how much could actually be completed in a sprint. Thad didn't like this idea. In the next sprint planning meeting, to point out the foolishness of working in such short sprints, Thad pushed the team to commit to what he thought was a ridiculously small amount of work. It turned out to be the right amount; for the first time the team finished all its work inside one sprint. As team members came to see the value of completing what they committed to, Thad's subtle efforts to force the team to overcommit were thwarted by the team's new insistence that it bring in to the sprint only what it could handle.

Although pushing the issue helped in Thad's case, the biggest factor in eradicating his resistance was time. It just took time (and a mounting pile of anecdotal evidence that it could be done) to sway Thad.

Saboteurs

It can be easy to mistake a saboteur for a skeptic—after all, some amount of uncertainty about any change can be a good thing. I made the mistake of confusing a saboteur with a skeptic while teaching a class at a search engine company. Elena, a participant in the class, was asking a lot of good, challenging questions. I didn't know her role in the organization, but because many class participants were deferential to her, I figured she was important in one sense or another, and so I spent a lot of time answering her questions. If I was right and she was an opinion leader, and if I could convert her by overcoming her objections one by one, I knew that would be a big step forward for this company.

At the end of the day, I met with the director who had invited me to teach that class in her company. We talked about how the class went and I told her how I hoped I'd made progress helping Elena to see the light. The director said, "I should have warned you about her. She hates Scrum. She runs a shared user experience design group and is completely opposed to everything about Scrum. She's been fighting it since we started six months ago. I was surprised to see that she'd signed up for your class."

Elena was a saboteur—opposed to Scrum and actively resisting it. Like most saboteurs, she had been soliciting others to her cause. Despite mounting evidence within her company that Scrum was helping create better products more quickly, she continued to argue that it would not. I asked Elena directly why she was so strongly opposed. She said, "I have the best stateroom on the Titanic and I'm not moving!"

In addition to some of the tools offered for overcoming the resistance of skeptics, the following tools have proven useful with saboteurs:

- **Success.** As long as there is any doubt about whether Scrum is the appropriate approach, saboteurs will use those doubts to spread resistance. "Yes, it worked on our web projects," they may grudgingly offer, "but, it won't work on our back-end projects." Success on many different types of projects is a surefire way of weakening those arguments.

- **Reiterate and reinforce the commitment.** Saboteurs need to know that the company is committed to the transition. Any sign of weakness and—like a lion eyeing a tasty-looking antelope—the saboteur will attack. Faced with a large number of saboteurs, a strong message from as high up the executive chain as possible will at least let them know resistance is futile.

- **Move them.** If possible, find another team, project, or division and move the saboteur there. Unless you are a small organization or are doing an

SEE ALSO

Sprints, and especially the value of producing something potentailly shippable by the end of each sprint, are covered in Chapter 14, "Sprints."

all-in transition, it is quite likely that a saboteur can continue to be a productive team member elsewhere—until Scrum starts to permeate that team, project, or division, that is.

- **Fire them.** This is the extreme end of moving someone. But if someone is opposed to a stated corporate direction and is actively resisting it, then this is quite possibly the appropriate action.

- **Be sure the right people are talking.** Chapter 4 introduced the idea of forming improvement communities as a way of identifying and spreading good practices and enthusiasm for Scrum through the organization. A thriving set of communities focused around topics of special interest can be invaluable in producing enough momentum to overcome resistance. Hearing how others within a community of practice are succeeding with Scrum can lessen a saboteur's resolve to continue resisting.

Elena was fortunate to work in a large organization in which she could be moved to a different department that was still taking a wait-and-see attitude toward Scrum. She eventually came around to the point where she is again a productive team member, though even today she will admit she is secretly waiting for a change back to the old way of working.

Diehards

Katherine worked as the director of metrics and measurement for a large division of a financial data provider. I had been told she was a supporter of the division's shift toward Scrum but that she had a few questions for me so that she could more effectively do her job of collecting process and product metrics. I have a natural interest in this subject, and such discussions are usually a great chance for me to learn something new. I was looking forward to meeting with Katherine as a chance to discuss some creative, innovative metrics.

Was I ever wrong! Katherine had mastered the art of appearing to support the transition to Scrum while trying to hold onto the status quo. Three years prior to our meeting, software development within this organization had been characterized by missed deadlines and buggy software that didn't meet customer expectations. At that time, Katherine was the newly hired test manager. She instituted some new procedures that dramatically improved things. As a result, teams seemed to be meeting their deadlines (mainly because schedules were padded by what I considered astounding amounts) and quality improved (by creating a separate test group that would spend months testing after a product was handed over to them).

For her efforts in solving these problems, Katherine had been promoted and was now running what was essentially a project management office (PMO). As she told me more about her background and about how she had previously helped her company by introducing various process improvements, I was sure I had found an ally in transitioning her division to Scrum. Instead, what I found was someone who had built herself a very nice empire (through good effort directed at earlier company goals). She was now so enamored of her current status, the number of people reporting to her, and her level of prestige that she was unwilling to consider further changes. Moses could have come down from the mountaintop with the ideal process engraved on stone tablets, and Katherine would have resisted.

Katherine, like other diehards, was opposed to Scrum not because of anything inherent in it but because she did not want to let go of the current state. She was very actively resisting the change but always in ways that allowed her to claim to be supporting it.

A common technique of diehards, and one Katherine employed, is to stall the transition by controlling resources. This is possible because diehards are often found at the middle and upper levels of management where they have enough status to want to keep it. In Katherine's case, she controlled a shared pool of testers. This allowed her to harm the transition by profligately moving testers between projects. There were always plausible reasons: A critical project needed an additional tester, another project needed the expertise of a specific tester, and so on. Katherine's tactics had the effect of ensuring that no team retained the same personnel from start to finish and that many Scrum teams didn't have a tester for the first few sprints.

Many of the tools appropriate for overcoming the resistance of the saboteur will work with the diehard as well. Some additional tools you may want to employ with diehards include

- **Align incentives.** Diehards are tied to the status quo because of the benefits (either tangible or intangible) that it brings them. If you find a lot of resistance from diehards, consider all incentives that exist in the organization and make sure each aligns well with being agile. I am not referring solely to financial incentives. Nonfinancial incentives such as who gets promoted or otherwise recognized should also be reviewed. If having a large number of people reporting to you creates clout in your organization, for example, you shouldn't be surprised when people resist losing their direct reports.

- **Create dissatisfaction with the status quo.** Diehards like the status quo. They are not opposed to Scrum because of what it is; they are opposed to it because they like how things are. So, try to create dissatisfaction with the current state. I don't mean to go create a crisis, but if one looms, point it out. If market share is declining, make sure people know. If calls to tech support are on the rise, show people. If an industry newsletter recently heaped praise on a competitor's product, hang copies of the article where everyone can see them. This is consistent with the advice of Stewart Tubbs, author of a textbook on small-group interaction: "A prescient manager is always looking for ways for the organization to improve

SEE ALSO

Chapter 20, "Human Resources, Facilities, and the PMO," provides advice on many human resources–related issues.

continuously. She or he is constantly on the lookout for ways to make the organization more effective, and looks to communicate these ideas as a way to generate dissatisfaction with the status quo" (2004, 352).

- **Acknowledge and confront fear.** Diehards resist in part because of the uncertainty of what their jobs will look like with Scrum. They are usually very happy with their current positions. Fear of an uncertain future can be very powerful. How will my role change? How will I be evaluated? What will come next in my career? These are all powerful questions often in the mind of the diehard. If you know the answers and are in a position to give them, do so. If the answers are unknown, say so but commit—if you can and if you value the work of the diehard—to working with him to find the answers. You can also help calm these fears by clarifying what is expected not just of the diehard but of others with whom he may work.

In Katherine's case, her vice president (Christine) and I sought to find the right role for her in the new organization. We talked with her about our confidence that her past experience in guiding the company toward dramatic process improvements put her in a key position for helping the company again. Christine clarified Katherine's role in the new organization. Unfortunately, Katherine's sense of identity and self-worth were so tightly coupled to the process that she had helped put in place that she could not help the company move beyond it. In the end, she left the company.

Followers

Like diehards, followers are more opposed to changing the status quo than they are opposed to adopting Scrum in particular. Unlike diehards, however, followers present passive resistance to the change. Dexter, a mid-level programmer at an e-commerce company was a follower. He asked questions like a skeptic but always with an undercurrent implying that he knew Scrum was a bad thing. Where a skeptic would ask, "How does Scrum work on projects where getting the user experience perfect is absolutely critical?" Dexter would ask, "Scrum doesn't work when getting the user experience perfect is critical, does it?"

I remember one conversation with Dexter in which he asked how many times I would be back to visit his company. "I'm scheduled back in July and October," I said. This was June.

"Nothing after that?" he asked.

"Maybe, but we haven't scheduled anything past October."

"Good. This will be done by the end of the year, then."

I was impressed by his enthusiasm, but I thought his timeline for adopting Scrum was a little aggressive considering the size of his company. "Well, probably not," I cautioned. "There will probably still be some work next year. Not everyone has even started running sprints. But you probably won't need me next year."

"Oh," Dexter replied, "I didn't mean it that way. I meant we'll be onto our next new process by then. After the Christmas shopping season is over, we always change our process."

No one had told me about these annual process changes prior to my first visit with this company, but considering the company's history of adopting a new process every January, it wasn't surprising that Dexter would take a wait-it-out approach to Scrum. In fact, many followers adopt this approach, reasoning that this change will be followed by some later change and they might as well skip a few along the way.

On his own Dexter didn't present a significant hurdle to a successful transition. But, have enough Dexters in your organization, and they can impede a successful transition. Fortunately, followers are not usually very vigorous in their resistance. They will put up minor, passive resistance, mostly hoping that the change goes away. In addition to some of the tools described already, there are a few more tools that can be useful in dealing with followers:

- **Change the composition of the team.** Some coworkers bring out the best in us; others bring out the worst. Changing the composition of the team will undoubtedly change the nature of resistance. Replacing a grumbling, always-negative saboteur with a skeptic may remove a follower's motivation for resisting.

- **Praise the right behavior.** Rather than focusing on changing the behavior of the followers, praise some aspects of appropriate behavior whether you observe it in a detractor or supporter. Followers will notice and resistance in some will weaken.

- **Involve them.** A great way to reduce the resistance of a fence-sitting follower is to involve her in the design of the new process. For example, you might ask a follower to join an improvement community figuring out how to do automated unit testing on your challenging legacy application or to work with others putting together a presentation for the sales group on how Scrum impacts your ability to put dates in contracts.

- **Model the right behaviors yourself.** Followers need someone to follow. Increase the odds that they follow someone who is exhibiting the right agile behavior by modeling those behaviors yourself. For example, given that collaboration is an essential part of Scrum, strive to demonstrate this in your interactions with others.

- **Identify the true barrier.** Following the model described in Chapter 2, "ADAPTing to Scrum," determine whether a follower is resisting because she lacks the awareness, desire, or ability to use Scrum. Then provide the appropriate support to break through that barrier. If she isn't aware of the reasons for transitioning to Scrum, have a private conversation in which you share them. If she currently lacks the ability to be agile, look for an opportunity to pair her with someone who can help her learn those skills.

THINGS TO TRY NOW

❑   Identify the five fiercest resistors in your organization.

❑   For each of the five fiercest resistors, decide whether each is most likely a skeptic, saboteur, diehard, or follower.

❑   Identify one action you can take to lessen or counter the resistance of each of the five fiercest resistors. Look for opportunities to find one action that will work for multiple resistors.

❑   Assess whether you have correctly set the stage for the transition by first building awareness and creating desire. Revisit these activities if needed.

Resistance as a Useful Red Flag

When introducing a complex change into a large organization, resistance will be inevitable. What isn't inevitable is the reaction of an organization's leaders to that resistance. Paul Lawrence, whom we heard from at the start of this chapter, describes an appropriate response.

> When resistance does appear, it should not be thought of as something to be overcome. Instead, it can best be thought of as a useful red flag—a signal that something is going wrong. To use a rough analogy, signs of resistance in a social organization are useful in the same way that pain is useful to the body as a signal that some bodily functions are getting out of adjustment. The resistance, like the pain, does not tell us what is wrong but only that something is wrong. And it makes no more sense to try to overcome such resistance than it does to take a pain killer without diagnosing the bodily ailment. Therefore, when resistance appears, it is time to listen carefully to find out what the trouble is. What is needed is not a long harangue on the logics of the new recommendations but a careful exploration of the difficulty. (1969, 9)

Be careful not to turn the need to handle resistance into an atmosphere of "us" against "them." The real goal is to create a feeling that the transition to Scrum is inevitable and that, as the Borg of Star Trek taught us, "resistance is futile." The need to foster this atmosphere does not give you carte blanche to ignore the feelings and reactions of employees or to steamroll Scrum into an organization. When an employee resists, an effective leader looks at the employee not as a problem to be solved but as a person to be understood (Nicholson 2003).

Additional Reading

Bridges, William. 2003. *Managing transitions: Making the most of change.* 2nd ed. Da Capo Press.

> The author is a general transition management expert rather than someone well versed in software development. His book is a standard on how individuals deal with transitions and contains a wealth of information on letting go of the past. There is also strong coverage of moving through what the author calls the "neutral zone," that time between when the old has been abandoned yet the new approach is not established.

Emery, Dale H. 2001. Resistance as a resource. *Cutter IT Journal,* October.

> Emery presents the view that a person's resistance can be viewed as a response to a change initiative and that the response carries with it information. That information can be used to learn about the person and hopefully get that person engaged in the change process. The article includes an informative list of four factors that influence whether someone resists.

Manns, Mary Lynn, and Linda Rising. 2004. *Fearless change: Patterns for introducing new ideas.* Addison-Wesley.

> This book presents 48 patterns that can be applied to any change initiative. Patterns range from the well known ("do food") to the lesser known, such as the value of designating a "champion skeptic," and many others that can help overcome resistance.

Reale, Richard C. 2005. *Making change stick: Twelve principles for transforming organizations.* Positive Impact Associates, Inc.

> Some of the 12 suggestions in this short book can be used to help overcome resistance. Sections on catching people doing something right and confronting fear are particularly useful. Other suggestions, such as align your culture, are too big to be adequately covered in the few pages devoted to them.

Chapter 7

New Roles

As we discussed in the previous chapter, teams and organizations resist Scrum for many different reasons. One likely source of opposition to adopting Scrum is confusion over the new roles that exist on a Scrum project. The roles of Scrum-Master and product owner are new ones without exact corollaries in the pretransition organization. It is common for an organization new to Scrum to struggle with filling these roles with appropriate individuals. Until people figure out what the new roles entail and which individuals have those skills, it is hard to put the right people in place.

In this chapter, I describe the new roles of ScrumMaster and product owner. For each role, we look at the responsibilities of the role, ideal attributes of candidates for the role, and how to overcome some common problems these roles present.

The Role of the ScrumMaster

Much has already been written about the job of the ScrumMaster in removing impediments to the team's progress (Schwaber and Beedle 2001, Schwaber 2004). Most ScrumMasters quickly grasp that part of their job. Where many falter—especially during the critical first 6 to 12 months of using Scrum—is in their relationships to their teams, which is why we will focus on that topic here.

Many who are new to the ScrumMaster role struggle with the apparent contradiction of the ScrumMaster as both a servant-leader to the team and also someone with no authority. The seeming contradiction disappears when we realize that although the ScrumMaster has no authority over Scrum team members, the ScrumMaster does have authority over the process. Although a ScrumMaster may not be able to say, "You're fired," a ScrumMaster *can* say, "I've decided we're going to try two-week sprints for the next month."[1]

The ScrumMaster is there to help the team in its use of Scrum. Think of the help from a ScrumMaster as similar to a personal trainer who helps you stick

---

1   Ideally, the ScrumMaster tries to get team members to decide this on their own. But, if they do not, the ScrumMaster's authority over the process allows for this decision.

with an exercise regimen and perform all exercises with the correct form. A good trainer will provide motivation while at the same time making sure you don't cheat by skipping a hard exercise. The trainer's authority, however, is limited. The trainer cannot make you do an exercise you don't want to do. Instead, the trainer reminds you of your goals and how you've chosen to meet them. To the extent that the trainer does have authority, it has been granted by the client. ScrumMasters are much the same: They have authority, but that authority is granted to them by the team.

SEE ALSO

For more on the meaning of potentially shippable, see "Deliver Working Software Each Sprint," in Chapter 14, "Sprints."

A ScrumMaster can say to a team, "Look, we're supposed to deliver potentially shippable software at the end of each sprint. We didn't do that this time. What can we do to make sure we do better the next sprint?" This is the Scrum-Master exerting authority over the process; something has gone wrong with the process if the team has failed to deliver something potentially shippable. But because the ScrumMaster's authority does not extend beyond the process, the same ScrumMaster should not say, "Because we failed to deliver something potentially shippable the last sprint, I want Tod to review all code before it gets checked in." Having Tod review the code might be a good idea, but the decision is not the ScrumMaster's to make. Doing so goes beyond authority over the process and enters into how the team works.

With authority limited to ensuring the team follows the process, the Scrum-Master's role can be more difficult than that of a typical project manager. Project managers often have the fallback position of "do it because I say so." The times when a ScrumMaster can say that are limited and restricted to ensuring that Scrum is being followed.

Attributes of a Good ScrumMaster

Today's surgeons are highly trained and skilled individuals who have had years of formal education followed by extensive internships. This was not always the case. Pete Moore has written that "the first surgeons had little anatomical knowledge, but plied their trade because they had sharp instruments and strong arms. They often did surgery in their spare time while working as the local barber or black-smith" (2005, 143).

Many organizations choose their first ScrumMasters in much the same way; but instead of seeking sharp instruments and strong arms, they look for management or leadership experience. As they become more experienced with Scrum, organizations eventually realize there are many more factors to consider in selecting ScrumMasters. To help save you from picking a ScrumMaster whose sole qualifications are strong arms and sharp instruments, I have listed the six attributes I have found to be common among the best ScrumMasters I've worked with.

Responsible

A good ScrumMaster is able and willing to assume responsibility. That is not to say that ScrumMasters are responsible for the success of the project; that is shared by the team as a whole. However, the ScrumMaster is responsible for maximizing the throughput of the team and for assisting team members in adopting and using Scrum. As noted earlier, the ScrumMaster takes on this responsibility without assuming any of the authority that might be useful in achieving it.

SEE ALSO

For more on whole-team responsibility, see Chapter 11, "Teamwork."

Think of the ScrumMaster as similar to an orchestra conductor. Both must provide real-time guidance and leadership to a talented collection of individuals who come together to create something that no one of them could create alone. Boston Pops conductor Keith Lockhart has said of his role, "People assume that when you become a conductor you're into some sort of a Napoleonic thing— that you want to stand on that big box and wield your power. I'm not a power junkie, I'm a responsibility junkie" (Mangurian 2006, 30). In an identical manner, a good ScrumMaster thrives on responsibility—that special type of responsibility that comes without power.

Humble

A good ScrumMaster is not in it for her ego. She may take pride (often immense pride) in her achievements, but the feeling will be "look what I *helped* accomplish" rather than the more self-centered "look what I accomplished." A humble ScrumMaster is one who realizes the job does not come with a company car or parking spot near the building entrance. Rather than putting her own needs first, a humble ScrumMaster is willing to do whatever is necessary to help the team achieve its goal. Humble ScrumMasters recognize the value in all team members and by example lead others to the same opinion.

Collaborative

A good ScrumMaster works to ensure a collaborative culture exists within the team. The ScrumMaster needs to make sure team members feel able to raise issues for open discussion and that they feel supported in doing so. The right ScrumMaster helps create a collaborative atmosphere for the team through words and actions. When disputes arise, collaborative ScrumMasters encourage teams to think in terms of solutions that benefit all involved rather than in terms of winners and losers. A good ScrumMaster models this type of behavior by working with other ScrumMasters in the organization. However, beyond modeling a collaborative attitude, a good ScrumMaster establishes collaboration as the team norm and will call out inappropriate behavior (if the other team members don't do it themselves).

Committed

Although being a ScrumMaster is not always a full-time job, it does require some-one who is fully committed to doing it. The ScrumMaster must feel the same high level of commitment to the project and the goals of the current sprint as the team members do. As part of that commitment, a good ScrumMaster does not end very many days with impediments left unaddressed. There will, of course, be times when this is inevitable, as not all impediments can be removed in a day. For example, convincing a manager to dedicate a full-time resource to the team may take a series of discussions over several days. On the whole, however, if a team finds that impediments are often not cleared quickly, team members should remind their ScrumMaster about the importance of being committed to the team.

One way a ScrumMaster can demonstrate commitment is by remaining in that role for the full duration of the project. It is disruptive for a team to change ScrumMasters mid-project.

Influential

A successful ScrumMaster influences others, both on the team and outside it. Ini-tially, team members might need to be persuaded to give Scrum a fair trial or to behave more collaboratively; later, a ScrumMaster may need to convince a team to try a new technical practice, such as test-driven development or pair program-ming. A ScrumMaster should know how to exert influence without resorting to a dictatorial "because I say so" style.

Most ScrumMasters will also be called upon to influence those outside the team. For example, a ScrumMaster might need to convince a traditional team to provide a partial implementation to the Scrum team. Or, a ScrumMaster might need to prevail upon a QA director to dedicate full-time testers to the project.

Although all ScrumMasters should know how to use their personal influence, the ideal one will come with a degree of corporate political skill. The term "cor-porate politics" is often used pejoratively; however, a ScrumMaster who knows who makes decisions in the organization, how those decisions are made, which coalitions exist, and so on can be an asset to a team.

Knowledgeable

Beyond having a solid understanding of and experience with Scrum, the best ScrumMasters also have the technical, market, or other specialized knowledge to help the team pursue its goal. LaFasto and Larson have studied successful teams and their leaders and have concluded that "an intimate and detailed knowledge of how something works increases the chance of the leader helping the team surface the more subtle technical issues that must be addressed" (2001, 133). Although ScrumMasters do not necessarily need to be marketing gurus or programming experts, they should know enough about both to be effective in leading the team.

Tech Leads as ScrumMasters

That we'd like ScrumMasters to have solid technical knowledge does not mean, however, that we simply anoint each team's tech lead as its ScrumMaster. In fact, because Scrum teams are self-organizing, there should not be a company-designated role such as "tech lead." However, when adopting Scrum it can be very tempting to take the former tech leads and search for equivalent roles where they can exert similar influence on the team and the product. Often this leads to designating tech leads as ScrumMasters. Although some tech leads make great ScrumMasters, never select someone as a ScrumMaster solely because of this, or any other, past role.

A few years ago I provided some initial training to a company, with the goal of helping its leaders decide whether they would adopt Scrum. Two weeks later, one of them called me and said that my training had convinced them, and they were proceeding with Scrum. In fact, she and a few others were in a meeting that moment discussing who their initial ScrumMasters should be, and they wanted my advice. She then said, "We don't have time for a lot of discussion on this. We have only one question: Can the tech lead on each team become the ScrumMaster for that team? Just give a yes or no answer." I began to reply, "Yes, they can, but…" and was about to explain the risks of this when she thanked me for my answer and hung up.

When I visited this client two months later, I was confronted with, "Why did you say we should make our tech leads our ScrumMasters?" Uh, I hadn't. Apparently they had encountered some of the problems I had tried to warn them about and had since found that having solid technical knowledge was only *one* of the desirable attributes of a ScrumMaster.

One of the risks in using a former tech lead as the ScrumMaster is that tech leads are used to providing direction to their teammates. And worse, team members are used to looking to their tech leads for decisions. Because a good Scrum-Master does not make decisions for the team, the former tech lead's history as a decision maker can work against the transition.

A second risk of converting tech leads into ScrumMasters is that they often do not have the requisite people skills. Although technical leads must have some interpersonal skills, ScrumMasters must be facilitators who can guide and lead self-organizing teams over which they have no authority. Author of *Collaboration Explained*, Jean Tabaka, shares similar concerns.

> I work primarily with Scrum teams, and those that struggle the most typically have a command-and-control project manager or a decision-oriented technical lead as ScrumMaster. Without a facilitative, servant-leader mode of team guidance, the agile adoption will be only a thin veneer over nonempowered, demoralized teams. (2007, 7)

All of this is not to say that tech leads should never be considered as possible ScrumMasters. Rather, the point is to be aware of these issues and not cavalierly decide that all tech leads in your organization will make great ScrumMasters. Perhaps the best way to assess a tech lead as a candidate for the ScrumMaster role is to look at how that person has used the leadership authority that came with the tech lead designation. Tech leads who took an "it's-my-way-or-the-highway" approach in the past will not make good ScrumMasters. On the other hand, tech leads who could have dictated decisions but instead worked to rally supporters to their viewpoint will probably do well.

Internal or External ScrumMasters

A common question is whether teams should use ScrumMasters from within the company or whether outside experts should be brought in. The long-term answer is easy: Having skilled ScrumMasters is a critical requirement and as such they should reside within the organization. You should not use contract ScrumMasters over the long-term.

But it is hard to learn a new skill until you've seen someone else demonstrate it. Learning how to lead without authority, when and how to nudge a team toward adopting new engineering practices, when it's OK to intervene, and so on can be difficult. Therefore, many organizations benefit from bringing in an outside consultant as a ScrumMaster initially. This outsider may act as the ScrumMaster to the team, but he should also serve as a mentor to prospective ScrumMasters within the team so that the organization can develop its own cadre of ScrumMasters.

Rotating the ScrumMaster

Some teams that struggle with choosing the best ScrumMaster decide that an appropriate strategy is to rotate the role among all team members. I don't advocate this, as I don't think it demonstrates an appropriate respect for the challenges and significance of the role. In my family, we rotate who cleans the table and loads the dishwasher. Any of us can do that job. We do not, however, rotate who cooks dinner. My wife is a far better cook than anyone else in the family. We want the cooking to be the best it can be, so we don't rotate that job. If you want your Scrum team to be the best it can be, I do not recommend that you make a habit of rotating the job of ScrumMaster.

However, there are some occasions when you may want to rotate. The most common is when you want to create learning opportunities. For example, if team members are struggling to understand the duties of the ScrumMaster, they may want to consider rotating each team member through the role. This may allow each to develop an understanding of what it means to be a ScrumMaster. Similarly, if a team identifies four or five good ScrumMaster candidates among its ranks, it may want to rotate among them, giving each a chance to try the role. Then by considering the performance of each, the team will hopefully be able to choose the most appropriate ScrumMaster.

Bob Schatz and Ibrahim Abdelshafi of Primavera Systems point out another reason why rotating might be useful.

> With time the team can begin to treat this position as their manager. And the person in that position typically detects and dutifully fills the apparent need. The result is a breakdown in the team's self-management practice. By rotating the responsibility at the start of each sprint, it diffuses the role and makes it a shared team responsibility and establishes a balance of power. (2006, 145)

So, although it is possible to rotate the job of ScrumMaster, I recommend doing it only for specific reasons, such as those just given, and only temporarily. Rotating should not be a permanent practice. There are simply too many problems with it, including the following:

- Someone who has rotated into the role usually has other, non-ScrumMaster tasks to perform during the sprint, and these often take priority.

- It's hard to train enough people to do the role well.

- Some people will use their time as ScrumMaster to try to push through changes to the process.

- Designating someone as ScrumMaster for a sprint or two does not automatically make someone value the job, which can lead to ScrumMasters who think Scrum is a mistake.

Overcoming Common Problems

Some of the common problems you may face in making sure that each team has the appropriate ScrumMaster and what you can do to address them include

Someone inappropriate takes the role. Sometimes the decision of who should be the ScrumMaster is made for you: someone just says, "I'll do it," and takes on the role. Often this is great—after all, good ScrumMasters are likely to be the ones who take on additional responsibility before being asked. But what if the person who volunteers is inappropriate for the role? Your response to this will depend on your role in the organization.

If you have some authority over the inappropriate ScrumMaster, the team, or the adoption of Scrum, meet with the volunteer and explain why you need someone different in the role. If appropriate, give the volunteer specific things you would like him to do to be considered as a ScrumMaster candidate later. And if the inappropriate person is already in the role of ScrumMaster? Even though it will be a bit more difficult, I still suggest removing the person from the role if you are convinced the person is truly inappropriate. In either case, act swiftly. An inappropriate ScrumMaster should be changed as soon as possible; I haven't met a team yet who felt an inappropriate ScrumMaster was removed too soon.

If you do not have authority over the ScrumMaster, team, or process, I still suggest you pursue a conversation with the person who has inappropriately assumed the ScrumMaster role. Approach the discussion from the perspective of having the team's best interests in mind. Try to accentuate the ScrumMaster's strengths and suggest that he might be able to find a better way of applying them to the project if he steps out of the ScrumMaster role.

The ScrumMaster is also a programmer/tester/other on the team. When it is impractical to have a dedicated ScrumMaster for a team, a decision must be made between a ScrumMaster who splits time between two or more teams and a ScrumMaster who is both a ScrumMaster and a programmer, tester, or other on the same team. Although either of these approaches can work suitably well, I tend to prefer that when necessary a ScrumMaster's time is split between two teams. Having a ScrumMaster who is also an individual contributor on the team carries many risks.

One risk is that the person may not have adequate time to devote to both roles. Another is that someone in a combined role will probably need to stay away from critical path activities because the person could be interrupted with ScrumMaster duties at any time. A more subtle risk is that other team members will not easily know whether they are talking to their ScrumMaster or to another individual contributor. Yet another risk is the ScrumMaster will have less credibility when protecting the team from outsiders. A dedicated ScrumMaster will have more credibility when saying, "We can't help. The team is busy," than will the ScrumMaster/individual contributor whose same message can be interpreted as "We can't help. I'm busy."

As risky as it can be for someone to be both ScrumMaster and a technical contributor on the project, it is a common situation. Awareness of these issues and a willingness to work through them as they arise is often the best solution.

The ScrumMaster is making decisions for the team. This problem can arise for two completely different reasons: it could be because the ScrumMaster misunderstands or is uncomfortable in the new role, or it could be because the team is used to someone else making decisions. In either case, the solution is the same. The ScrumMaster should be taken aside and reminded that being a ScrumMaster is about providing guidance, not answers.

As a new ScrumMaster, one of the first things I had to learn was how to count. When we'd be in a meeting, struggling with some vexing problem, the team would look to me to tell them the solution. Having previously been the team leader I was tempted to blurt out "the answer." But I needed the team to learn how to find the right answers themselves, and so I sat there quietly counting to myself. 1, 2, 3.... I counted well into the hundreds on a few occasions, but this helped me learn to keep my mouth shut. And it helped the team learn not only how to make those decisions but also that I wouldn't do it for them.

The Product Owner

I think of the ScrumMaster as the person who ensures that the team is working well together, that impediments to progress are quickly removed, and that the team is moving efficiently toward its goal. I think of the product owner as the person who makes sure the team is aimed at the right goal. A good team needs both roles to succeed. The product owner points the team at the right target; the ScrumMaster helps the team get to that target as efficiently as possible.

Roman Pichler, author of *Agile Product Management with Scrum: Creating Products that Customers Love*, stresses the importance of the product owner: "The product owner has the authority to set a goal and shape the vision. The product owner is not just a project manager who now also writes requirements and does a little bit of prioritization." Thinking of the product owner as the provider of a team's goal helps make certain aspects of the product owner's job clear. For example, the product owner is clearly responsible for defining and prioritizing the product backlog that expresses the goal. Similarly, the product owner is responsible for making sure the project earns a good return on the investment made in it.

Responsibilities of the Product Owner

Compiling an exhaustive list of the responsibilities of the product owner would be difficult. Every application exists within its own context of company culture, individual and team competencies, competitive forces, and so on. This context strongly influences how the product owner role is performed in different companies. So instead of providing a checklist of product owner responsibilities ("must attend sprint planning meeting"), I find it more helpful to think in terms of two things that a product owner provides the team: a vision and boundaries.

SEE ALSO

See *Agile Product Management with Scrum: Creating Products that Customers Love* by Roman Pichler for a thorough discussion of the product owner role.

Providing Vision

Many of the product owner's responsibilities involve establishing and communicating the vision for the product. The best teams are those whose passion has been ignited by a compelling vision shared by the product owner. Who will we be selling to? What is unique about our product? What are our competitors doing? How will our product evolve over time? Of course, the questions are different for an application or service that is being delivered to a group of in-house users, but having a shared vision is important for motivating a team and creating a long-term connection between those developing the product and those using it.

Beyond having a clear vision in mind, the product owner must elucidate that vision for the team. The product owner does this through creating, maintaining, and prioritizing the product backlog. There is a lot of dissension among Scrum-Masters and teams as to whether the product owner is the one who actually writes the product backlog. I am firmly in the camp of I-don't-care. It doesn't matter to me who performs the physical act of writing the product backlog; what does matter is that the product owner is the one who makes sure it happens. If the product owner delegates this to a business analyst and the analyst gets sidetracked and fails to write the product backlog, it is still the product owner who is responsible.

Beyond ensuring that the product backlog exists, the product owner adds detail to the vision by answering questions team members will have: Do you want it to work this way? What did you mean when you said such-and-such? Although the product owner can delegate or distribute the responsibility for answering these questions, the product owner cannot delegate the responsibility that they indeed get answered. A product owner can say, "Talk to Nirav if you have questions about how the shopping cart and checkout features should work," but if Nirav isn't responsive or helpful, a good product owner will step in and answer questions personally, find out why Nirav is unable to do so, designate a different person, or find some other solution.

SEE ALSO

The product backlog is a prioritized list of features to be added to a product. It is fully described in Chapter 13, "The Product Backlog."

Providing Boundaries

Vision and boundaries can be thought of as competing aspects of the project. The vision shows what the product can become. The boundaries describe the realities within which the vision must be realized. Boundaries are provided by the product owner and often come in the form of constraints, such as

- I need it by June.
- We need to reduce the per-unit cost by half.
- It needs to run at twice the speed.
- It can use only half the memory of the current version.

Often when I tell groups that the product owner is allowed to dictate things such as this—especially the date—I am met with angry responses. "No," they tell me, "estimates are up to the team. All the product owner does is prioritize the work." Although those statements are true, the product owner is also responsible for defining the boundaries that will determine the success of the product.

Most experienced Scrum team members will readily agree that it is within the product owner's purview to say, "We need to develop at least this much of the product backlog or the product won't be worth shipping." But many of these same experienced people resist when similar statements are made about deadlines.

But, let's see what Takeuchi and Nonaka had to say in their study of the six teams that formed the foundation of Scrum and that were the subject of the first paper on Scrum back in 1986.

> Fuji-Xerox's top management asked for a radically different copi-
> er and gave the FX-3500 project team two years to come up with
> a machine that could be produced at half the cost of its high-end
> line and still perform as well. (139)

Here, we clearly have a team that is given a challenging problem—match the performance of the company's best current copiers but at half the cost—and a deadline for solving the problem. There is nothing wrong with this. Product own-ers go wrong when they overly constrain a problem or when they make a solution impossible. Had Fuji-Xerox's management given that team the same problem but only one month to solve it, the team would have seen the futility in the situation and not even tried. The problem as presented to that team presumably left the team plenty of operating room in which to find a solution. A part of the product owner's job that is more art than science is providing just enough of a boundary around the project so that the team is motivated to solve the difficult problem before them but not providing so many boundaries that solving the problem be-comes impossible.

When brainstorming solutions to a challenging problem, common advice is to think "outside the box." However, there is evidence that better solutions emerge more easily from thinking that is done "inside the box" as long as the box has been properly framed (Coyne, Clifford, and Dye 2007). When we're told to think outside the box, they say, the total lack of constraints can be unsettling.

> Imagine a random product you are trying to improve in a typical
> facilitated brainstorming session. Outside-the-box possibilities
> could include making the product bigger or smaller, lighter or
> heavier, prettier or more rugged (or changing its appearance in
> any of a hundred ways). Further ideas could involve making the
> product more expensive or less or maybe breaking it into parts
> or bundling it with other products. They could involve chang-
> ing the product's functionality, durability, ease of use, or the way
> it fits with other products. Or its availability, affordability, or re-
> pairability. How do you know which dimensions are fruitful to
> explore? Without some guidance, people cannot judge whether
> they should continue in the direction of their first notion or
> change course altogether. They cannot handle the uncertainty,
> and they shut down. (2007, 71)

The product owner's job is to create the new box—the boundaries—in which the team will think. This new box prevents the team from getting lost in the infinitude of possible solutions and gives team members a basis for making and comparing choices. Boundaries for that new box are determined by the most important constraints for the business, which may involve things like minimum guaranteed functionality, dramatically faster performance, reduced resource consumption, and, yes, in some cases the date.

Each Team Needs Exactly One Product Owner

SEE ALSO

Schedule is one side of the infamous iron triangle of scope, schedule, and resources. The iron triangle is discussed in Chapter 15, "Planning."

On a team that is new to Scrum, the ScrumMaster job can be very time consuming. The ScrumMaster will be busy training team members on Scrum itself, encouraging them to think in different ways about the problems they encounter, removing impediments to the team's progress, and more. Early on, this might even be a full-time job, depending on the newness of the team and the types of impediments team members face. Over time, however, things improve. Eventually the ScrumMaster has removed many recurring impediments, and the team itself has begun to master Scrum and has embraced its self-organizing nature. As these changes occur, the team needs less and less of their ScrumMaster's time. If we were to graph a team's demands on its ScrumMaster's time, it would look something like Figure 7.1.

SEE ALSO

Self-organization is discussed in detail in Chapter 12, "Leading a Self-Organizing Team."

FIGURE 7.1

A team's time demands on their product owner and ScrumMaster move in different directions.

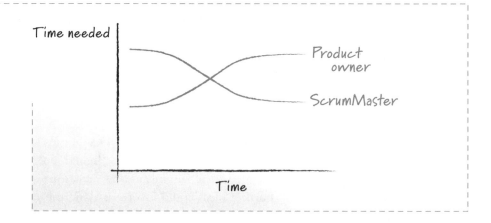

Contrast this with the team's need for its product owner. When the team first adopts Scrum, it will not be very good at it. It will struggle with how much detail to put on the product backlog, how much work can be completed in a sprint, how to work well together within the sprint, and so on. Team members will be learning new practices and new ways of working together. The team will not be very fast—at least not compared to how fast it will be after it gets good at Scrum. As the team speeds up (through its own improvements and from the ScrumMaster gradually removing impediments), it will be completing more work each sprint. This means members will have more questions for their product owner. Therefore, as the team's efficiency increases, so will its demands on the product owner's time. This is likely the case even as team members learn the domain and take on more responsibility themselves.

This inverse relationship between a team's demands on the product owner's and the ScrumMaster's time is shown in Figure 7.1. The lines in this figure show that although it may be acceptable to have an experienced ScrumMaster work with two or possibly even three teams (depending on how much help each team needs at the time), it is not advisable to share one product owner across more than two teams. Instead, each team should ideally have its own dedicated product owner. The product owner job is very challenging. Part of the job is outward-facing: talking to customers and following market trends. Another part of the job is inward-facing: working with the team to build the product. When a job involves both inward- and outward-facing duties, the outward, customer-facing duties always seem to win. Any developer who is responsible for both new development and customer support can confirm that customer-facing issues almost always win.

SEE ALSO

The topic of scaling the product owner role for large projects is described in detail in Chapter 17, "Scaling Scrum."

Just as a product owner should work only with one team, each team should work only with one product owner. I have seen occasions where having two product owners assigned to a team works, but this is usually a result of someone in the organization not wanting to make the hard call of saying, "Your product owner is so-and-so." Find someone to make the hard call, designate one product owner for the team, and then encourage that person to solicit all sorts of helpful input and feedback from those who also could have been the product owner.

A team with two product owners will inevitably fall into the trap of "Mom said no; let's go ask Dad." Of course, only the most dysfunctional (or perhaps desperate) teams will get the "wrong" answer from one product owner and go ask the same question of the other. Even they know they will eventually be found out and will be called on their behavior. However, most teams with two product owners will go so far as to think about which product owner will give the most satisfying answer before they choose which one to ask.

A Product Owner Team

In some cases, the product owner role can be too much for one person. Researchers Angela Martin, Robert Biddle, and James Noble found that the product owner role is "consistently under more pressure than the developers and other participants in the project" (2004, 51). Ron Jeffries, one of the inventors of the Extreme Programming process and a Scrum trainer, agrees: "It was only after the first book or two on XP came out that we fully realized the load a single XP Customer/ Scrum product owner is taking on. It's clear that they'll need to be a group."

A common solution is the use of a *product owner team*. Splitting the duties of the product owner across a product owner team is fine as long as there remains one person on that team who can be singled out as the person with ultimate responsibility and authority, a "the-buck-stops-here" individual. Even with a product owner team, each development team needs to have one identifiable, consistent person they can go to for answers. As Ken Schwaber and Mike Beedle have written, "The product owner is one person, not a committee" (2001, 34). Make sure each team can identify one person people can go to for decisions. A good Scrum team moves far too quickly to wait for all questions to be answered by committee. A product owner will never be able to instantly answer all questions the team may have; occasionally telling the team, "I need to run this by my colleagues," is fine. But, well-founded caution should not be replaced by de facto decision-by-committee.

Attributes of a Good Product Owner

NOTE
Remembering these five attributes is easy. Putting together the first letter of each spells ABCDE.

As when describing what to look for in selecting or hiring a good ScrumMaster, I've culled the long list of desirable product owner traits down to five must-have attributes.

Available. By far the most frequent complaint I hear from teams about their product owners is that they are unavailable when needed. When a fast-moving team needs an answer to a question, waiting three days for an answer is completely disruptive to the rhythm it has established. By being available to the team, a product owner demonstrates commitment to the project. The best product owners demonstrate their commitment by doing whatever is necessary to build the best product possible. On some projects this includes doing things like assisting in test planning, performing manual tests, and being actively engaged with other team members.

Business-savvy. It is essential that the product owner understand the business. As the decision maker regarding what is in or out of the product, the product owner must have a deep understanding of the business, market conditions, customers, and users. Usually this type of understanding is built over years of working in the domain, perhaps as a past user of the type of product being developed. This is why many successful product owners come from product manager, marketing, or business analyst roles.

Communicative. Product owners must be good communicators and must be able to work well with a diverse set of stakeholders. Product owners routinely interact with users, customers, management within the organization, partners, and, naturally, others on the team. Skilled product owners will be able to deliver the same information to each of these different audiences while at the same time tailoring their message to best match the audience.

A good product owner must also listen to users, customers, and perhaps most important the team. Especially as team members learn more about the product and market (as they should over time, especially on a Scrum project), they will be able to offer valuable suggestions about the product. Additionally, all teams will have much to say to the product owner about the technical risks and challenges of the project. Although it is true that the product owner prioritizes all work for the team, the wise product owner will listen to her team when it recommends some adjustments in those priorities based on technical factors.

Decisive. Another common complaint teams make about their product owners is their lack of decisiveness. When team members go to the product owner with an issue, they want a resolution. Scrum puts a lot of pressure on teams to produce functionality as quickly as possible. Teams are frustrated when a product owner responds to a question with, "Let me call a meeting or convene a task force to work on that." A good team will understand that this is sometimes necessary, but teams are very perceptive at knowing when a product owner is actually just trying to avoid making a hard decision. Just as bad as a product owner who won't make a decision is the product owner who makes the same decision over and over but with different answers. A good product owner will not reverse prior decisions without a good reason.

Empowered. A good product owner must be someone empowered with the authority to make decisions and one who is held accountable for those decisions. The product owner must be sufficiently high up in the organization to be given this level of responsibility. If a product owner is consistently overruled by others in the organization, team members will learn to go to those others with their important questions.

The ScrumMaster as Product Owner

One common consideration is whether the ScrumMaster and product owner roles should be combined. No. In the vast majority of times I've seen this done, the results have been disappointing. Not only does combining these roles put a lot of power in one person's hands, but it also creates confusion for both team members and the ScrumMaster/product owner hybrid. A certain amount of tension should exist between these roles. Product owners continually want more, more, more features. ScrumMasters protect their teams by pushing back against the product owner when they feel that pushing their teams harder would be detrimental. When the roles are combined, this tension is removed.

With an eye toward full disclosure, I feel compelled to add that two of the most successful Scrum projects I've participated in or witnessed had a combination ScrumMaster/product owner. There are tremendous advantages to having a single person who has a deep understanding of the market, has the technical and collaborative skills of a ScrumMaster, and can effectively balance them. Toyota essentially combines the ScrumMaster and product owner roles into its single chief engineer role. The Toyota chief engineer is someone who is most definitely an engineer and could likely engineer any part of a new vehicle but who also has a deep understanding of the market and likely purchasers of the vehicle being engineered.

So, the combined ScrumMaster/product owner model can be successful. However, I suspect that there are very few individuals who are good at both jobs and who are good at doing them both at the same time. Even if you suspect you are one of them or can identify these people within your organization at the start of the transition to Scrum, I still recommend using separate individuals in these roles, at least at the start.

Overcoming Common Problems

There are many potential pitfalls when selecting the initial product owner. Some of the most common early-stage problems and what you can do to address them include

The product owner delegates decision making but then overrules the decision maker. To fit the new duties of the product owner into their schedules, some product owners delegate decisions about specific parts of the product. Other product owners enlist a business analyst to be a "feature owner" over some part of the system. This can work well because the product owner has more time to dedicate to areas that are not as easy to delegate.

SEE ALSO

Establishing a product owner hierarchy like this is a common scaling technique and is described in Chapter 17.

Problems arise when the product owner says that decision-making authority has been delegated but then continues to approve or sometimes reverses decisions. Before delegating, product owners should be sure they are really willing to delegate without later second-guessing. Because of the pressure of the short, timeboxed sprints, Scrum teams often move much more quickly than they did before transitioning. It is inevitable that some decisions that the product owner delegates will turn out to be wrong, and these should be revisited. What we want to avoid, however, are situations where the product owner says, "Get your answers from Dave; he owns this part of the system," and then consistently overrules Dave's answers.

My advice to a new and overloaded product owner is to free some time by delegating just beyond the point at which you're comfortable. You may be pleasantly surprised and find no important decisions to reverse. But you'll occasionally find some decisions you would have made differently. Often the best thing to do in this case is the same thing we're all taught when learning to drive: If the car starts to slide, steer into the slide. Rather than pull against the decision (assuming it is not a horrendous one), allow that decision to persist through the end of the sprint; then decide if it should be changed. When the cost of reversing a decision is compared against all the other valuable work on the product backlog, you may find that the decision wasn't so bad after all.

The product owner pushes the team too hard. Product owners are often under pressure to deliver financial results to the company; more features delivered sooner is one way for them to achieve it. As I've said, I have no objection to a product owner who announces at the start of a project, "We need to build a product that is smaller, better-performing, and cheaper than our competitor's, and we need to do it in three months less than we spent on the last product." As long as a challenging goal like that is accompanied by appropriate freedom in how the goal is achieved, the team will do its best. The problems arise when the team is kept under constant and changing pressure from sprint to sprint. One difficult goal of "do this amazing thing in 6 months" is in many ways less stressful for the team than 13 successive two-week sprints of "I need more, more, more!" If you have product owners who are pushing teams this way, the ScrumMasters should first push back and then work with the product owners to set longer-term goals for the teams while ensuring teams have commensurate degrees of freedom in how those goals are achieved.

The product owner wants to cut quality. Cutting quality is an oh-so-tempting decision when trying to deliver a challenging set of features by a difficult date. It can lead to the short-term appearance of having met the objectives established at the start of the project. Eventually, however, the cost of having cut quality becomes apparent as more post-release bugs than usual are reported, the team's velocity decreases, and customers clamor for the product to behave as they thought it would.

Ken Schwaber has called quality a "corporate asset" (2006). As such, no one except the chief executive has the authority to sacrifice quality in exchange for achieving a short-term goal such as making a release date. A decision to cut quality may be the appropriate one; I can't tell you otherwise without knowing the full context of a situation. But, that decision is one that needs to be made sufficiently high up in the organization and with such openness that no one is surprised by the negative impacts that will almost certainly follow.

Selecting product owners who understand this is sometimes challenging in organizations that are consistently focused on this quarter's numbers. Pushing back against attempts to reduce quality is the job of the ScrumMaster. The ScrumMaster does not need to prevail in these early disagreements. The ScrumMaster does, however, have to succeed in making the decision visible.

Time is on the ScrumMaster's side. If the ScrumMaster successfully raises the visibility of decisions to cut quality, he should eventually be able to win later arguments against reducing quality. "Remember on the Gouda project how I told you that cutting quality on version one would hurt us during version two?" the ScrumMaster can say. "Well, here are the graphs of velocity on the two projects. Note that version two had a lower velocity even though we added two experienced people. That was because we left bugs behind during version one (here's a graph showing that) and because the team didn't feel it had the time to do a good job of keeping its code clean. We even skipped the automated unit tests on a few modules. Here's a comparison of the number of defects found during the six months following release, broken down by whether the module had automated unit tests. It's up to you if we do this again on this project, but I think you know my opinion."

Our product owner is in a different city than the development team. With more projects being developed by remote teams, this is an increasingly common situation. Both the team and product owner in this situation should assume some of the burden of overcommunicating with the other. I have worked with many remote product owners, and it can work very successfully as long as the product owner does the following:

SEE ALSO

For more on the challenges of distributed development, see Chapter 18, "Distributed Teams."

- Remains engaged in the project
- Establishes a rapport with the team
- Performs all usual duties of the role
- Is available to the team for phone calls for at least some part of the day, even if it is after the usual workday for the product owner
- Responds by e-mail or phone when not available in person

New Roles, Old Responsibilities

The roles of product owner and ScrumMaster are critical for becoming a high-performing Scrum team. In this chapter we've looked at the responsibilities of the people in these jobs, attributes we'd like our product owners and ScrumMasters to possess, and how to overcome some common problems that occur when introducing these roles into an organization.

Although the roles of product owner and ScrumMaster are new, the responsibilities are not. High-performance teams have always known they needed to do the things described in this chapter. On a Scrum team, individuals are asked to look beyond their explicit roles to find ways to help the team accomplish its goals. In the next chapter, we look at what this new emphasis on teamwork and shared responsibility means for existing roles in the organization.

Additional Reading

Davies, Rachel, and Liz Sedley. 2009. *Agile coaching.* The Pragmatic Bookshelf.
This book is full of practical, immediately useful advice for any ScrumMaster. It covers everything from how to help the team improve to how to help yourself improve.

Fisher, Kimball. 1999. *Leading self-directed work teams.* McGraw-Hill.
The self-directed work teams of Fisher's book are the self-organizing teams of an agile project. His book offers guidance appropriate to ScrumMasters.

James, Michael. 2007. A ScrumMaster's checklist, August 13. Michael James' blog on Danube's website. http://danube.com/blog/michaeljames/a_scrummasters_checklist.
In making his argument that a great team needs a full-time ScrumMaster, rather than one who works with two or more teams, Michael James presents a rather exhaustive list of work to be performed by the ScrumMaster.

Kelly, James, and Scott Nadler. 2007. Leading from below. *MIT Sloan Management Review*, March 3. http://sloanreview.mit.edu/business-insight/articles/2007/1/4917/leading-from-below.
This article presents useful information for those not in authority positions who nonetheless realize they can still influence the direction of the organization.

Pichler, Roman. Forthcoming. *Agile product management with Scrum: Creating products that customers love.* Addison-Wesley Professional.
The most complete coverage available of the role of the product owner. Pichler clarifies the key differences between traditional and agile product management while providing useful tips to product owners.

Schwaber, Ken. 2004. *Agile project management with Scrum.* Microsoft Press.
Schwaber's second book is full of anecdotes about teams using Scrum both successfully and unsuccessfully. In addition to chapters dedicated to the product owner and ScrumMaster roles, other valuable advice on performing those roles is spread throughout the book.

Spann, David. 2006. *Agile manager behaviors: What to look for and develop. Cutter Consortium Executive Report*, September.
In this extensive report, Cutter consultant David Spann addresses the question of what attributes to look for in what he calls an "agile manager," but which corresponds closely to the ScrumMaster role of this chapter. He starts with a list of 22 candidate behaviors but reduces this to a list of 8 preferred behaviors to look for when hiring an agile manager.

Chapter 8

Changed Roles

The previous chapter focused on the two new roles on a Scrum project—Scrum-Master and product owner. But changes to a Scrum project's team members go beyond the introduction of two new roles. For example, the self-organizing nature of a Scrum team eliminates the role of the technical team leader, individuals are asked to look beyond their specialties and help the team in any way possible, emphasis is shifted from writing about requirements to talking about them, and teams are required to produce something tangible by the end of each sprint. Because these changes alter the roles and relationships within the team and organization, they often contribute to some of the challenges organizations face when adopting Scrum.

This chapter will describe the primary adjustments individuals must make as they transition from traditional roles to Scrum. The focus will be on how these roles change, rather than on a thorough description of each role. I won't, for example, describe everything a tester does as part of testing an application. I will instead focus on changes in how a tester works on a Scrum project. I will discuss the roles of analyst, project manager, architect, functional manager, programmer, database administrator, tester, and user experience designer.

> While reading about these roles, keep in mind that any team member who is involved in developing a product or software system is first and foremost a developer. When I use a term like *tester*, I mean a developer with specific skills or an interest in testing. Similarly, *analyst* is used to refer to a developer who prefers to work on analysis tasks but who will work on any high-priority task needed by the team.

NOTE

Analysts

With an intimate knowledge of the product and strong communication skills, some analysts will tend to shift into product owner roles. This is especially common on large projects that make use of a hierarchy of product owners. Someone with product manager on her business card, for example, may act as the chief

SEE ALSO

Scaling the product owner role is discussed in Chapter 17, "Scaling Scrum."

product owner for the overall product, spending most of her time looking outward at users and the market. An individual with analyst on her business card, on the other hand, may act as product owner for the various teams, working with the chief product owner to translate her vision into product backlogs for her teams.

Many teams find that having an analyst on the team continues to be very beneficial, although the ways in which the analyst works will change. On traditionally managed projects, the analyst's mission seemed to be to get as far ahead of the team as possible. On a Scrum project, just-in-time analysis becomes the goal. The analyst's new aim is to stay as slightly ahead of the team as possible while still being able to provide useful information to the team about current and near-term features.

Analysts can be instrumental in achieving the goal of shifting the emphasis from writing about requirements to talking about them. Because analysts are not working as far ahead of the team as they may be used to, they need to become more comfortable sharing information with the team more informally, rather than through a large document. As much information as possible should be shared through verbal discussion, but analysts will still need to document some requirements, especially when working on a distributed team. Often though, what the analyst writes will be less formal—more often a wiki than a document with a signature page.

SEE ALSO

Shifting the emphasis from documents to discussions is described in Chapter 13, "The Product Backlog."

On traditional projects, analysts often become intermediaries through whom other team members and the product owner communicate. On a Scrum project the analyst should become more a facilitator of team–product owner discussion than an intermediary. Team members and product owners need to talk. Rather than be the conduit for all conversation, the good agile analyst focuses on making sure those conversations are as productive as possible given the time constraints the team or product owner may be under. This may mean that the analyst steers the product owner and team toward talking about one user story rather than another because that is where there is more risk of going astray. Or it may mean that the analyst conveys a top-level understanding of a new feature to the team before bringing the team and product owner together to discuss the details.

SEE ALSO

User stories are an agile way of describing features. They are described in Chapter 13.

On a traditional project, an analyst may say to the team, "I've talked to our key stakeholder, understand what he wants, and have written this document describing it in detail." By contrast, on a Scrum project, the same analyst should say, "I've spoken to our product owner and have a feeling for what he's after. I wrote these six user stories to give you a start, and I've got a bunch of additional questions to ask the product owner. But I want to make sure that I bring along a couple of you when we have those discussions."

With all this talk of analysts looking ahead, it can be tempting to think that analysts work a sprint ahead of the team. They don't. Gregory Topp, an analyst with Farm Credit Services of America, describes how using Scrum has allowed him to concentrate on the current sprint: "Before Scrum, I had to focus on requirements that were not going to be developed for several weeks, if not months. Now, I focus on the current sprint (two weeks for us), so more time can be spent on user story details, development, and testing." An analyst's first priority is to achieve the goals of the current sprint. An analyst on a Scrum team will assist in testing, will answer questions (or track down answers to questions) about features being developed, will participate fully in all regular sprint meetings, and so on.

However, it is quite possible that these activities will not fully consume the analyst's time. Time that is not needed to complete the work of the current sprint can be used to look ahead. However, being a part of the team on this sprint and spending some time looking ahead is not the same as working a sprint ahead of the team. Topp explains how jumping too far ahead actually put him behind: "I tried working ahead a sprint or two, defining user story details. I found that this caused the current sprint to suffer. I also found that many times the details of a user story changed by the time the team actually started working on the story."

A common question is whether the effort analysts spend looking ahead should be included on the sprint backlog. My recommendation is to include on the sprint backlog any specific analysis tasks that can be identified during sprint planning. For example, suppose the team is working on an application that approves or rejects loan applications. If the product owner and team agree that the next sprint will include work on calculating the applicant's credit score, then preliminary analysis tasks related to that should be identified, estimated, and included in the sprint backlog. On the other hand, if the next sprint's work is unknown, no specific tasks related to the next sprint should be included on the sprint backlog.

Overall, many analysts enjoy the change to Scrum even though they relinquish the role of sole interpreter of customer desires. Two years after adopting Scrum, Topp commented on how his relationship with others on the team had changed.

> Because we are all on the same team and all work on the same user stories at the same time, the team seems to have more unity. Before using Scrum, it seemed each function (analyst, programmer, tester, DBA) was done in a silo. There was more finger-pointing when in that mode. Now using Scrum, the team is all focused on a small set of stories. The finger-pointing has been eliminated with an "as a team" mindset.

Project Managers

On a project using a sequential development process, the project manager has the difficult job of ensuring that the product a customer wants is the one that is developed. To do this, the project manager must try to manage everything about the project, including scope, cost, quality, personnel, communication, risk, procurement, and more. Some of these responsibilities really belong to others. Scope control, for example, rightfully belongs with the customer. No one else is in the position to make the necessary trade-off decisions that will arise during product development, as priorities, team velocity, and market conditions shift. Prioritization is not a static, one-time, all-at-the-start activity that can be managed by a project manager. Yet time and again, sequential projects demand that project managers make educated guesses to deliver the right product.

On Scrum projects we acknowledge the untenable role of the project manager and eliminate it. Eliminating the role, though, does not mean we can do away with the work and responsibilities. As you might guess, since self-organizing teams are a core tenet of Scrum, a great deal of the responsibility previously shouldered by the project manager is transferred to the Scrum team. For example, without a project manager to assign tasks to individuals, team members assume the responsibility of selecting tasks themselves. Other responsibilities shift to the ScrumMaster or product owner.

Former project managers often assume one of the roles that have taken on some part of their past responsibilities—the project manager becomes either a ScrumMaster, product owner, or team member, depending on experience, skills, knowledge, and interests.

Some people became project managers because they considered it the next step in a desirable career path, yet they don't enjoy project management. These individuals miss the technical challenge of working as a programmer, tester, database engineer, designer, analyst, architect, or so on. Many of these individuals will take advantage of the elimination of the project manager role to return to work they found more satisfying.

Other project managers have used their roles to become knowledgeable about the business and its customers. A project manager in this situation will leverage that knowledge into a role as a product owner. This can be an excellent fit, especially for the project manager who is having a hard time completely relinquishing the ability to tell the team what to do. As part of their role, product owners are allowed to tell the team a bit of the "what to do" as long as they stay largely away from telling them how to do it. This can satisfy a former project manager whose nature makes it hard to stop occasionally directing the team.

If a project manager can overcome the old habits of directing the team and making decisions for it, it is likely such a project manager can become a good ScrumMaster. This is the most common new role for project managers in organizations adopting Scrum. The new role will likely be difficult at first for the former project manager as she learns to bite her tongue and let the team learn how to work through its own issues and make decisions. Often, new ScrumMasters are put in the challenging position of coaching teams at something that they are not yet good at themselves—being agile. The best strategies for a ScrumMaster in this situation include the following:

- **Stick as close as possible to doing Scrum by the book.** Initially follow the advice of this or another Scrum book closely. Or engage an on-site trainer or coach and follow her advice to the letter. Only begin customizing the process after you have real, hands-on experience with it.

- **Talk to other ScrumMasters as much as possible.** If there are multiple ScrumMasters in your organization, form a community of practice with the other ScrumMasters and share good and bad experiences. Look to learn by extracting lessons from commonalities among these experiences. If you are the only one in your organization, find outside ScrumMasters with whom you can share stories and compare approaches.

SEE ALSO

Communities of practice are described further in Chapter 17.

- **Learn as much as you can as quickly as you can.** Read books, articles, blogs, and websites. Look into local agile interest groups and attend their meetings. Try to attend one or more of the major agile or Scrum conferences.

Doris Ford, a software engineering manager with Motorola, was a classically trained project manager and a Project Management Professional (PMP). However, despite having a traditional background in project management, Doris's approach has always been about supporting and enabling her teams. Because of that, she was able to easily move from project manager to ScrumMaster. She writes of how her job has changed with Scrum.

> Over the years in managing agile development I have learned not to sweat the task details. As a traditional project manager, I always needed to stay on top of who was doing which tasks, what were their dependencies, and would they be done on time. I spent countless number of hours just asking these questions to get the answers in attempt to meet the scope/schedule/budget/ quality constraints and reporting upwards on the progress (sometimes using earned value). In an agile environment I had to learn to trust the team members that they would identify and do the tasks necessary to complete the scope for each sprint. It was hard letting go at first, but I quickly learned that the team could do this. I now spend the majority of my time supporting the team members by addressing impediments that they raise and keeping external noise from diverting their focus.

Why the Title Change?

If it's possible for a project manager to become a team's ScrumMaster or product owner, why do we need to change the person's title? Let's consider the term

ScrumMaster. Years ago, when I first started running Scrum projects, the term *ScrumMaster* didn't exist, and it never dawned on me to call the role anything but *project manager.* This worked well enough. But, I was hiring new individuals into these roles; I was clear with these new hires about my expectations for how they'd interact with the team. I avoided domineering, command-and-control-style individuals. Also, these new project managers reported to me, which allowed me a lot of influence over how they interacted with their teams. Calling them *project managers* worked fine.

As our company continued to succeed and grow, we began to acquire other companies. In those companies I would inherit project managers who sometimes did have very traditional mindsets about the role of the project manager. I was confronted with helping them shift that mindset to one more compatible with agile development. I found this much harder than just hiring project managers with a collaborative approach suitable to self-organizing teams.

Years later in a discussion with Ken Schwaber, he helped me understand why transitioning existing project managers had been more difficult than I had anticipated. Schwaber informed me that by allowing the project managers to retain their titles, I was allowing them to think that the changes were less all-encompassing than they were. He invented the word *ScrumMaster* in 1997 in part because it would remind everyone that this was not just the project manager role with a few additional responsibilities removed or added. Schwaber told me that "the vocabulary of Scrum is a vocabulary of change. The words are often intentionally ugly—burndown, backlog, ScrumMaster—because they remind us that change is occurring."

Although I recommend it, you do not necessarily need to banish the title *project manager.* If you or your organization is enamored of it, continue to use it. But be mindful of Ken Schwaber's advice and my experience that using the old words will slow or prevent the adoption of the new approach. Retaining an old title discourages thinking in the new way. Further, if people are unwilling to relinquish something as insignificant as a job title, they will probably also be unwilling to make the far harder changes necessary to adopt Scrum.

Architects

Many architects have worked for years to deserve the august title *architect.* They are rightfully proud of their knowledge, experience, and ability to propose elegant solutions to technical and business challenges. I find that many of the concerns raised by architects faced with adopting Scrum can be put into these two categories:

- Will people still implement the architectures I tell them to?

- How can I ensure we build an architecturally sound product without an up-front architecture phase?

The answer to the first of these concerns depends entirely on the architect in question. Many architects may find that very little about their jobs changes. Solutions recommended by these architects are implemented because other developers respect them and know their advice is likely to be good. For example, if one of my coworkers has a reputation for having made sound architectural decisions in the past, and I observe her making good architectural decisions on this project, I will be inclined to go to her with architectural questions. I'll do that even if we're a self-organizing team and no one is forcing me to get a second opinion on my decisions.

The second concern is largely unfounded. As we will see in the section, "Work Together Throughout the Sprint," of Chapter 14, "Sprints," and in the section, "Design: Intentional yet Emergent," of Chapter 9, "Technical Practices," the architectural needs of a product are used in conjunction with business objectives to drive the prioritization of the product backlog. This allows an architect the ability to focus attention and effort on architectural uncertainties within the application. On an architecturally complicated or risky product, the architect will need to work closely with the product owner to educate the product owner about the architectural implications of items on the product backlog. All product owners are aware that they need to listen to the marketplace, users, or customers for input into product decisions. Good product owners also know to solicit the opinion of the technical team about the priorities. Although the ultimate decision is the product owner's, good product owners consider all viewpoints when prioritizing work.

Andrew Johnston of AgileArchitect.org has written, "In an agile development the architect has the main responsibility to consider change and complexity while the other developers focus on the next delivery" (2009). Judicious sequencing of work into sprints can help a team gain key knowledge sooner, avoid or discover risks with sufficient time to react, and minimize the total cost of development.

The Non-Coding Architect

Non-coding architects are likely to see the biggest shift in what they do. These are the ones that Scott Ambler calls "ivory tower architects" (2008b). The mere presence of a non-coding architect is a well-known harbinger of trouble; Scrum projects are well rid of them. Some non-coding architects will look on Scrum as a chance to again do some of the programming they hopefully enjoyed earlier in their careers. These architects will be welcome contributors to Scrum teams. They will be respected for the depth of their knowledge and experience and their ability to roll up their sleeves and get into the code.

Beware of the architect who resists a revised role that requires hands-on contributions to projects. In many cases these non-coding architects took their careers in that direction as a way to get out of hands-on programming. One such architect, Tom, confounded me when I first met him. He talked a good game and sounded knowledgeable about all the right technologies. However, he was the first developer I had ever met who enjoyed meetings. He was always looking to schedule more meetings. As I got to know Tom better, I realized that his technical knowledge was very superficial—he wasn't as good as I had thought. I soon realized why he liked the team to spend so much time in meetings: in an unnecessary meeting all attendees are equally productive and valuable. It's when team members return to their desks and start doing real work that the often dramatic differences between developers start to show up. Tom's preference for unnecessary meetings was a self-preservation technique—the more time the team spent in meetings, the longer it would take everyone to realize that Tom wasn't very good.

To be a valued contributor, someone with a business card reading *architect* does not need to code full-time. In fact, it's quite possible for a sprint or two to pass without an architect writing any production code. The distinction I want to draw is between architects who can still code and those whose coding skills are behind them. Software architect Johannes Brodwall says that "the biggest changes to my role as an architect have been that, formally, the architect no longer has the power to dictate technical solutions. Instead, an architect has to be an advisor and a facilitator. As an advisor, I better still be able to do the job I'm giving advice about."

Functional Managers

Functional managers, such as development managers, QA directors, and so on, who are used to working in a matrixed manner will continue to work that way on Scrum projects. A typical functional manager will likely experience some diminution in power after the transition, but this will depend greatly on how the role was defined in the organization prior to transitioning.

Functional managers usually retain the job of assigning individuals to projects. They will be expected to continue to make these decisions based on the competing needs of all projects, project locations, developmental needs and career aspirations of individuals, and so on. In some organizations, functional managers are accustomed to going beyond assigning individuals to projects and have been involved in the assignment of tasks to individuals within their groups. They will no longer do this after transitioning to Scrum. Individual selection of work is a fundamental aspect of how the members of a team self-organize and must be left to the team.

The Leadership Role of the Functional Manager

Functional managers have always been leaders. Broad leadership trends over the years have affected individual style. While I was growing up, for example, my father managed Sears stores. This was back in the era when Sears was the world's largest retailer. My father's management style was very much top–down. He would establish goals, quotas, and other measurements; communicate them to store employees; and then measure each employee against those targets. This was also an era when prevailing wisdom was that a good manager could manage anything. My father should presumably have been able to take his experience managing a retail store and manage a bank or manufacturing operation with equal skill. My father was operating in the bottom-left quadrant of Figure 8.1, which is from *The Toyota Way* by Jeffrey Liker (2003, 181).

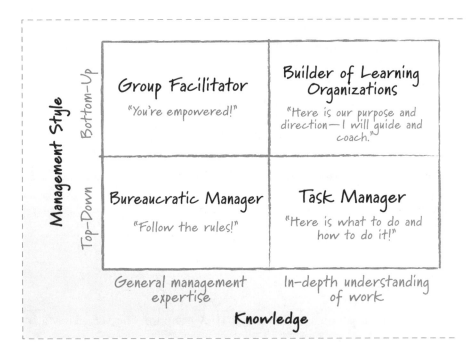

FIGURE 8.1

Different types of functional managers as determined by type of expertise and management style. Adapted from *The Toyota Way*, Jeffrey Liker, copyright The McGraw-Hill Companies, Inc.

A different type of manager, or perhaps one working in a different era than my father, might have applied her general management skills in a bottom-up manner. This manager would be in the top left of Figure 8.1. In the bottom right of that figure we see a manager with a deep understanding of the work and a top-down style. This manager—who is quite common on software projects—tells his team both what to do and how to do it.

In an organization using Scrum, functional managers should operate in the top-right quadrant, where they combine a deep understanding of the work with a bottom-up style. A functional manager is responsible for providing guidance and coaching to members of the group. ScrumMasters and product owners also provide guidance and coaching, but their views are limited to a single project or product. A functional manager will have a broader perspective, including the ability to establish cross-project standards and set expectations for quality, maintainability, reusability, and many of the other -ilities or nonfunctional requirements.

Functional managers also retain responsibility for developing the people in their groups. Securing the budget and time to send them to conferences, challenging them with appropriate projects, and encouraging them to join or form communities of practice are all part of the functional manager's role.

SEE ALSO

Improvement communities were introduced in Chapter 4, "Iterating Toward Agility." Communities of practice are more generally described in Chapter 17.

Personnel Responsibilities

In most organizations, functional managers will retain responsibility for writing periodic reviews of the personnel in their departments. Although the functional manager has hopefully always incorporated input from each employee's coworkers and customers into the review, the need to do so is greater in a Scrum environment because the employee will likely be working less closely with the functional manager on a day-to-day basis.

SEE ALSO

Periodic performance reviews are discussed in Chapter 20, "Human Resources, Facilities, and the PMO."

In many organizations, functional managers also retain responsibility for making hiring and firing decisions. Neither the ScrumMaster nor the product owner has this level of authority over individuals on the product development teams.

After the organization adopts Scrum, most functional managers find themselves with more time available than they had before. This time is most often used to stay in closer touch with their direct reports, to know more about each project the group's employees are working on (by attending various sprint reviews and so on), and to pay more attention to cross-project standards and future directions.

Programmers

What do programmers do on a Scrum team? They program. They test. They analyze. They design. They do anything necessary to help the team complete the work committed to for a sprint. Although it is OK to have specialists on a Scrum team, specialists need to be willing to work outside their specialties whenever needed for the greater good of the team. There are exceptions. A game development project may, for example, benefit from specialists in artificial intelligence programming. Because of the highly specialized nature of their product, these specialists may do nothing outside their specialty. The majority of programmers on a Scrum team, however, should be willing to contribute in any number of ways to optimize the throughput of the overall team. This means they will test when necessary, sometimes program in a nonpreferred language, and so on.

SEE ALSO

The subject of specialists is considered in detail in Chapter 11, "Teamwork."

One of the most striking changes for programmers on a Scrum team is that they can no longer sit in their cubicles and wait to be told exactly what to program. They need to become active participants in understanding product requirements. Surprisingly, there are many people who simply want to be told what to work on. I've heard this expressed as "if they tell me what to work on and I do it, then I can't be fired." Programmers on a Scrum team—like all others on the team—are expected to share in the responsibility for the overall success of the product. When this responsibility is fully felt, it is easier to do the things that go beyond one's normal job description.

Programmers will also be expected to talk to customers and users. The amount of this can be adjusted up or down based on the programmer, the organization, the strengths of other team members, and the nature of the project. Programmers do not need to develop the personalities of gregarious, glad-handing salespeople. But they do need to be comfortable occasionally talking to a user or customer, even if it's just over the phone.

Similarly, programmers can expect to spend more time interacting with their coworkers. A programmer may not be allowed to come in at 11 and clamp headphones on until quietly leaving at 7. Instead, programmers may be expected to sit in a group space, engage in discussions, help others with problems, and participate in pair programming.

SEE ALSO

Pair programming, which entails two programmers sharing one computer, is discussed more in Chapter 9.

These changes can be quite unsettling for the many programmers (including myself) who got into this field because we thought we could sit alone in our cubicles all day. Prior to my first programming job, I worked in a six-foot by four-foot totally enclosed dark room developing photos all day. I would pop out for regularly scheduled breaks and lunch; otherwise I was alone in the dark all day and loved it. Moving to the lighted world of cubicles was a big change. Moving from quiet cubicles to an energetic, talkative culture is an even bigger change. Programmers on a Scrum team will be expected to make this transition. Fortunately, though, the change isn't that hard for most of us. We may like to be alone, but we find participating in structured conversations (as in the meetings and decision-making discussions on a Scrum project) much easier than unstructured conversations as at a cocktail party.

Beyond the communication and interaction changes, programmers will almost certainly experience changes in how they do their work. Many of the technical practices described in Chapter 9 will be new to them. The team may not choose to adopt all of these practices at first (or ever in some cases), but I suggest all be considered and tried.

Database Administrators

Data professionals, whether they go by the title of database administrators, database engineers, or something else, can be among the most resistant to adopting Scrum. Much of what the preceding section said about programmers will also be true about database administrators. Additionally, data professionals will be faced with learning how to do incrementally what has traditionally been viewed as a part of a project's up-front work.

Standard advice in database design has been to do a complete analysis of the system's needs, create a logical or conceptual database design, and then map the concepts to the constraints of a real-world database during physical database design. Success at this series of steps is predicated on a full and accurate analysis up front. The traditional data professional's view was best summed up to me by a fellow traveler on a plane from Chicago to Sacramento. He was a vice president of database development for a relatively large healthcare company. His view on the world was "applications change; data is forever."

This type of thinking leads to an intense focus on doing a complete analysis up front. This is nice in theory, but while we're taking the time to do that complete analysis, the world is continuing to evolve. Users' needs are changing. Competitors are releasing their products. Databases need to evolve to support the evolving applications built on them.

In Chapter 14, I am going to make the point that user experience design, architecture, and database design are all special cases of the same challenge: working incrementally on something that is thought about holistically. Much of a DBA's day-to-day work will not change significantly, but how the DBA approaches and schedules that work will change dramatically and will be discussed in the "Work Together Throughout the Sprint" section of that chapter.

Testers

For years the common approach to testing has been based on Philip Crosby's definition of quality: conformance to requirements (1979, 16). If quality is conformance to requirements, then those requirements better be written down. This has led many testers to an overzealous pursuit of a perfect requirements document against which they can confirm that the system conforms. However, as nice as conformance to requirements may be, conformance to users' needs is even better. In using Scrum we acknowledge that it is impossible to perfectly predict all user needs.

Just as programmers can no longer say, "Hand me the perfect spec; then go away while I make the system do exactly what you requested," testers cannot say, "Hand me the perfect requirements document and I'll make sure the system does everything in it." Each of these attitudes (and they've been prevalent ones in traditionally managed projects) leads to an abdication of responsibility. When statements like these are voiced, the programmer or tester who says them is relinquishing accountability for the ultimate success of the project. "Just tell me what to do and I'll do it," each is saying. Instead, each needs to be thinking about the product and asking questions about each feature and how it adds to (or detracts from) the overall product.

Because Scrum teams shift focus during requirements gathering from writing about requirements to talking about them, conversations with the product owner become the tester's primary way of finding out how a new feature should behave. A tester is likely to talk with the product owner about how a feature should work, how quickly it should perform, what acceptance criteria must be passed, and so on. Testers are not limited to acquiring this information solely from the product owners. As appropriate, testers should also talk with users, customers, and other stakeholders.

SEE ALSO

Shifting from writing about requirements to talking about them is covered in the section "Shift from Documents to Discussions" in Chapter 13.

As with programmers, working in such an interactive environment can be uncomfortable for testers who are transitioning to Scrum. Many testers, like their colleagues, entered software development with the expectation that they could sit in a cubicle with little human interaction on a daily basis. Not anymore. Testers on a Scrum team will need to become accustomed to more frequent and meaningful conversations with their coworkers and, in many cases, people outside the team.

Along with giving up on the myth that a perfect specification can be written in advance, one of the biggest changes facing testers is learning how to work iteratively. Conceptually this shouldn't be a hard thing to do. If we think of each sprint as its own project, then the testing for each project/sprint is done within that sprint. It's not as simple though as proclaiming that the last week of each sprint shall be reserved for testing. This doesn't work and instead creates miniature waterfalls inside each sprint. During the first few sprints, testers will face an immense challenge. During that time the programmers are also learning how to work iteratively and probably won't be good at it either. The team will probably overcommit to what can be done in a sprint, and the programmers will probably not have any of the planned features fully coded until very near the end of the sprint. So they will attempt to hand code to testers on the eighteenth day of a 20-day sprint. After individuals in these roles learn how to work in an agile manner, these eleventh-hour handoffs will disappear.

SEE ALSO

For advice on how testers, programmers, and others should work together, see the section "Do a Little Bit of Everything All the Time" in Chapter 11.

An increased emphasis on test automation becomes a hallmark of Scrum teams. Even teams that have struggled for years to make progress in automating tests find that the short sprints of Scrum make test automation a necessity. Over time this reduces the reliance on manual testers: those who read a script, push a button, and note the results. These testers often find themselves being asked to learn one or more of the test automation tools used by the team. While some test

SEE ALSO

For why a team may use more than one test automation tool, see "Automate at Different Levels" in Chapter 16, "Quality."

automation tools rely on what might as well be called programming to create the tests, not all do. I have met only a handful of manual testers who have been unable to transition to making significant contributions to their teams' test automation efforts. On the other hand, I've met many who are afraid of this change. Time, practice, training, and pairing (including with a programmer) should be sufficient to overcome the fears.

Lisa Crispin, coauthor with Janet Gregory of the book *Agile Testing*, recalls that when she shifted to working on an agile team, the first thing she noticed was that she needed to be proactive.

> Don't sit and wait for things to come to you. Be proactive! We testers can't wait for testing tasks to come to us. We have to get up and get involved and figure out what to do. Collaborating with programmers is new to a lot of testers. (Although it wasn't to me, I always elbowed my way in at the start of every project no matter what our process was.) Collaborating with customers is also new to a lot of testers. It's way out of the comfort zone for a lot of people. Programmers are busy people and kind of scary, sometimes. When I was the only tester on a team of eight programmers, even though most of them were guys I had worked with for years at another company, it took a lot of courage to ask for help.

OBJECTION

"If I work too closely with others on the team, I will develop 'programmer eyes,' causing me to see everything from their perspective, rather than from the viewpoint of a tester."

It's hard to see how working more closely with programmers will cause testers to lose so much perspective that they can no longer test the software. Database professionals have worked closely with programmers for years without becoming so contaminated. For decades, testers have advocated doing both white-box testing (in which they can see the internals of the system) and black-box testing (in which they cannot). If working with a programmer can lead to developing "programmer eyes," it seems logical to believe that a tester who has done white-box testing would similarly lose perspective and not be able to do black-box testing. Fortunately, this isn't the case.

Though many of the changes brought by Scrum will be uncomfortable at first, most testers will enjoy their new ways of working after getting used to them. Jyri Partanen is a QA manager with Sulake, developers of Habbo, a virtual world averaging over eight million unique visitors each month. Partanen describes the transition required of testers.

> Testing is a profession where old habits tend to last. In the case of transitioning to agile, sticking to the old ways of doing things may lead to a half-hearted implementation of the spirit of agile. Usually the distress the testing engineers have is related to job security and the changes the upcoming agile transition may bring to their day-to-day tasks. This is, however, an unnecessary concern. Based on my own experience and the experience of others who actually have completed the transition to agile with QA personnel, I can say with confidence that the change has been without a doubt a smart move. Testing engineers in agile teams have more influence in the development process and, what's even more important, on the end product.

User Experience Designers

User Experience Designers (UEDs) often have a legitimate concern with adopting Scrum. Although they are accustomed to working iteratively, they prefer to run their iterations in advance of the rest of the project. On a Scrum project, however, we don't want to do all of the UED work before beginning other development activities.

My favorite descriptions of how agile designers work have come out of Autodesk in Toronto. Lynn Miller (2005) and Desirée Sy (2007) have written about the approach they have used to integrate design into an agile process. I have worked on dozens of projects on which the teams and designers embraced their advice.

According to Miller and Sy, there should be two parallel tracks of work on the project: one for development and one for interaction design. Figure 8.2 depicts these two tracks and the interaction between them. The essential idea here is that UED work always precedes development work by at least one sprint. UEDs are given a headstart on the project through a combination of an initial sprint zero and a focus in sprint one on features with few or no user interface implications.

The approach shown here can work well but brings with it the risk that UEDs view themselves as a separate team. Lynn Miller sketched the first version of this diagram and agrees that it must not be interpreted to imply that there are separate teams.

> Whenever I have taught this concept I have always stressed that the designers should not think of themselves as a separate team

and that tight and frequent communication is essential to make the concept work. It has always been a failing of the diagram that it seems to suggest separation when that never was my intent.

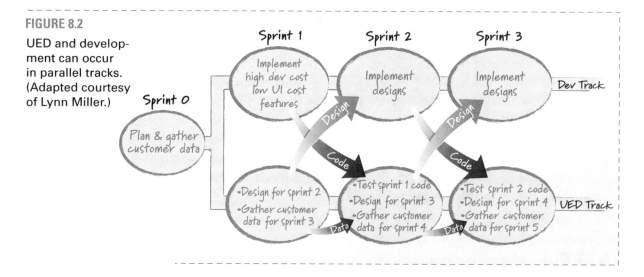

FIGURE 8.2

UED and development can occur in parallel tracks. (Adapted courtesy of Lynn Miller.)

It is essential that UEDs view themselves as part of the team. The idea of cross-functional teams is fundamental to Scrum; the team needs to include every-one necessary to go from idea to implementation. What would prevent a testing group from preparing its own version of Figure 8.2 showing parallel tracks of programming and testing sprints?

If I were to meet a UED in the hallway of your company and ask, "What do you do?" I might get a response like this: "I'm a user experience designer. I work one sprint in advance of the developers. My job is to make sure that when they start a sprint I can give them a design for what they'll develop in that sprint." This answer corresponds with Figure 8.2, but it's not an answer I like. Instead I'd prefer to hear, "I'm a user experience designer. I'm on the development team, and my primary job is to make sure we finish whatever work we commit to for the sprint. But that doesn't take up all my time, so I spend a good amount of it looking ahead at what we're going to build in the next sprint or two. I then gather data, mock up designs, and do whatever I can so that when we start on a feature in a future sprint, we're able to finish it in that sprint."

Both of these fictitious quotes describe exactly the same work. In both cases the UEDs are working with the team during the sprint to resolve issues about that sprint, but they are also looking ahead. However, the two different answers present different mindsets about the work. First and foremost, I want UEDs to feel a part of the team and that their top priority is delivering whatever is committed for the current sprint. Beyond that, their job is to look ahead in exactly the same way everyone expects a product owner to be looking ahead at what competitors are doing, what users will want next, and so on.

I'm not alone in thinking that an agile mindset is critical for UEDs in making the transition to Scrum. Well-respected usability expert Jakob Nielsen concurs.

SEE ALSO

In Chapter 14 we will examine in much greater detail how user experience designers are able to overlap their work effectively with the work of others on the team.

> For user experience practitioners who support agile teams, the main change is in mindset. Having good, general user experience knowledge will help you understand how to change traditional design and evaluation methods to meet your agile team's different focus. Ultimately, however, you must both believe in yourself and embrace agile development concepts if you want to succeed. If you're prepared to change your practices and take on the responsibility, there are great opportunities to improve your effectiveness and your impact on the teams you support. (2008)

Three Common Themes

In this chapter we considered the changed roles of analysts, project managers, architects, functional managers, programmers, database administrators, testers, and user experience designers. In doing so, three major themes reasserted themselves:

- **Work incrementally.** Always strive to produce a potentially shippable product increment within the sprint.
- **Work iteratively.** Functionality can be revisited in subsequent sprints.
- **Work beyond your specialty.** To create something potentially shippable by the end of the sprint, individuals need to be willing to work outside their specialties occasionally.

As you go forward, you'll find it helpful to keep these themes in mind as general heuristics about how individuals should work on a Scrum team.

Additional Reading

Ambler, Scott. n. d. Agile Data Home Page. http://www.agiledata.org.
A useful website that collects some of prolific author Scott Ambler's writings on agile development in data-intensive environments.

Crispin, Lisa, and Janet Gregory. 2009. *Agile testing: A practical guide for testers and agile teams.* Addison-Wesley Professional.
A comprehensive guide to testing on an agile project. The book begins with ten principles for what agile testing is and then describes the organizational changes that will be felt by a testing or QA group. The core of the book is a four-quadrant view for describing all testing, which many teams have found useful.

Highsmith, Jim. 2009. *Agile project management: Creating innovative products.* 2nd ed. Addison-Wesley Professional.

> The most popular book on agile project management. The second edition adds chapters on release planning, scaling, governance, and measure to an already complete table of contents.

Jeffries, Ron. 2004. *Extreme programming adventures in C#.* Microsoft Press.

> An intriguing book in which we read along as Ron Jeffries teaches himself C# by pair programming with Chet Hendrickson. The book isn't intended specifically to teach C# programming. Rather, it is an excellent introduction to the type of fast-feedback programming practiced on Scrum teams.

Johnston, Andrew. 2009. The role of the agile architect, June 20. Content from Agile Architect website. http://www.agilearchitect.org/agile/role.htm.

> This entire site is dedicated to information for agile architects. I found this to be the most useful article on the site. It describes the five key objectives and seven golden rules of the agile architect.

Krug, Steve. 2005. *Don't make me think: A common sense approach to web usability.* 2nd ed. New Riders Press.

> This is the best of the books to cover a discount approach to usability. Experienced user experience designers may find it too simplistic and that it shortcuts too much research, but many teams have found it helpful.

Marick, Brian. 2007. *Everyday scripting with Ruby: For teams, testers, and you.* Pragmatic Bookshelf.

> This excellent book is aimed at testers who need to learn basic scripting skills using Ruby, probably as part of working on an agile team. However, the book will appeal to anyone who needs a good introductory book on Ruby.

Sliger, Michele, and Stacia Broderick. 2008. *The software project manager's bridge to agility.* Addison-Wesley Professional.

> Sliger and Broderick are both Scrum trainers as well as Project Management Professionals (PMPs). They have targeted this book directly at PMPs like themselves who are making the switch to Scrum or any agile process.

Subramaniam, Venkat, and Andy Hunt. 2006. *Practices of an agile developer: Working in the real world.* Pragmatic Bookshelf.

> This short book collects nearly 50 tips aimed at programmers on any agile project. Each tip (such as "Let Design Guide, Not Dictate") includes a description of the practice and how it should feel when it is being done well.

Chapter 9

Technical Practices

New titles, roles, and responsibilities aren't the only changes Scrum teams are asked to make. For a Scrum team to be truly successful, it must go beyond adopting the basic, highly visible parts of Scrum and commit to real changes in the way it approaches the actual work of creating a product. I've observed teams who work in sprints, conduct good sprint planning and review meetings, never miss a daily Scrum, and do a retrospective at the end of each sprint. They see solid improvements and may be as much as twice as productive as they were before Scrum. But they could do so much better.

What these teams are missing—and what stops them from achieving even more dramatic improvements—are changes to their technical practices. Scrum doesn't prescribe specific engineering practices. To do so would be inconsistent with the underlying philosophy of Scrum: Trust the team to solve the problem. For example, Scrum doesn't explicitly say you need to test. It doesn't say you need to write all code in pairs in a test-driven manner. What it does do is require teams to deliver high-quality, potentially shippable code at the end of each sprint. If teams can do this without changing their technical practices, so be it. Most teams, however, discover and adopt new technical practices because it makes meeting their goals so much easier.

In this chapter we look at five common practices that were made popular by Extreme Programming and have been adopted by many of the highest-performing Scrum teams. We see how these practices are derived from a quest for technical excellence. Finally, we look at how the technical practices of a Scrum team intentionally guide the emergent design of the software system.

Strive for Technical Excellence

Like most kids, when my daughters drew or painted a particularly stunning masterpiece, they would bring it home from school and want it displayed in a place of prominence—namely the refrigerator. One day at work I coded a particularly pleasing use of the strategy pattern in some C++ code. Deciding that the refrigerator door was suitable for displaying anything we're particularly proud of, onto the fridge it went! Wouldn't it be nice if we were always so pleased with the quality of our work that we proudly displayed it on the fridge along with our kids' artwork? Although you probably won't go as far as taping your code, tests, or database schema on your fridge, producing fridge-worthy work is a goal shared by many Scrum teams.

In this section we will look at common technical practices used by Scrum teams to improve the quality of their work: test-driven development, refactoring, collective ownership, continuous integration, and pair programming. While I just referred to these as common practices, the truth is that they are not so common. These practices are well regarded and lead to higher quality, but because they can be hard to put into practice, they are used less often than they should be. Each, however, is a practice that Scrum teams should consider adopting. Because there are many great books and articles available on each of these practices, I will introduce each only briefly and will reserve the bulk of my comments for ways to introduce the practice into your organization and to overcome common objections to it.

SEE ALSO

For specific recommendations of reading material that will help you learn more about the technical practices themselves, see the "Additional Reading" section at the end of this chapter.

Test-Driven Development

If you were to look at how programmers write code on a traditional development team, you would find that they typically select a portion of the program to tackle, write the code, attempt to compile it, fix all the compile errors, walk through the code in a debugger, and then repeat. This is summarized in Figure 9.1. This process is very different from a test-driven approach, which is also shown in that figure. A programmer doing test-driven development works in very short cycles of identifying and automating a failing test, writing just enough code to pass that test, and then cleaning the code up in any necessary ways before starting again. This cycle is repeated every few minutes, rather than every few hours.

SEE ALSO

This cleaning up of the code is called refactoring. It is discussed in detail in the next section of this chapter.

FIGURE 9.1

The microcyclic nature of traditional and test-driven development.

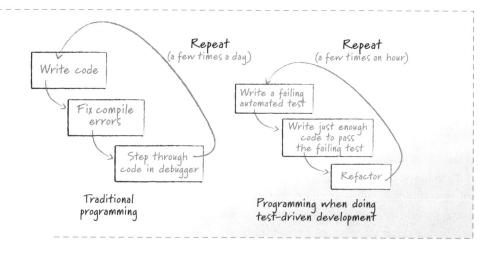

I find test-driven development (TDD) invaluable. One of the biggest reasons is that it ensures that no untested code makes it into the system. If all code must be written in response to a failing test, then if we do nothing else, we at least achieve full code coverage with TDD. You might think a test–right–after approach would achieve the same result. However, I've found that when programmers make a commitment to write their unit tests "right after" they finish implementing a feature, they often do not do so. The pressure to get started programming the next feature can be tremendous. So programmers tend to write tests for only a subset of the new functionality or put testing on a list of things to get to later, and then find that later never comes.

It is appropriate to think of TDD as being as much a design practice as a programming practice. After all, the tests a programmer writes and the order in which they are written guide the design and development of a feature. A programmer doesn't create a list of 50 small unit tests and then randomly choose which to implement first. Instead each test is selected and sequenced so that the uncertainties of the feature are addressed early. In this way, the selection and implementation of tests does indeed drive the development process, resulting in a design that, at least in part, emerges from the needs of the system.

There is some debate about whether TDD leads to more robust or otherwise better designs.[1] But there is no doubt that TDD is helpful as a practice that helps programmers think through their designs. A design that is hard to test, for example, may indicate poorly structured code. My recommendation is to do TDD for its testing benefits; any potential design improvements it brings are a bonus.

SEE ALSO

The idea of driving development with tests has also been scaled up to what is known as acceptance test–driven development, a topic covered in Chapter 16, "Quality."

"I am working on a complex system. I need to do some architectural work first."

OBJECTION

Yes, on a complex or large system, you probably do. There is nothing to say that TDD as a micro-level practice cannot be effectively combined with a small amount of up-front architectural thinking. In fact, later in this chapter, the section "Design: Intentional yet Emergent" introduces the idea that being agile is about finding the right balance between anticipation and adaptation. The question of how much, if any, architectural thinking to do up front is best considered with achieving that balance in mind.

---

1   For an example, see Abby Fichtner's blog at http://haxrchick.blogspot.com/2008/07/tdd-smackdown.html, which includes a link to a video-recorded debate between Jim Coplien and Robert Martin.

OBJECTION

"Always writing a test first is bound to take longer; I don't have time to waste."

There is evidence that doing TDD takes about 15% longer than not doing TDD (George and Williams 2003). But there is also evidence that TDD leads to fewer defects. Two studies at Microsoft found that the number of bugs found went down by 24% and 38% with the use of TDD (Sanchez, Williams, and Maximilien 2007, 6). So, yes, TDD may take longer initially, but the time will come back to the team in the form of reduced bug fixing and maintenance time.

THINGS TO TRY NOW

❑ Commit to spending at least one full day in the coming week doing test-driven development. If you've never done TDD before, you will likely need to work with another programmer to get the hang of it. Even if your partner doesn't have TDD experience either, it will be easier to learn together.

❑ Getting comfortable with how to write a failing test before writing the implementation can be difficult. It's a very different way of working. One way to gain a better understanding of it is to try *gang programming*. Gather four to eight programmers in a conference room equipped with a laptop and projector. Pick a programmer to start coding while everyone else looks at the projected source code. Find one failing test you can write, and then have the programmer write the code that makes the test pass. After 15 minutes or so, pass the laptop to another programmer. Continue writing code and passing the laptop until the task is complete.

❑ If trying TDD on your full application is too difficult right now, find an ancillary project you can try it on. How about that data conversion program everyone has been putting off? Or the stand-alone program one of the system administrators asked for last month?

Refactoring

Consider the classic definition offered by Fred Brooks in *The Mythical Man Month* of what happens as a software system is modified over time.

> All repairs tend to destroy the structure, to increase the entropy and disorder of the system. Less and less effort is spent on fixing original design flaws; more and more is spent on fixing flaws introduced by earlier fixes. As time passes, the system becomes less and less well-ordered. Sooner or later the fixing ceases to gain any ground. Each forward step is matched by a backward one.

> Although in principle usable forever, the system has worn out as
> a base for progress. (1995)

Fortunately, since 1975 when Brooks first wrote this, our industry has learned ways to modify systems such that the system does not decay further with each modification. The ability to modify without introducing decay is essential to Scrum because Scrum teams build products incrementally. As Ron Jeffries says, "In agile, the design simply must start simple and grow up. The way to do this is refactoring."

Refactoring refers to changing the structure but not the behavior of code. Let me give you an example. Suppose a programmer has two methods that each contain three identical statements. These three common statements can be extracted from both methods and put into one new method that is called from both of the old locations. This refactoring (formally known as *extract method*) has slightly improved the readability and maintainability of the program because it is now more obvious that some code is reused and the duplicated code has been moved to a single place. The structure of the code has been changed while its behavior has not.

Refactoring is not only crucial to the success of TDD, but it also helps prevent code rot. Code rot is the typical syndrome in which a product is released, its code is allowed to decay for a few years, and then an entire rewrite is needed. By constantly refactoring and fixing small problems before they become big problems, we can keep our applications rot free. Robert C. Martin calls this the Boy Scout Rule.

> The Boy Scouts of America have a simple rule that we can apply
> to our profession: Leave the campground cleaner than you found
> it. If we all checked-in our code a little cleaner than when we
> checked it out, the code simply could not rot. (2008, 14)

"If they wrote it right the first time, they wouldn't need to refactor now."

OBJECTION

This is kind of like saying, "If Toyota built better cars, they wouldn't need oil changes, new tires, or any maintenance ever." Applications will need maintenance; refactoring is choosing to do it a little at a time when doing so is cheap. Most of the managers or product owners I've met who take a "you aren't allowed to refactor" stance do so because teams have abused the ability to refactor in the past. A typical example is the team that reserves the last three days of every ten-day sprint for refactoring. Another is the team that tells its product owner, "No, we can't do that important feature this sprint because we need to refactor what we wrote the last sprint." If the whole team needs three days to refactor every sprint, that's a sign of different troubles. If the team has planned refactorings that are so large they have to turn down features the product owner would like included, the refactoring probably belongs on the product backlog itself.

THINGS TO TRY NOW

❑ Start a refactoring backlog of all the things you want to clean up. If the team is collocated, simply write it on a big sheet of paper hanging somewhere. If not, use the electronic equivalent. You want the list to be as informal as possible. The goal is to fix all the issues and then destroy the list. Institutionalizing the refactoring list in a custom-built database with a custom web client, RSS feeds, and iPhone support will encourage the list to remain forever.

❑ Learn the refactorings that can be performed automatically by your integrated development environment.

❑ When a refactoring opportunity is identified, have team members write it on an index card. Post the cards in a small, delineated area on a wall in the team room. As the area fills, feel mounting pressure to complete one or more refactoring.

❑ At the end of your next two-hour-long programming session, spend 20 or 30 minutes cleaning up something you noticed as you were touching or looking at existing code.

❑ During your next retrospective, facilitate a discussion about refactoring with your teammates, including the product owner. At what threshold should refactoring switch from a personal decision to a whole-team decision? Clearly, I can rename a poorly named variable I come across without a team discussion. What if the developers come across a two-day change; can they just make it, or does the product owner need to approve the effort first?

Collective Ownership

Collective ownership refers to all developers feeling ownership over all artifacts of the development process, but especially of the code and automated tests. Because of the fast pace of a Scrum project, the team needs to avoid the trap of saying, "That's Ted's code. We can't touch it." Collective ownership encourages each team member to feel responsible for all parts of the program so that any programmer can work on any module of the program. When modifying a module, the programmer then shares responsibility for its quality with the module's initial writer.

Collective ownership is not intended to cause a free-for-all in the coding. Programmers will still tend to have certain areas they specialize in and prefer to work in, but everyone on the team shares the following responsibilities:

- Ensure that no developer becomes so specialized he can contribute only in one area.

- Make certain that no area becomes so intricate that it is understood and worked upon by only one developer.

A natural benefit of fostering a feeling of collective ownership is that it encourages developers to learn new parts of the system. In doing so they generally also learn new ways of doing things. Good ideas used in one part of the application are more quickly propagated to other areas as programmers moving in and out of parts of the application carry the ideas like pollen.

"It's my code; I don't want to have to fix anyone else's bugs."

I don't blame you, but keep in mind they are also fixing your bugs. In fact, from my experience a team practicing collective ownership will write cleaner code (and presumably therefore have fewer bugs). No one wants to look bad in front of coworkers. If some code is "mine" and no one will see it, I might be tempted to get a little sloppy; not so if anyone can see my code at any time. For proof of this look no further than your guest bathroom. Which do you keep cleaner: the bathroom only you use or the one that visitors are likely to see?

"I don't want anyone else looking at my code and making judgments about my skills, character, upbringing, and so on."

This is a natural fear. The best way over this fear is to write better code. If you always did your best to write high-quality code, any judgments others made would be positive. If you're not confident in your ability to write high-quality code, pair as often as you can with other programmers as a way of improving.

"Development is faster if each person owns one part of the system."

This depends entirely on the time frame over which we are measuring. If you and I are building a throwaway system over the next two weeks, it will indeed most likely be faster for each of us to own one part of the application. If, however, we are part of a much larger effort and are going to have to maintain the system for the long term, the learning, cross-training, and other benefits of collective ownership weigh heavily in its favor.

- ❑ Pretend that the owner of any critical area is away on vacation and nearly impossible to reach. For a couple of sprints, make the deliberate decision that the "obvious person" is never allowed to take on tasks related to that area of expertise. If the area expert is needed, that expert is available by phone only—literally call the person who is sitting two cubicles away.
- ❑ The next time you work in code that is difficult to work with, fix it—even if it was written by someone else. If you feel that this is overstepping your authority, ask the original programmer to work with you in making the code easier to use.

Continuous Integration

Creating an official nightly build of a product has been known as an industry best practice since at least the early 1990s. Well, if a nightly build is a good idea, building a product continuously is an even better one. Continuous integration refers to integrating new or changed code into an application as soon as possible and then testing the application to make sure that nothing has been broken. Rather than checking in code perhaps every few days or even every few weeks, each programmer on a Scrum team running continuous integration is expected to check in code a few times each day—and to run a suite of regression tests over the entire application.

Continuous integration is usually achieved with the help of a tool or script that notices when code has been checked into the version control system. Cruise Control was the first product to gain popularity for automating continuous integration. It could build a product, run as many tests as desired against it, and could then automatically send a notification to the developer who broke the build (or to the entire team). Cruise Control could also send build results to additional feedback devices such as lava lamps, ambient orbs, spare monitors, LED displays, and more.

Some teams opt for a manual approach, in which developers initiate the build and test for each check-in. I strongly recommend against this. Although it is possible to be successful with a manual approach to continuous integration, my experience is that developers will occasionally skip the build and test. It is just too tempting to occasionally think, "I changed only two lines and it worked on my machine." It's also tempting to forgo the build and test when checking in code after your planned quitting time for the day: "Yikes, it's almost six o'clock," a developer may think. "I'm sure this works and I don't want to wait 15 minutes for the tests to finish…." Given the ease with which a continuous integration tool can be configured, it is almost always one of the first things I coach teams to do.

For most developers, the first exposure to automated continuous integration is eye-opening. I know it was for me. I'd become very accustomed to the benefits of a nightly build but had somehow never made the mental leap that if once a day is good, many times a day would be better. After working in a continuously integrated environment for a day, I was hooked. Not only could we eliminate all risk of big integration issues at the end of a project, but also the entire development team would be receiving near-real-time feedback on the status of the product.

"Maintaining a build server and all those tests takes time away from other work."

A Scrum team will require a suitable automated testing environment regardless of whether it also does continuous integration. So, the only additional overhead is that of setting up and maintaining the build server environment. For most applications this investment will be paid back within the first month by the time saved on integration issues.

"Our system is too complex; it takes hours to run a full integration test—we can't build continuously."

These days it is not uncommon to encounter a Scrum team with a test suite that takes hours to run. The solution is normally to partition the test suite rather than abandon the idea of continuous integration. Stephen Marsh and Stelios Pantazopoulos worked on the TransCanada pipeline project and did exactly this.

> Several months into the project it became evident that running the full regression test in under fifteen minutes was not possible. As a result the regression test was split into two: a smoke test and a full test. The first ran after every check-in and included all test scripts from the current delivery milestone [sprint] and a subset of scripts from past milestones. The second ran once an hour and included all test scripts from all milestones. The first proved to be complete enough the majority of the time. Only on rare occasions did the second one fail. (2008, 241)

❑ An official nightly build is a must for any Scrum team. Getting at least this much in place should be one of the first things you do if you don't have it already. The effort to get a nightly build in place will be paid back within a month at the most, so there's no excuse to be without one. Plan this into your next sprint.

❑ If you already have a nightly build, take the next step and start building continuously.

❑ If you have a continuous build, but no tests run as part of it, add some. Chapter 16 introduces the test automation pyramid. Getting the first test of each type from this pyramid is a hurdle. But after the first test has been integrated, the rest come much more easily.

Pair Programming

Pair programming is the practice of having two developers work together to write code. It originated from the idea that if occasional code inspections are good, constant code inspections are better. Many of the practices just described are made easier through the use of pair programming. Learning how to do test-driven development is made easier when working together. Feelings of collective ownership are created when code is produced in pairs. And having the discipline to leave the code cleaner than you found it comes easier when another developer is sitting beside you.

Clearly, there are some benefits to pair programming. That's why I invented it. OK, I didn't really invent it, but I like to think I did. I did happen across it out of true necessity, which is, after all, the mother of invention. In 1986 I was hired by Andersen Consulting in its Los Angeles office. On my first day on the job I completed a skills survey. I marked myself as "proficient" with the C programming language, even though I was very much a beginner at the language. But, I reasoned, I'm studying it every night after work, and I will be proficient by the time they read this skills survey. Unfortunately for me, they read the survey the next day. And on the day after that I was on a plane from Los Angeles to the New York office to a project that desperately needed C programmers.

After arriving in New York, I met another programmer who had also been transferred because he knew C. I knew I couldn't deceive him, so I came clean and confessed my exaggeration on the skills survey. "Ugh," he said, "I lied, too." Our solution was that we would work together—pair programming, although we didn't call it that. We figured that between us we were as good as one "proficient" C programmer. And, we reasoned, if we worked together on everything, they wouldn't know which of us to fire.

It worked like a dream. He and I worked together for much of the next eight years at three different companies, pairing as much as possible, especially on anything difficult. We wrote some amazing and incredibly complex products, always with low defect rates. We also felt that even though there were two heads for every pair of hands on the keyboard, we were highly productive when working this way.

Since those early, positive experiences with pair programming, I've been hooked. I knew it was a good way to write code. On the other hand, many of us in this industry (myself included) were first attracted to this work because we could sit in a cubicle with our Sony Walkman playing (yes, it was that long ago) and not have to talk with anyone all day. Even now, there are days when I enjoy nothing more than listening to some loud music on my headphones while code is flowing from my fingers as fast as I can type. Because I still relish those days, I have a hard time ever mandating to a team that they must do pair programming 100% of the time.

Fortunately, most teams have realized that the vast majority of the benefits of pairing can be achieved even when it is not done all day, every day. So, when coaching teams, I always push them to adopt pair programming on a part-time basis; use it for the riskiest parts of the application. I encourage teams to find the guidelines that help them pair enough, while stressing that enough is somewhere greater than 0%, but also acknowledging that I can understand the reasons they may have for wanting it to be less than 100%.

There are many advantages to pair programming, even for teams who do it less than 100% of the time. Although most studies show a slight increase in the total number of person-hours used when pairing, this is offset by a decrease in the total duration of the effort. That is, while pairing takes more person-hours, fewer hours pass on the clock (Dybå et. al 2007). Although projects are always under financial pressure, the overriding concern is not so much person-hours as time to market. Pair programming has also been shown to improve quality. In a survey of studies, Dybå and colleagues found that each study showed an improvement in quality with pair programming. Additionally, pair programming facilitates knowledge transfer and is an ideal way to bring new developers up to speed on the application. It is also an effective practice for working in uncharted territory or solving difficult problems in known parts of the system.

"It costs more; I don't want to pay two programmers to do the job of one."

OBJECTION

Pair programming will cost more in the short term. However, that additional initial cost may very likely be paid back with shorter schedules and with higher quality, leading to lower maintenance costs down the road. Rather than take industry studies as your proof either way, prove this to yourself. Pair on the most difficult modules and see if they have fewer defects and are easier to maintain later, perhaps in comparison to similar modules from other programs done without pair programming.

"We're in a hurry. We can't have two programmers on one task."

Actually, if you're in a hurry this is the time you need pair programming the most. I've already mentioned that pairing leads to shorter project durations (while increasing overall effort, or person-hours). Additionally, there is even some evidence (Williams, Shukla, and Anton 2004) that pairing is an effective way to counter Brooks' Law ("adding manpower to a late software project makes it later"). In other words, if you have an aggressive deadline or are tempted to add people to a late project, these are ideal times to incorporate pair programming.

OBJECTION

"When working on a tough problem, I need some quiet time to think through the problem."

Talk with your pairing partner and agree to separate for an hour or whatever you need to think through the problem. When you resume pairing, start by sharing any insights either of you had.

THINGS TO TRY NOW

❑ In your next sprint planning meeting, commit to doing some pairing. Make the commitment explicit by adding tasks to the sprint backlog: "Mike and Bob pair for two hours," "Mike and Mehta pair for an afternoon," and so on. This is a good way to at least get comfortable with pairing. It is too easy to put off pairing with a vague commitment to try it sometime in the near future. Having tasks in the sprint backlog, though, acts as a constant nagging reminder, and, as a result, is much more likely to result in action.

Design: Intentional yet Emergent

Scrum projects do not have an up-front analysis or design phase; all work occurs within the repeated cycle of sprints. This does not mean, however, that design on a Scrum project is not intentional. An intentional design process is one in which the design is guided through deliberate, conscious decision making. The difference on a Scrum project is not that intentional design is thrown out, but that it is done (like everything else on a Scrum project) incrementally. Scrum teams acknowledge that as nice as it might be to make all design decisions up front, doing so is impossible. This means that on a Scrum project, design is both intentional and emergent.

A big part of an organization's becoming agile is finding the appropriate balance between anticipation and adaptation (Highsmith 2002). Figure 9.2 shows this balance along with activities and artifacts that influence the balance. When doing up-front analysis or design, we are attempting to *anticipate* users' needs. Because we cannot perfectly anticipate these, we will make some mistakes; some work will need to be redone. When we forgo analysis and design and jump immediately into coding and testing with no forethought at all, we are trying to *adapt* to users' needs. All projects of interest will be positioned somewhere between anticipation and adaptation based on their own unique characteristics; no application will be all the way to either extreme. A life-critical, medical safety application may be far to the anticipation side. A three-person startup company building a website of information on kayak racing may be far toward the side of adaptation.

Foretelling the agile preference for simplicity, in 1990, was speaker and author Do-While Jones.

I'm not against planning for the future. Some thought should be given to future expansion of capability. But when the entire design process gets bogged down in an attempt to satisfy future requirements that may never materialize, then it is time to stop and see if there isn't a simpler way to solve the immediate problem.[2]

Scrum teams avoid this "bogging down" by realizing that not all future needs are worth worrying about today. Many future needs may be best handled by planning to adapt as they arise.

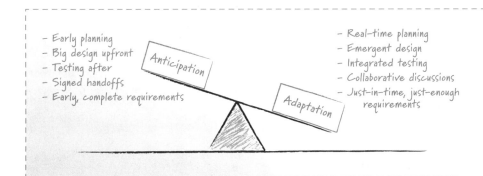

- Early planning
- Big design upfront
- Testing after
- Signed handoffs
- Early, complete requirements

Anticipation

Adaptation

- Real-time planning
- Emergent design
- Integrated testing
- Collaborative discussions
- Just-in-time, just-enough requirements

FIGURE 9.2

Achieving a balance between anticipation and adaptation involves balancing the influence of the activities and artifacts on each side.

Getting Used to Life Without a Big Design

As Scrum teams begin to become adept at the technical practices described in this chapter, they will naturally begin to shift further away from anticipating users' needs and more toward adapting to them. This will result in a number of changes for the agile architect or designer to become accustomed to. The new realities caused by this shift include the following:

- **Planning is harder.** Estimating, planning, and committing to deliverables is already hard; it becomes more difficult in the absence of an up-front design. A lot of thinking goes into creating an up-front design. Some of that thinking is helpful in estimating how long things will take and in combining estimates into plans. The upside to forgoing the big up-front design, however, is that the work that needs to be estimated is often simpler so that individual features can be estimated more quickly and easily.
- **It is harder to partition the work among teams or individuals.** Having a big, up-front design in hand makes it easy to see which features should be developed simultaneously and which should be developed in sequence. This makes it easier to allocate work to teams or individuals.

---

2   Jones' 1990 article, "The Breakfast Food Cooker," remains a classic parable of what can go wrong when software developers over-design a solution. I highly recommended reading it at http://www.ridgecrest.ca.us/~do_while/toaster.htm.

- **It is uncomfortable not to have design done.** Even though we've always known that no up-front design can be 100% perfect, we took comfort in its existence. "Surely," we reasoned, "we've thought of all the big things so any changes will be minor."
- **Rework will be inevitable.** Without a big up-front design, the team will certainly hit a point where it needs to undo some part of the design. This two-steps-forward-one-step-back aspect of iterative development can be unsettling to professionals trained to identify all needs and make all design decisions up front. Fortunately, refactoring and the automated tests created during test-driven development can keep most rework efforts from becoming very large.

Doing a large, up-front design became popular because of the belief that doing so would save time and money. The cost of the up-front design plus the cost of adjustments was viewed as less expensive than the many small changes necessary with emergent design. The situation can be visualized as shown in Figure 9.3, with the question being which weighs more?

FIGURE 9.3

The costs of significant up-front design and analysis plus occasional expensive changes are weighed against the costs of frequent but smaller changes on a Scrum project.

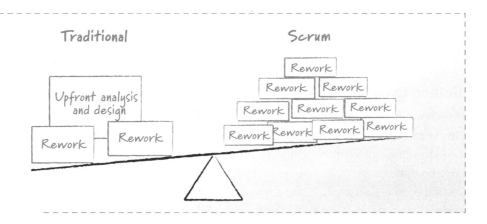

In the past, it was entirely possible that doing a large, up-front design would save time and money. After all, Barry Boehm demonstrated in *Software Engineering Economics* (1981) that defects are more expensive to fix the later in the development process they are discovered. But the technical practices employed by good Scrum teams can dramatically alter the equation. When a team uses good technical practices—test-driven development, a heavy reliance on automated unit tests, refactoring, and pair programming among them—it may find itself in the situation where it is cheaper to adapt to user needs by reworking the application more often than it is to anticipate those needs and rework only occasionally.

Figure 9.3 shows that in traditional development there is a large cost on upfront analysis and design. This investment keeps down the number of later changes. But when a change is needed, it is relatively expensive to make because the change violates the primary assumption that change will be largely unnecessary. By contrast, the Scrum view shows many more changes, but the size of each bit of rework is smaller. This is the result of anticipating that change will be needed, but not knowing exactly where. Because of that, a Scrum team pursues technical excellence, always keeping the code well factored, with as simple a design as possible, and with a suite of automated tests for early detection of regression problems. So, while there are more occasions for rework, each is less of a setback.

Guiding the Design

When I hear attacks on the lack of design on a Scrum project, the attacks usually start from the position that technical members of the team have no influence on the order in which features are added to the system. This is a faulty premise. In fact, one of the best things a Scrum team can do to ensure the scale shown in Figure 9.3 is tipped in the right direction is to influence the order in which items are worked on.

However, we read in Chapter 7, "New Roles," that prioritizing the product backlog is the responsibility of the product owner. Although that is true, the chapter also pointed out that a good product owner will listen to the advice of the team. Standard Scrum guidance is that the product owner prioritizes based on some nebulous concept of "business value." Although this may be true, it is a bit simplistic. The real job of the product owner is to maximize the delivery of features over some period of time. This may mean getting less "business value" now in favor of getting more later. In other words, a good product owner remains focused on ensuring that the product contains as much business value as possible when it is released but lets the team invest in the technical aspects of the product as appropriate because doing so pays later dividends to the product as well.

Especially early on a new project, the team should encourage the product owner to select product backlog items that will maximize learning and drive out technical uncertainty or risk. This is what I meant earlier by saying design on a Scrum project is both intentional and emergent. The design emerges because there is no up-front design phase (even though there are design activities during all sprints). Design is intentional because product backlog items are deliberately chosen with an eye toward pushing the design in different directions at different times.

An Example

As an example of how the product backlog items can be sequenced to influence the architecture of the system, consider a workflow system I worked on. The system supported a fund-raising company that produced specialized T-shirts and similar products. School-age children would go door to door selling these items. The sales revenue would be split between the company and the organization the kids represented, such as a school, sports team, or other group. For each sale, the kid would complete a form and send it to the company, where it was scanned, sent through an optical character recognition (OCR) process, and converted into an order. To keep shipping costs down, orders from the same organization were batched together and sent back to the organization, after which the kids would hand-deliver the items.

Our software handled the entire process—from when the paper was received by the company until the shipment went out the door. Kids have notoriously bad writing and are bad spellers, so our system had to do more than just scan forms and prepare packing lists. There were various levels of validation depending upon how accurately we thought each order form had been read. Some forms were routed to human data-entry clerks who were presented the scanned form on one side of the screen, the system's interpretation on the right, and an additional space to make corrections.

Because thousands of shirts were processed on the busiest days, this process needed to be as automated as possible. I worked with the product owner, Steve, to write the product backlog. After that I met with the development team to discuss which areas of the system were the highest risk or we were the most uncertain about how to develop. We decided that our first sprint would focus on getting a high-quality document to run through the system from end to end. It would be scanned, go through OCR, and generate a packing list. We would bypass optional steps such as deskewing crooked pages, despeckling pages, and so on but would prove that the workflow could be completed from start to finish. This wasn't highly valuable but it was something that needed to be done, and it let the developers test out the general architecture. After we accomplished this, we had a basic database in place and could move documents from state to state, triggering the correct workflow steps.

Next the developers asked the product owner if they could work on the part of the system that would display a scanned document to a human, who would be able to override the scanned and interpreted values. This was chosen as the second architectural goal of the project for three reasons:

- It was a manual step, making it different from the workflow steps handled already.
- Getting the user interface right was critical. With the volume of documents flowing through this system, saving seconds was important. We wanted to get early feedback from users to allow time to iterate on usability.
- After this feature was added, users could start processing shirt orders.

The project continued in this way for a few months and was ultimately tremendously successful, meeting all of the prerelease targets for reliability and throughput. A key to the success was that the product owner and technical personnel worked together to sequence the work. The closest the team got to a design phase was the first afternoon in the conference room when we identified risky areas and dark corners and decided which one we wanted to tackle first. From there the design emerged sprint by sprint, yet was intentionally guided by which product backlog items were selected to illuminate the dark corners and risks of the project.

THINGS TO TRY NOW

- ❑ Facilitate a discussion between the team and product owner on how much influence technical factors should have on how the product owner prioritizes the product backlog.
- ❑ Before the start of the next sprint planning meeting, identify the top five technical uncertainties on the project and the risk associated with each. See if there are product backlog items that could be moved slightly up in priority that could create the learning necessary to eliminate these uncertainties.

Improving Technical Practices Is Not Optional

The technical practices described in this chapter are ones I would expect to see in use by a top-performing team. Of course, there is room to argue that these practices may not be necessary 100% of the time on your application. All of the practices, though, are ones that members of a good Scrum team should be experienced with. Continuous integration is merely the natural extension of a nightly build, which is a bare minimum for a team to be agile. Skill at refactoring and a mindset of collective ownership can be established over time with any team. Practices such as pair programming and test-driven development lead to higher quality code, which is a goal of every Scrum team.

Used together, these practices result in high-quality, low-defect products. Chapter 1, "Why Becoming Agile Is Hard (But Worth It)," included metrics on the improvements in quality and defect rates agile teams can experience. These improvements are the result of teams deliberately enhancing their technical skills and incorporating better practices.

As a result of these improvements, good Scrum teams are able to shift the balance between anticipation and adaptation further to the side of adaptation. Minimizing, and in some cases eliminating, up-front analysis and design activities saves both time and money. In an aptly titled article, "Design to Accommodate Change," Dave Thomas, founder of Object Technology International, which was responsible for the early Eclipse development, summarizes how achieving this balance helps make change less painful.

> Agile programming is design for change....Its objective is to design programs that are receptive to, indeed expect, change. Ideally, agile programming lets changes be applied in a simple, localized way to avoid or substantially reduce major refactorings, retesting, and system builds. (2005, 14)

Additional Reading

Ambler, Scott W., and Pramod J. Sadalage. 2006. *Refactoring databases: Evolutionary database design*. Addison-Wesley.

    The first five chapters of this book clarify the role of the data professional in the agile organization. The chapters that follow are a compendium of well-thought-out ways to evolve a database design. Each refactoring includes descriptions of why you might make this change, trade-offs to consider before making it, how to update the schema, how to migrate the data, and how applications that access the data will need to change.

Bain, Scott L. 2008. *Emergent design: The evolutionary nature of professional software development*. Addison-Wesley Professional.

    I've been waiting for someone to write the book proving how effective designs can emerge without being entirely thought-through up front. I'd hoped from its title that this would be that book. It isn't, but it is an excellent description of how code should be developed on an agile project. Included are top-notch chapters on many of the technical practices described in this chapter.

Beck, Kent. 2002. *Test-driven development: By example*. Addison-Wesley Professional.

    This slim book will not teach you everything you need to know about test-driven development. (For that, see *Test Driven: TDD and Acceptance TDD for Java Developers* by Lasse Koskela.) Where Beck's book excels is at showing how TDD works and why you might want to try it.

Duvall, Paul, Steve Matyas, and Andrew Glover. 2007. *Continuous integration: Improving software quality and reducing risk*. Addison-Wesley Professional.

    This book covers everything you'll ever need to know about continuous integration. It covers how to get started, incorporate tests, use code analysis tools, and even evaluate continuous integration tools.

Elssamadisy, Amr. 2007. *Patterns of agile practice adoption: The technical cluster*. C4Media.

    This book covers all of the technical practices recommend here (and more) and is an excellent choice if you are looking for one book that covers all of the technical practices in more detail. While full of good advice, the book is written in typical pattern style, where each practice is described in a fixed manner, which I find doesn't hold my attention well after awhile.

Feathers, Michael. 2004. *Working effectively with legacy code*. Prentice Hall PTR.
Introducing new technical practices and committing to technical excellence is challenging enough on a new project; it's even harder on a legacy application. Michael Feathers' excellent book provides practical and immediately useful advice on doing so.

Fowler, Martin. 1999. *Refactoring: Improving the design of existing code*. With contributions by Kent Beck, John Brant, William Opdyke, and Don Roberts. Addison-Wesley Professional.
The bible of refactoring. Today's integrated development environments can do a lot of refactorings for us, but it is still useful to go back to the original source and see the catalog of refactorings presented here. One of my favorite chapters is on "Big Refactorings," which are often the ones that are most challenging.

Koskela, Lasse. 2007. *Test driven: TDD and acceptance TDD for Java developers*. Manning.
This is the most thorough book on test-driven development and is appropriate for those new to TDD and those with lots of experience. Koskela doesn't shy away from the hard topics and presents advice on such often-ignored topics as TDD for multi-threaded code and user interfaces. The book takes a holistic approach to TDD, even including nearly 150 pages on acceptance test–driven development.

Martin, Robert C. 2008. *Clean code: A handbook of agile software craftsmanship*. Prentice Hall.
The title page inside this book features the statement, "There is no reasonable excuse for doing anything less than your best." The book then proceeds to present a compendium of practices for writing clean code. Topics range from the commonplace (meaningful names) to novel (test-driving an architecture and emergence). This is a must-read for all programmers.

Meszaros, Gerard. 2007. *xUnit test patterns: Refactoring test code*. Addison-Wesley.
This encyclopedic book covers everything a programmer might possibly want to know about the popular xUnit family of unit testing tools. The book starts with the basics but quickly moves on to thoroughly cover advanced topics as well.

Wake, William C. 2003. *Refactoring workbook*. Addison-Wesley Professional.
A well-organized and easily accessible introduction to refactoring. The book is full of Java code examples for you to refactor and is a combination of a refactoring primer and exercises to drive home the point. The last third of the book is made up of four programs for you to refactor.

SEE ALSO
Acceptance test–driven development is described in Chapter 16.

PART III

Teams

Most teams aren't teams at all
but merely collections of individual relationships with the boss.
Each individual vying with the others
for power, prestige and position.

—Douglas McGregor

Chapter 10

Team Structure

It is perhaps a myth, but an enduring one, that people and their pets resemble one another. The same has been said of products and the teams that build them.

> The system being produced will tend to have a structure that mirrors the structure of the group that is producing it, whether or not this was intended. One should take advantage of this fact and then deliberately design the group structure so as to achieve the desired system structure. (Conway 1968; commonly referred to as "Conway's Law")

If it is true that a product reflects the structure of the team that built it, then an important decision for any Scrum project is how to organize those individuals into teams. Factoring into this decision are considerations of team size, familiarity with the domain, the channels of communication, the technical design of the system, individual experience levels, the technologies involved, the newness of those technologies, where team members are located, competitive and market pressures, expectations about project schedule, and much more.

In this chapter we look at the importance of two critical factors to be considered when deciding how to structure Scrum teams: keeping teams small and orienting each team around the delivery of end-to-end user-visible functionality. We also look at the importance of having the right people on each team and not overloading those individuals by forcing them to split time among too many teams. We conclude the chapter with nine questions to ask when starting a multi-team project.

Feed Them Two Pizzas

I was working on a project for a bioinformatics company when the CEO asked me to provide her with an estimate of how long the project would take. The application was large, the domain complicated, and the team mostly new. Because the domain was so complicated, our team was made up of some very smart Ph.D. scientists, who knew only a little about programming, and some very smart programmers, most of whom had taken no more than a class or two in biology or genetics. No one on the team was great at both the science and the development.

After a bit of research and work with the team I returned to the CEO with an estimate of something like 100 person-years. In other words, if we used all 40 people on the team, we could finish the project in about two and a half years. I don't think that number was too shocking to her, but it was a big number, so she asked me, "What's the cheapest way we could write it?" My answer: "Take Steve, the scientist with the best understanding and aptitude for programming, and have him go spend 10 years working in a great software company doing nothing but learning how to be a great programmer. Then have him return to our company and spend 30 years working alone to write the program. It'll take 40 years, but it's your cheapest option." She should have been quite pleased with my answer—after all, I'd taken the 100 person-year initial estimate and offered her a way to cut it by more than half. Alas, 40 years was just a bit too long for her to wait.

As this story illustrates, a team offers the advantage of getting things done far more quickly than one person could, but with that advantage comes a potentially large amount of communication overhead. Knowing that, what is the ideal team size for Scrum projects? Generally accepted advice is that the ideal Scrum team size is five to nine individuals. While I agree with this, putting a number to it makes me nervous. If you're thinking about your ten-person team right now you may feel inclined to return this book, demand a refund, and give up on Scrum.

Don't.

Rather than take the five-to-nine person guideline too literally, I prefer how Amazon.com thinks its about its teams. Amazon refers to them as "two-pizza teams," meaning a team that can be fed with two pizzas (Deutschman 2007). As humorous as that is, it's actually useful. If ordering food for the occasional team lunch is a hassle, it could be a good indicator that the team has become too large.

SEE ALSO

Scrum projects scale through the use of teams of teams. For information on large Scrum projects, see Chapter 17, "Scaling Scrum."

The largest single Scrum team that I worked with where I was content to leave them alone was 14 people. The team, its ScrumMaster, and I had all looked at possible ways to split them up, but no solutions we came up with seemed better than leaving them intact. I've also worked with one team of 25 that insisted it should be one team rather than more. They were wrong; there was too much communication overhead on a single team of that size.

Why Two Pizzas Are Enough

To be fair, there are some advantages to large teams. Large teams may include members with more diverse skills, experiences, and approaches. Large teams are not as much at risk to the loss of a key person. They may also provide more opportunities for individuals to specialize in a technology or a subset of the application.

On the other hand, there are even more advantages to small teams. These include the following:

- **There is less social loafing.** Social loafing is the tendency for people to exert less effort when they believe there are others who will pick up the slack. Members of small teams are less prone to social loafing. Social loafing was first demonstrated by psychologist Max Ringelmann in the 1920s when he measured the pressure exerted by individuals and teams pulling on a rope. Groups of three exerted only two-and-a-half times (not three times) the average individual pressure. Groups of eight exhibited less than four times the individual average. Ringelmann's and related studies have shown that individual effort is inversely related to team size (Stangor 2004, 220).

- **Constructive interaction is more likely to occur on a small team.** Stephen Robbins, author of *Essentials of Organizational Behavior*, a best-selling textbook on organizational behavior, has concluded that teams of more than 10 to 12 people have a difficult time establishing feelings of trust, mutual accountability, and cohesiveness. Without these, constructive interaction is difficult (2005).

- **Less time is spent coordinating effort.** Small teams spend less time coordinating the efforts of team members. This is true both in the aggregate and as a percentage of total project time. As a simple example, we all know that the effort just to plan a meeting for a large team can be overwhelming.

- **No one can fade into the background.** With large teams, there is lower participation in group activities and discussions. Similarly, the disparity in the amount of participation among team members increases. The problems can prevent a group of individuals from jelling into a cohesive, high-performing team.

- **Small teams are more satisfying to their members.** With a small team, one person's contributions are more visible and meaningful. This is perhaps one reason why research has shown that participation on a large team is less satisfying to team members (Steiner 1972).

- **Harmful over-specialization is less likely to occur.** On a large project, individuals are more likely to take on distinct roles (Shaw 1960). For example, one developer chooses to work only on the user interface. This creates wasteful hand-offs of work between team members and reduces the amount of learning that occurs when individuals are more willing and likely to work beyond specific job roles.

SEE ALSO

The problems with hand-offs will be considered in Chapter 11, "Teamwork."

One interesting study of team size looked at 109 different teams. The small teams had 4 to 9 members while the large teams had 14 to 18. The researchers reached several conclusions.

Members of smaller teams participated more actively on their team; were more committed to their team; were more aware of the goals of the team; were better acquainted with other team members' personalities, work roles, and communication styles; and reported higher levels of rapport. The data also show that larger teams are more conscientious in preparing meeting agendas compared to smaller teams. (Bradner, Mark, and Hertel 2003, 7)

Hmm. With a small team I can have many compelling advantages. Or I can staff a larger team and get better meeting agendas.

Small Team Productivity

Given the strength of these advantages to small teams, we would expect small teams to be more productive than large teams. Doug Putnam of QSM found exactly that after studying 491 projects with team sizes from 1 to 20 people. Since 1978 QSM has been collecting data on software productivity and estimates. The company maintains the software development industry's most thorough metrics database, including data on application size, effort, industry, and more. As such, the QSM database is uniquely valuable for comparing different types of projects.

From the QSM database of over 7,000 projects, Putnam narrowed the data set to 491 projects completed between 2003–2005 that delivered between 35,000 and 95,000 new or modified lines of source code.[1] Project sizes were evenly distributed from 1 to 20 team members. As shown in Figure 10.1, Putnam found that the smaller the team size, the more productive each team member was. However, the difference between teams sized from 1.5 to 7 people was very small.

FIGURE 10.1

The average productivity per person on teams of various sizes. Printed with permission from QSM, Inc. All rights reserved.

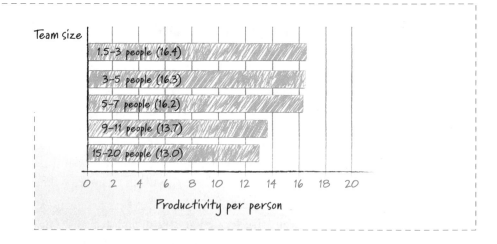

---

1   Lines of code is, of course, a much maligned metric and deservedly so in many cases. However, in a database of this size, I believe it is a reasonable proxy for the size of a project and can therefore be used in productivity calculations.

Putnam looked also at the total development effort that goes into projects. Not surprisingly, he found that smaller teams complete projects with less total effort. Putnam concluded that "larger teams translate into more effort and cost. The trend appears to have an exponential behavior. The most cost-effective strategy is the smallest team; however the extreme nonlinear effort increase doesn't seem to kick in until the team size approaches nine or more people." These results can be seen in Figure 10.2.

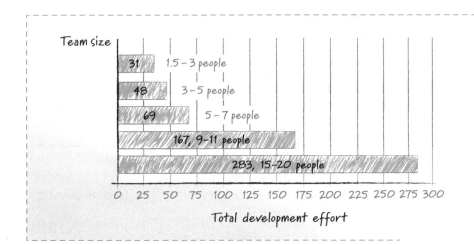

In most cases, however, we are not concerned with minimizing the total development effort; schedule is always a major consideration. After all, we rarely have 40 years to wait for a lone developer to finish what we need by next spring. The impact of team size on overall schedule is shown in Figure 10.3. This figure shows that a 5- to 7-person team will complete an equivalently sized project in the shortest amount of time. Smaller teams took slightly longer. Notice again the dramatic increase with teams of 9 to 11 people.

An additional study described in the *Communications of the ACM* compared the productivity of large and small teams. Long-time industry veteran Phillip Armour writes of this research.

SEE ALSO

There are, of course, projects that cannot be done with a single two-pizza team. Scrum teams scale by having teams of teams rather than one immense team. For more on scaling, see Chapter 17.

> Large teams (twenty-nine people) create around six times as many defects as small teams (three people) and obviously burn through a lot more money. Yet, the large team appears to produce about the same amount of output in only an average of twelve days less time. This is a truly astonishing finding, though it fits with my personal experience on projects over thirty-five years. (2006, 16)

With all of the strong reasons in favor of small teams, I don't think I'll be placing any orders for three pizzas any time soon.

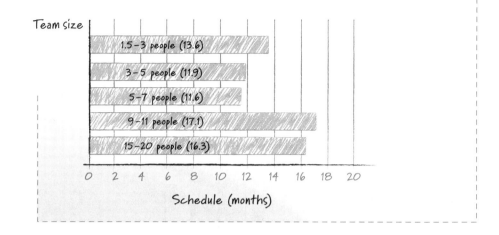

OBJECTION

"There are too many disciplines on my project for us to have small teams. There are analysts, programmers, database developers, client-side programmers, middle-tier programmers, testers, test automation engineers, and more. I can't possibly have a five- to nine-person team."

Although a project may require work in that many disciplines, it almost certainly does not require a dedicated expert in each area. On a nine-person team with each person responsible solely for one discipline, it will be difficult or impossible to balance the workload of each team member. A team structure where some people may work only within one discipline but where others can move between two or more makes it much easier for the team to balance the workload of the different disciplines. Having at least some people work across disciplines also instills a better sense of whole-product responsibility rather than "I just do such-and-such."

THINGS TO TRY NOW

❑ If your team has nine or more people, try splitting into two teams after the current sprint. Work that way for at least two sprints before discussing whether it was better.

❑ For each team with five to nine people, consider splitting into two teams.

Favor Feature Teams

When I first began to consult for a certain California–based game studio, its teams were organized around the specific elements and objects that would exist in the video game it was developing. There was a separate team for each character. There were weapons teams, a vehicle team, and so on. This led to problems, such as weapons too weak to kill the monsters, colors too dark to show secret passages, and obstacles that frustrated even the most patient player.

On more traditional, corporate projects, we see equivalent problems when teams organize around the layers of an application. For example, a typical early-stage mistake for the project whose architecture is shown in Figure 10.4 would be to have four teams: a rich client team, a web client team, a middle-tier team, and a database team. Creating *component teams* such as these leads to a variety of problems including

- Reduced communication across the layers
- A feeling that design by contract is sufficient
- Ending sprints without a potentially shippable product increment

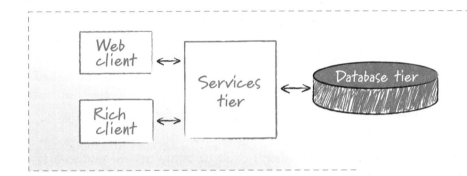

FIGURE 10.4

A typical three-tier architecture.

If structuring teams around the layers of an architecture is the wrong approach, what's better? Rather than organizing around components, each team on a project can ideally be responsible for end-to-end delivery of working (tested) features. A feature team working on the application shown in Figure 10.4 would, for example, work across all layers of the architecture. It might develop one feature that involves the database layer, the services tier, and the rich client user interface. In the same or next sprint, it would develop a feature going across the web client, services tier, and database tier.

There are many advantages to organizing multiteam projects into feature teams:

SEE ALSO

The importance of delivering end-to-end functionality is discussed further in Chapter 14, "Sprints."

- **Feature teams are better able to evaluate the impact of design decisions.** At the end of a sprint, a feature team will have built end-to-end functionality, traversing all levels of the technology stack of the application. This maximizes members' learning about the product design decisions they made (Do users like the functionality as developed?) and about technical design decisions (How well did this implementation approach work for us?).

SEE ALSO

More problems with hand-offs are described in Chapter 11.

- **Feature teams reduce waste created by hand-offs.** Handing work from one group or individual to another is wasteful. In the case of a component team, there is the risk that too much or too little functionality will have been developed, that the wrong functionality has been developed, that some of the functionality is no longer needed, and so on.

- **It ensures that the right people are talking.** Because a feature team includes all skills needed to go from idea to running, tested feature, it ensures that the individuals with those skills communicate at least daily.

- **Component teams create risk to the schedule.** The work of a component team is valuable only after it has been integrated into the product by a feature team. The effort to integrate the component team's work must be estimated by the feature team, whether it will occur in the same sprint during which it is developed (as is best) or in a later sprint. Estimating this type of effort is difficult because it requires the feature team to estimate the integration work without knowing the quality of the component.

- **It keeps the focus on delivering features.** It can be tempting for a team to fall back into its pre–Scrum habits. Organizing teams around the delivery of features, rather than around architectural elements or technologies, serves as a constant reminder of Scrum's focus on delivering features in each sprint.

OBJECTION

"My application is too complex; I can't possibly deliver end-to-end functionality in one sprint."

Learning how to identify small pieces of functionality is one of the first big hurdles for a new Scrum team. I remember my first Scrum project: Initially there were times we struggled to find anything we could deliver in less than six weeks. Looking back on that system many years later, I now see many ways we could have split that work. In fact, I see enough ways to split the work now that we could have done one-day sprints if we had wanted to.

As they gain experience, team members will find many more ways to split features while still delivering end-to-end functionality within each sprint. When doing so looks impossible, it is usually because teams are not structured appropriately. Before giving up, reconsider the individuals and skills on the team.

Use Component Teams Sparingly

Although you should strongly favor the use of feature teams, there will be occasions when creating a component team is appropriate. A component team, as I'm using the term here, is a team that develops software to be delivered to another team on the project rather than directly to users. Examples of component teams include a team developing an object-relational mapping layer between the application and the database or a reusable user interface widget team.

It is important that a component team still produce high-quality, tested, potentially shippable code by the end of each sprint. However, the new capabilities created by a component team are usually meaningless on their own. Think back for a moment to the examples I just gave. The object-relational mapping layer developed by one of the component teams is of interest to end users only through the context in which it is used by feature teams. But what about the team developing the reusable user interface widgets such as custom drop-down lists, data entry grids, and so on? These are certainly of interest to end users, right? Yes, but again only within the context of other features. An end user is not interested in a new data entry grid until it is embedded onto a page or screen.

Build Components Only As Feature Teams Ask for Them

Because the work of a component team is delivered to another team, it is those teams who usually act as the product owner for the component team. If your team needs deliverables from my team, then you will act as the product owner to my team. As such you will have all the responsibilities of a good product owner. At the start of a sprint, you will need to help prioritize what I work on. At the end of the sprint you will accept or reject it, providing feedback to me on what has been produced.

It will be hard for you to prioritize my work and provide feedback on it if my team is working far in advance of yours. Because of this, a component team should not develop new capabilities until one or more feature teams is ready for them. When a component team works far in advance of what feature teams need, it resorts to guessing at what capabilities are needed next. All too often this results in components or frameworks that are not usable by the feature teams. All new capabilities, including those built by component teams, should be developed within the context of externally visible functionality.

Rob was the senior developer on a component team developing an object-relational mapping layer that would be used by many of the 15 feature teams on the project. Rob's team was initially tasked with choosing between developing this technology in-house or using a commercial or open-source product. Members made the questionable decision to build it themselves. Anxious to prove the correctness of this decision, Rob and team tried aggressively to get ahead of the needs of the feature teams. Rather than working closely with one or more feature teams, Rob's component team made some big guesses about the grand design. For two months (two sprints) members didn't deliver anything to the feature teams. After the third month, when they finally delivered an initial version, it did not meet the needs or expectations of the feature teams.

What Rob's team should have done instead was work very closely with the feature teams and add new capabilities in the context of the features being delivered by the feature teams. This would have forced a much closer collaboration between the component team and the feature team, increasing the chances of delivering what was needed. Rob's team could have, for example, delivered only the ability to write fixed-length text data to the database in the first sprint. Feature teams who received that capability would not have been able to write numeric data, dates, and so on to the database. And they would not have been able to *read* any data. But, the feature teams could have done one thing—write fixed-length text data—and from that could have provided feedback to Rob and his team on the usability of the component.

Perhaps the best way to ensure that a component team hears the feedback it will need to create useful functionality is to staff the component team temporarily with people from the feature teams. A developer assigned to a component team who knows he will soon be moving back to a feature team will be more likely to make sure the work of the component team will be usable.

Deciding When a Component Team Is Appropriate

Whenever possible, form feature teams rather than component teams. I like to start out with the assumption that all teams on a multiteam project will be feature teams. I'm willing to back away from that assumption, but I only want to do so in the face of evidence that forming one or more component teams will be in the best interest of the product. I suggest considering a component team only when most of the following statements are true:

SEE ALSO

For more on the evils of multitasking, see "Put People on One Project," later in this chapter.

- **The component team will build something that will be used by multiple feature teams.** If a component will be used by only one feature team, have that feature team build it. This ensures that the new capability is built within the context of that team's needs and expectations, which makes the implementation more likely to be used. Even when a component team will build something useful to multiple teams, a better strategy is often to have one feature team build the functionality it needs and then have subsequent teams refactor and generalize the functionality as their needs arise.

- **Using a component team will reduce the sharing of specialists.** On some multiteam projects, some highly specialized disciplines are shared across many teams. Although some sharing of specialists is usually necessary, too much of it can be detrimental as the specialist's time becomes too fragmented. You may want to consider creating a component team if doing so will make more manageable the extent to which specialists are shared across many teams.

- **The risk of multiple approaches outweighs the disadvantages of a component team.** If we choose to build a shared component or service by having multiple feature teams contribute to the effort, there are two related risks to be aware of. First is the risk that each feature team implements a different solution to the same problem. Second is the risk that the feature teams each build on top of what prior feature teams have done but do so without a cohesive vision. These risks could be great or small, depending on what shared functionality is being built. When the risk of multiple approaches is high, a component team is a valid option.

- **It will get people talking who might not talk otherwise.** People tend to talk more with those on their team than those outside their team. This is true even on a Scrum project. In fact, it may be especially true on a Scrum project because team members on Scrum projects come to identify so strongly with their teams. You can use this to your advantage by creating teams from people who need to work together but who might not naturally talk to each other. If past experience shows that a project's artificial intelligence programmers do not talk often enough, this can help justify the short-term use of a component team, as long as there are other reasons for doing so.

- **You can see an end to the need for the component team.** A component team should not linger around forever, like my in-laws after the holidays. The team should develop the functionality it has been pulled together to create and then disband as soon as possible. When first forming a component team, it is not necessary to know when it will disband; however, you should have some idea of either how long it will exist or what will be delivered by the time the team has fulfilled its purpose. Because a component team is a deviation from the ideal of having all feature teams, you should be reluctant to create a component team that looks as though it might exist forever.

While acknowledging the occasional benefits of using a component team, I want to stress again that the vast majority of teams on a large project should be feature teams. Wes Williams and Mike Stout have described what happened at Sabre Airline Solutions when beginning with component teams.

> Stories weren't complete from a user perspective. Teams were working on different features at different times with different acceptance criteria. There was a lot of rework coming back into the system. Teams were blaming each other for incomplete functionality, failing builds, tests, etc. In hindsight…the teams

should have been structured along functional or feature lines. (2008, 359)

Who Makes These Decisions?

Ideally, the team makes decisions about how it is structured. If the team is to be trusted with solving the problem of how to build the product, it seems appropriate to trust it with the decision about how to structure itself to do so. However, though team members are accustomed to making technical decisions, they usually do not have a lot of experience making team organization decisions. So, initially the team may not be in the best position to design its own structure.

I've introduced Scrum to hundreds of teams. One of the things I've noticed is how frequently someone's initial exposure to Scrum results in an opinion like, "Scrum sounds wonderful for our company, and it will be great for all the other groups but not mine." Architects add, "After we do the up-front architecture, I can really see how this will help the programmers and testers." User experience designers say, "After we've done the up-front usability research, I can really see how this will work for the architects, programmers, and testers." Testers take the initial view, "It will be wonderful to have everyone working so closely together and then handing off to us for a big round of integration testing."

If we ask team members with these common initial mindsets to design the structure of their multiteam project, it shouldn't surprise us when they come back with plans for an architecture team, a programming team, a user experience team, and a test team. Of course I'm generalizing, but the tendency to think this way is so prevalent that it will be tempting to organize that way as well.

Initially, then, it is likely that functional managers, project managers, Scrum-Masters, or those driving the transition to Scrum will make the decisions about how to organize the teams. These decision makers should solicit nonbinding input from their teams, especially from team members with past experience with Scrum or other agile methodologies.

What's Right Today May Be Wrong Tomorrow

An important thing to remember when selecting an appropriate team structure is that no team structure is forever. If the current team structure is impeding a team's or project's ability to use Scrum, that issue should be raised during an end-of-sprint retrospective. You don't want to continually change team structures, as team members need time to jell, but if the current structure is clearly wrong, change it.

As team members gain more experience with Scrum, it will be appropriate for them to become more involved in team structure decisions, including which teams are needed, whether each is a feature or component team, and who should be on each team.

❑ Make a list of all teams on your current project. Identify whether each is a feature team or a component team. For each component team, consider the statements in the section, "Deciding When a Component Team Is Appropriate." Consider restructuring the team if not all statements were true.

Self-Organizing Doesn't Mean Randomly Assembled

The ability for a team to self-organize around the goals it has been given is fundamental to all agile methodologies, including Scrum. In fact, the Agile Manifesto includes self-organizing teams as a key principle, saying that "the best architectures, requirements, and designs emerge from self-organizing teams" (Beck et al. 2007). As part of deciding how best to achieve the goal given them, some teams will decide that all key technical decisions will be made by one person on the team. Other teams will decide to split the responsibility for technical decisions along technical boundaries: Our database expert makes database decisions, and our most experienced C# programmer makes C# decisions. Still other teams may decide that whoever is working on the feature makes the decision but has the responsibility of sharing the results of the decision with the team.

There are two key points here: First, not every team will choose to organize themselves the same way, and that's OK. Second, making use of the collective wisdom of the team will generally lead to a better way of organizing around the work than will relying solely on the wisdom of one personnel manager. However, the benefit of allowing a team to self-organize isn't that the team finds some optimal organization for its work that a manager may have missed. Rather, it is that by allowing the team to self-organize, it is encouraged to fully own the problem.

A common criticism of self-organizing teams is, "We cannot just put eight random individuals together, tell them to self-organize, and expect anything good to result." Well, I don't know if that's true, but when we are putting together a two-pizza Scrum team, we are definitely not doing so with eight randomly selected individuals. In fact, those in the organization responsible for initiating a Scrum project should expend a lot of effort in selecting the individuals who will comprise the team.

In the original paper describing Scrum, Takeuchi and Nonaka identified "subtle control" as one of its six principles. They list staffing decisions as a key management responsibility.

> Selecting the right people for the project team while monitoring shifts in group dynamics and adding or dropping members when necessary [is a key management responsibility]. "We would add an older and more conservative member to the team should the balance shift too much toward radicalism," said a Honda

SEE ALSO

Chapter 12, "Leading a Self-Organizing Team," describes how leaders exert subtle, positive influence.

executive. "We carefully pick the project members after long deliberation. We analyze the different personalities to see if they would get along." (1986, 144)

Getting the Right People on the Team

If you are a personnel manager or otherwise influence team composition in your organization, some of the factors to consider are the following:

- **Include all needed disciplines.** As a cross-functional team, it is important that all skills necessary to go from idea to implemented feature be represented on the team. Initially this may mean that team size is slightly larger than desired. But, over time, individuals on a Scrum team will learn some of the skills possessed by their coworkers. This is a natural result of being on a Scrum team. As some team members develop broader skills, other individuals can be moved onto other teams.

- **Balance technical skill levels.** Subject to considerations of team size, you should strive to balance skill levels on the team. If a team has three senior programmers and no less-experienced programmers, the senior programmers will need to code some low-criticality features that they could find boring. Not only might a junior programmer have found such features enjoyable to work on, that programmer would also benefit from learning through association with the senior programmers.

- **Balance domain knowledge.** Just as we strive to balance technical skills, we should strive for a balance between those with deep knowledge of the domain in which we are working or the problem we are attempting to solve. This is not to say that if we have the opportunity to assemble a team entirely of domain experts we shouldn't take it. Rather, we should consider the long-term goals of our organization. One of those goals is likely the build up of domain knowledge throughout the organization. You'll have a hard time achieving that if you put all of the domain experts on one team.

- **Seek diversity.** Diversity can mean many different things—gender, race, and culture being just three among them. Perhaps equally important can be how individuals think about problems, how they make decisions, how much information they need before making a decision, and so on. Homogeneous teams reach consensus more quickly than do heterogeneous teams, but they do so by failing to consider all options (Mello and Ruckes 2006).

- **Consider persistence.** It takes time for team members to learn to work well together. Strive, therefore, to keep team members together who have worked well together in the past. When forming a new team, consider how long members will be able to work together before some or all are dispersed to other commitments.

> **"We can't self-organize because we have a dominating former technical lead who makes all decisions before we even have a chance to discuss the issue."**

If possible, take the dominating personality aside and inform her of the issue. Let her know that even in situations where she may know the "right" thing to do, she should sometimes refrain from voicing her opinion before others have a chance to express their thoughts. Ask her if she thinks the team would make the right decision if she were to present her thoughts as an opinion rather than as an unchallengeable decision. Enlist her assistance as a mentor to the others—her job should be not just making sure the right decisions are made but that team members grow such that they will make the right decisions on their next projects, where she may not be there for them.

> **"My team won't self-organize; team members are too passive and look to me to lead."**

If they look to you, look back right at them. If you are the team's Scrum-Master, make sure they know that your job is to support them, not to make decisions for them. If you are a team member, you do not need to subjugate your opinions and keep quiet all the time. However, you should look for ways to engage others by not making the decision in all cases. For example, try asking questions of others before giving your opinion.

> **"The team is too junior; members don't have enough experience to self-organize."**

If they have enough experience to build a software product, they probably have enough experience to figure out how to organize themselves. If not, provide them with training or coaching. Often, this objection really masks the objection of, "I don't trust the team to self-organize in the way I want them to." Too bad. Exert subtle control over the team in who you put together to form the team and the goal you give that team, not in how it does its day-to-day work.

Put People on One Project

Individuals assigned to work on multiple projects inevitably get less done. Multitasking—attempting to work on two projects or two things at once—is one of the biggest drains on project team performance. Yet it has unfortunately become one of the busy manager's most frequently used tools. The reason for this, I believe, is that multitasking creates the illusion of progress and gives the manager the feeling that a problem has been solved. Really, though, in many cases the problem has been made worse.

Consider the case of Jon, a director of database engineering who managed a staff of database administrators (DBAs) who were woefully outnumbered by the programmers, testers, and other types of developers in his company. Jon was faced with allocating himself and his staff of five across more projects than they could handle. His solution was to create a spreadsheet like the one shown in Figure 10.5. Jon's spreadsheet allowed him to allocate DBAs across the various projects, which he did down to the 5% level. Five percent of an 8-hour day is 24 minutes. Through this spreadsheet Jon was telling Bill he could spend 24 minutes each on the Napa and PMT projects, Ahmed could spend the same on PMT and Spinwheel, and so on.

FIGURE 10.5

A portion of Jon's project staffing spreadsheet.

	Napa	Connect	SpongeBob	Dodge City	DB2 Mitigation	Enigma	PMT	Spin Wheel
Bill	5%		15%	50%		25%	5%	
Ahmed		90%					5%	5%
Siv	25%			25%	25%	25%		
Tor	25%		50%		10%		15%	
Robert		20%					5%	75%
Jon	5%	10%	10%	10%		5%	10%	

Did Jon really think that Bill would stop working on the Napa project after 24 minutes each day? Of course not. But he probably did think that Bill had enough control over his schedule that he could be close to $24 \times 5 = 120$ minutes in a week. What Jon was really doing in this situation was taking a problem (the correct allocation of resources) that he couldn't solve and pushing it down to the members of his team. What Jon should have done instead was push this problem up to his own manager.

Pushing problems toward the team is often a wonderful strategy. In fact, delegating problems to the team is at the heart of Scrum. However, when a problem is pushed toward the team, the team needs to be given the authority to solve the problem. In the case of Jon and his DBAs, it was obvious that one solution to consider was doing fewer concurrent projects. Without being empowered to enact that solution, they were put into an impossible-to-solve situation.

And they didn't solve it any better than Jon did. They invoked the age-old policy of "work on the project of whoever is screaming the loudest."

Time on Task Decreases with Too Many Tasks

Kim Clark and Steven Wheelwright studied the impact of multitasking on productivity. Their findings, shown in Figure 10.6, indicate that the total amount of time on task goes up when a person has two tasks to work on. After that, however, Clark and Wheelwright found that time on task decreased. In fact, with three tasks the amount of time on task decreased so much it was less than when an individual had only one task to work on (1992, 242).

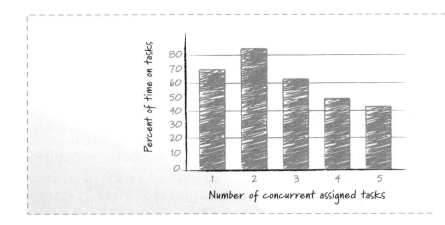

FIGURE 10.6

The amount of time spent on value-adding tasks decreases with three or more concurrent tasks.

If you have only one task to work on it is almost a certainty that you will occasionally be unable to work on that task. You will become blocked by waiting for someone to return a phone call, answer an e-mail, approve the design, or so on. And so it makes sense that the Clark and Wheelwright study shows that a person with two tasks to work on spent more time on task than did someone with only one task. However, consider that Clark and Wheelwright did this research in the early 1990s.

What's changed since then? For starters how about e-mail, instant messaging, the proliferation of mobile telephones, and any number of ways in which we communicate? My theory is that the bars in Figure 10.6 need to be shifted one space to the left to reflect today's faster pace. I remember clearly the job I had back in 1992 when Clark and Wheelwright published their results. I remember times back then when I was at my desk and thought, "I'm caught up; I have nothing to do right now." Of course, I haven't thought that since 1992.

The pace of the world has accelerated dramatically. Just being a good corporate citizen takes more time now than it did in 1992. There's more to read, more to process, and more for each person to do. Merely being an employee should count today as a first task for each of us. The first project we are on counts as a second, and we are then already optimally productive. Any further projects we are assigned just make us less productive.

One of the main reasons that multitasking is so horrible is the task-switching cost involved. There is tremendous overhead in getting started on one task, switching to another, and then switching back to the first. The more tasks or projects we are involved in, the more likely we are to be interrupted while working on them. One study of members of a software development team found that team members are interrupted every 11 minutes (Gonzales and Mark 2004). If you're reading this chapter at the office, it is likely that you were interrupted at least once while reading.

THINGS TO TRY NOW

❏   If you are a manager, make a list of your direct reports and the projects each is on. If anyone is on more than two projects, immediately find a way to change that. If you've already achieved this, see if you can reduce someone's allocation from two projects to one. Assess the situation after two sprints.

When Multitasking Is OK

All of this is not to say that we should never allow multitasking on our projects. It is sometimes helpful. The key is to remember that a person who is multitasking and shared across multiple projects is likely to get less total work done than if she had been dedicated fully to just one of those projects.

Let's again consider Jon and his DBAs. Suppose each DBA could complete "20 database tasks" per day assuming that all database tasks are the same size. A DBA fortunate enough to work on only 1 project would achieve this level of performance. However, a DBA on 2 projects might complete only 16 database tasks per day. And a DBA on 3 projects might complete only 14 database tasks per day.

Although these reduced levels of productivity may look quite bad, they may not be. Suppose 1 of our DBAs is assigned to 2 projects and is to split her time equally between them. She will be able to complete 8 database tasks on each project. This may be the optimal use of her time if neither of the projects needs 20 database tasks done in a day. If neither project needs more than 8 database tasks a day from her, then she is better split between both projects than dedicated entirely to 1. From this we can extract the following guidelines:

- In general, and for the majority of a project's team members, multitasking is to be avoided.
- Multitasking may be acceptable if a person cannot be fully or nearly fully utilized on a single project. If we look back to Figure 10.5 and Jon's DBAs, we see that the Connect project was allocated three people

with a total allocation greater than 100%. A better solution would likely have been to allocate a single person but for 100% of his time.

- Rather than have everyone multitask a little, it is better to have a few people multitask a lot. Figure 10.6 illustrates how the largest drop in time on task occurs after a person takes on the first task too many. In Jon's case, a better solution would have been to do anything possible to have two or three of his DBAs not have to multitask, even if that meant the others had to multitask even more.

The Corporate Form of Multitasking

Individuals feel compelled to multitask because the organizations in which we work attempt to multitask as well. The corporate form of multitasking is pursuing too many concurrent projects. When an organization takes on too many projects, people become shared across multiple projects, which leads to individual multitasking. The detrimental effect of multitasking then causes those projects to take longer, which leads to more multitasking near the end of the project when "we need to get started" on the next project.

An eight-year study of projects at a dozen companies and published in *Harvard Business Review* concluded that "projects get done faster if the organization takes on fewer at a time" (Adler et al. 1996). Corporate multitasking—attempting to make progress on too many concurrent projects—is what created the situation that Jon found himself in earlier in this chapter when he resorted to allocating his people to the 5% level.

Mary and Tom Poppendieck urge organizations to limit work to capacity. An organization that has more projects running concurrently than can be adequately staffed is attempting to work beyond its capacity. As they write, "If you expect teams to meet aggressive deadlines, *you must limit work to capacity* (2006, 134, emphasis is theirs).

Stopping the Treadmill

One of the happiest days of my life as a consultant was when I explained the impact of personal and corporate multitasking to the general manager of a large division of a big company. I could tell the message resonated with her. She asked me to follow her as she rose from her desk. We walked to a conference room near her office. She pointed toward a huge number of sticky notes stuck to the widest wall in the conference room and said, "We just made our plan for next year. There it is. Do you think we're doing too much?"

Her division had well over 100 developers but the wall was full. We talked about the plan, the number of concurrent projects, and the ripple effect that would occur if one project was substantially late. She knew they were planning to do too much, and I confirmed this for her. She convened a meeting for the next day of the vice presidents and directors who had made the plan and instructed them to start taking projects off the board. A look of relief (and surprise) went across the faces of everyone present. They had each known that the plan they had created the week before was overly ambitious and would not happen. However, no one had been willing to say so.

I checked back with this general manager a year later and was delighted—but not surprised—to hear that her division had just completed its most successful year ever. Part of that was attributable to the adoption of Scrum and the improvements it brought across her department. But an equal part of the success was attributable to the focus that was brought to each project by having fewer projects in progress at one time.

As this anecdote shows, often the best way to stop multitasking is to stop cold turkey. However, the reason I was so impressed with this general manager is that she is one of the few I have seen with the courage to do that. If you can't stop immediately, or if you're not in a position within the organization to make such a far-reaching decision, there are other things you may want to try.

Don't start a new project until it can be fully staffed. Avoid the temptation to start a new project with just a few analysts and maybe one programmer. Try to get everyone to agree that new projects will be started only when they can be staffed with all disciplines represented. This isn't to say you need to wait to start a large project until all 50 developers are available. Starting a new project only when at least one full team can be fully and appropriately staffed will help adjust the rate at which new projects are started to closer to the rate at which they can be developed.

Include ramp-up and wind-down time in enterprise plans. If, like the general manager in this section's story, you put together a big, annual plan, be sure to include the time necessary to start and stop the various projects. All too often a team provides an estimate of six months, and six months are reserved on an enterprise calendar. However, even on a Scrum project (especially from a new Scrum team), there may be a month or two of wind-down. During this time at least a subset of the team may be needed for high-priority bug fixes or to implement great, new ideas that were discovered only upon release. Failing to plan for some of this will cause unexpected periods of overlapping projects.

Institute simple rules. Gaining agreement on simple rules can help lead to the right organizational behavior. A simple rule such as "No one can be assigned to more than two projects" can work wonders. Johannes Brodwall, chief scientist with Steria in Norway, suggests one simple rule.

Everyone on the team must be at least 60% allocated to the team. Sixty percent seems to be a magical number, which says to people, "This is the most important thing." With 60%, when one task suffers, it is usually one of those 10% or 20% tasks. So this structure guides people to be more dedicated to their primary team.

Go slow but go. I can totally respect the leap of faith required to believe that doing fewer concurrent projects will lead to more projects being completed. Even if they believe that completing projects more quickly will ultimately lead to increased productivity, people will be uncomfortable postponing or canceling large-scale projects. So, start small: Remove one project from the first quarter plan and see how it goes.

Guidelines for Good Team Structure

This section presents a set of guidelines to consider in designing an appropriate team structure. Each guideline is presented in the form of a question to be asked of a current or proposed team. The questions are intended to be asked iteratively. Ask each question of a current or proposed team, changing the structure as appropriate based on the answer. As the structure changes, reask the questions until you can answer "yes" to each.

Does the structure accentuate the strengths, shore up the weaknesses, and support the motivations of the team members? People don't enjoy being on a team where they are not able to make use of their strengths or are constantly required to do things they are bad at. Good team members are willing to do whatever is necessary for the success of the project, but that doesn't relieve us from the goal of trying to find a team structure that accentuates the strengths of as many team members as possible.

Does the structure minimize the number of people required to be on two teams (and avoid having anyone on three)? A well-conceived team structure for an organization that is not attempting to do too many concurrent projects will reduce multitasking to a tolerable level. If the organization is not attempting too many concurrent projects, yet more than 10–20% of all team members belong to more than one team, consider an alternative team design or deferring some projects.

Does the structure maximize the amount of time that teams will remain together? If other factors are equal, you should favor a design that allows team membership to persist over a longer period. It takes time for individuals to learn to work well together. Amortize the cost of that learning over a longer period by trying to leave teams together as long as possible, ideally even finding a team structure that can outlast the current project.

Are component teams used only in limited and easily justifiable cases? Most teams should be created around the end-to-end delivery of working features. In some cases, it is acceptable to have a component team developing reusable user interface components, providing access to a database, or similar functionality. But these should be exceptions.

Will you be able to feed most teams with two pizzas? Given the compelling productivity and quality advantages of small teams, the majority of teams in a good design should have five to nine members.

Does the structure minimize the number of communication paths between teams? A poor team structure design will result in a seemingly infinite number of communication paths between teams. Teams will find themselves unable to complete any work without coordinating first with too many other teams. Some interteam coordination will always be required. But, if a team that wants to add a new field on a form is required to coordinate that effort with three other teams, as I've seen, then the communication overhead is too high.

Does the structure encourage teams to communicate who wouldn't otherwise do so? Some teams will just naturally communicate with each other. An effective team design encourages communication among teams or individuals who should communicate but may not do so on their own accord. In fact, one valid reason to put someone on two teams is that doing so will increase the communication between those teams. If lack of communication between two teams is a concern, splitting a person's time between those two teams is easily justified.

Does the design support a clear understanding of accountability? A well-designed team structure will reinforce the concept of a shared, all-teams accountability for the overall success of the project while providing each team with clear indicators of its unique accountabilities.

Did team members have input into the design of the team? During the early stages of your transition to Scrum, this may not be possible. Individuals may not yet have enough experience delivering working, tested, ready-to-use products by the end of each sprint. Similarly, some individuals may be initially too resistant to Scrum to contribute to team structure discussions in constructive ways. In these cases, it is acceptable for managers outside the team to design an initial team structure.

While doing so, however, they should remember that this is a responsibility that will eventually need to be turned over to the team as a whole.

Onward

In this chapter we've looked at why Scrum teams should be kept small and used the analogy of being able to feed each team with two pizzas. To further enhance a team's ability to rapidly, correctly, and efficiently develop software products, we also considered whether teams should be structured around features or components. We concluded that in structuring multiple teams, we should seek to favor feature teams and try to avoid the use of component teams, while acknowledging they will occasionally be appropriate.

Next we dispensed with the myth that a self-organizing team is a random collection of individuals. As with any team, team members should be chosen with effort and care. We also looked in detail at the need to structure teams in such a way as to minimize the need for individuals to belong to two or more teams. Finally, we concluded with nine guidelines for structuring teams.

In the next chapter we turn our attention to the subject of teamwork. We look specifically at what the members of a single, two-pizza team can do to work well together during a sprint.

Additional Reading

DeMarco, Tom, and Timothy Lister. 1999. *Peopleware: Productive projects and teams*. 2nd ed. Dorset House.

> It is impossible to say enough good things about this book. I remember the day in 1989 when my CEO told me, "After reading *Peopleware* this weekend, I am going to completely change our development group." She did, and the group excelled because of it. This book is full of advice on helping teams achieve their fullest potential.

Goldberg, Adele, and Kenneth S. Rubin. 1995. *Succeeding with objects: Decision frameworks for project management*. Addison-Wesley Professional.

> This book precedes the agile movement but still contains some of the best advice on various team structures. Two chapters include a summary of various team structure options, how to choose among them, and case studies of how six teams chose to organize.

Hackman, J. Richard. 2002. *Leading Teams: Setting the stage for great performances*. Harvard Business School Press.

> The premise of this book is that a leader's job is to design and support teams that can manage themselves. It includes an excellent chapter ("Enabling Structure") on how to structure teams.

Chapter **11**

Teamwork

Teamwork is at the heart of every agile process. The Agile Manifesto proclaims that we are to favor "individuals and interactions over process and tools" (Beck et al. 2001), meaning great software comes from great teams. Scrum itself derives its name from the view that a product development team should behave much like a rugby team—a group of individuals moving the ball down field as a unit. Considering the central importance of teams to successful agile development, it should be no surprise to encounter a chapter called "Teamwork."

Scrum teams succeed together and fail together. There is no "my work" and "your work" on a Scrum team; there is only "our work." This is a radically different way of working for most people, especially those used to working in specialty silos or those who have developed a habit of doing only what they're asked to do. Teams that break free of this mind-set rightly feel a sense of satisfaction and accomplishment. Too many teams, however, stop improving at the point where they begin functioning as a unit, missing out on many of the advantages Scrum can bring. To become a truly high-performing Scrum team requires a concerted effort toward continuous learning and improvement.

In the following sections, we explore whole-team responsibility, collaboration, and the role of specialists on a Scrum team. We also look at how Scrum teams can work effectively during a sprint by doing a little bit of everything all the time. The chapter concludes with advice on how to go beyond a basic level of functionality by fostering team learning, eliminating sources of knowledge waste, and eliciting a commitment from the team to continuous improvement.

Embrace Whole-Team Resposibility

One of the first steps to becoming a functional Scrum team is to come to terms with whole-team responsibility. When I teach, my favorite questions are the ones starting with "Who is responsible for…." It doesn't matter how someone ends that question, my answer is always the same: the team.

Not wanting to fully evade such questions, I will expand further. Suppose the question was, "Who is responsible for the product backlog?" I will answer that although the whole team is responsible, it is the product owner I'll go talk to about making it happen. The whole team should feel responsible for all aspects of the product. Quality is a whole-team responsibility. Clean code is a whole-team responsibility. Having a well-formed product backlog is a whole-team responsibility. And so on.

As Jon Katzenbach and Douglas Smith, authors of the best-selling *The Wisdom of Teams*, wrote, "No group ever becomes a team until it can hold itself accountable as a team" (1993, 60). Yes, there will be specific individuals who should feel additional responsibility for some of these items. But that doesn't relieve the team from sharing full-team responsibility for the overall product and all aspects of its development.

Although having clean, well-written code may seem to be something only the programmers can do anything about, that isn't the case. Suppose a tester notices that a handful of bugs appear, are fixed, and then reappear in one part of the application. This may be evidence to the tester that this particular code has become difficult to maintain. Exactly what the tester does with this information is up to the tester and the culture of the team. The tester may, for example, share the concern with a programmer who has worked in that area, with the whole team during a daily scrum or retrospective, or with the product owner. Which approach the tester selects is unimportant. That the tester takes action out of a sense of responsibility for having well-written code is what matters.

Lisa Crispin, long-time agile tester and coauthor with Janet Gregory of *Agile Testing*, recalls how she first learned that on an agile team she was not solely responsible for quality.

> My title at my last job prior to joining my first agile team was "Quality Boss." I thought I was in charge of quality. I had a lot of input to release decisions, and in fact, I had the keys: I was the only one who could release. Our first iteration on my new XP team, the server crashed if two people logged on to the app at the same time. I was appalled and deemed it unacceptable. Our coach had to have a talk with me and explain that I wasn't in charge of quality. In fact, our customer was in charge. The customer worked for a start-up company and wanted bells and whistles that could be shown to their potential customers. They had no need for two users being logged in at the same time—that wasn't what they were prioritizing—so the programmers hadn't written code to support it. This was a huge mind-set change to me.

"If everyone is responsible then no one is responsible. For everything that needs to be done there needs to be one throat to choke."

From a manager's perspective it can be nice to always be able to point to one person and say, "That's who I'll blame if things go wrong." But the "one throat to choke" argument is false. Historically, there may be one person who takes the blame for things when they go wrong, but that doesn't mean that person was responsible for the failure. Take the case of a sports team. At the start of a new season, who on a sports team do we say we'll hold responsible for winning the championship? The coach? The owner? The star player? Teams that win championships find a way to win games, no matter the circumstances. If the game plan isn't working, the coach and players adapt. If the star player is having a bad day, someone else steps up. The whole team feels responsible for winning somehow, some way. If the team loses, it may be tempting to blame one person or another, but the team members know that each one of them is accountable for the loss. It's never just one person's fault. In reality, there is no single, wringable neck.

Consider a nonsports analogy. If both parents were involved in raising a child (and assuming one of them isn't abusive or obviously negligent), which parent is the one throat to choke if a child grows up to be a convicted felon? There is a reason we call it a parental unit. Raising a child is a team effort.

The only way to ever create an environment of shared ownership and responsibility is to let go of the notion of having one throat to choke. That doesn't mean no one is responsible. That means that on a successful team, the team members must do their part, or even go beyond a perceived role, to ensure that the team reaches its goals.

"But my annual review is based on what I do, not what my team does."

Indeed it probably is and, if not altered, that will work against your organization's successful long-term adoption of Scrum. We do not need to completely abandon individual assessments, but periodic performance reviews should include a significant component measuring achievement of team goals. This topic is discussed in more detail in Chapter 20, "Human Resources, Facilities, and the PMO."

Nurture Whole-Team Commitment

SEE ALSO

As a result of the shift to whole-team responsibility, individuals will often be called on to perform work outside their specialties. Changes in the day-to-day work of various individuals are described in Chapter 8, "Changed Roles."

Along with shared responsibility must come a shared commitment to achieving the goals the team accepts. One of the worst things I've ever heard at the end of a sprint was a programmer who said, "But I finished my tasks," when the product owner complained that sprint backlog items were left incomplete. This programmer may indeed have finished his tasks, but his tasks were only one part of the work his team had committed to finish and only a small portion of the work required to move the product forward.

During sprint planning, the team plans the work of the coming sprint. Although I do not recommend that this planning include selection of tasks by individuals ("I'll do this, you do that...."), such early allocation of work is common among teams new to Scrum. During these early sprints, I remind teams I coach that these allocations are to be treated tentatively. The team's goal is to finish all of the product backlog items it has committed to for the sprint. This is a whole-team commitment, not a commitment by each person to complete the tasks he or she has signed up for.

In some organizations, it will be difficult to shift from a culture of "I am responsible for and commit to completing my tasks" to a culture of shared, whole-team responsibility. Until this shift occurs, however, teams will find it difficult to complete the selected product backlog items for a sprint. With whole-team commitment, the team member who is ahead of schedule will help the one who is behind such that hopefully each finishes on time. Without a whole-team commitment, it is almost certain that many product backlog items will be "90% done" at the end of the sprint, as each waits on a last bit of work from the person who was a little behind schedule.

THINGS TO TRY NOW

❑ In your next sprint planning meeting, do not have individuals sign up for specific tasks. Go ahead and identify who is likely to work on which tasks so that everyone can agree to the product backlog items to be completed. But, don't write any names next to tasks, and let the assignments emerge during the sprint. After the sprint, discuss how it went.

❑ Swarm on one product backlog item at a time: Have the entire team commit to working on one product backlog item until it is finished before moving on to the next. This is a great way for team members to learn to work together, even if it may be overly restrictive as a permanent practice.

Rely On Specialists but Sparingly

A common misconception is that everyone on a Scrum team must be a generalist—equally good at all technologies and disciplines—rather than a specialist in one.

This is simply not true. What I find surprising about this myth is that every sandwich shop in the world has figured out how to handle specialists, yet we in the software industry still struggle with the question.

My favorite sandwich shop is the Beach Hut Deli in Folsom, California. I've spent enough lunches there to notice that they have three types of employees: order takers, sandwich makers, and floaters. The order takers work the counter, writing each sandwich order on a slip of paper that is passed back to the sandwich makers. Sandwich makers work behind the order takers and prepare each sandwich as it's ordered. Order takers and sandwich makers are the specialists of the deli world. Floaters are generalists—able to do both jobs, although perhaps not as well as the specialists. It's not that their sandwiches taste worse, but maybe a floater is a little slower making them. When I did my obligatory teenage stint at a fast food restaurant, I was a floater. I wasn't as quick at wrapping burritos and making tacos as Mark, one of the cooks. And whenever the cash register needed a new roll of paper, I had to yell for my manager, Nikki, because I could never remember how to do it. But, unlike Mark and Nikki, I could do both jobs.

I suspect that just about every sandwich shop in the world has some specialists—people who only cook or who only work the counter. But these businesses have also learned the value of having generalists. Having some generalists working during the lunch rush helps the sandwich shop balance the need to have some people writing orders and some people making the sandwiches.

What this means for Scrum teams is that yes, we should always attempt to have some generalists around. It is the generalists who enable specialists to specialize. There will always be teams who need the hard-core device driver programmer, the C++ programmer well-versed in Windows internals, the artificial intelligence programmer, the performance test engineer, the bioinformaticist, the artist, and so on. But, every time a specialist is added to a team think of it as equivalent to adding a pure sandwich maker to your deli. Put too many specialists on your team, and you increase the likelihood that someone will spend perhaps too much time waiting for work to be handed off, which is the subject of the next section.

❑ In your next sprint planning meeting, agree that one specialist on the team will not work in that specialty for the duration of the sprint. The specialist can advise others who do the specialty work but cannot do the work personally. The goal is not so much to broaden the specialist's skill set as it is to develop those skills in other team members. Discuss how this worked during the retrospective. Consider repeating it with the same person. Consider trying it with a different specialist.

THINGS TO TRY NOW

Do a Little Bit of Everything All the Time

Teams used to a sequential development process have become accustomed to hand-offs between specialists. Analysts hand their work to designers who hand it to programmers who pass it on to testers. Each of these hand-offs includes some overhead in the form of meetings, documents to read and perhaps sign, and so on. In part because of this overhead, the hand-offs tend to be of large amounts of functionality. In the purest meaning of a waterfall process, the entire application is handed from group to group.

Teams that are new to Scrum often do not go far enough in eliminating these hand-offs. They often make the assumption that the programmers should finish programming a product backlog item before handing it off to the testers. This results in lengthy delays at the start of a sprint, when the testers are waiting for a first product backlog item to be handed to them. On a Scrum project, the unit of transfer between disciplines should be smaller than an individual product backlog item. That is, although there will always be some hand-offs (not everyone can be working on everything all the time), the amount of work being transferred from one person to the next should generally be as small as possible.

As an example, suppose a team is developing a new eCommerce application. The team chooses to work on this user story: *"As a shopper, I can select how I want items shipped based on the actual costs of shipping to my address so that I can make the best decision."* A discussion should ensue among those who are interested in or who will be involved in developing this feature. Let's suppose that includes the product owner, a business analyst, a tester, and a programmer. Their initial discussions are around the general requirements implicit in this feature—things like which shipping companies do we support (FedEx? DHL? and so on), do we want to support overnight delivery? two-day delivery? three-day? and so on.

As these discussions occur, the individuals involved will naturally be thinking about how to get started. On a traditional project, each would be able to start however he or she wanted (after the work was handed over). On a Scrum team, however, how to get started should be a collaborative discussion among those who will work on this feature. For this example, let's assume that the programmer makes the case that it will be easier for some reason to start with FedEx. The tester agrees. The analyst states an intention to investigate DHL and learn more about the parameters that affect DHL shipping costs. The analyst's goal is to have that information available by the time the programmer and tester finish with FedEx.

When the programmer knows enough to get started coding, she does so. The product owner, analyst, and tester discuss high-level tests. (Will our site ship any odd-sized items like skis?) After that discussion, the tester turns the high-level list of tests into concrete tests (boxes of this size and weight going to that destination). The tester creates test data and automates the tests. Some automation may be possible without any interim deliverables from the programmer. Full automation may require getting an early version from the programmer. While the tester is thinking of the concrete tests, he should also inform the programmer of any test cases that the programmer may not be considering while she's programming. When the programmer and tester have finished, they add support for calculating FedEx shipping costs into the build, complete with automated tests. Graphically, this can be depicted as shown in Figure 11.1.

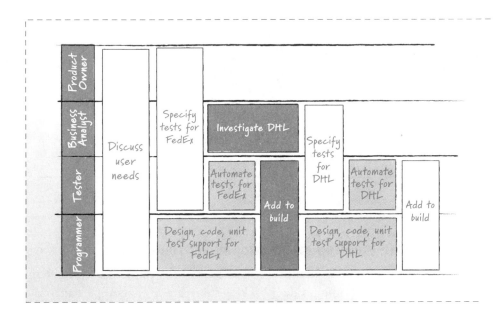

FIGURE 11.1

These four individuals work closely together on one product backlog item rather than handing it to each other.

Next, the programmer and tester check in with the business analyst, who has hopefully learned more about calculating DHL shipping costs. The process is repeated, and support for DHL shipping calculations is added to the application when the programming and testing are complete. The key element in Figure 11.1 is that the team has learned to work by doing a little of everything all the time. Rather than an analysis phase (done without the programmer and tester) followed by a programming phase followed by a testing phase, a little of each of those activities is happening at all times.

Don't Wait Until the End of the Sprint to Finish Everything

A symptom of continuing to hand off work in overly large chunks will be a tendency for no product backlog items to be finished until the last few days of the sprint. Testers on teams that work this way often complain that they are given nothing to test until two days before the end of a sprint and are expected to test everything that quickly. The best way to expose this problem is to create a chart of the number of product backlog items finished as of each day in the sprint. An example can be seen in Figure 11.2a.

As the ScrumMaster on a team, I often just hang this chart in the team area with no fanfare or explanation. Team members soon figure out the problem a chart like this exposes and hopefully start to find ways to finish product backlog items sooner. The result will often be similar to Figure 11.2b, which shows a much smoother flow through the sprint.

FIGURE 11.2

Charting the number of product backlog items finished as of each day in the sprint can expose the problem of handing off large pieces of work.

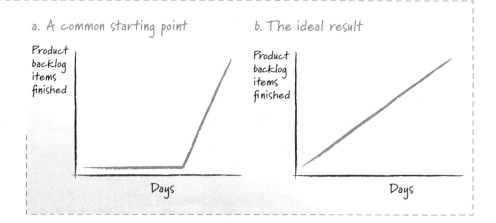

a. A common starting point

Product backlog items finished

Days

b. The ideal result

Product backlog items finished

Days

Mix the Sizes of the Product Backlog Items You Commit To

When planning a sprint, pay attention to the sizes of the product backlog items you are committing to. Some product backlog items are more complex than the FedEx/DHL example given in this section. Some product backlog items will require a week or more of programming time before the programmer can give something even beginning to be testable to a tester. That's OK. Not everything can be split as small as we might like.

You want to avoid bringing a bunch of items like this into the same sprint. Doing this will shift too much testing work to the end of the sprint. Instead of planning a sprint with, for example, three very large items that cannot be partially implemented, bring one or two large items into the sprint along with two or three smaller items. Some of the programmers can work on the large items, handing them over to testers whenever possible. The remaining programmers can work on the smaller items, ensuring a somewhat smoother flow of work to testers early in the sprint.

THINGS TO TRY NOW

❑ Commit to having one-third of the planned product backlog items done by the midpoint of your sprint.

❑ Post a chart like the one shown in Figure 11.2.

❑ For the next three sprints, start by having programmers and testers find a suitable approximate midpoint of each product backlog item. Commit to adding it to the nightly build as soon as this midpoint is reached rather than only after the item is done.

Foster Team Learning

If your team has embraced the concept of whole-team commitment, has reduced its reliance on specialists, and is doing a little bit of everything all the time, you have probably made great strides in improving how you work together. This is when most teams become complacent. Don't. There are still opportunities for improvement. To become a truly high-performing team and to realize all of the benefits that Scrum has to offer, your team must proactively seek out new ways to learn and share knowledge.

Some learning occurs naturally—a user tells the product owner that she likes how a feature behaves or a programmer discovers that scalability needs cannot be met using a particular technology. Other learning is sought deliberately. This is the learning we are interested in right now. Rather than passively waiting for learning to occur, the most effective teams and their leaders take a very active role in optimizing the rate and significance of learning.

Ensure Learning Conditions Exist

In the proactive pursuit of team learning as a goal of the project, there are five conditions that are necessary for team learning to occur:

- Teams must be designed for learning.
- Individuals must have concrete ways of sharing knowledge.
- Leaders must reinforce the importance of learning.
- Teams need to be presented with motivating challenges.
- A supportive learning environment must exist.

These are described in the following sections.

Design Teams for Learning

As we discussed in the previous chapter, managers and others often have significant influence over the composition of a team. They should use this responsibility to create teams from individuals who, when combined, will be more than the sum of their parts. These individuals should be diverse enough that new, creative ideas are generated but not have so many differences that the team fails to jell.

The best thing a manager can do for a newly functional team is to allow it to remain together for as long as possible. A team needs time to learn how to work well together; constantly altering who is on the team forces the team to start this process over each time a new member is added or leaves. Richard Hackman, a Harvard professor and authority on teamwork, cites a study that indicates that "R&D teams do need an influx of new talent to maintain creativity and

SEE ALSO

In the next chapter, Chapter 12, "Leading a Self-Organizing Team," we will see how managers and other leaders should use this influence and responsibility.

freshness—but only at the rate of one person every three to four years" (Hackman and Coutu 2009).

Find Concrete Ways to Share Knowledge

Lew Platt, former CEO of Hewlett-Packard, once said, "If HP knew what HP knows, it would be three times more profitable." For companies to be successful, teams must have concrete ways to share what they have learned not just with each other but with the rest of the organization as well. One way Scrum teams attempt to do this is through Scrum's many built-in communication forums. Daily scrums disseminate information among the members of one team and possibly a few additional attendees; sprint reviews typically spread knowledge a bit further, especially if they are attended by stakeholders and members of other teams; and, in large organizations, the scrum of scrums allow teams to share information with representatives from all other Scrum teams. Scrum teams also have tools designed to help them share knowledge. Wikis and big visible charts give an at-a-glance view into the current state of the sprint and the project among team members and any who view it.

Beyond these communication devices, high-performing Scrum teams find ways to talk with people on other teams directly. It is common, for example, for database developers to talk with other database developers and for user interface designers to talk to other user interface designers. In many environments these conversations are entirely informal and unplanned, but that does not need to be the case. Large Scrum projects and departments often form communities of practice, where groups of like-minded or like-skilled individuals can meet regularly to talk and share not only common problems but also the solutions they have discovered. Communities of practice are a wonderful means of sharing knowledge among teams.

SEE ALSO

Communities of practice are described in Chapter 17, "Scaling Scrum."

Exhibit Behavior That Reinforces Learning

Team members will interact in ways they see modeled by those they consider leaders in the organization or to their team, including product owners, any functional managers to whom team members report, and other executives and managers in the organization. To foster the right kind of behavior, then, team and organizational leaders should demonstrate the type of learning behaviors they would like to see on their teams.

For example, I recently attended a meeting at which a team and its product owner, Michael, were pitching a new product idea to an executive committee. One member of this committee, a VP named Sean, was particularly adept at questioning Michael and the developers. He asked hard questions intended to help the team (and the other committee members) identify holes in the product plan. Sean was not grilling Michael to make him squirm or to shoot down his ideas. His questions (Can you give me three reasons why a prospect would buy our product instead of a competitor's? Would those reasons be sufficient?) were designed to initiate a dialogue in which he engaged as an active participant. Because Sean—a senior leader in the company—was sincerely willing to learn during this dialogue, his behavior created and reinforced similar learning-conducive behavior in those who witnessed it.

Beyond asking questions that lead to a sincere, learning-focused dialogue, Edmondson, Bohmer, and Pisano identify three additional behaviors leaders should exhibit to reinforce learning:

- **Be accessible.** Leaders need to be available to team members rather than locked away behind closed doors, three floors up.
- **Ask for input.** Asking team members for input is a sure way to let them know that their opinions are valued and desired. If you ask them for input into decisions you need to make, they will be more likely to do the same of each other. If you ask the team for input, be sure later to demonstrate how that input was used or why it couldn't be acted upon.
- **Serve as a "fallibility model."** By admitting your own mistakes, you demonstrate to others that bugs, bad decisions, and problems can be discussed without repercussion (2001).

Give Teams a Motivating Challenge

The way in which a challenge is presented to the team influences how team members will respond to it. Imagine a product owner who needs a certain set of features delivered by a firm deadline that appears to be impossible. The product owner could present this challenge to the team as a fait accompli: "I need these features by that date and there's no flexibility. Make it happen."

This isn't how Curt, a product owner, presented a similar challenge to his southern California team. Instead, Curt first acknowledged the difficulty of the task he was about to put before the team. He then outlined what was needed and by when. Without any false tone of doom or threat of penalty, he explained the importance of achieving the goal. He concluded by emphasizing the importance of each person to achieving the goal. Five months later the team delivered enough functionality to avoid the initial crisis, which bought them another six months to deliver the full release.

In the first situation the product owner threw a problem over the wall at the team. In the second, Curt acknowledged the difficulty of the challenge but maintained a positive outlook on the team's ability to rise to the occasion. He then worked with the team to find a suitable initial release—just enough to keep the company's largest customer happy and as much as the team could do. This helped establish a positive environment on the project, which led to the dialogue and discussion necessary for learning.

Create a Supportive Learning Environment

I remember being less than impressed when I took my daughter, Delaney, to her first day of preschool. The place looked a mess. Rather than one big bookshelf or two to hold all the school's books, there were lots of small bookshelves all over the large room that would be my daughter's home two mornings a week. There were no orderly rows or circles of chairs; instead, chairs, bean bags, cushions, and small couches were all over the place. Every inch of wall space was covered with posters, large cut-out letters, maps, or something similar. My wife explained that while the place looked messy to me, it was actually a well-organized space intended to be conducive to learning by four- and five-year-olds like Delaney.

Similarly, it is up to leaders and managers in aspiring Scrum organizations to create supportive learning environments for their teams. Whereas creating a learning environment for little kids consists mostly of arranging the physical layout of the room (being sure a book is never far from reach), creating a learning environment for a Scrum team will involve organizational, social, and psychological changes. Organizations with a supportive learning environment exhibit the following characteristics:

- **Psychological safety.** One of the best ways to learn is to try something, make a mistake, and then do it a better way. Other ways to learn include asking questions and engaging in debate. If someone doesn't feel safe doing these things, they won't. Product owners, ScrumMasters, functional managers, and others must find ways to create a feeling of safety around these activities; otherwise, team members will not risk trying new things for fear of failing, looking stupid, or suffering similar repercussions. Creating psychological safety is particularly important when transitioning to Scrum because of the expertise shift that occurs. It's likely that certain individuals are accustomed to being viewed as experts, perhaps in the technology, the code base, or the domain. Transitioning to Scrum disrupts existing expertise and introduces the need for new expertise. Organizational leaders (and, in fact, all team members) need to create psychological safety so that, for example, the company expert on multithreaded Java programming is willing to ask rudimentary questions about automated unit testing. Failure to do so usually results in the expert resisting the transition.

- **Appreciation of differences.** Individuals on a team need to appreciate rather than attack differences. When everyone has the same background, the same skills, approaches a problems with the same style, or so on, the result can be a lack of creative thinking. As Harvard professor and author of *Leading Teams*, Richard Hackman puts it: "Every team needs a deviant, someone who can help the team by challenging the tendency to want too much homogeneity, which can stifle creativity and learning. Deviants are the ones who stand back and say, 'Well, wait a minute, why are we even doing this at all? What if we looked at the thing backwards or turned it inside out?'" (Hackman and Coutu 2009)

- **Openness to new ideas.** Scrum teams are often asked to meet difficult challenges: develop this faster than we've done similar projects before, do that project with fewer resources, and so on. To rise to meet these challenges, team members often have to look beyond the tried-and-true. An openness to new ideas—and occasionally to the temporary failures and setbacks this creates—is vital.

- **Time for reflection.** Teams need time apart from the fast pace of iterative development in which to reflect upon what they are doing and how they are doing it. Real-time learning in action is the best way for a team to learn, and this is helped by daily scrums. But most teams find that somewhere between a half hour and a half day every sprint spent finding ways to improve is time well spent.

❑ If a team includes members who are expert at some aspect of the current way of working but who feel threatened by the changed technical practices Scrum inspires, this is an excellent time to bring in an external coach. The lead developer who is struggling to get her head around test-driven development and mock objects often feels less threatened learning this new skill from an outsider than from someone on the team whom she is normally mentoring.

THINGS TO TRY NOW

Eliminate Knowledge Waste

While establishing an environment conducive to team learning, we must simultaneously strive to eliminate organizational impediments that cause knowledge waste. Knowledge waste refers to either lost opportunities to learn or learning less than we could have from a situation. Lean development expert Allen Ward divides knowledge waste into three categories: scatter, hand-off, and wishful thinking (2007).

Scatter happens when anything breaks the flow of work. At the individual level, scatter refers to the many things that distract us or break our day into small pieces, making it difficult to do substantive work. At a project level, scatter occurs when the team is interrupted, such as when it is asked to stop what it's doing and work on a different feature, when a person is added to or removed from the team, or when the team is harassed for updates on its progress toward an urgent task.

There are two main causes of scatter—barriers to communication and poor tools. Communication barriers can be physical, such as the 5,000 miles or two floors between team members. Barriers to communication can also, however, be the result of corporate policies ("all database change requests must be in writing") or skill deficiencies, such as the inability of two groups to communicate because they lack a common vocabulary. Ed Catmull, cofounder of Pixar, makers of *Toy Story*; *Finding Nemo*; *The Incredibles*; *Monsters, Inc.*; and other movies, acknowledges these barriers.

> Getting people in different disciplines to treat one another as peers is just as important as getting people within disciplines to do so. But it's much harder. Barriers include the natural class structures that arise in organizations: There always seems to be one function that considers itself and is perceived by others to be the one the organization values most. Then there's the different languages spoken by different disciplines and even the physical distance between offices. (2008, 70)

By poor tools, Ward was not specifically referring to the software products that are such a part of our day-to-day lives. The poor tools that cause scatter are the standardized practices that are so common in a typical development process. For example, one company I consulted to had failed to anticipate the effect of a change to the database shared by multiple applications. This led to a new rule that every new feature must be accompanied by a *database impact report*. The vast majority of application changes, of course, had no database impact, but this standardized report was required nonetheless. Rather than mandating that all projects complete a standard form, a more appropriate response would have been to clarify the responsibility of all project teams to consider and communicate impacts to the database. Responsibility for results, not process adherence, should be the goal.

THINGS TO TRY NOW

❑ In your next sprint retrospective, identify at least a dozen causes of scatter affecting your team. Pick two to work toward eliminating over the next month. Look for items that cause scatter within a single day and for items that create scatter across the span of a project.

Ward defines a *hand-off* as a separation of knowledge, responsibility, action, and feedback. Hand-offs occur everywhere you look in a sequential software development process. The results of analysis are handed off to architects who hand the architecture off to programmers. Programmers then hand off code to testers. Most written documents on a project are produced to enable a hand-off. Not all hand-offs are of artifacts, however. Holding a traditional project manager accountable for meeting project specifications and deadlines she didn't contribute to is an example of a responsibility hand-off.

Cross-functional teams became popular, at least in part, as a response to the trouble caused by hand-offs on traditional development projects. Think back to the earlier section of this chapter, "Embrace Whole-Team Resposibility." The main point of that section was that although there may be one person we look to for certain tasks, just about everything is the responsibility of the whole team. The more the whole team is involved and the more the whole team feels this shared responsibility, the fewer hand-offs there will be. By eliminating hand-offs we eliminate problems created by waiting and by the need to transfer knowledge from one person to another.

Ward's third category of knowledge waste, *wishful thinking*, is not simply optimism. Wishful thinking refers here to making decisions without adequate information to support those decisions. Late projects are the most obvious result of wishful thinking. Choosing a date, creating a specification, and hoping the project will run exactly as planned with no unexpected changes is the ultimate in wishful thinking. Discarded knowledge is a second type of wishful thinking. Discarded knowledge is the failure by teams to capture acquired knowledge in useful formats. When a team finds and fixes a rare bug but fails to add an automated test to prevent that bug from being detected later, it is discarding knowledge. It is wishful thinking for the team to think that the bug will never recur.

It is hard to overstate the importance of team learning. I meet too many teams who are much improved over how they were before they adopted Scrum but that have failed to improve since. Continuous improvement is part of Scrum; failing to learn and wasting the knowledge gained are serious deficiencies.

Encourage Collaboration Through Commitment

Tommy Lasorda, long-time manager of the Los Angeles Dodgers baseball team, has said, "My responsibility is to get my twenty-five guys playing for the name on the front of their shirt and not the one on the back" (LaFasto and Larson 2001, 100). Team learning will only get you so far in your quest to become a high-performing, agile team. To keep your self-organizing team working as a unit instead of a collection of individuals, you must constantly reenergize and focus it toward shared goals. To do this you must find ways to renew team members' commitment to their purpose and to each other. There are a number of things you can do to build and nurture this kind of commitment.

Involve widely. One of the most common complaints I hear from programmers, in particular, is that they do not want to be treated like "code monkeys." They use this term to mean someone who is told exactly what to code and has had all creativity (and fun) stripped from the job. You can avoid treating developers like code monkeys by involving them in as many project activities as practical. This is why, for example, I advocate including all developers in product backlog story-writing

SEE ALSO

For information on conducting a story-writing workshop, see *User Stories Applied for Agile Software Development* (Cohn 2004).

workshops. The broader the picture of the project and product that team members see, the more fully engaged in the project and committed to it they will be.

Find an igniting purpose. London Business School professor Lynda Gratton uses the term "hot spot" to refer to a place and time when "working with other people was never more exciting and exhilarating and when you knew deep in your heart that what you were jointly achieving was important and purposeful" (2007, 1). For a hot spot to form, you need what she calls an "igniting purpose," which is "something that people find exciting and interesting and worth engaging with" (13).

In the mid-1990s I worked at a company that had the igniting purpose of revolutionizing healthcare by changing how patients interacted with providers. This company was built around nurses in a call center, supported by developers writing systems for them. Every week the head nurse sent an e-mail summarizing important information for the week. Much of it was mundane: how many new clients were added, how many calls were answered, the average time to answer calls, and so on.

What wasn't mundane and what stoked the company's igniting purpose was the summary of patients' lives we'd saved. I remember one particular call the head nurse e-mailed us about. The caller was a man who had pain in his upper-left back. He wanted to know if he should go to a doctor or just take ibuprofen. By asking a few questions and being guided by the expert system within our software, the nurse determined the caller was having a heart attack. She dispatched an ambulance to his house even before he hung up, thereby saving his life. An igniting purpose does not have to be as lofty as saving lives. It just has to be something that excites and interests the team members so that they are anxious to be a part of it.

Tap into existing intrinsic motivation. Beyond seeking a teamwide igniting purpose, you should also feed team members' existing motivations. These will differ from team member to team member, but a project that is structured such that each individual's unique, personal goals are aligned with project goals will generate the desired commitment. Perhaps a Java developer wants to gain some experience with C#. Is there an opportunity to do that on this project? Perhaps a tester wants to gain some leadership experience. Can he be given responsibility to lead the effort to select a vendor who will develop some outsourced components?

Beware the least motivated team member. One highly motivated and skilled individual often makes each of his teammates a little better. One unmotivated team member, on the other hand, can drag the whole team down with him. Christopher Avery describes the devastating effect of one bad apple.

> In my experience when a freeloader comes into a team and can't be rejected because of bureaucratic policy, the other hardworking

members of the team immediately and drastically reduce their work level and channel their attention and commitment to other parts of their lives. (Avery, Walker, and O'Toole 2001, 97)

Help everyone understand their relevance to the goal. No one wants to feel superfluous or that they are making only ancillary contributions to a project. It is difficult for team members to fully engage and commit to a project's goals if they do not feel their contributions are significant. Product owners are an obvious source for helping everyone feel important and relevant to the goal, but relevance-boosting comments can come from anyone on the team.

Build confidence. While knowing that the challenge before them will not be easy, team members do want to feel confident they can achieve it. Confidence doesn't come from making the goal easier but from belief in ourselves and our teammates. People enjoy working with those who boost their confidence. A confident team will commit to almost any goal.

Remember that creating commitment is not a one-time effort. Teams need periodic reenergizing to renew their commitments both to the project and to each other. In *Teamwork Is an Individual Skill*, Christopher Avery suggests that while calendar years and quarterly boundaries are good times to reenergize, "the best time to reorient a team is any time you notice that the sense of shared direction has been lost or that energy has decreased" (107).

THINGS TO TRY NOW

- ❑ Does your team have an igniting purpose? Can all team members express it? Would each do so in roughly the same terms? If not, ask the product owner to facilitate a chartering session as described in the "Energize the System" section in Chapter 12.
- ❑ Do you understand what motivates every other person on your team? If not, find out. How? Ask.
- ❑ Do others understand your motivation? If not, tell them.

All Together Now

Creating the right sense of teamwork can be challenging. ScrumMasters can help by ensuring that the team embraces the concept of whole-team responsibility and whole-team commitment to deliver working software at the end of each sprint. The team might struggle at first to break long-held habits of specialization and hand-offs. Minimizing individual task assignments and doing a little bit of everything all at once in a sprint are essential to shifting from sequential development to working as a team. After a team is working well together and delivering what it has committed to during each sprint, the team deserves to feel pride and a sense of accomplishment. Don't fall into the trap, though, of being satisfied with merely being a functional Scrum team. Becoming a high-performing, agile team requires that you continue to learn and improve. Foster team learning, eliminate sources of knowledge waste, and keep your team's collaborative spirit alive by eliciting its commitment and finding ways to renew it throughout the project.

The next chapter looks at ways in which leaders can further influence self-organizing teams, leading them forward toward high performance and optimal productivity.

Additional Reading

Avery, Christoper M., Meri Aaron Walker, and Erin O'Toole. 2001. *Teamwork is an individual skill: Getting your work done when sharing responsibility.* Berrett-Koehler Publishers.
 The premise of this book is that each individual needs to take responsibility for the performance of the team. Avery provides details and anecdotes about how any team member can improve the performance of the overall team.

Katzenbach, Jon R., and Douglas K. Smith. 1993. *The wisdom of teams: Creating the high-performance organization.* Collins Business.
 An early classic on the subject of teams that has stood the test of time. Covers every aspect of teams including the stages they progress through, who should be on them, who should lead them, the role of management in working with them, and more.

Larson, Carl E., and Frank M. J. LaFasto. 1989. *Teamwork: What must go right/what can go wrong.* SAGE Publications.
 The authors spent three years studying and interviewing 32 highly successful teams across a broad spectrum. Included were a cardiac surgery team, a team that climbed Mt. Everest, championship sports teams, an airplane design team, and even the team at McDonald's that invented Chicken McNuggets. From this they distilled eight characteristics of a high-performing team.

Chapter 12

Leading a Self-Organizing Team

One of the earliest models for organizational change was put forth by Kurt Lewin in the 1940s. In Lewin's model, change is a three-step process: "unfreezing" the current situation so that change may occur, transitioning to a new state, and then "refreezing" the new state so that it persists. Many subsequent organizational change models are similar to Lewin's in depicting extended periods of relative stability punctuated by brief times of transition.

Although this may have been Lewin's world in the early 1900s, the world today is much different. Change no longer happens in short spurts that interrupt long periods of relative stability. Instead, rather than moving from one state of equilibrium to another, organizations in the 21st century operate under far-from-equilibrium conditions. Despite the turmoil and frenetic pace this leads to, there are benefits. An organization in equilibrium, and that seeks to return to equilibrium when pushed away from it, is one that resists change (Goldstein 1994, 15). Organizations that operate far from equilibrium become better suited to continuous change. As such, it is up to an organization's leaders and change agents to keep the organization in these far-from-equilibrium conditions.

Leaders do this by periodically agitating the organization. By stirring up, exciting or calming, pushing, shaking up, stimulating, and rearranging the organization, leaders are able to keep the organization from achieving an equilibrium from which it will resist moving. This keeps the organization on its toes and better able to respond to or create change. Agitating the organization becomes a fundamental way leaders and change agents continually move the organization toward becoming more and more agile.

So, who are these leaders and change agents? It's difficult to answer that without knowing the specifics of a given organization, but when I say leaders, I am addressing anyone with influence or authority over the team. That includes managers, who can hire and fire team members. It includes the product owner, who determines the scope of the product or system to be developed. It includes the ScrumMaster, who can introduce small but significant changes to the process. And it includes organizational change agents working to introduce or spread Scrum.

In the following sections, we look at how these leaders, managers, and change agents can influence the self-organizing path of a team or company. You'll learn about three conditions that must exist for self-organization to occur and how leaders can alter those conditions. You'll also learn how organizations evolve, and you'll encounter seven ways that leaders, managers, and change agents can exert influence on the evolution of their organizations.

Influencing Self-Organization

Self-organization is a fundamental concept in agile software development. The Agile Manifesto includes the principle, "The best architectures, requirements, and designs emerge from self-organizing teams" (Beck et al. 2001). Yet a common misconception is that because of this reliance on self-organizing teams, there is little or no role for leaders of agile teams. Nothing could be further from the truth. In *The Biology of Business*, Philip Anderson refutes this mistaken assumption.

> Self-organization does not mean that workers instead of managers engineer an organization design. It does not mean letting people do whatever they want to do. It means that management commits to guiding the evolution of behaviors that emerge from the interaction of independent agents instead of specifying in advance what effective behavior is. (1999, 120)

Self-organizing teams are not free from management control. Management chooses for them what products to build or often chooses who will work on their projects, but they are nonetheless self-organizing. Neither are they free from influence. Early references to Scrum were clear about this. In "The New New Product Development Game" from 1986, Takeuchi and Nonaka write that "subtle control is also consistent with the self-organizing character of project teams." Then in *Wicked Problems, Righteous Solutions* in 1990, DeGrace and Stahl describe how managers exercise indirect control over a self-organizing team.

> To be sure, control *is* still exercised; but, it is subtle and much of it is indirect. It is exercised by selecting the right people, creating an open work environment, encouraging feedback from the field, establishing an evaluation and reward system based on group performance, managing the tendency for going off in many directions early on and the need to integrate information and effort later on, tolerating and even anticipating mistakes, and encouraging suppliers to become involved early without controlling them. (159)

A Scrum team's job is to self-organize around the challenges, and within the boundaries and constraints, put in place by management. Management's job is to come up with appropriate challenges and remove impediments to self-organization.

That being said, the fewer constraints or controls put on a team, the better. If leaders overly constrain how a team solves the challenge given to it, self-organization will not occur. The team will shut down; because it has already been told so much about the challenge and how to solve it, it will wait to hear the rest.

So how does an agile leader achieve the subtle balance between command and influence? One way is to understand how slight changes in three team-related conditions can have a tremendous impact on how teams organize, and thereby how they perform. These conditions are containers, differences, and exchanges.

Containers, Differences, and Exchanges

In her doctoral dissertation, Glenda Eoyang describes three conditions that, when altered, influence how a team will self-organize: containers, significant differences, and transforming exchanges (2001).

A container is some boundary within which self-organization occurs. Imagine you are at a movie theater that does not preassign seats. The physical boundaries of the theater form a container within which you and other filmgoers self-organize into seats. Another set of filmgoers are in the adjacent theater, and they have self-organized within their physical container. The two containers (theaters) are distinct, so filmgoers in one theater cannot be said to have self-organized with filmgoers in the other theater. Containers do not need to be physical. As the following examples illustrate, they can also be behavioral, organizational, and conceptual:

- Everyone working on the San Jose campus
- Everyone working in Building A-3
- Everyone working in the software development department
- Everyone programming in Ruby
- Everyone who is Norwegian
- Everyone who belongs to the Agile Alliance
- Everyone on the Capricorn project team

Differences among individuals inside the container also influence how they will self-organize. Without differences among members of our Scrum team, it wouldn't matter who does which work or whether the individuals interact. Because we would all be equivalently skilled in all ways, each member of the group would work in isolation. Fortunately, there always are differences among the individuals on a software development team. These include technical expertise, domain knowledge, power, gender, race, education, connections to others in the company, problem-solving approach, and so on. The types and degrees of these differences influence how a team self-organizes.

Finally, transforming exchanges influence how a team organizes in response to a challenge. A transforming exchange is an interaction between members within a container in which one or more of the individuals is changed or influenced by that interaction. For example, I meet with my project's product owner who answers my questions about how a feature should work. This is a transforming exchange because I leave with new knowledge. It is not always information that passes between individuals in a transforming exchange; it might be money, power, energy, or any number of other things. A team motivated by a conversation with its product owner has experienced a transforming exchange: Energy was created and passed to the team.

What do these three conditions mean for leaders and change agents? By adjusting containers, amplifying or dampening differences, or altering exchanges, leaders can influence how a team or teams self-organize. This is one form of the *subtle control* mentioned at the start of this chapter. For example, suppose one team member, Jeff, is domineering and no one is willing to stand up to him. This team has self-organized—it has chosen to let Jeff make all key decisions. As the Scrum-Master for this team, you recognize that this will impede the team's efforts to improve. You consider having a private conversation with Jeff, but that is unlikely to change much. You contemplate stepping in and overruling some decisions he makes, but if you do it once the team will expect you to continue to do so, which won't be good.

Stumped, you begin to think about the containers, differences, and exchanges that are influencing how this team has chosen to self-organize. You realize that you could influence the situation by decreasing the differences among team members. As a result, you decide to add someone else to the team who will sometimes stand up to Jeff. Or you may decide to exert subtle control over the team by altering the exchanges. To do so, you suggest to the enterprise architecture team that someone from the group attend key meetings. No matter the specific problem, if you see that the team has self-organized in a way that impedes it, it is your responsibility to find a way to agitate, stir up, or otherwise disturb the status quo, so that the team adjusts, hopefully reorganizing in a more productive way.

In *Facilitating Organization Change*, Eoyang and coauthor Edwin Olson advocate exactly this type of approach.

> The role of the change agent is to use an understanding of the evolving patterns to shift the container, differences, or exchanges to affect the self-organizing path, to observe how the system responds, and to design the next intervention. The objective of this

action-oriented experimentation is to anticipate, adapt, and influence, not to predict or control the behavior of the system.
(2001, 16)

"This doesn't sound right. How can a team be self-organizing if some boss or change agent is controlling things from behind the scenes?"

Self-organization does not mean a collection of individuals is free to do whatever it wants. The individuals self-organize around a problem that is presented to them by the organization. ("We want a product that does this.") The containers, differences, and exchanges put in place by the organization influence, but do not determine, how a team organizes itself around the problem.

Keep in mind also that a change agent is not fiddling with a team's or project's containers, differences, or exchanges for her own pleasure. The change agent is doing it as part of helping the team become the best that it can be.

Adjusting Containers

Colin, a development director at a medical software company, was frustrated by one team's inability to produce working software by the end of its sprints. He wasn't disappointed with the amount of work being done each sprint; the team seemed to be doing a reasonable amount of work each time. He was frustrated because rather than finishing five items by the end of a sprint, the team would instead be "half done" with ten. He knew this wasn't how a Scrum team should behave.

Colin and I discussed the situation and I presented the CDE (Container, Difference, Exchange) model. Colin felt that the right people were talking and that he didn't need to change the current exchanges or introduce new ones. We discussed differences among team members and agreed that one possible remedy was to move an experienced agile developer onto the team. Such a developer would be able to help the team understand the problems with how it had been working. Unfortunately, there were no experienced agile developers available for this team.

In discussing the containers that enclosed this team, Colin realized that a possible solution was to expand the team's responsibilities. Contributing to its challenges in finishing work, he decided, was the fact that this team was dependent on low-level functionality being developed by another team. Colin decided to merge the two teams. By merging them, he could make the combined team entirely responsible for work that used to span two teams. This would eliminate

SEE ALSO

The importance of finishing each sprint with working software is discussed in Chapter 14, "Sprints."

SEE ALSO

The merits of feature and component teams are described in Chapter 10, "Team Structure."

one opportunity for excuses about why something wasn't finished by the end of a sprint. In a later e-mail to me, Colin described his thought process.

> Only part of their problems were caused by delays waiting for the other team. But they'd become accustomed to leaving product backlog items half finished. By adding responsibilities and new members to the team, it would be a chance for me to re-stress my expectation that having a few things done at the end of a sprint was better than having more things started.

Colin's approach of expanding the responsibilities to expand the container is just one possible way of adjusting containers to influence the team. It and some others are summarized in Table 12.1.

TABLE 12.1

Ways to use containers to influence how a team self-organizes.

Change the number of people on the team.
Change who is on the team.
Introduce a new container, such as a community of practice.
Give the team more or less responsibility.
Change the team's physical space. Give team members more or less space. Remove or lower cubicle walls. Move everyone together on the same floor.

THINGS TO TRY NOW

- ❏ List all of the containers that members of a team work within. Do the containers seem appropriately sized and scoped? Are there too many? too few?
- ❏ For each container, decide if it has a positive, negative, or neutral impact on the team's performance.
- ❏ Identify the container that you think currently exerts the most influence on the team. Should changes be made to that container?

Amplifying or Dampening Differences

Carey, a development director who initiated her company's adoption of Scrum, was troubled by a recent but sustained drop in velocity on one of her teams. The quality of its work remained high, but the team was getting less done now than it was a few months ago. During regular, 30-minute, one-on-one meetings she had with each of her employees, she asked some members of this team why they thought this had happened. She followed that up by attending the team's next sprint retrospective.

What Carey learned was that the team had made a few ill-considered architectural decisions six to nine months back. She put together what she learned from the retrospective, her monthly team member meetings, and what she already knew of team member personalities. Carey concluded that while some bad decisions are inevitable, some of this team's bad decisions were the result of team members not adequately questioning one another.

I had previously introduced Carey to thinking about containers, differences, and exchanges as a light-touch way for her to guide her teams. She told me later that she had used the approach in this situation. By thinking through the CDE model, Carey knew that insufficient differences existed between team members. She decided that she could best help this team by amplifying those differences. She did so through one of my favorite techniques: She asked a lot of probing questions.

Carey had always been a hands-off director, but she decided this team needed more of her attention. She began to drop by when she saw the team holding impromptu meetings. During these meetings she asked questions intended to pull out dissenting opinions. She asked questions such as the following:

- What alternative approaches have you considered and rejected before accepting this one?
- What could go wrong with this approach?
- What has to go right for this approach to work?
- What could make us regret this decision?
- Is there any information we don't have that would help us be sure of this?

Even when Carey agreed with the prevailing opinion, she asked hard questions, poking for flaws and hoping others might voice even better opinions.

Another good way to amplify differences is to change how the team makes decisions. For example, if a team currently makes decisions by a majority vote, ask members to require consensus for the next two sprints. Do the opposite if they currently require consensus. These and other approaches for dampening or amplifying differences are shown in Table 12.2.

Introduce a new team member with significantly more power, experience, knowledge, or so on.
Ask hard questions of the team to ensure different viewpoints are heard.
Change the team's decision-making style.
Encourage dissenting viewpoints.

TABLE 12.2

Ways to amplify or dampen differences to influence how a team self-organizes.

❏ For each way in which team members differ (such as technical knowledge, domain knowledge, industry experience, tenure with the company, respect, problem-solving style) rate the differences from one to ten. From this, do team members appear too different? too similar?

❏ Identify one difference that if amplified would improve team performance. Could someone be added to the team who would amplify that difference?

❏ Identify one difference that if dampened would improve team performance. Could someone be removed from the team who would dampen that difference?

Altering Exchanges

A leader or change agent in the organization can also influence a team by altering the exchanges in which team members participate. Alejandro, a technical lead at a video game development studio, was attending his third sprint review of the day when he noticed a problem. Each team included an artificial intelligence (AI) programmer. The AI programmers were responsible for the behavior of the bad guys who would attack the player in the game. Alejandro picked up on statements in the sprint reviews that told him each team was programming its AI a bit differently. Not only would this lead to inconsistent game play, but it was also a duplication of some of the effort.

I met Alejandro after he had encountered and solved this problem. His solution was to introduce a new exchange. Because the AI programmers were not talking to each other often enough, Alejandro decided the AI programmers should meet once a week with no one else present. Although not one of the AI programmers himself, Alejandro had enough personal authority in the organization that he was able to convince them this was a good idea. During a two-week sprint, AI programmers met on the day after sprint planning so that each would be aware of what the others had committed to and would be working on. A second meeting was held around the start of the second week, giving them a chance to compare progress and expectations.

Alejandro introduced a community of practice, a group of like-minded or like-skilled individuals. We saw the use of communities of practice in Chapter 4, "Iterating Toward Agility," as the basis for the organization's Enterprise Transition Community and the improvement communities that help the organization adopt Scrum. We will see them in more detail in Chapter 17, "Scaling Scrum." In addition to introducing a community of practice, additional techniques for altering exchanges are shown in Table 12.3.

Add or remove people from an exchange.
Formalize or deformalize an exchange.
Change how an exchange occurs (face-to-face conversation, document).
Change the frequency of an exchange.

TABLE 12.3

Ways to alter exchanges to influence how a team self-organizes.

Now that we've looked at three factors that influence how a team self-organizes around the challenge it is given, let's look at ways leaders can keep the team or company evolving over time.

❑ Who outside the team do you wish the team would talk to more often? Is there a way to encourage such exchanges?

❑ Diagram the intensity of interaction among team members. Draw a circle for each person. Then draw lines between pairs of team members who interact. Use color or thickness to indicate intensity or frequency. Do you see any problems?

❑ Observe the team carefully for a sprint: Are the right people involved in all exchanges? Should some exchanges involve more (or fewer) people?

THINGS TO TRY NOW

Influencing Evolution

Many years ago I worked for a CIO, Jim, who was well-known in the company for frequently reorganizing his department. A joke made the rounds that if you didn't like Jim's current organization, you should just wait a day. He didn't reorganize us daily, but it did feel that way at times. Jim's reorganizations are just one example of how the company today is not the same as the company last week. Companies evolve. Organizational evolution comes in response to environmental factors, competitive forces, strengths and weakness of employees, and other influences.

Evolution is the result of three elements: variation, selection, and retention. Philip Anderson explains the connectedness of these three elements with the example of the giraffe. Through a random mutation a giraffe is born with a longer-than–normal neck. This is *variation*. The longer neck helps this particular giraffe reach food that other giraffes cannot. This makes that giraffe more likely to breed successfully, which is known as *selection*. Finally, the giraffe passes the gene for longer necks to its descendants, which is known as *retention* (1999, 120–1).

Organizations also evolve through variation, selection, and retention. An organization needs sufficient variation among employees, teams, processes, and the like so that a variety of results can be achieved. There must also be a sufficient definition of success so that employees can distinguish between variations that lead to desirable outcomes and those that do not. In effect, variation and selection lead to someone in the organization noticing that "when we did more of such-and-such, it led to better results." Finally, there must be sufficient mechanisms in place to reinforce behaving in the new, better way. If culture or human resources policies run counter to a new way of behaving, the new way will not be retained.

Leaders and change agents do not sit idly by while their organizations evolve. Instead, they help guide the organization's evolution through variation, selection, and retention.

> Self-organization proceeds from the premise that effective organization is evolved, not designed. It aims to create an environment in which successful divisions of labor and routines not only emerge but also self-adjust in response to environmental changes. This happens because management sets up an environment and encourages rapid evolution toward higher fitness, not because management has mastered the art of planning and monitoring work flows. (Anderson 1999, 119)

Phillip Anderson suggests seven levers that leaders can use to guide an evolving organization. These are summarized in Table 12.4. We have already covered *choose people* (similar to altering containers or amplifying differences) and *reconfigure the network* (similar to exchanges) in our earlier discussion of the CDE model. The remaining levers form the basis for the sections that follow.

TABLE 12.4

Techniques a leader can use to influence how an organization evolves.

Select the external environment.
Define performance.
Manage meaning.
Choose people.
Reconfigure the network.
Introduce vicarious selection systems.
Energize the system.

Select the External Environment

Self-organization and evolution occur in response to the environment in which the team works. Leaders can have a significant amount of influence on that environment. By *environment* I mean more than simply a team's physical work space. There are many more important environmental factors under the influence of leaders. Leaders, for example, control or influence the business the organization is in. They determine the organization's approach to innovation: Is the company an innovator or a fast follower? Leaders also control the type of projects to be worked on and the rate at which new projects are introduced to the organization. Each of these factors will influence how an organization evolves and adapts.

Julie was the general manager of a large division of a software company. She was responsible for approximately half of her company's 500 developers. Scrum began in a grass-roots manner within her division. When early results proved promising, she initiated a plan to spread Scrum to all teams within a year. As part of doing this, Julie also slowed the flow of new projects into the organization. This wasn't because Scrum teams were developing more slowly; they were, in fact, developing quickly. But her early experiences with Scrum helped her realize that the organization was trying to do too many projects at the same time. Experiences with her initial Scrum teams had proven to her the benefits of allowing people to be dedicated to one or possibly two teams. To achieve that, she needed to match the flow of incoming projects more closely to the rate at which projects were being completed.

SEE ALSO

The issue of doing too many concurrent projects is discussed in "Put People on One Project" in Chapter 10.

Define Performance

Organizations and organisms evolve to fit their environments. According to the principle of selection, those traits most likely to help an individual or group survive in the organization will be the ones retained. It is the organization's leaders and managers who define what traits help groups or individuals survive. If agile values such as openness and transparency lead to survival in the form of promotions and public praise, those behaviors will be the ones individuals select.

Leaders and managers can exert a great deal of influence in how they define successful performance. For example, they define the organization's attitude toward trade-offs between short- and long-term performance. An organization that favors long-term success will be more likely to invest in training, support working at a sustainable pace, be willing to allow employees time to explore novel ideas, and will not exchange meeting a near-term deadline for unmaintainable code.

Manage Meaning

Individuals in a self-organizing system evolve in response to the messages they receive. Messages can be generated from within the system itself or fed into the system from outside it. Managers and leaders manage the meaning of these messages by providing context to help employees interpret the messages. Much of this context is provided in the stories, myths, and rituals that leaders repeat. Leaders select and tell stories through which they wish employees to interpret current situations.

I recall my first (and last) day with what was to have been a new client. The development director tried to impress me by saying, "Every night at 5:00 p.m., the general manager goes outside and counts the number of cars in the parking lot. He's going to do that every night as long as there's a problem."

This story was rapidly becoming part of the corporate folklore. It was being told so that people would know what type of behavior was expected and accepted by the new general manager.

I knew that if the general manager had this attitude, this company's Scrum adoption was doomed. I couldn't resist trying to reframe the story to support the behavior I hoped to see: "That's wonderful," I said. "I can't wait to meet him. Any boss who would go into the parking lot at 5:00 p.m. and count the number of people who are still there so he can send them home is someone I want to meet." My attempt fell flat, and my later meeting with the general manager fell even flatter. Even after I pointed out the environmental problems inhibiting the company's Scrum adoption, the general manager had no desire to send a different message.

Introduce Vicarious Selection Systems

The primary selection system that should govern organizational evolution is long-term market success. Products that generate profits should displace products that do not; team structures that lead to profitable products should displace those that do not; and practices that lead to profitable products should drive out those that do not. This, of course, takes years. Additionally, with many changes occurring in the organization simultaneously, it is impossible to fully isolate the effect of one variation. To accelerate and improve the rate of evolution, managers can introduce vicarious selection systems.

A vicarious selection system is a process for selecting desirable projects, products, or behaviors but that does so without the lengthy feedback of a market-driven selection system. Google's policy of allowing developers to spend 20% of their time on projects of their own choosing is a vicarious selection system. So is Google's policy of allowing developers to move freely between teams and projects "any time they want, no questions asked" (Yegge 2006). Because developers want to work on projects that are successful, ground-breaking, or otherwise desirable to Google, these are well-designed vicarious selection systems; they select in the short term the same projects, products, or behaviors that the market would have eventually found desirable in the long term. New projects that fail to attract attention are more likely to fade away. Or, in evolutionary terms, they will not be selected and retained.

Vicarious selection systems are common in organizations. Many organizations have a system where one employee can nominate a coworker for a small cash bonus. When not used to encourage individual over team performance, such rewards can be useful at communicating the type of behavior desired in the organization.

Unfortunately, not all vicarious selection systems are good predictors of the behavior that the market would select. Managers must take care when putting a vicarious selection system in place. James, a vice president of development, did not carefully consider one of the vicarious selection systems in use within his organization: praise. James thrived on chaos and always needed an emergency to handle. If emergencies didn't exist, he always seemed able to stir one up. He excelled at handling emergencies and praised others with similar skills. James's employees learned that their boss valued crisis resolution skills more than he valued skills that avoided crises in the first place.

Energize the System

Teams and organizations rely on energy. Unless energy is pumped in, the team or organization will suffer from entropy. Managers and leaders provide the energy that sustains self-organization and evolution by inspiring and challenging employees. Challenges create gaps between a product's current state and one that is envisioned, or between a group's current and desired levels of performance. When a group is inspired to accept a challenge, it self-organizes around how to achieve it.

In their book *Teamwork*, Larson and LaFasto focus on the power of presenting a team with a "clear, elevating goal" (1989, 27). In *Hot Spots*, Lynda Gratton came to a similar conclusion, saying that high-performing teams need an "igniting purpose" (2007, 3). Bill Gates's famous "Internet Tidal Wave" memo from May 1995 created an igniting purpose within all of Microsoft. After describing some of the ways the Internet would change Microsoft's products and business, Gates presents a clear, elevating goal, saying that Microsoft must "first embrace the Internet and then extend it." He concludes with a final bit of motivation.

> The Internet is a tidal wave. It changes the rules. It is an incredible opportunity as well as an incredible challenge. I am looking forward to your input on how we can improve our strategy to continue our track record of incredible success.

In *Agile Project Management*, Jim Highsmith stresses the importance of starting each project with a charter—a short, memorable vision of why the project is being undertaken or what it is to deliver. An appropriately chosen charter can provide team members with a clear, elevating goal and spark an igniting purpose in a memorable way. Highsmith provides three techniques for chartering a project:

- Write a one- or two-sentence summary of the project or product (an "elevator statement").
- Design the box the product would ship in (even if it would never ship in a box).

- Write a product description constrained to fit on one page (2009).

In addition to these chartering tools, I occasionally use two others:

- Write the imaginary press release you would like to accompany the product release.
- Write the product review you would like to appear in magazines.

One of my clients used the magazine review to great effect. This client develops antispyware software and had recently been designated as "runner-up" by a magazine in its product-of-the-year awards. For many products, being the second best in its class would be quite desirable. The second-best film of the year probably does well at the box office. But for a product that most users buy only one of, being second best is a problem.

I advised the team's ScrumMaster, Erin, to have all members involved in chartering the next version of the product by writing the review they would like to read. They did. The envisioned review was then hung in a variety of strategic places within the team's work space. Six months later the new version of the product was released and was reviewed again by the same magazine. This time the product was given the Editor's Choice award for best antispyware product. The team's achievement was due in part to the ScrumMaster pumping energy into the system in the form of a clear, elevating goal that led to an igniting purpose.

THINGS TO TRY NOW

- ❏ Make a list of all the vicarious selection systems in your organization. What formal and informal mechanisms influence or decide which projects, types of behavior, approaches, and so on succeed and are propagated into the future? Are any of these at odds with adopting Scrum? What can you do, and whose help do you need, to eliminate them?
- ❏ Is the team sufficiently energized? If not, create a project charter using one of the techniques outlined.
- ❏ Identify all individuals outside the team and the messages they are sending the team. Does the team have the right context in which to interpret those messages? Can you prevent the team from receiving inconsistent messages, especially about conflicting project goals such as quality, scope, and schedule?

There's More to Leadership Than Buying Pizza

While watching a tennis match, you may notice that the player receiving the serve stays on her toes rather than standing flat-footed. This stance allows the player to be ready for any ball, whether the serve is left or right, deep or short. Leaders and change agents involved in transitioning an organization to Scrum want the organization always on its collective toes, ready to go left, right, or any which way. An organization on its toes is ready for whatever change confronts it. Such an organization becomes accustomed to continuous incremental change, is rarely surprised by change, and will be able to assimilate change more quickly.

Leaders, managers, and change agents keep an organization on its toes by altering its containers, differences, and transforming exchanges. Leaders influence the direction in which an organization evolves by pulling one of Anderson's seven levers.

There is more to self-organization than buying pizza and getting out of the way. There are subtle and indirect ways through which leaders influence teams. It is impossible for a leader to accurately predict how a team will respond to a change, whether that change is an altered container, new standards of performance, a vicarious selection system, or so on. Leaders do not have all the answers. What they do have is the ability to agitate the organization toward becoming more agile.

Additional Reading

Anderson, Philip. 1999. Seven levers for guiding the evolving enterprise. In *The biology of business: Decoding the natural laws of enterprise*, ed. John Henry Clippinger III, 113–152. Jossey-Bass.

> This is one of the better chapters in an excellent book. In it, Anderson lays out the principles of organizational evolution and presents the seven levers described in the "Influencing Evolution" section of this chapter.

Goldstein, Jeffrey. 1994. *The unshackled organization: Facing the challenge of unpredictability through spontaneous reorganization*. Productivity Press.

> This is one of the earliest books on self-organization within corporations. Highlights include the multiple real and anonymized case studies of self-organization in a variety of companies.

Olson, Edwin E., and Glenda H. Eoyang. 2001. *Facilitating organization change: Lessons from complexity science*. Pfeiffer.

> This excellent book builds on ideas in Eoyang's doctoral dissertation on self-organization and applies them specifically to organization change. It presents the model that organizational change can be influenced through the containers, differences, and exchanges that are put in place or encouraged by change agents in the organization.

Chapter 13

The Product Backlog

The biggest question looming at the start of a project is, what exactly are we building? We know the general shape of the system to be built. We may know, for example, that we are building a word processor. But there are always dark corners yet to be explored or issues yet to be settled about how specific features will work. Will our word processor include an interactive table design feature, or will tables be designed by entering values into a series of screens?

When using a sequential development process, we try to start with a lengthy, up-front requirements-gathering phase during which the product is presumably fully specified. The idea is that, by thinking longer, harder, and better at the outset of the project, no dark corners will be encountered during the main development phase of the project.

A Scrum team forgoes a lengthy, up-front requirements phase in favor of a just-in-time approach. High-level feature descriptions may be gathered early, but they are minimally described at that time and are progressively refined as the project progresses. They are documented in a *product backlog*, which is a list of all desired functionality not yet in the product. It is maintained by the product owner and kept in priority order, which is why a product backlog is sometimes called a *prioritized feature list*. Unlike a traditional requirements document, a product backlog is highly dynamic; items are added, removed, and reprioritized each sprint as more is learned about the product, the users, the team, and so on.

In this chapter we look at three changes organizations need to make to effectively work with a product backlog. First, we look at the need to shift from writing about a product's features to talking about them. Second, we see why it's important for detail to be added progressively rather than for all of it to be documented up front. Third, we see why specification by example should be a team's preferred approach to documenting a product's functionality. The chapter concludes with an acronym for remembering key attributes of the product backlog.

Shift from Documents to Discussions

There is a grand myth about requirements—if you write them down, users will get exactly what they want. That's not true. At best, users will get exactly what was written down, which may or may not be anything like what they really want. Written words are misleading—they look more precise than they are. For example, recently I wanted to run a three-day public training course. My assistant and I had discussed this, so I sent her an e-mail saying, "Please book the Hyatt in Denver," and reminded her of the dates. The next day she e-mailed me, "The hotel is booked." I e-mailed back, "Thanks," and turned my attention toward other matters.

About a week later she e-mailed me saying, "The hotel is booked on the days you wanted. What do you want to me do? Do you want to try another hotel in Denver? A different week? A different city?" She and I had completely miscommunicated about the meaning of "booked." When she told me "the hotel is booked," she meant, "The room we usually use at the Hyatt is already taken." When I read "the hotel is booked," I took it as a confirmation that she had booked the hotel like I had requested. Neither of us did anything wrong in this exchange. Rather, it is an example of how easy it is to miscommunicate, especially with written language. If we had been talking rather than e-mailing, I would have thanked her when she told me "the hotel is booked." The happy tone of my voice would have confused her, and we would have caught our miscommunication right then.

Beyond this problem, there are other reasons to favor discussions over documents.

Written documents can make you suspend judgment. When something is written, it looks official, formal, and finished, especially when fancy formatting has been applied. Awhile back a client whose office I'd visited many times decided we would have an off-site meeting near the company's office. The client sent me very detailed directions from my hotel to a country club where we were to meet:

- Turn left out of your hotel onto North Commerce Parkway and go 0.4 miles
- Turn left on SW 106th Avenue and go 0.2 miles
- Turn right on Royal Palm Boulevard for 1.1 miles
- Turn left onto Town Center

But I couldn't turn left onto Town Center! After 1.1 miles on Royal Palm, I found myself at an intersection, but Town Center went only to the right. I had been told to turn left but that road was called Weston Hills Boulevard. I could see the Country Club to the left, and it seemed like I should turn there. However, the directions had been very specific and correct to this point so I continued forward. I went another two miles, watching the country club fade past me on the left. Eventually it was clear that the one instruction had been wrong, so I turned around and turned on Weston Hills instead of Town Center as was written in the directions. Suppose instead of these directions my client had simply said, "Head toward our office the same way you usually do. But when you see the country club, turn left. I don't know the name of that street, but you can't miss the country club."

With a written document, we don't iterate over meaning as we would in conversation. A few years back I read a requirements document that described a Windows Explorer–like interface for managing folders of data. One requirement said, "The name of the folder can be 127 characters." I was fairly certain that the requirement should have said that the folder name could be a *maximum of* 127 characters. But this was a bioinformatics application, and there were some unusual requirements such as text fields that could contain only the letters A, C, G, and T. A folder name of exactly 127 characters was a little surprising, but it was not impossible to fathom for this particular application.

Because a specific length was given, I presumed it must have been chosen for a good reason. It may not have been. Yet the nature of a requirements document made me much less likely to question the "127" mandate than I would have been had the analyst and I been talking. If we had, our conversation would have been punctuated with exchanges such as, "So what you're saying is…," "If I understand you, that means…," and "Doesn't that imply…." These questions are intended to ensure that a transfer of understanding has occurred, that I understand what you've said. This iterating over meaning is missing in documents.

Written documents decrease whole-team responsibility. One of the goals of shifting to Scrum is to get the whole team working together toward the goal of delivering a great product. We want to strip our development process of bad habits that work against this goal. Written documents create sequential hand-offs, which deprive the team of a unity of purpose. One person (or group) defines the product; another group builds it. Two-way communication is discouraged. Through the written document, one team member is saying, "Here's what to do," and others are expected to do it. This type of master-and-servant relationship is unlikely to create strong feelings of engagement on the part of the servants. Rather than feeling responsible for the success of the product, they feel responsible for doing what is described in the document. Discussions have the opposite effect: Whole team discussions lead to greater buy-in by all team members.

SEE ALSO

Whole-team responsibility and the problems with hand-offs were covered in Chapter 11, "Teamwork."

<table>
<tr><td>OBJECTION</td><td>"I can't get rid of all documents—my project has ISO 9001 (or similar) requirements, and everything has to be documented and traceable."</td></tr>
</table>

As I'll describe in the next section, you don't need to get rid of all documents. Eliminate those you can and keep others as short as possible, even considering whether they can be automatically generated. It is also important to recognize that you can document for posterity, while still relying on conversation during the project.

Don't Throw the Baby Out with the Documentation

These weaknesses of written communication are not to say we should abandon written requirements documents—absolutely not. Rather, we should use documents where appropriate. Because the Agile Manifesto says that we favor "working software over comprehensive documentation" (Beck et al. 2001), agile has been misinterpreted as being against documentation. The goal in agile development is to find the right balance between documentation and discussion. In the past we've often been skewed way too far toward the side of documents.

SEE ALSO

The section "Learn to Start Without a Specification," later in this chapter will show the power of specifying behavior in test cases.

We should also remain aware that requirements documents are just one form of documentation that may exist on a project. Other artifacts will exist: Test plans, executable test cases, and even code document the behavior (or intended behavior) of the system.

Because code and automated test cases will be produced to deliver a product, an experienced Scrum team learns to lean heavily on these artifacts. It will augment these forms of documentation with a written requirements document to the extent that such a document is helpful or required for regulatory, contractual, or legal purposes. A written requirements document will still be useful on many projects. Tom Poppendieck, coauthor of books on lean software development, has said that "when documents are mostly to enable handoffs, they are evil. When they capture a record of a conversation that is best not forgotten, they are valuable."

Use User Stories for the Product Backlog

User stories are the best way to shift the focus from writing about features to talking about them. A user story is a short, simple description of a feature told from the perspective of the person who desires the new capability, usually a user or customer of the system. User stories are often written on index cards or sticky notes, stored in a shoe box, and arranged on walls or tables to facilitate planning and discussion. As such, user stories strongly shift the focus from writing about features to discussing them. User stories typically follow a simple template:

As a <type of user>, I want <some goal> so that <some reason>.

Other templates are possible. The following template, for example, is promoted as putting the value of the user story at the front: *In order to <achieve value>, as <type of user>, I want <some goal>.* Having used both formats, I still prefer starting with *as a <type of user>.* For reasons why, see http://blog.mountaingoatsoftware.com/advantages-of-the-as-a-user-i-want-user-story-template. More important than the format of the written part of the user story, though, is that the conversations surrounding the story occur.

User stories can be stored in a software tool (and there are many reasons why you may choose to do so), but whenever possible I prefer to write on simple 3" × 5" index cards. Although a user story is often written on an index card or sticky note, the text written there is only the beginning. The story card is not meant to be a complete feature description in the same way we would view "The system shall…" statements in a software requirements specification. Instead, the story card serves as a two-way promise between the development team and the product owner. Team members promise they will talk to the product owner before beginning work on the story; the product owner promises to be available when the team is ready to talk.

The team's promise to talk to the product owner before beginning work is important because it frees the product owner from concerns that every last detail must be written on the card. Indeed, this is one of the reasons for using such a lightweight, apparently unimportant medium as index cards. They serve as a constant reminder that the card does not need to hold all the details. The details will come out during conversations between the product owner and the team.

The product owner's reciprocal promise of availability is important because it allows the team to accept work into a sprint without having considered all details, because doing so is impossible anyway. The product owner does not need to be constantly available to the team, although this is helpful and does lead to higher productivity. Rather, what the product owner is promising is to be accessible; it won't take two weeks to schedule a phone call, for example.

OBJECTION

"I can't possibly put my requirements on index cards."

That's fine. Projects with distributed teams, very large teams, traceability requirements, or similar needs often require the use of a software tool. A good tool can improve high-level product planning, what-if scenario discussions, and broad communication. However, teams using software tools rather than pen-and-paper are much more likely to struggle with the shift from documents to discussion that Scrum requires. A team using a tool is much more likely to fall into a number of dangerous traps, including

- Writing overly long feature descriptions
- Having only a subset of the team (business analysts) working to understand users' needs
- Resisting the need to split user stories so that complete stories can be delivered within a sprint
- Holding on to stories that are no longer needed because it's actually easier to keep them than to delete them from the tool

I would never go so far as to say you cannot be agile when using a tool to manage your product backlog. I will, however, say that you can be more agile with pen-and-paper than with a tool. Whenever this low-tech option is possible, use it.

"I'm already good with use cases; do I really need to switch to user stories?"

Use cases are an alternative method for expressing the functionality of a system. If you—and the rest of the team including the product owner—are good with use cases, there may be no reason to switch. However, use cases were intended to be much larger than is common for a user story.

In *UML Distilled*, Martin Fowler says that use case originator Ivar Jacobsen expects about 20 use cases for a ten person-year project. That's six person-months per use case. Fowler goes on to say he likes smaller use cases, perhaps having 100 for a ten person-year project. Assuming two-week sprints, a six-person team would take more than two sprints for each Jacobsen-sized use case. The same team could finish just over two Fowler-sized use cases per sprint.

This conflicts with data I've collected from dozens of Scrum teams and hundreds of sprints showing that six-person teams average six to nine user stories per two-week sprint. This indicates that Scrum teams do best with units of work that are smaller than a typical use case. So, although you can have use cases on your product backlog, be aware that you'll probably want to write far smaller ones than were intended by their originator.

"We write back-end software that no users ever see, so user stories don't make sense for us."

The word *user* in *user stories* makes the approach sound more limiting than it is. User stories have been successfully applied in all sorts of domains. A story that reads, *"As the loan authorization system, I want to receive all data as valid, well-formed XML so that I don't have to worry about syntax checking,"* is perfectly valid. Additionally, although I find writing stories in the *As a <type of user>, I want <some goal> so that <some reason>* format to be best, it may not be best for all projects. If that syntax doesn't fit what you're developing, write the backlog in another format. I've had success with Feature-Driven Development's feature syntax of

> *<action> <result> <object>*

Examples using this syntax would include the following:

- Assess the risk of a loan.
- Authorize a cash withdrawal from an account.
- Activate the "service now" light on the dashboard.
- Calculate the frequency of haplotypes.

- ☐ If it doesn't already exist or isn't in good shape, write your product backlog. Invite all project participants to a meeting and do this collaboratively on index cards. Remind attendees that the text on a story card serves as a promise to have a future discussion; not every detail needs to be included.

- ☐ Print all of the documents that were written on the last project or a typical project. With everyone present, discuss how long each took to write and maintain, whether it was used later, and what would have happened (good or bad) if it had not been written. While doing this, create a pile of documents you agree will be useful on the current project and others you can dispense with.

- ☐ If you are currently using a tool to manage your product and sprint backlog, give it up for at least two sprints. At the end of the planned number of sprints, use the retrospective to discuss how it went. See if you can abandon the tool altogether or reduce your reliance on it toward the use of conversation or paper.

- ☐ In your next sprint retrospective, ask team members to write down the software tool they would most like to stop using. When everyone has finished, share the answers. If one or two tools have been consistently named, discuss the pros and cons of eliminating the tool and then consider dumping it.

Progressively Refine Requirements

When starting a new project, the struggles of the previous project are fresh in our minds. In reflecting on those struggles, a common conclusion is that if we'd only tried harder or done more of something, we might have done better. Although this may sometimes be true, in the case of requirements-gathering it is often not. No matter how long or how hard we work at the start of the project to identify all desired features, we cannot succeed. There are always some things that users and developers cannot be expected to think of until they start to see the system take shape.

Emergent Requirements

These features that we cannot identify in advance are called *emergent requirements*. When someone identifies an emergent requirement, she usually announces it to other team members and users by saying, "Seeing that makes me think of this..." or, "That gives me an idea..." or even occasionally, "Holy crap, we never thought about..." There will always be some things that we think of only after we can see the software. One reason Scrum puts so much emphasis on having working code at the end of each sprint is to create a situation where emergent requirements can be discovered sooner rather than later.

Emergent requirements exist on every nontrivial project, and they can cause problems. For example, emergent requirements make it impossible to perfectly predict schedules. Similarly, an up-front design phase will always be imperfect because it will be impossible for the designers to consider the emergent requirements until they do, in fact, emerge.

When using a sequential development process, project managers handle emergent requirements by adding contingency buffers to the plan and by devoting significant energy to proactive risk management. When an emergent requirement appears, it is viewed as a failure of the plan. In contrast, a Scrum team accepts that requirements will emerge, no matter how carefully team members plan. And rather than view emergent requirements as a failure of the plan, they are viewed as a result of planning either too early or in too much detail.

The first step in dealing with emergent requirements is to acknowledge that we cannot think of everything. After acknowledging that some requirements will emerge as we build the system, it is easier to accept the idea that we don't need (and in fact cannot have) a perfect requirements document up front that specifies all the details of the system to be built. In fact, rather than strive for this degree of completeness, we are better off to specify features with different levels of precision based on when the feature will be worked on.

"I understand that things will change—that requirements can emerge. But I need to specify all requirements at the start of the project because the requirements become part of the contract."

As much as we'd like to lock down requirements in a contract, we can't. We can pretend requirements are locked down and won't change, but some always do. The best contracts reflect this or at least acknowledge that change will happen. Trond Pedersen describes it this way, "Complaining about requirement change is like complaining about the weather. You can't really change the way the world is, but you can find ways to deal with it. Don't make an offering to Thor [the Viking god of thunder] to make the rain stop; get an umbrella."

The Product Backlog Iceberg

Fortunately, it is easy to write a product backlog that contains features written with different levels of detail. The product backlog items that a team will work on soon must be known in sufficient detail that each can be programmed, tested, and integrated within a single sprint. This leads to the user stories at the top of the product backlog being small but reasonably well understood. User stories that are further down are larger and understood in less detail. These *epic* user stories are left large, often known only in enough detail that each can be estimated approximately and then prioritized. This leads the product backlog to take on the shape of an iceberg, as shown in Figure 13.1.

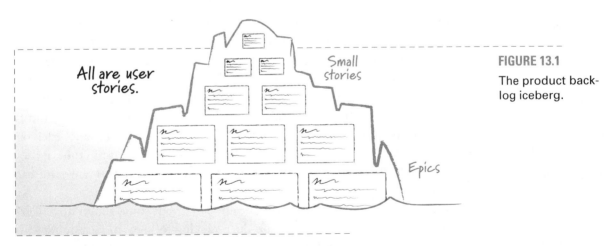

FIGURE 13.1

The product backlog iceberg.

At the top of the product backlog iceberg are the small features the team can fully implement within a sprint. As we look further down the product backlog iceberg (and therefore further into the future), items on the backlog become increasingly larger until we reach the waterline. The team has no idea what lurks beneath there; those are features that haven't even been discussed yet.

Grooming the Product Backlog

As items are developed and removed from the top of the product backlog, the iceberg develops a flat spot at the top and loses its shape. To counter this effect, time must occasionally be spent *grooming the product backlog*. Grooming the product backlog does not refer to combing its hair. Like me, most product backlogs have no hair. Rather, I use *groom* here in the same sense that this morning's ski report said my local mountains have "groomed, packed powder" and that the *Oxford American Dictionary* defines as meaning "to look after." A team needs to groom, or look after, its product backlog.

A good rule of thumb seems to be that about ten percent of the effort in each sprint should be spent grooming the backlog in preparation for future sprints. This time may come from one individual (perhaps an analyst) whose role on the team is largely focused on the backlog. Or it may represent smaller efforts coming from each team member.

Conversations about the product backlog are not limited to a single time or meeting; they can happen any time and among any team members.

> It's the conversations about user stories that enable developers to understand what needs to be built. [A ScrumMaster needs to] encourage conversations about the user stories to keep happening—before planning meetings, in planning meetings, and after planning meetings. (Davies and Sedley 2009, 75)

Your goal should not be to begin each sprint with a perfect understanding of the product backlog items that will be developed during the sprint. A good Scrum team does not need a perfect understanding of a feature before it starts working on it. Rather, at the start of the sprint, the feature needs only to be sufficiently understood that the team has a reasonably strong chance of finishing it during the sprint. Instead of striving to understand all features up front, we want a just-in-time, just-enough approach to understanding features on the product backlog. Large features are split apart and details added to small features just in time as they move up the backlog. Each is described in just-enough detail that the team can complete it during the sprint.

This is not to say that a team cannot choose to put some time into understanding items further down on the product backlog iceberg. In fact, doing so is often necessary. If the team thinks an item further down the product backlog may have an impact on items above it, it can put some effort into understanding it. This often results in the item being split into multiple, smaller product backlog items. However, given our history of favoring up-front understanding of all features, teams should be careful to make sure there is a real need to better understand an

SEE ALSO

Looking ahead down the product backlog is often done by analysts, user experience designers, and others with similar skills. How to do so is described in Chapter 14, "Sprints," in the sections "Prepare in This Sprint for the Next," and "Work Together Throughout the Sprint."

item before putting more early effort into it than would otherwise be warranted based on the item's position on the product backlog.

"We'll never find time to groom the product backlog. We can barely keep up with our coding tasks."

Remember that Scrum requires you to plan for change. Time must be budgeted for grooming the product backlog. It may not be needed in every sprint, but you'll need to do it often enough to keep small, sprint-sized items at the top of the product backlog while deferring investment in items that will be worked on further in the future.

Why Progressively Refine Requirements?

It can be comforting to start a new project by identifying "all" of the requirements. However, because every project has some emergent requirements, it can't be done. Fortunately, there are advantages to progressively refining requirements, including the following:

- **Things will change.** Over the course of a project, priorities will shift. Some features that were initially thought to be important will become less so as the system is shown to potential users and customers. Other needs will be discovered and have to be properly prioritized. If we acknowledge that change is inevitable, the advantages of structuring your product backlog like an iceberg become more apparent. The features most likely to change are those that will be done further into the future; to account for the increased likelihood of change, these features are described only at a high level.

- **There's no need.** Novelist E.L. Doctorow has written that "writing a novel is like driving at night in the fog. You can only see as far as your headlights, but you can make the whole trip that way." Software development is the same way. My headlights don't illuminate everything between me and the horizon because they don't need to. They light the way far enough for me to see and respond at the speeds my car can safely travel. The iceberg-shaped product backlog works similarly. Enough visibility is provided into upcoming items that teams see far enough into the future to avoid most issues. The faster a team goes, the further ahead in the product backlog it will need to peer.

- **Time is scarce.** Nearly all projects are time constrained. We want more than will fit in the time allotted. Treating all requirements as equivalent is wasteful. With a limited supply of one of a project's most critical resources (time), we need to be protective of it. If it is sufficient for now to describe a future feature at a high level, this is all that should be done. When that future feature needs to be better understood—whether because it has moved to the top of the product backlog or because we expect it to influence the implementation of another feature—we can describe it in more detail.

Progressive Refinement of User Stories

An agile requirements process must support the creation of requirements at the various levels shown in the product backlog iceberg of Figure 13.1. Team members must be able to easily create large, placeholder requirements that lie at the bottom of the product backlog iceberg, later disaggregate them into medium-size items, and eventually split them into small-enough pieces that each can be delivered by the team in a single sprint. Just as user stories work well in shifting the emphasis from writing about requirements to talking about them, they also fit well onto the product backlog iceberg. This is because of the ease with which we can move between large and small user stories.

A large user story is typically referred to as an epic. Although there is no magic size at which we start calling a user story an epic, generally an epic is a user story that will take more than one or two sprints to develop and test. Because a team must be able to completely finish a user story within the sprint in which it starts it, this means that epics will be split into smaller user stories before work begins on them. Let's look at an epic and how it may be split into smaller pieces. Consider the following:

- As a user, I am required to log into the system so that my information can only be accessed by me.

This may not appear to be an epic, and it may not be one in all cases. However, for our purposes, let's assume that the product owner clarifies that this simple story is intended to cover everything to do with logging in—requesting a new password, changing the password, and so on. It is about more than pressing a *Login* button on one screen. Based on this, the team decides the story will probably take two or three sprints to develop and test. This makes it an epic. Because it's an epic, it is split into smaller stories, each of which the team thinks can be completed within a single sprint. Here's one possible set of smaller user stories:

- As a registered user, I can log in with my username and password so that I can trust the system.
- As a new user, I want to register by creating a username and password so that the system can remember my personal information.
- As a registered user, I can change my password so that I can keep it secure or make it easier to remember.

- As a registered user, I want the system to warn me if my password is easy to guess so that my account is harder to break into.

- As a forgetful user, I want to be able to request a new password so that I am not permanently locked out if I forget it.

- As a registered user, I do not want to be sure if it was the username, password, or both that was wrong when my login attempt fails so that someone trying to impersonate me will have a harder time doing so.

- As a registered user, I am notified if there have been three consecutive failed attempts to access my account so that I am aware if someone is trying to access my account.

After an epic is split into smaller stories, I recommend that you get rid of it. Delete it from the tool you're using or rip up the index card. You may choose to retain the epic to provide traceability, if that is needed. Or you may choose to retain the epic because it can provide context for the smaller stories created from it. In many cases, the context of the smaller user stories is obvious because the epics should be split in a just-in-time manner as noted earlier. When an epic is ripped up and turned into smaller user stories shortly before the team begins work on it, remembering the context of the small stories is much easier.

Some Epics Are So Large They Split into Epics

In the case of a much larger epic than our password example, the split may occur in multiple steps: first into some medium-sized stories (perhaps epics themselves), then later into smaller ones. As an example of a larger epic, consider this user story from a company developing software for use by large retail stores:

- As a vice president of marketing, I want to review the performance of historical advertising campaigns so that I can identify profitable campaigns worth repeating.

The idea was that the vice president would be able to browse through statistics on various past advertising campaigns and select the best ones to repeat. For example, which worked best: the television ads during *Desperate Housewives*, the twice-a-day radio ads, the Thursday newspaper inserts, or the e-mail campaign?

It was clear to all involved on this project that this initial story was too large to complete in one of their two-week sprints. So the story was split in two:

- As a vice president of marketing, I want to select the time frame to use when reviewing the performance of past advertising campaigns so that I can identify profitable ones.

- As a vice president of marketing, I want to select which type of campaigns (direct mail, TV, e-mail, radio, and so on) to include when reviewing the performance of historical advertising campaigns.

The team felt that these stories, while smaller, might still be too large to complete within a sprint, so they were split further. The story about selecting the time frame to use was split into three stories:

- As a vice president of marketing, I want to set simple date ranges to be used when reviewing the performance of past advertising campaigns so that I can pick an exact set of dates.

- As a vice president of marketing, I want to select seasons (spring, summer, winter, fall) to be used when reviewing the performance of past advertising campaigns so that I can view trends across multiple years.

- As a vice president of marketing, I want to select a holiday period (Easter, Christmas, and so on) to be used when reviewing the performance of past advertising campaigns so that I can look for trends across multiple years.

After this final split, the team felt the stories were small enough to complete during a sprint and stopped there. Notice though that even these stories may not be trivial to implement. Selecting holiday ranges such as "from Good Friday through Easter Sunday" or from "Thanksgiving until Christmas" will be difficult because the dates move around from year to year. There was a chance the team could have considered these too big.

In many cases it will be possible to go from a large epic near the waterline of the iceberg directly to small, implementation-size stories. Whether you choose to go through the intermediate step of splitting a large epic into multiple smaller epics will be up to you and largely driven by the context of the project.

Adding Conditions of Satisfaction

Eventually stories are small enough that splitting them further is no longer helpful. At this point it is still possible to progressively refine the requirement by adding *conditions of satisfaction* to the user story. A condition of satisfaction is simply a high-level acceptance test that will be true after the user story is complete. As an example, let's reconsider the following story:

- As a vice president of marketing, I want to select a holiday season to be used when reviewing the performance of past advertising campaigns so that I can identify profitable ones.

We've already established that this is small enough for the team to complete in a sprint. So let's continue to progressively refine this requirement by working with the product owner to add its conditions of satisfaction. To do so, we turn the index card over (metaphorically if you're using a product backlog management tool or wiki) and write the following conditions of satisfaction:

- Make sure it works with major retail holidays: Christmas, Easter, President's Day, Mother's Day, Father's Day, Labor Day, New Year's Day.

- Support holidays that span two calendar years (none span three).

- Holiday seasons can be set from one holiday to the next (such as Thanksgiving to Christmas).

- Holiday seasons can be set to be a number of days prior to the holiday.

Progressive refinement by adding conditions of satisfaction helps the team members by telling them the product owner's expectations for that feature. These can be expectations about what will be included and about what will not be. For example, given the conditions of satisfaction for this story, it's clear that we do not need to support Chinese New Year. Although I seize every opportunity to enjoy a spicy Chinese meal, it is not exactly a big shopping holiday here in the United States. Of course, the product owner could have made this even more obvious by explicitly stating, "Does not need to support Chinese New Year." But even that is probably not necessary because the conversations that support this written part of the user story should bring out details such as that.

> **THINGS TO TRY NOW**

❑ Convert your existing product backlog to user stories. Print each current product backlog item on an index card. Group similar cards on a large table or flat surface. For high-priority groups of cards, write individual user stories. Be aware that there will probably not be a one-to-one correlation between old product backlog items and new user stories. For lower-priority groups, replace each group with a single epic. Paper clip or staple the old cards behind the new epic, so you'll have them for reference when it's time to split the epic into sprint-size user stories.

❑ During your next sprint planning meeting, make sure that each user story you are bringing into the sprint has clearly identified conditions of satisfaction by the time that meeting ends. During the following sprint retrospective, discuss whether having these identified was helpful.

Learn to Start Without a Specification

Because a Scrum team shifts its focus from writing requirements to talking about them and then progressively refines those requirements over the course of the project, the team is left without the comfort of starting with a traditional specification document. Many groups—quality assurance and technical writing foremost among them—will find this very disconcerting. Part of transitioning to Scrum and achieving long-term success with it will be learning how to comfortably get started on a project without a "complete" specification document.

First, I should be clear that the goal is not to throw out what may be a useful document. What we want instead is to use a specification document appropriately. Apart from meeting regulatory or compliance needs, the primary appropriate use of a specification document is to convey information that is best done in writing. Complex or detailed calculations such as might be found in scientific and mathematical applications are good examples, but there can be many others.

One of the dangers of specification documents is that they are seldom kept up to date. Before you write a document, ask yourself if you are willing to commit to updating the document. If not, either think twice about writing it or consider putting an expiration date on the document, similar to the "best if used by" date on a milk carton.

Specify by Example

Another thing you may want to do is change how you write your specifications. Consider specifying a product through examples. Examples are a wonderful way to communicate the desired behavior of a system, especially when augmented with conversations and some small amount of explanatory written text. Gojko Adzic, author of the book *Bridging the Communication Gap*, describes the value of using examples to explain behavior.

> Working with real-world examples helps us communicate better because people will be able to relate to them more easily. It is also easier to spot inconsistencies between realistic examples. Developers, business people, and testers all need to participate in the discussion about examples. Developers learn about the domain and get a solid foundation for implementation. Testers obtain the knowledge they need firsthand, and they can influence the development by suggesting important cases for discussion. (2009, 32)

To see how this works, suppose we are building a system for use within our company that will automatically approve or reject requests for time off. The first thing our product owner wants is for the system to automatically approve requests that are for fewer days than the employee has already accrued. She writes a user story to describe this: *"As an employee, I want a request for up to my earned vacation time to be automatically approved so that I don't need to wait for someone to approve it manually."* The product owner, perhaps working with a tester, then elaborates by providing the examples shown in Table 13.1.

TABLE 13.1

days_accrued	days_requested	approved?
6	5	Yes
5	6	No
5	5	Yes

Examples showing that a request for more time off than has been accrued will not be automatically approved.

The rows of Table 13.1 show different test cases. The first two columns show the test data of those test cases. The final column indicates what the result of the test should be. So, the first row describes an employee who has accrued six days of time off and has requested five days. In the final column we can see that this request should be approved.

This is an admittedly simple illustration of specification by example, so let's see what happens when the product owner writes the next user story: *"As an employee who has been here more than a year, I want automatic approval of a time-off request that is up to five days more than I've currently accrued."* Specifying this through examples, the product owner creates Table 13.2.

TABLE 13.2

days_accrued	days_requested	employed_over_1_year	approved?
10	11	No	No
10	11	Yes	Yes
10	11	No	No
10	15	Yes	Yes
10	16	Yes	No

A slightly more involved example begins to show the power of specification by example.

Table 13.2 is still fairly simple but hopefully it starts to show the power of specification by example.[1] I won't create more detailed examples, but notice how specification by example becomes even more helpful as the scenarios become more complex. For example, in the preceding user stories the number of days accrued was fixed. In many companies time off is accrued monthly. So a request that might be rejected today could be one that would be approved if the date of the desired time off is three months into the future. To specify a situation such as that with examples, we would add to the table such columns as the request date,

---

1   This example has been intentionally kept simple so as to show how specification by example works. A more thorough implementation of the same example but showing better ways to construct equivalent tables has been provided by Jeff Langr, author of *Agile Java*. His implementation is available at www.informit.com/articles/article.aspx?p=1393274.

the time off start date, and the rate of accrual. Explaining a detailed requirement such as this through a combination of conversations and examples increases the likelihood that what the product owner thinks she's asked for is what the developers build.

Specification by example becomes extremely powerful when the examples can be turned into automated tests. This is not as far-fetched as it may seem. One of the biggest benefits is that we can instantly tell if the specification is out of date—run the automated tests, if they pass then the application conforms to the specification. The tests become self-verifying specifications. They both express detailed design decisions and automatically verify that the application conforms to that specification.

This is exactly the approach taken by Trond Wingård, an agile project manager in Norway. Wingård's team made extensive use of FitNesse, a wiki for creating executable tests and specifications in the form of tests. His project's approach is shown in Figure 13.2 and described by Wingård as follows:

> We have a policy that all requirements and tests should be in FitNesse—no exceptions. Even if we find that we need some manual tests, they too should be described in the FitNesse wiki, not somewhere else. The front page contains a list of nine "user epics" linked to a page for each epic. On each of those pages, the epic is described in user story format, followed by a list of each of the user stories that make up this epic. Each story corresponds to an item on the Product Backlog and is linked to the story's page. On a story page, the story is described followed by a grouped list of Conditions of Satisfaction. These COS are grouped, and each group has its own page with FitNesse tests for them. This structure was very easy to set up and easy to grasp and is a real help for the team.

SEE ALSO

FitNesse, available from www.fitnesse.org, is my favorite tool for doing this. It allows you to create and run tests that specify functionality by example almost exactly as shown here. Another popular tool is Cucumber.

FIGURE 13.2

A series of FitNesse wiki pages that go from high-level requirements written as epics all the way to test cases for each user story.

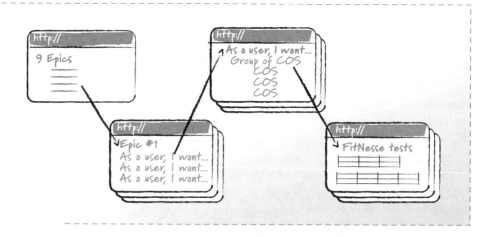

Cross-Functional Teams Reduce Documentation Needs

A common objection to getting rid of or reducing the scope of specification documents is that these documents are the only way some groups learn what is expected of the system. A QA group, for example, may reason that without a specification document it will not know which behavior is expected and which is buggy. In an organization's pre-Scrum days this would likely have been true. The programmers may have met on their own, made decisions, and then relayed the decisions to the testers through specification documents. After years of exposure to working this way, it would be fair for testers to assert that without the specifications they won't know what to test.

On a Scrum project, however, the programmers and testers work as one team. There is no programming team that hands off work to a testing team. Instead, there is a cross-functional, multidisciplinary team. The testers don't need the same type of documents because work isn't handed off to them in the same way it was in the past. In fact, work isn't handed off to them at all. A tester should be part of the discussion whenever what would have gone in the document is discussed.

Back in my pre-agile days, I often found myself in the middle of arguments between the programmers and testers on a project. The testers complained that programmers weren't keeping documents up to date; the programmers complained that they didn't benefit from the documents. After hearing these same arguments repeated on a handful of projects, I came to the realization that those who benefit from a document should be the ones to write it. Because the testers were the ones who claimed to benefit from the detailed specifications that the programmers were not maintaining, they became the ones responsible for writing and maintaining the document. Not only did this solve my problem, it introduced the additional benefit of forcing the programmers and testers to talk earlier and more frequently so the testers would have the information they needed to write their document. Johannes Brodwall reports using a similar strategy.

> Testers were used to getting very vague, yet very detailed documents and had to try to reinterpret these as test cases. With a more agile approach, the tester is actually the one who's responsible for writing the detailed specification in the first place. Today, we have the tester write the "specification" in terms of testable scenarios at the beginning of an iteration.

Make the Product Backlog DEEP

Roman Pichler, author of *Agile Product Management with Scrum: Creating Products That Customers Love*, and I use the acronym DEEP to summarize key attributes of a good product backlog.

- **Detailed Appropriately.** User stories on the product backlog that will be done soon need to be sufficiently well understood that they can be completed in the coming sprint. Stories that will not be developed for awhile should be described with less detail.
- **Estimated.** The product backlog is more than a list of all work to be done; it is also a useful planning tool. Because items further down the backlog are not as well understood (yet), the estimates associated with them will be less precise than estimates given items at the top.
- **Emergent.** A product backlog is not static. It will change over time. As more is learned, user stories on the product backlog will be added, removed, or reprioritized.
- **Prioritized.** The product backlog should be sorted with the most valuable items at the top and the least valuable at the bottom. By always working in priority order, the team is able to maximize the value of the product or system being developed.

Don't Forget to Talk

Although a project's product backlog will be written somewhere—typically on index cards or entered into a software tool—the product backlog is not a one-to-one replacement for a traditional project's requirements document or use case model. Just as important as what is written in the actual product backlog are the conversations that surround it. These conversations occur when the team and product owner work together to brainstorm items for the initial product backlog And they happen during a sprint as the team and product owner progressively refine their understanding of a feature. In looking to improve your team's use of the product backlog, don't forget the importance of these conversations.

Additional Reading

Adzic, Gojko. 2009. *Bridging the communication gap: Specification by example and agile acceptance testing.* Neuri Limited.

This excellent book describes the reasons why communicating about requirements is difficult. It then proposes specification by example as the solution. Particularly valuable is the chapter on selecting examples. The book also includes a chapter on tools that facilitate specification by example.

Cao, Lan, and Balasubramaniam Ramesh. 2008. Agile requirements engineering practices: An empirical study. *IEEE Software*, January/February, 60–67.

The authors of this academic research paper studied requirements gathering at 16 software development organizations that were using agile approaches. From this study

they identified the benefits and challenges of using a handful of specific agile requirements practices.

Cohn, Mike. 2004. *User stories applied: For agile software development.* Addison-Wesley
Professional.
This book is a thorough explanation of working with user stories. In it I write about
identifying user roles, writing user stories, conducting story-writing workshops, the
six attributes of good user stories, and even how to plan a project with user stories.

Mugridge, Rick, and Ward Cunningham. 2005. *Fit for developing software: Framework for
integrated tests.* Prentice Hall.
Fit, the Framework for Integrated Tests, is an open source product. It can be used to
create human-readable automated tests that can specify behavior through examples,
similar to the tables shown in the last section of this chapter. The first 180 pages are
readable by anyone on the project, technical or not, and show how Fit can benefit
a project. The next 150 or so pages are meant for those with a programming background and dive into the specifics of using Fit.

Chapter 14

Sprints

Like all of the agile processes, Scrum is an iterative and incremental approach to software development. Although the terms *iterative* and *incremental* each have a unique meaning, they are often used together. Let's briefly tease them apart so we can better understand their meanings.

Incremental development involves building a system piece by piece. First one part is developed, then a next is added to the first, and so on. Alistair Cockburn describes incremental development as primarily a "staging and scheduling strategy" (2008). An incremental approach to developing an online auction site might involve first developing the capability to create accounts on the site, next developing the capability to list items for sale, and then developing the capability to bid on items, and so on.

By contrast, iterative development is what Cockburn refers to as a "rework scheduling strategy" (2008). An iterative development process acknowledges the impossibility (or at least improbability) of getting a feature right the first time. In building an online auction site iteratively, we may first develop a preliminary version of the full site, get feedback on it, develop a subsequent version of the full site that incorporates the feedback, and repeat the process as needed.

So in an incremental process, we fully develop one feature and then move onto the next. In an iterative process, we build the entire system but do so imperfectly at first, using subsequent passes across the entire system to improve it. The weaknesses inherent in being only iterative or only incremental disappear when they are combined, as they are in Scrum.

In this chapter we examine how Scrum's sprints combine iterative and incremental development. We consider the importance of ending each sprint with working software that is valuable to the system's users or customers. You will see why it's necessary for the whole team to work together during the sprint. Along the way, we also look at how a Scrum team ensures that it finishes one sprint prepared for the next, the importance of setting and sticking with a goal for the sprint, and the need to timebox how long the team has to achieve a goal.

Deliver Working Software Each Sprint

By the end of each sprint, a Scrum team is required to produce working software. Working software is software that is both complete and potentially shippable. Working software is required from both feature teams and component teams. Learning how to deliver working software each sprint is one of the biggest challenges that a new Scrum team must overcome. Yet doing so is critical to becoming agile. In fact, it's so important that one of the four values given in the Agile Manifesto states that we are to value "working software over comprehensive documentation" (Beck et al. 2001). Agile methodologies emphasize working software for three key reasons:

SEE ALSO

Feature and component teams were described in Chapter 10, "Team Structure."

- **Working software encourages feedback.** A team can collect more and better feedback if it shows (or better, gives) a functioning but partial product to users than if it provides those users with a document about what the product will do. Not only will users provide better feedback from being able to see and touch the product, they will be more likely to engage in the request to provide feedback in the first place. A 50-page product specification is too likely to get buried and ignored.

- **Working software helps a team gauge its progress.** One of the biggest risks on a project is not knowing how much remains to be done. When too much of a system is allowed to linger too long in an unfinished state, it is extremely difficult to know how much effort will be required to bring the system to a shippable state. By emphasizing working software and requiring the delivery of some portion of user value in each sprint, Scrum teams avoid this problem.

SEE ALSO

More on adjusting scope can be found in the section "Favor Scope Changes When Possible" in Chapter 15, "Planning."

- **Working software allows the product to ship early if desired.** In today's competitive and rapidly changing world, the option to ship early (even if that means delivering fewer features) can be very valuable. Putting the software in or near this position at the end of every sprint provides this option.

Defining Potentially Shippable

In the mid-1990s, it became popular for teams doing iterative and incremental development to set the target of periodically bringing the application to a "Zero Defect (ZD) milestone." Jim McCarthy, former director of the Microsoft Visual C++ group, wrote and spoke often about ZD milestones.

> Zero defects does not mean that the product does not have bugs, or missing functionality; it means that the product achieves the quality level that had been set for that milestone. The product is tested to that effect. The essential point of ZD milestones is that

nobody makes the milestone until everybody does, and nobody leaves it until everybody does. This enables the team to discover what aspects of the project are in trouble.

At a milestone, the team and its leadership also have the opportunity to perceive the whole project status simultaneously, to draw conclusions about erroneous practices, to remedy bad design decisions, and to reorganize for peak performance…The team develops extraordinary focus and introspection about each and every milestone. (2004)

Although McCarthy's ZD milestone is still a good target for many teams, Scrum teams set their sights higher and target the delivery of potentially shippable software at the end of each sprint. But what does *potentially shippable* mean? To fully define *potentially shippable* would require knowledge of the domain and application that only the team, including its product owner and ScrumMaster, will have. In fact, one thing any new team should do is discuss and agree on a definition of *done* that defines a potentially shippable product increment appropriate for its environment. Each product backlog item brought into a sprint will then be expected to comply with these criteria before being considered complete. Chapter 13, "The Product Backlog," introduced the idea of conditions of satisfaction as acceptance criteria for individual user stories. In many ways, the elements that comprise a team's definition of done are like conditions of satisfaction that are applied across all user stories on the product backlog.

As an example, ePlan Services, which offers retirement accounts to small companies, defines *done* to include "coded, tested, checked-in, well-written, integrated, and has automated tests." Each product backlog item the team works on needs to comply with these expectations in addition to its item-specific conditions of satisfaction. Consider this ePlan Services user story: *"As a user, I can pay account maintenance fees by credit card so that fees are not taken from my after-tax retirement account."* For this user story, let's say that the product owner provided the following conditions of satisfaction:

- Accept Visa, MasterCard, and American Express.
- Do not store credit card information in our system.
- Process all transactions in a secure manner.

So not only would these conditions of satisfaction have to be met, but also the conditions set forth in the project-specific definition of done (coded, tested, checked-in, well-written, integrated, and has automated tests) would need to be met.

"Our application is too complex to be developed incrementally."

Usually this argument means that it's too hard to think of ways to build the product incrementally, rather than it is actually impossible to do. When I am presented with this argument, I ask the person making it to tell me where some natural breakpoints are in the application. She will usually provide me with three or four parts of the system, and she will be correct that each is too large to fit into a sprint. However, once she acknowledges that we can work incrementally (even if the increments are too large at this point in the discussion), I've won the argument that "our application is too complex to be developed incrementally." At that point we both agree it is possible; we just need to find ways to split the logical pieces of functionality so that each can be developed within a sprint.

Next, I make the point that while we want to deliver potentially shippable pieces of the product each sprint, we do not need to end each sprint with a cohesive product. That is, while the product needs to be solid at the end of each sprint, we call it *potentially* shippable as a reminder that the developed features may not be sufficient yet to be truly shippable.

Identifying Potentially Shippable Guidelines

Although it is up to the organization or team to establish an appropriate definition of done for its context, there are certain guidelines that are applicable across most Scrum projects in most organizations.

Potentially shippable means tested. Although the exact definition of what constitutes potentially shippable belongs either to the organization or the team, I can't think of a situation in which it would be OK for the team to leave testing out of this definition. By the end of the sprint, we must have the expectation that new features are bug free and that no bugs were introduced into old features. For some products, we may not be 100% sure of this, but we would always like to be as close to sure as possible. That being said, special-purpose types of testing such as integration testing, performance testing, usability testing, and so on may not be performed every sprint. Rather, these types of testing can be performed in release sprints that may be inserted following every handful or so of regular sprints.

As an example of the proper use of a release sprint, consider a bank I worked with that had a large legacy application on a mainframe. It consisted of a few million lines of COBOL code that was being maintained by a handful of developers using the same sequential process they'd used for two decades. There was little active development on this part of the system, which was fortunate because testing this beast took three weeks of manual effort.

The bank also had a relatively small, 300,000-line Java application that provided web-based access to the same financial data. Both applications shared the same database. This meant that it was possible for the web application to write data to the database that would adversely affect the COBOL application. The web application had been written mostly by a Scrum team.

As a good Scrum team should, the web team targeted a potentially shippable product at the end of each sprint. Members defined *potentially shippable* as well-written and tested to a point that they were reasonably sure no important (money-affecting) bugs remained. This involved writing the best code they could and adding to and then running a complete set of automated tests on the web application. This put the web application in a potentially shippable state in their minds. Going from potentially shippable to shippable required an occasional release sprint during which the three weeks of manual testing of the mainframe application was performed.

Potentially shippable does not necessarily mean cohesive. Just because a product is potentially shippable doesn't mean anyone wants us to actually ship it yet. Sometimes it takes two, three, or more sprints for a feature set to come together in a minimally useful manner. However, during the sprints leading up to that point, the team should still strive to put the product into a potentially shippable state by the end of each sprint.

As an example, consider a company that was adding printing and print preview to its product. During sprint planning, the team decided it could not add printing and print preview within the same sprint. With the product owner's blessing, the team elected to work on print preview first. It successfully completed print preview by the end of the sprint. At that time, print preview was rock solid; it was well-written, thoroughly tested, and the product could have been shipped with it. However, who would want a product with print preview but without printing? Still, the lack of a cohesive feature set after that first sprint does not prevent the product from being potentially shippable. If someone had wanted it with only print preview, the team could have shipped it.

Potentially shippable means integrated. A potentially shippable product does not exist as 14 different collections of source code. On a multiteam project, the teams should define done such that it includes integrating development streams. To the extent possible, integration should be done continuously throughout the sprint.

SEE ALSO

For more on integrating the work of multiple teams, see Chapter 17, "Scaling Scrum."

OBJECTION

We can't run sprints at the start of our project; a certain amount of infrastructure needs to be built first.

Developers new to Scrum will often concede that iterative and incremental development seem feasible after a sufficient amount of the application has already been written but will be impossible until then. I disagree. Even infrastructural elements can be built incrementally. During early sprints it is often necessary to work mostly or entirely on the infrastructural aspects of the product. I'll concede that it is often difficult to find ways to demonstrate the value of this work to end users, but it's OK to sometimes struggle in that regard, especially early on. Just because something is hard is no reason to abandon it. Instead, find ways to split those early infrastructural pieces into smaller pieces that can fit within a sprint. One way I do this is to think about the natural points where I might call a coworker over and say, "Hey, check out the cool new thing I just got working." Whenever something is done enough that a coworker can provide feedback (even if it's just the positive reinforcement of "good job"), it is likely to be a reasonable chunk of functionality to target for an early sprint.

Finding these natural points can help ensure that even a team's earliest sprints will still contain something visible or of value to a user or customer, which is the topic of the next section.

THINGS TO TRY NOW

❑ Have the product owner and team discuss and agree on what *done* means for the end of a sprint. Post the definition where all can see it daily.

❑ As a team, make a list of all the problems you have individually experienced on past projects by letting a product get too far from shippable. Discuss what could be done to overcome these problems.

Deliver Something Valuable Each Sprint

As though making sure each sprint ends with working software isn't challenging enough, Scrum teams are also required to deliver something valuable to the system or product's users or customers each sprint. The definition of what is valuable to users or customers can be stretched quite easily and maliciously. For example, a team can say that upgrading all developer desktops to the newest version of their preferred operating system allows them to develop more quickly so that new features make it to customers more quickly. Although this may very well be true, the intent is that each sprint should deliver something of immediate value to users or customers that they can see. Because one of the benefits of working in sprints is the ability to generate feedback from users and customers at the end of each sprint, a team will get better feedback if at least some of the work done each sprint results in features that users can see.

As an example of what I mean by user-visible features, suppose that a single team is developing a website that will allow people to search for houses for sale. At one of the sprint planning meetings, the product owner wants to add the ability for users to enter any combination of 20 search parameters and see a nicely presented list of matching houses. The team tells the product owner that this is too much to complete in a single sprint. The work must be split and done over two sprints. The team and product owner discuss it and come up with the following options of what they could complete in the coming sprint:

1. The team focuses only on the back-end search. At the sprint review, users will see text-only results of searches run from a command line.

2. The team focuses only on the user interface. At the sprint review, users will see fully functional screens but only with mocked-up data rather than data retrieved from the database.

3. The team splits its time between the back-end search and the user interface. At the sprint review, the team shows an application that supports 10 of the 20 planned search fields and a user interface that, while functional, is incomplete.

Which of these approaches is best? First, let me state that there are times when each may be appropriate. However, in general, the third approach listed here is the one you should prefer. In that approach the team has sent what Andy Hunt and Dave Thomas call a "tracer bullet" through the application. According to Dave Thomas, a tracer bullet is an attempt to "produce something really early on that we can actually give to the user to see how close we will be to the target. As time goes on, we can adjust our aim slightly by seeing where we are in relation to our user's target" (Venners 2003).

But what about options one and two? If I were coaching this team I might allow either of these approaches, but only if it we could not find a way to send a tracer bullet through the feature, as with the third option. Of the first two choices, I vastly prefer the first (delivering the back-end and showing that it works through a command-line interface). In that scenario, the team is able to demonstrate that the desired feature works; it just isn't pretty yet and hasn't been added to a web page. If shown this in a sprint review, most users or customers would agree that the functionality represents a step forward.

The second choice—developing only the user interface—is not appealing to me. Although it can be argued that completing only the back-end or only the front-end of a feature are two sides of the same coin, I do think there's a difference. When the team shows only the back-end functionality, no one will mistakenly think the feature is done. Minimally, some stakeholder may think "all we need to do is slap a user interface on it." But in the case where a team presents only the user interface part of a feature, it will be tempting for some stakeholders to think that the feature is done since they can see it.

So, although the first two options here do provide value to users of the system, teams should prefer sending a tracer bullet through the application. I mention the alternatives but consider them valid only in the case when a team absolutely cannot instead send a tracer bullet through the application.

Unobservable Features

Although not all products include functionality that is visible to end users, every product does have functionality that is visible to someone. For example, suppose that, instead of one team, five teams are working on our houses-for-sale website. Four are feature teams developing functionality that site visitors will see. The fifth team is a component team building a common data access layer that is being used by the feature teams.

SEE ALSO

See Chapter 10 for a discussion of the relative merits of feature and component teams.

This fifth team may be tempted to think that nothing it is building is user visible. The fallacy in this thinking is obvious when that team realizes that its users are the other four teams, rather than the end users. The fifth team, which we'll call the data access team, is interested in getting feedback from its users—the programmers and testers on the four other teams. So it is to those teams that functionality should be visible. This means that in its sprint review, the data access team could demonstrate a purely technical feature (such as a cascading delete in the database) that we would not want a feature team to demonstrate in its sprint review.

Johannes Brodwall worked on a project for a new version of a system for batch processing of payments sent in electronic files. Although this system had tremendous value to its customers, it is a good example of a system with not much to see. Brodwall describes how the team members solved the problem.

> For our most recent sprint review, we ran four weeks of data from the production system on the new system. The demo was a web page that collected the output of the new system and compared it to the output of the old system. The web page listed the number of transactions that had differing results as a table. These transactions were categorized into varying groups of deviation by column (for example, some things should be processed differently) and by each individual day on the rows. Each cell was clickable to show the exact transactions that had deviated. Even though we didn't "show the system," we did show this report. This helped the team and product owner build confidence that the new software would work when shipped.

I have seen many situations like the one Brodwall describes. The team takes on a slight bit of extra work to produce something more demonstrable and engaging for the sprint review. What always intrigues me is how often this slight detour proves valuable to the team as well. Often this small bit of extra effort helps the team test the system and more easily investigate unexpected test results.

"Our deadline is 18 months away; the overhead of delivering value in every sprint is unnecessary."

A person making this argument does not yet see the value of working iteratively. Done properly, working iteratively does not require a great deal of overhead. Yes, automated tests will be needed so that teams don't waste weeks manually retesting every sprint. But working iteratively does not require a team to do a great deal of additional work at the end of each sprint that it should not do anyway. All that is necessary is that the team find logical breakpoints where work can be tied up and demonstrated.

"We can't deliver value for the first few months."

This belief is very common on projects of a year or more. When countering this position it is important to remember that the two primary benefits of delivering value each sprint are the ability to solicit feedback as early as possible and the assurance that the team members are never in a position to deceive themselves (even unintentionally) about their progress.

I will grant that on some projects we may not be able to get useful end-user feedback for a few months, but I still want complete, working, tested functionality each sprint. If that functionality is not quite yet something that my end users will be able to see (or see the value of), then I make sure that my product owner can understand the value of what's been completed. With the product owner acting as a rigorous judge of whether the team has taken a step in the right direction (always preferring working software over documentation), the team is unlikely to take steps that result in a lot of activity but little forward progress.

❑ At the end of each of the next three to five sprints, make sure your software is in the hands of real users. If a formal release isn't practical for your type of product, find friendly first users who can provide feedback on the new functionality. After the final sprint, consider whether this was useful.

❑ For each product backlog item you develop in the next three sprints, have the team explicitly identify a person or audience to whom that item will be valuable. After three sprints, discuss what you learned from doing this and whether it was valuable to you.

Prepare in This Sprint for the Next

I got a call from a development director who needed some coaching for her three teams. Their early use of Scrum was going well except that sprint planning was taking each team three days. I couldn't fathom how this was possible, so I was anxious to visit these teams and see what they were doing. I pictured them locked in a conference room for the entire three days, either endlessly debating how to break out the tasks of each product backlog item they were working on or breaking each task out in unnecessary detail. What I found instead were billiard ball sprints.

Billiard Ball Sprints

Shoot a billiard ball across the table and into another ball and—whack!—the second ball is sent rolling across the table. With billiard ball sprints, the team finishes one sprint, isn't ready to start the next, and—whack!—the start of the next sprint is pushed into the future. The second sprint often starts in name, but the team is so unprepared to do the work of that sprint that it spends days learning about what is expected. This is what was occurring at my client who called with the complaint of three-day sprint planning meetings.

The best way to avoid billiard bill sprints is to follow the Boy Scout motto: Be prepared. Expend a little effort in each sprint preparing for the following sprint. Ken Schwaber recommends allocating about 10% of a team's available time in any sprint toward preparing for the next sprint (2009). I've found this to generally be about the right amount as well. The team should, of course, adjust this amount up or down based on its experience.

SEE ALSO

Grooming the product backlog, as described in Chapter 13, is one way time is spent in this sprint preparing for the next.

Only Pull into a Sprint What Can Be Completed

We already know that a team should not pull a user story or other product backlog item into a sprint if it is clearly too large to be completed. An epic user story that will take months to complete should be split into much smaller pieces so that each can be completed within a sprint. The same is true of user stories that are too vague; if a story is not sufficiently well understood that it can be completed in a sprint, it should not be brought into the sprint. Instead, the team needs to spend some effort learning about the story first.

Notice I used the phrase sufficiently understood rather than fully understood. A user story on the product backlog does not need to be fully thought through, with every last detail worked out, before it is pulled into a sprint. In fact, we don't even want items to be *fully* thought through. The product owner and other team members will still collaborate on the story during the sprint. But, each user story pulled into the sprint must be understood in enough detail that, when augmented by discussions during the sprint, it can be completed during the sprint.

To see how this works, let's consider the case of user experience design. Some user stories need a lot of user experience design; others do not. For example, suppose the team has chosen to implement a user story that says, *"As a user, I can view an About dialog with copyright, version number, and company contact information so that I can find contact information for the company."* I suspect that even within a short, two-week sprint, the user experience designers can mock up a few screens, run them by a few users, incorporate any feedback, and have screen designs programmed and tested. In other words, this user story is fine as is. A short description scrawled on an index card is sufficient for that story to be designed, coded, and tested within one sprint.

Next, consider a team adding features to a recently launched eCommerce site. The team is shown a new user story: *"As an existing customer, I can cancel an order that has not yet shipped so that I can change my mind without cost."* This involves new workflows that have not been considered as part of launching the basic, initial eCommerce site. During the sprint planning meeting, the team's user experience designers identify the following tasks:

- Create three initial mock-ups in Photoshop, 12 hours each
- Schedule demos with 15 users, 2 hours
- Conduct four demo sessions, 8 hours total
- Meet to discuss design changes, 4 hours
- Create new design in Photoshop, 8 hours
- Schedule second round of demos, 2 hours
- Conduct four second demo sessions, 8 hours total
- Write HTML and CSS incorporating final changes, 16 hours

This is quite a bit more work than was needed on the story for the *About* dialog. Team members discuss this and decide that it will not be possible to do all of this work, plus code the full screen into the application and test it, all within one sprint. But they reason that if at least the first demo sessions were done this sprint, they would be able to complete the user story in the next sprint. And so, this is what the team decides to do.

Notice that when the second sprint starts and the team pulls this story into its sprint, it is are still not starting with a fully specified user story. Final details will be worked out during the sprint. The amount of detail that must accompany a product backlog item as it is pulled into a sprint is the minimum amount necessary so that the item can go from product backlog item to running, tested feature in one sprint. This will be different for each product backlog item.

OBJECTION

"This doesn't sound like Scrum. Scrum teams are supposed to produce a potentially shippable product increment every sprint."

The team is still expected to produce a potentially shippable product increment. But it is shortsighted to think that all of a team's time during a sprint should be spent directly on that sprint's product increment. Team members spend time on all sorts of valuable activities that are unrelated to creating the current sprint's product increment. Interviewing prospective new team members, for example, is investing time that will not be paid back until after the new member joins the team (and is up to speed). Estimating product backlog items so that the product owner can prioritize the product backlog is not directed at this sprint's product increment, yet is valuable. Time spent making sure that enough work is understood in just enough detail that it can be completed in the next sprint is similar to these cases.

THINGS TO TRY NOW

❏ Discuss the product backlog. Identify the top five items in need of advance thinking. For each, discuss who needs to think about it (an architect? user experience designer? database designer? other?) and decide how many sprints in advance that should begin.

❏ In your next three sprint reviews, discuss whether each product backlog item included just-enough detail and whether it was added just in time.

❏ For a sprint or two, track the amount of time spent thinking ahead. Is it enough? too much? Remember that normally about 10% of a team's available time should be spent looking ahead.

Work Together Throughout the Sprint

Apple has always been known as a highly innovative company. Its Apple II, Macintosh, and iPod were some of the most significant innovations in the personal computer era. Steve Jobs, founder of Apple, was asked how the company had so consistently innovated great products. He answered in the form of a story.

> You know how you see a show car, and it's really cool, and then four years later you see the production car, and it sucks? And you go, What happened? They had it! They had it in the palm of their hands! They grabbed defeat from the jaws of victory! What happened was, the designers came up with this really great idea. Then they take it to the engineers, and the engineers go, "Nah, we can't do that. That's impossible." And so it gets a lot worse. Then they

take it to the manufacturing people, and they go, "We can't build that!" And it gets a lot worse. (Grossman 2005, 68)

What Jobs is referring to is the deep collaboration that should exist on an experienced Scrum team. Rather than handing off work from group to group, a Scrum project is characterized by cross-functional teams working together. At Apple "products don't pass from team to team. There aren't discrete, sequential development stages. Instead, it's simultaneous and organic. Products get worked on in parallel by all departments at once—design, hardware, software—in endless rounds of interdisciplinary design reviews" (Grossman 2005, 68).

This is, of course, easier said than done. One of the easiest traps to fall into is performing work serially within the sprints. A team in this trap may decide that the first week of a sprint will be for analysis, the second week for design, the third for coding, and the fourth for testing. A serial approach to completing the work of a sprint is clearly inefficient. There's too much sitting around, too much specialization, and too many hand-offs. Fortunately, even though many Scrum teams start this way, most quickly see the problems. When they do, they start to look for ways to overlap work. The goal should be to overlap as much as possible the various activities required to go from idea to shippable feature.

At first, finding ways to improve the overlap of activities will seem difficult. But most teams soon realize that many of the agile engineering practices help. Writing automated unit tests, for example, reduces the number of bugs, which allows programming to continue later into the sprint while still allowing time for other testing. Test-driven development (especially acceptance test–driven development) merges analysis, design, and coding activities with testing.

SEE ALSO

The section "Do a Little Bit of Everything All the Time" in Chapter 11, "Teamwork," offered suggestions on how team members can overlap their work.

SEE ALSO

Information on these practices was provided in Chapter 9, "Technical Practices."

Avoid Activity-Specific Sprints

A good ScrumMaster will continually nudge team members toward adopting improved technical practices that help them learn how to overlap their work. If a team doesn't learn effective ways to do this, team members may settle on a less desirable approach: activity-specific sprints. An activity-specific sprint is as bad a practice as it would be an acronym. In this approach, the team decides to use one sprint for analysis and design, a second sprint for coding, and a third for testing, as shown in Figure 14.1. In this approach, the team is split in thirds with the analysts working one sprint ahead of the programmers and the testers working one sprint behind them.

This can be a very alluring approach. Not only does it seemingly solve the problem of how to overlap work but it also allows each type of specialist to work mostly with others of their own kind, which many may prefer until they become used to the close collaboration of a Scrum team. Unfortunately, the same disadvantages apply to activity-specific sprints as apply to activity-specific teams: too many

SEE ALSO

For more on the problems with activity-specific teams, see "Favor Feature Teams" in Chapter 10.

hand-offs and a lack of whole-team responsibility. Activity-specific sprints also have three additional disadvantages:

- **There is increased schedule risk.** Planning how much work can be done in a sprint will be more error prone because the effort is highly dependent on the quality of the work done in the prior sprint. The programmers, for example, will not know how much of their time will be needed in a testing sprint until the testers start testing. This means those programmers won't know how much work to pull into their concurrent coding sprint.
- **It takes longer to go from idea to running, tested feature.** Not only is this bad itself, it will also extend the time it takes to get feedback from customers, users, or others.
- **It doesn't really solve the problem of overlapping work.** When all work is done within one sprint, the entire team moves at the same pace. Team members help each other and work outside their disciplines to ensure they complete their work. When we introduce activity-specific sprints we allow the different subteams to progress at different rates. This causes work to build up in front of some subteams. Not only is effort wasted in having teams go faster than the slowest team, but the work that piles up may contain defects that will not be discovered until the work is processed by downstream teams.

FIGURE 14.1

Activity-specific sprints are a bad idea.

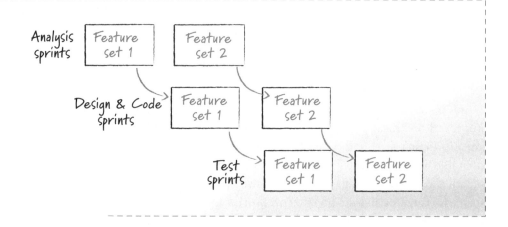

Replace Finish-to-Start Relationships with Finish-to-Finish Ones

One of the biggest problems with activity-specific sprints is that they create what are known as finish-to-start relationships. In a finish-to-start relationship, one task must finish before the next can start. For example, a Gantt chart on a sequential project may show that analysis must finish before coding can start and that coding must finish before testing can start. Good Scrum teams learn that this is not true; many activities can be overlapped. What is important is not when tasks start but when they finish. Coding cannot finish until analysis finishes and testing cannot finish until coding finishes. These are known as finish-to-finish relationships and are reinforced by Scrum's sprint mechanism. All work is done at the end of the sprint, or it is returned to the product backlog.

With a little experience, most teams are able to see how to overlap some types of work and create finish-to-finish relationships between them. Teams easily find ways to overlap discussions of what users need and programming. They also soon find ways to overlap programming and testing. These activities lend themselves to iterative and incremental approaches: Get a few details from the users about what they need and then build a little of it; build a little and then test what you've built.

Other activities do not appear to be as amenable to an iterative, incremental approach. User experience design, database design, and architecture are often cited as work that needs to be done up front. Failing to view these activities holistically will, the argument goes, lead to downstream problems.

Overlapping User Experience Design

Let's look more closely at user experience design (UED) to see how some Scrum teams have successfully integrated user experience designers into their sprints. Understanding how this has been done for UED will also provide guidance on how to do this with database design, architecture, or other activities that may not initially seem as well suited to agile development.

On traditionally managed projects, UED is generally viewed as an up-front activity, preferably completed before other software development activities begin. UED work progresses in its own series of phased activities, typically starting with an assessment of current work practices and user needs and concluding with the creation of user interface designs. Eventually, user interface designs are created and assessed in an iterative manner. A variety of potential interfaces is shown to likely users, feedback is collected, and revisions are made, which are again shown to likely users. So, user experience designers are somewhat accustomed to working in an iterative manner. It's just that they're used to executing those iterations in advance of the rest of the project beginning. On a Scrum project, however, we don't want to start with an up-front UED phase. We instead want user experience designers working alongside other team members. The importance of designers working closely with the rest of the team is confirmed by Desirée Sy, an agile interaction designer at Autodesk.

> In addition to keeping in touch with the whole agile team through the daily scrum, we work with developers very closely throughout design and development.... Interaction designers need to communicate every day with developers. This is not only to ensure that designs are being implemented correctly, but also

so that we have a thorough understanding of technical constraints that affect design decisions. (2007, 126)

During a sprint we want all team members, regardless of personal specialty, working together. But remember that during a sprint, the team has two goals: complete the planned work of the current sprint but also prepare for the coming sprint. Naturally, different team members will spend unequal amounts of their time on these different goals. Most programmers spend the majority of their time adding new features. User experience designers, on the other hand, will likely spend the majority of their time learning about upcoming features. They will be creating the additional detail that gets attached to complex product backlog items. But—and this is critical—they also spend time refining and answering questions about designs being programmed and tested in the current sprint. Even though a team's designers (or architects or technical designers) may spend time looking ahead, they remain members of the team working on this sprint.

The result is something like what is shown in Figure 14.2. This figure shows that while coding and testing one part of the product backlog, the user experience designers will spend some of their time (perhaps a majority of it) looking further down the product backlog at upcoming items. Yet, it remains one team working on one sprint at a time.

FIGURE 14.2

User experience designers are on the current sprint but spend some of their time looking forward.

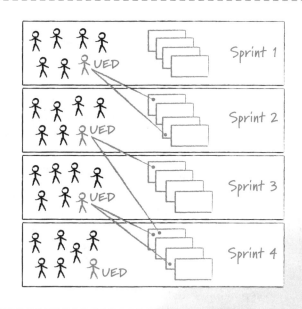

Think Holistically, Work Incrementally

But what about the concern that UED (and similar work like architecture and database design) must be done holistically? The answer comes in how work is selected from the product backlog. Figure 14.2 shows how the user experience designers on a team often put some (or even most) of their effort toward work in a later sprint. On an application with significant UED concerns, the product owner (with guidance from knowledgeable team members) needs to prioritize the backlog with an eye toward resolving open UED issues.

The product owner and designers think holistically about the system, deciding where they most need to acquire new knowledge. These areas become the focal points for the UED work of the next sprint. Designers then work on the system in what agile interaction designer Desirée Sy refers to as "design chunks" (2007, 120). A design chunk is a small, sprint-sized piece of the system that builds into the overall design. Sy says that "interaction designers are trained to consider experiences holistically, so breaking designs into pieces—especially into pieces that do not initially support workflows—can be difficult at first, but it is a skill that comes with practice. Design chunking yields many benefits" (2007, 120).

One of the benefits to working iteratively in design chunks is that it reduces the amount of wasted effort that would sometimes go into features that are later dropped. Working this way allows a team to shift user experience designers (or architects or database designers) to the most important problems at just the right times. Sy found that just-in-time design ultimately results in better designs.

> We have found that the new agile user-centered design methods produce better-designed products than the "waterfall" versions of the same techniques. Agile communication modes have allowed us to narrow the gap between uncovering usability issues and acting on those issues by incorporating changes into the product. (2007, 112)

Lynn Miller, the director of user interface development at Autodesk, believes there are advantages to designers looking ahead on the product backlog and designing for those user stories slightly in advance of the rest of the team working on them. She identifies three benefits: First, there is no wasted time "creating designs that [are] not used." Second, "usability testing of features and contextual inquiry for design [can be done] on the same customer trips." Third, because designers are able to get "timely feedback," if there is "a sudden change in the market (like new competing software being released)," they can find out about it "right away and... act accordingly" (2005, 232).

These benefits are echoed by Marissa Mayer, Google's vice president for search products and user experience.

In the case of the Toolbar Beta, several of the key features (custom buttons, shared bookmarks) were prototyped in less than a week. In fact, during the brainstorming phase, we tried out about five times as many key features—many of which we discarded after a week of prototyping. Since only 1 in every 5 to 10 ideas work out, the strategy of constraining how quickly ideas must be proven allows us to try out more ideas faster, increasing our odds of success. (Porter 2006)

In many ways, this manner of working through a design is no different from what good designers have always done. No user experience designer locks the door, spends weeks coming up with the "perfect design," and then emerges to hand it over ready for implementation. A good designer instead thinks about the overall design and identifies the open issues that will have the most impact on the ultimate design. The good designer then seeks to address those open issues through discussions with users, prototypes, design reviews, and even quiet contemplation. As one set of open issues is resolved (or at least narrowed to a smaller set of options), the next set of issues is tackled. The skilled and experienced designer is already doing what I've described: thinking holistically but working iteratively toward solutions.

Architecture and Database Design

I've claimed that user experience design, architecture, and database design are three specialized cases of the same general problem: working iteratively on activities that have traditionally been completed in an early phase of a sequential development process. To support this claim, let's look at how architectural decisions were made on a commercial product developed in an agile way.

Klaus was the architect at a medium-sized company that was beginning to develop a product to manage workflows of scientific data. Although the product owner, Robin, had strong opinions of what needed to be in the product, she knew that it would be important to start development on a solid foundation. With that in mind, while prioritizing work for the early sprints she carefully considered Klaus' suggestions about which user stories should be developed early to provide that solid foundation.

In the first sprint, the team added functionality to read comma-separated value (CSV) files. The product would eventually need to read many different file formats, but Klaus and the others suggested starting simple. The work of this first sprint didn't eliminate many architectural uncertainties, but it did start the team off with a successful first sprint. It also gave it the ability to easily get data into the system, which everyone involved knew would benefit the team during subsequent sprints.

For the second sprint, the team could have continued by adding support for reading all the other file formats that would eventually be needed. But Klaus was not very concerned with those. From his perspective these were not big architectural risks or areas of uncertainty. If the system could load a CSV file, it could eventually load an XML file, and so on. What did worry Klaus were the extensive data visualization needs for the product. The hope was to use a commercial visualization package. But, if that didn't deliver the needed performance on the product's extremely large data sets, the backup plan was to write the visualization features themselves. So, for sprint two, the team and product owner agreed to incorporate two different visualization libraries that were being considered and to create one simple visualization with each. This wouldn't resolve Klaus' concerns about achieving acceptable performance, but it would teach the team what was involved in using each of the two commercial products.

For sprint three, Klaus recommended developing a complicated visualization with each third-party product. This would enable the team to gauge the performance and suitability of each. Fortunately, one of the commercial products performed at the required level. So, in the fourth sprint, the team used that product to develop two other complicated but very different visualizations as a further test of the product.

Also, during the fourth sprint, the team began work on some of the math capabilities needed in the product. For example, as Klaus explained it in an e-mail to me, users needed to be able to instruct the system to "add the values in the fourth and ninth fields of an imported file and then filter the data set to include only items where that sum is at least twice the value in the first field." The viability of doing this was not a concern to Klaus, but he suggested to the product owner that it be started early for two reasons. First, while there were many ways to design this type of functionality, the approach selected would influence many subsequent design decisions. Second, there were hundreds of various rules such as this to add to the product, and developing the first few now would allow them to add two additional teams who would focus solely on the development and testing of the many rules. Table 14. 1 summarizes the work done in each sprint and the reasons why.

As you can see from this example, Klaus kept the overall architecture and design of the product in mind but used the sprints to iteratively address the decisions that needed to be made. Work was always prioritized by the product owner, and each sprint delivered some new amount of working software. But, some of the functionality to be developed each sprint was done at the suggestion of the project's architect and his teammates. Database design and user experience design considerations can be similarly factored into decisions about what to work on.

Sprint	Goal	Reason
1	Import data from comma-separated files.	Start simple. Be able to easily get data into the system since all subsequent work relied on having data to act on.
2	Create the same simple data visualization using two separate commercial packages.	Start to see what was involved in using the two candidate products.
3	Develop a complicated visualization with each product.	See if one of the products could handle complex visualization needs.
4	Develop two new but very different visualizations. Add initial math functions.	Confirm suitability of selected visualization product. Determine best approach for adding math functions and create base for rapidly adding similar rules by a second team.

Keep Timeboxes Regular and Strict

When I first started doing iterative and incremental development (even a bit before doing what today we'd call agile development), I made the mistake of not having all of our sprints be the same length. We would meet at the start of a sprint to plan the work of that sprint. One item on the agenda of those early sprint planning meetings was to decide how long that sprint would be. We would bounce around in a seemingly random manner between lengths of two to six weeks.

We would make the decision about how long each sprint should be based on how big we felt the work was, how much of it we needed to deliver before our users could see it, who was planning to be out of the office ("We better make this a three-week sprint as Kristy is gone the entire second week."), and how energized or tired we felt. There were a lot more six-week sprints at the start of the project. (There were a lot more long lunches then as well.) And there were a lot more two-week sprints near the end.

Allowing our sprint lengths to vary seemed right at the time—and I have to admit it wasn't a conscious decision; we just did it without ever discussing whether it was a good idea. It was later that I discovered the benefits of fixed sprint lengths:

- **Teams benefit from a regular cadence.** When sprint lengths vary, team members are often a little unsure of the schedule. "Is this the last week?" and "Do we ship this Thursday or next Thursday?" become common questions. Having a regular cadence of anything from one to four weeks helps teams settle into a work rhythm most suited to them.

- **Sprint planning becomes easier.** Both sprint planning and release planning are simplified when teams stick with a constant sprint length. Sprint planning is easier because over the course of typically two to five sprints, the team learns about how many hours of work can be planned into a sprint.

- **Release planning becomes easier.** As we will see in the next chapter, Scrum teams derive their release plans empirically (whenever possible). They estimate the size of the work to be done on a project and then measure the amount completed per sprint. If sprint lengths shift around, measuring a team's velocity becomes harder: There is no guarantee that a four-week sprint will complete exactly twice as much as a two-week sprint. Normalizing velocity to be "velocity per week" works somewhat but is needless extra work when sprints are kept the same length.

- **It's what Richard Feynman would do.** Nobel-prize winning physicist Richard Feynman recounts the story of getting tired of having to choose what to have for dessert each evening. From that point on, he resolved he would always choose chocolate ice cream (1997, 235). Choosing a sprint length at the start of each sprint is a waste of energy. Experiment with a couple of lengths, make a decision, and stick with it until there is a significant reason to change.

In stressing that your sprints should all be the same length, I am not suggesting you become obsessive about this. Pick a day of the week that works well in your environment and start all sprints on that day. I like starting sprints on Fridays so that we can pack that day full with the sprint review, retrospective, and planning meetings. Putting all of these on Mondays makes us dread Monday even more than usual.

But there may be occasions when it would be best to deviate slightly from this schedule. Holidays can be a common cause of this. In the United States it is common for individuals to take extra time off around the Thanksgiving and Christmas holidays. A team that routinely does two-week sprints may find itself with half the number of person-days during a sprint that includes one of these holidays. In that case, the team may benefit from a three-calendar-week sprint, as this would yield closer to the usual number of person days.

<table>
<tr><td>

OBJECTION
</td><td>

"There are times when changing sprint length makes sense. I don't want a rigid rule to prevent us from doing it."
</td></tr>
</table>

Granted. No guideline such as this needs to be turned into an unwavering rule. Suppose we are doing two-week sprints and have three weeks left before a big trade show at which we want to show our product. We would very reasonably be able to run either a single three-week sprint or follow the usual two-week sprint with a one-week sprint. It would be unnecessarily rigid for us to lose the chance to put one more week of functionality into the product just because of how sprint end dates line up with the trade show schedule.

Never Extend a Sprint

A second mistake you can make in how you execute sprints is not treating the timeboxes as strict. No matter what, sprints finish on time. Do not arrive at the planned finish date and decide you need to add a couple of more days to finish the work.

Now in the grand scheme of let's say a year-long project, does extending the deadline of the first sprint by a couple of days really hurt? Yes, absolutely. If the team members decide to extend that first sprint, they have just learned that it is OK to miss deadlines. It's not OK to miss deadlines, even deadlines so early in the project that missing them may not appear to have a big impact.

Keeping sprints strictly timeboxed reinforces the idea of continually moving the project forward. Every so many weeks the team must deliver some new potentially shippable product increment. If the timeboxes are allowed to vary ("Let's run a six-week sprint this time because we're working on architectural elements") or are occasionally extended ("We just need three more days"), this valuable discipline is lost.

To strictly enforce the sprint deadlines means that teams will occasionally need to drop work they had planned on completing during the sprint. Hopefully they can somewhat offset this unfortunate but realistic situation by occasionally adding work to a sprint. As we will discuss in Chapter 15, dropping work is not the end of the world as long as work is done in priority order.

As soon as there is any indication that not all planned work can be completed, the product owner meets with the rest of the team to discuss what to do. Hopefully this meeting occurs early enough in a sprint that the product owner can make choices about what should be completed and what should be dropped. If the team doesn't discover the problem until the 18th day of a 20-day sprint, the product owner will not have much leeway in what to drop; the product owner will need to drop whatever feature isn't yet finished.

"We need the flexibility to respond to client or customer pressures."

Being highly responsive to bug reports or feature requests is a goal many organizations set. This is often a good goal, but it is important to understand that the real goal is to respond quickly overall and over time rather than to one specific request. (Understanding, of course, that sometimes the one specific request is from the customer who represents 80% of your business.) In fact, more important to most customers than an occasional quick fix from us is confidence in the date by which we promise to have a fix. Working in strict timeboxes allows us to better have this predictability: we know the dates on which our next sprints will come out, so it becomes a question merely of in which sprint we will work on the request.

❏ If you've been using variable-length sprints, pick whatever length seems best and commit to sticking with it for the next two months. At that time evaluate if you should change.

❏ If you've been doing four-week or monthly sprints, try going to two-week sprints. They might feel too fast at first, so commit to running three before deciding whether to make the change permanent.

❏ Break my guideline against vacillating between different sprint lengths by running two one-week sprints. Athletes training to run a marathon mix in some amount of speed work during which they run faster than their intended marathon pace. Occasionally going faster than normal helps improve our long-term sustainable pace. At the retrospective, discuss how the one-week sprint went and see if there are things from it you can incorporate when returning to your regular sprint length.

Don't Change the Goal

Some of my early experiences as a programmer were in the litigation consulting department of a large consulting company. One challenge of working in that domain was the inevitability of change. Our bosses—the attorneys running a case—would have us begin a project that was to take a few weeks. Inevitably, though, partway through that project they would come running into our programming bullpen yelling, "Stop what you're doing! The other side has asked for such-and-such. Now we need you to…" and they would redirect us toward a new project that would need to be completed before we could return to the original project.

Because of this background, one of the initial things I found appealing about Scrum was its emphasis on leaving the goal of the sprint alone. Scrum takes a two-pronged approach to change. Nothing is allowed to change within the sprint. The team commits to a set of work on the first day and then expects its priorities to remain unchanged for the length of the sprint. However, although no changes are allowed into the sprint, the entire world may be changing outside it.

Scrum's stance against mid-sprint change may seem detrimental to the success of the project. After all, sometimes the changes are so important that they need to be done. And other times new information may make worthless the work the team is currently engaged in. In both cases I encourage you to take—at least initially—Scrum's hard-line stance against mid-sprint change.

To see why, let's consider examples of both types of these seemingly legitimate causes of mid-sprint change. First let's consider the case of the product owner discovering some important new requirement that she says needs to be done instead of the work the team is engaged in. Sometimes this will happen. When it does I suggest making the change in sprint goal visible. Scrum does this by having the team announce an *abnormal termination* to the sprint, which is followed by immediately planning a new sprint to include the newly discovered, high-importance feature. Raising the visibility of changes in sprint goals is important because it makes them less likely to happen. In too many organizations, the only ones who see the constant redirection of the team are the team members themselves. Scrum's approach of not letting change into a sprint but being willing to abnormally terminate and start a new one raises the visibility of the cost and frequency of change. This will cut down on the mid-sprint changes thrown at the team. Only the most important changes will justify abnormally terminating.

What about the case where new information is learned that makes the planned work of the sprint less desirable? As in the prior case, yes sometimes a team will learn something that means it should stop work on some part of a sprint. For example, a goal of the current sprint may be to add a particular feature specifically to help make a sale to a large client. In the middle of the sprint the client tells you his company has had a budget freeze and can't buy your product even if it has the new feature, or that it's been acquired and will be forced to use your competitor's product, or any of a number of similar situations. In these cases it may absolutely make sense to stop work on this feature, depending on its general desirability to other customers and how far along the work is. However, situations like these happen less often than most people who are new to Scrum think.

A far more common situation is the one Janis found herself in. As the product owner for a bioinformatics application, she had worked with the team to design a very involved screen for searching for complex data. It wasn't perfect, but no one had any better ideas, and everyone was generally happy with the screen. At the next sprint planning meeting, everyone agreed to develop the search screen as prototyped.

Progress went well during the first half of the team's two-week sprint. On the morning of the seventh day, Janis announced that she'd had an epiphany the night before. She showed the developers a sketch she'd done of a better search screen. It was completely different from what the team was seven days into. And it was undeniably better. Everyone agreed. At this point, Janis and the rest of the team had a decision to make:

- Cancel the current sprint and start a new sprint focused on the search screen that everyone agreed was better.
- Continue work on the one that just seven days earlier everyone felt was good enough.

Some might think this an easy decision: The new screen was undeniably better, so the developers should shift to working on it. However, Scrum helped them ask the question a bit differently: Ship the product with the good-enough search screen plus seven days of additional features, or ship it with only the better search screen? The decision was Janis's but the whole team weighed in with opinions. Collectively, the team decided to finish the good-enough search screen. The improved search screen was added nine months later in a subsequent version.

Break the Habit of Redirecting a Team

Through years of being allowed to constantly redirect their teams, organizations have become addicted to doing so. Often teams are interrupted not because the product owner discovered a critical, sudden customer need or other valid interruption but because the product owner or other stakeholders failed to think ahead. They've become used to working this way and aren't aware of the negative impact it has on their development teams.

I noticed this at one company that sold business-to-business services. Much of its business was created through relationships with partners. Adding a new partner involved five to ten hours of work from the development team. The team had come to view this work as unplannable because it didn't know how many partners the salesperson would need added during one of their two-week sprints.

I decided this was hurting the throughput of the team, so I met with the salesperson. I told him that from then on the team would only add partners who had signed contracts prior to the start of the sprint. He surprised me by saying that wouldn't be a problem with him. He told me that a big selling point to partners was that the company updated its website every two weeks. Prospective partners would understand that partner launches would now be tied to the updates and that if they wanted to launch by a given date they would need the contract signed by the start of that sprint. This salesperson had no problem working in a way that was more beneficial to the team; he just wasn't doing it before then because no one had asked or made the cost of the current way of working visible to him.

Relax the Hard-Line Stance Later

I usually advise Scrum teams to start by taking a firm stance against mid-sprint changes. This is not because I am opposed to redirecting a team or because I want to slavishly obey a Scrum rule. It is because I want to help those outside the team learn that there is a cost to redirecting the team. Of course, sometimes redirecting a team mid-sprint is necessary. But, all too often teams are redirected because it's easy to do and because someone didn't think ahead. I relax this hard-line stance against change after I see that the organization no longer thinks of every new request as an emergency worthy of a mid-sprint change.

OBJECTION	**"Being responsive is what has made us successful, and users expect that of us."**

Indeed, many organizations have built successful relationships with their users or customers by being exceptionally responsive to their requests. However, many of these organizations also find themselves weighed down by needing to be constantly hyper-responsive. From my experience what customers really want is predictability. Most understand that non-critical bugs cannot be fixed instantly. They understand when told something like, "This is definitely an important issue and we want to get to it as quickly as possible. We make system patch releases available every two weeks. It's too late to schedule this into the release going out on Friday, but you'll have this in the release two weeks after that." Because they have not received this level of predictability from software development organizations in the past, they've learned that the best thing to do is to clamor for all fixes *now*.

OBJECTION

"Scrum is about being flexible; if a change arises in the middle of a sprint we should be able to make it."

Scrum is also about maximizing the delivery of value by a team over an extended period. One good way of doing so is to allow the team to retain focus on one goal before redirecting it toward another. Improving an organization's flexibility in responding to strategic changes is different from becoming overly responsive to the short term, which often leads to unsatisfying long-term results.

Get Feedback, Learn, and Adapt

Each sprint can be viewed as an experiment. The product owner and team meet at the start of the sprint to identify the most valuable experiment they can perform. The experiment involves the creation of some amount of new functionality in the form of working software. This new increment of the product is held to the standard of being potentially shippable so that feedback on the experiment can be maximized. At the end of a sprint, the experiment is evaluated. The team as a whole learns from it.

Much of the learning will be about the product: What do users like? What do they dislike? What do they find confusing? What do they want next? What features does the new increment help them think of that they hadn't thought of before? But perhaps an equal part of the learning will be about the team's use of Scrum itself: How much work can we do in a sprint? What gets in our way? What could help us go faster? Are we achieving "done" software every sprint?

Most of this learning would be useless if Scrum were not also iterative. Sprint by sprint, the product owner, team, and ScrumMaster are able to revisit partially satisfactory but working implementations and improve upon them. Additional fields are added to the data search screen. A user interface is taken from acceptable to excellent based on the feedback received. Performance is tuned in the most important parts of the system based on data collected. Plans are updated and work reprioritized based on a better understanding of how much can be completed within the three-month deadline.

Iterative and incremental development is about generating feedback, learning from it, and then adapting what we are building and how we are building it. Sprints provide teams the mechanisms for doing this.

Additional Reading

Appelo, Jurgen. 2008. We increment to adapt, we iterate to improve. *Methods & Tools*, Summer, 9–22.

> Appelo's article presents excellent descriptions of what iterative and incremental development are and describes how each brings something important but different to agile development.

Cockburn, Alistair. 2008. Using both incremental and iterative development. *Crosstalk*, May, 27–30.

> This article provides excellent definitions for both incremental and iterative development and argues for why they should be used together.

Larman, Craig, and Victor R. Basili. 2003. Iterative and incremental development: A brief history. *IEEE Computer*, June, 47–56.

> A survey of iterative and incremental development tracing its roots back to the 1950s and proving that incremental and iterative development is not a passing fad.

Sy, Desirée. 2007. Adapting usability investigations for agile user-centered design. *Journal of Usability Studies* 2 (3): 112–132.

> The best description available of how to integrate user experience design into an agile process.

Chapter 15

Planning

"We're agile; we don't plan" and "We'll be done when we're done" were common statements in the early years following the publication of the Agile Manifesto. I suspect that many people on some of the early agile teams that took this stance knew that they were giving up something valuable when they threw planning out the window. But, theirs was a natural reaction to the prior cultures in which they'd worked. Too many developers hated planning because the plan had never been of any personal benefit to them. Instead, plans were often weapons used against the developers: "You said you'd be done by June; it's June. Make it happen."

As inappropriate as it was for some organizations to use plans as weapons, it was equally inappropriate to throw planning out altogether. As a former vice president of engineering for a handful of companies where agile development had been central to our success, I also knew that Scrum teams could and should plan. In fact, not only can agile and Scrum teams plan, according to research by Kjetil Moløkken-Østvold and Magne Jørgensen, agile teams often plan more accurately than teams using a sequential process (2005).

Planning is a fundamental aspect of Scrum. Scrum teams commit to always working on the features with the highest value. To do this, the team and product owner must have an estimate of how much a feature will cost to develop; otherwise they are prioritizing on desirability alone. Similarly, it is important to estimate how long a feature will take to develop—a feature that misses a critical market window will deliver much less value. Clearly, for a Scrum team to live up to its promise of working in priority order, planning must be an essential practice.

In this chapter we look beyond the basics and consider some planning challenges I see many organizations still facing well into their adoption of Scrum. We start by looking at the need to progressively refine plans rather than starting with fully detailed plans. We next look at why overtime is not a solution to schedule problems. After that, I make the argument that organizations should learn to favor changing scope rather than the other critical project planning parameters of schedule, resources, or quality. Finally, the chapter concludes with advice on separating the estimates created by a team from the commitments the team makes.

Progressively Refine Plans

In Chapter 13, "The Product Backlog," we learned that the product backlog should be progressively refined. Capabilities that will be added well into the future are initially put on the product backlog as epics and later split into smaller user stories. Eventually these stories are so small that they do not need to be split further. But they are then refined one last time by adding conditions of satisfaction that describe high-level tests, which will be used to determine whether the story has been completed.

A good Scrum team takes a similar approach to planning. Just as an epic describes the essence of a feature but leaves out specifics, an early plan captures the essence of what will be delivered but leaves the specifics for later. Subsequent plans add the necessary details but only when that detail can be supported by the knowledge gained through the project thus far. Leaving details out of an initial plan does not mean we cannot make commitments about what will be included when a project is finished. We can still make commitments, but those commitments must leave room for changes commensurate with the amount of uncertainty on the project.

For example, consider the case of a team developing a new web-based genealogy product. The team has a firm deadline in six months and needs to be able to convey exactly what will be delivered by then. The team can provide a lot of detail about the most important features (which will have been prioritized highest on the product backlog). If manually drawing family trees is a high priority, the initial plan will include a great deal of detail about that feature. The product backlog might mention showing a layout grid, snapping items to a grid, showing rulers, manually inserting page breaks, and so on.

A feature further down the product backlog will include less detail. We might write, *"As a user, I want to upload photos so that I can attach them to a person in the family tree."* This gives the team and product owner the flexibility later to support only JPG and GIF files even though the initial hope had been to support seven or eight image formats.

OBJECTION

"We do outsourced, contract development. Our customers want to know before they sign the contract which file formats they'll get. I can't leave details like that out."

Although deferring implementation details allows the team more flexibility in finding the best solution, you don't need to progressively refine all feature descriptions. If image file formats are critical to your customers, then you're right. These should be detailed in the product backlog and plans that accompany the contract. Other, less critical features can be refined as they rise to the top of the product backlog.

There are many advantages to progressively refining a plan. Chief among them are the following:

- **It minimizes the time investment.** Planning is necessary, but it can be time consuming. The time spent estimating and planning is best viewed as an investment; we want to invest in planning only to the extent that our effort is rewarded. If we create a detailed project plan at the start of the project, that plan will be based on many assumptions. As the project progresses, we'll find that some of our assumptions were wrong, which will invalidate plans based on them.

- **It allows decisions to be made at the optimal time.** Progressively refining the plan helps the team avoid falling into the trap of making too many decisions at the outset of the project. Project participants become more knowledgeable about their project day by day. If a decision does not need to be made today and can be safely deferred until tomorrow, we should defer making that decision until everyone is one day smarter.

- **It allows us to make course changes.** One thing we can always be certain of is that things change. Planning enough that we know the general direction but not all of the specifics leaves the team with the flexibility to alter course as more is learned. Notice that I've carefully avoided the common phrase *course correction*. There is no one "correct course" that is known in advance.

- **It helps us avoid falling into the trap of believing our plans.** No matter how well we understand that the unexpected can happen and that no plan is safe from change, a thorough, well-documented plan can fool us into believing everything has been thought of. Progressively refining a plan reinforces the idea that even the best plan is subject to change.

- ❑ Review a current release plan. Identify parts of the plan that are prematurely precise or detailed.

- ❑ Make a list of the reasons why your organization creates plans that are prematurely precise. Are there specific individuals or groups that demand such plans? Could they be persuaded to start with less detail? If so, meet with them and present the reasons for doing so.

THINGS TO TRY NOW

Don't Plan on Overtime to Salvage a Plan

Long ago, when I first started managing software developers, I thought it would be the easiest job in the world. In my experience, and as a programmer, it seemed that programmers routinely underestimated how long things would take. I thought that all I would need to do as a manager would be ask individuals to create their own estimates and then keep the heat on them to meet those estimates. Because

<p>the estimates would be low more often than not, I reasoned that we'd finish earlier than if I prepared a schedule for the team.</p>

the estimates would be low more often than not, I reasoned that we'd finish earlier than if I prepared a schedule for the team.

This worked quite well for the first few months. As a non-Scrum team back in the 1980s, many of the first tasks on the schedule had loosely defined deliverables. Analysis was done when we called it done. Design was done when the deadline for design being done arrived. The first few features to be programmed were finished on schedule. I made a few team members work overtime to meet the deadlines—after all, they were the ones who gave those estimates, not me. The overtime wasn't excessive: a few extra hours this week, maybe half a day next Saturday. But after a few months of this I noticed we were working more overtime and it wasn't helping as much. Corners we had cut during earlier crunch periods were coming back to haunt us. We were also either finding or making more bugs than before.

My solution back then? More overtime.

No, it didn't work. It also didn't work on the next few projects where I repeated the cycle. But I did eventually learn that teams cannot be pushed infinitely hard and that beyond a certain point, working more hours in a week will move the team backward rather than forward.

In the early days of Extreme Programming this was known as the *forty-hour workweek*, based on the eight-hour day common in the United States. Soon, though, the principle was renamed to *sustainable pace* to reflect that many countries have a standard different from 40 hours and that it is sometimes acceptable to work longer than 40 hours in a week. Watch any marathon, and each runner will seem to be running at a personally sustainable pace. After all, the runner will keep it up for 26.2 miles. Look more closely, however, and you'll notice that the pace is not entirely consistent from mile to mile. Each works a little harder going up the hill and maybe recovers slightly coming down it. At the finish line, most accelerate and sprint at a pace that is not sustainable beyond the finish line.

Sustainable pace should mean the same to a Scrum team: Most of the time the team runs at a nice, even pace, but every now and then team members need to kick it up a gear, such as when nearing a finish line or perhaps attacking a critical, user-reported defect. Working overtime occasionally does not violate the goal of working at a sustainable pace. Authors of *Extreme Programming Explained* Kent Beck and Cynthia Andres concur.

> Overtime is a symptom of a serious problem on the project. The XP rule is simple—you can't work a second week of overtime. For one week, fine, crank and put in some extra hours. If you come in on Monday and say "To meet our goals, we'll have to work late again," then you already have a problem that can't be solved by working more hours. (2004, 60)

Learning the Hard Way

When Clinton Keith was the CTO of High Moon Studios, a developer of Triple-A video games, he learned the hard way to take seriously this admonishment against more than one week of overtime. The video game industry is one of the few that still has a dominant annual trade show. Theirs is called the Electronic Entertainment Expo, or E3. Important upcoming titles are shown at E3, and deals are struck between studios and publishers. It is natural for teams to put in overtime leading up to the biggest showcase of the year for their games. Not only do team members want their games to show well to the press and possible business partners, but they also want to impress their friends from other companies who will be at the show.

For years, Keith had encouraged his teams to work overtime for the months leading up to E3. But, now that he and High Moon had embraced Scrum, teams had been working at a consistent and sustainable pace. Still, old habits die hard. With a few weeks left before the show, Keith asked his teams for some mandatory overtime. As Kent Beck might have predicted, velocity did go up in the first week, as shown in Figure 15.1. But in the second week, although velocity was still higher than without the overtime, it was below that of the first week. By the third week, velocity was insignificantly above the pre-overtime pace. In the fourth week of overtime, velocity was actually below what the team had been achieving at its sustainable pace (Keith 2006).

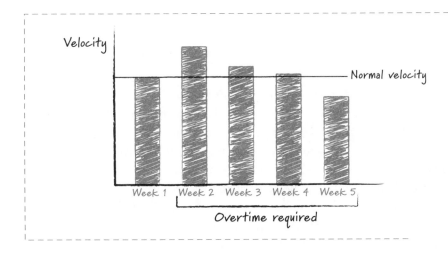

FIGURE 15.1

High Moon Studios found that subsequent weeks of overtime actually lowered velocity. Printed with permission of Clinton Keith, Agile Game Development.

Although ingrained habits might be difficult to break, after a manager experiences something like this and sees hard evidence from his teams that extended periods of overtime are counterproductive, the lesson finally sinks in.

Getting There

The argument in favor of working at a sustainable pace says that teams get more done that way than they do when cycling between an unsustainable pace and a recovery period. Graphically, this is shown in Figure 15.2. The team working at a sustainable pace completes the same amount of work each period of time. The team working at an unsustainable pace exceeds that amount of work during some periods. But during other periods it is recovering from having worked unsustainably and complete less work. In Figure 15.2 the question is whether the area under the sustainable pace curve (representing the total work done by that team) is greater than the area under the unsustainable pace curve. Another way to think about this is if you have five kilometers to run, will you be faster running at a consistent pace or alternating periods of all-out sprinting and walking?

FIGURE 15.2

The amount of work completed is shown by the area under each line.

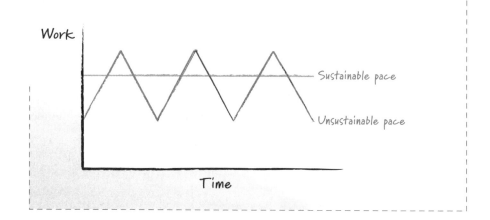

Intellectual arguments that working at a sustainable pace is most productive are unlikely to convince most doubters. After all, do you really believe a tortoise (at its sustainable pace) could beat a hare (with its sprint/sleep strategy)? I know Aesop's fables are supposed to reinforce great truths, but I'd have to see it to believe it. The same can be said of the truth of sustainable pace; most organizations need to collect their own data to be convinced that overtime is not a solution to long-term schedule problems. After you see the data for your teams (like Clinton Keith did in Figure 15.1), it's easy to see that prolonged overtime does not increase productivity.

Unfortunately, getting people to try working at a sustainable pace so that you can even collect that data is no easy feat. I've found the following arguments helpful in pleading that case:

- **Working at a sustainable pace leaves extra capacity for when you need it.** If a team is constantly running at an all-out pace, it will not have the extra reserve of energy for the time when extra effort is truly necessary.

- **It leaves time for more creativity.** Real productivity comes not just from working more hours but from occasionally coming up with creative solutions that either dramatically shorten the schedule or vastly improve the product. Teams working at a sustainable pace will be more likely to have the mental energy to come up with these ideas.

- **Stop arguing that our brains are exhausted after six hours a day.** Teams need to stop telling management that their brains are exhausted after six hours of hard thinking and that working beyond that is impossible. Many executives work 12 hours or more per day. Maybe that work is less brain intensive, but developers will get nowhere telling such executives that it is impossible to program for more than six hours. Besides, how many developers who make this argument during their day jobs go home and contribute at night to an open source project for fun? As passion increases, so does productivity.

- **It's worth a try.** If an experiment will result in useful, objective data, most decision makers will support the experiment, as long as it's done at the right time. Early in the project, when there's less apparent time pressure, start collecting data about the team's velocity when working at a sustainable pace. Later, when overtime is mandated, don't argue against it. Instead, try to gain the agreement that you'll continue the overtime more than a few weeks only if the data shows that velocity has increased.

If Not Overtime, What?

Extended overtime is a popular tool because it's cheap, easy, and occasionally effective. It takes nothing more than a manager saying, "I expect you here on Saturday," and has an immediate cost of no more than an occasional pizza. If we wish to establish a culture in which we eliminate such an attractive, seemingly free tool as overtime, we need to offer something in its place.

Tony Schwartz and Catherine McCarthy of the Energy Project believe they have the solution. They point out that time is a finite resource—we cannot add hours to our day. Energy is different, they say: We can add energy. We know this intuitively. There are days we come into the office energized and are hyperproductive. And then there are the days we do little more than watch the clock. If we can add energy to the team, it will have more of the former and fewer of the latter days (2007).

One of the best ways of adding energy is increasing passion. The more passionate people are about their projects, the more likely they are to fully engage on them each day. The product owner is the key here. Product owners need to convey a compelling vision around the product being developed so that team members are enthusiastic about working on it.

SEE ALSO

Suggestions on how to convey this compelling vision were given in the section, "Energize the System," in Chapter 12, "Leading a Self-Organizing Team."

Another good technique advocated by Schwartz and McCarthy is to take brief but regular breaks (2007). A 20-minute walk outside or a quick chat with a coworker works to restore focus and energy to the main task. As a personal example, I used 30-minute sprints to write this book. At the start of each writing sprint I would turn off all distractions such as e-mail and my phone. I would then turn over a 30-minute sand timer. At the end of each half hour I could either turn the timer immediately back over if the writing was going well, or I could grant myself five or ten minutes to check e-mail, return a call, or just look outside.

Francesco Cirillo has long advocated a similar approach he calls "pomodoro," which is Italian for tomato. In Cirillo's pomodoro approach, team members work in 30-minute increments. At the start of each increment, a tomato-shaped kitchen timer is set for 25 minutes. The team works diligently during that time with no distractions from e-mail, the phone, or so on. When the timer goes off, team members take a five-minute break. During these five minutes they can walk around, stretch, share stories, and so on but are discouraged from doing things like talking about work or checking e-mail. Every fourth pomodoro, Cirillo encourages a longer break of from 15 to 30 minutes (2007).

Cirillo's advice of a longer mental break twice a day fits with human ultradian rhythms. These are 90- to 120-minute cycles during which the body moves between high- and low-energy states. Psychologist Ernest Rossi says that "the basic idea is that every hour and a half or so you need to take a rest break—if you don't...you get tired and lose your mental focus, you tend to make mistakes, get irritable and have accidents" (2002).

THINGS TO TRY NOW

❑ Commit to running the next two or three sprints without any overtime. After doing that, evaluate how much work was completed, the quality of that work, and the creativity and energy of team members during the sprint.

❑ Consider trying Cirillo's pomodoro approach or a less rigid variation of it. Work for 30 or 60 minutes without interruption. Then take a five- or ten-minute break to look outside, walk around the building, or talk to coworkers.

Favor Scope Changes When Possible

The Project Management Institute (PMI) has long drawn the "iron triangle" shown in Figure 15.3. The iron triangle is meant to show the interdependent relationships between scope, cost (resources), and schedule. It is often drawn by a project manager and handed to the project's customer accompanied by the words, "Pick any two." By this the project manager means that as long as he has some flexibility in one of the three dimensions, he can meet the customer's expectations on the other two.

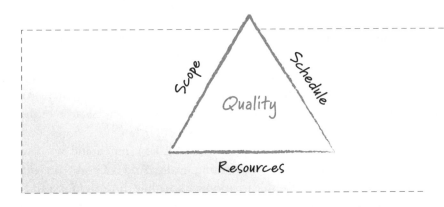

FIGURE 15.3

The iron triangle illustrates the relationship between scope, resources, and schedule.

Shown in the center of the iron triangle of Figure 15.3 is quality. This is because quality—like the federal agents who arrested Al Capone—is considered untouchable. Unfortunately, this is rarely the case; as such, quality is often used as a fourth side of the iron "triangle."

As part of transitioning to Scrum, key project stakeholders, developers, and product owners will need to learn to make changing scope their first choice. It is far easier to lock down the schedule, resources, and quality of a project. This does not mean that we don't sometimes instead fix the scope of the project and allow the schedule or resources to vary. However, our bias should be toward adjusting scope to fit available resources and schedule.

Considering the Alternatives

To see why we should favor changing scope over the other options, suppose we are part of a team that has just finished the ninth month of what we expected to be a 12-month project. At this point everyone realizes that the full scope of the project cannot be delivered on schedule with the current team. What are our choices?

Cut Quality?

Perhaps we should cut some quality corners—skip a little testing, leave a few bugs unfixed. Reducing quality is rarely explicitly considered, yet it is often the go-to option when the project is running behind. If we reduce quality, perhaps by altering our definition of what bugs must be fixed before we ship and perhaps by skipping the stress testing, in our scenario we may succeed in finishing the project in three months. The problem is that reducing quality is short sighted. These decisions, if made, will come back to haunt the team on the next release. The team will probably be under equivalent deadline pressure then but will also have to find a way to pay off the technical debt they racked up to meet the last deadline.

Scrum teams have learned that the best way to go fast is by keeping the quality of the system high throughout its development. In 1979, Philip Crosby wrote that "quality is free" and that "what costs money are the unquality things—all the actions that involve not doing jobs right the first time" (1). So if we try to meet our deadline in three months by cutting quality between now and then, there is a good chance that we will only succeed in slowing ourselves down because of the rework and instability in the system, even over the short term.

A further problem with cutting quality is deciding how much and what to cut. It is hard to predict the impact of shortcutting quality. And if Crosby is right, attempts to shortcut quality could result in a longer schedule. Imagine for a moment that you've been asked to move a deadline up from six months to five and that for some reason everyone (including you) agrees that cutting quality is the way to do this. How much quality would you need to cut to shorten the schedule by a month? Specifically, which items would you choose to test less and how much less? Which validation steps would you skip? The difficulty of these questions illustrates how unpredictable cutting quality is as an attempt to shorten a schedule.

Add Resources?

What about meeting the planned schedule by adding resources? Tossing a few (or a few dozen) more developers onto the team ought to bring the schedule in, many will think. Unfortunately, it's not that simple. In *The Mythical Man-Month*, Fred Brooks wrote that "adding manpower to a late software project makes it later" (1995, 25). With 3 months left in our 12-month project, it is quite possible that the time spent training the new team members, the additional communication overhead, and so on will negate the benefit the additional developers bring over such a short period. If we were 1 month into our 12-month project when we realized we wouldn't be able to deliver everything on schedule, adding people may have made more sense, because they would have had longer to contribute.

Even if we were to debate the relative merits of adding people and when it is too late to do so, what we cannot debate is that the impact of adding people is unpredictable. Because we cannot be positive of the impact, adding resources is risky.

Extend the Schedule?

So if we can't ensure success on our hypothetical project by either reducing quality or increasing resources, that leaves us with changing the scope or the schedule. Let's first consider changing the schedule. From the development team's perspective, changing the schedule is a wonderful option. If our project cannot be delivered in the originally planned three remaining months, all we need to do is estimate how much additional time is needed and then announce that as the new schedule. Apart from the difficulty of successfully re-estimating the completion date, there is little risk to the developers in adjusting the schedule.

Unfortunately, adjusting the date can be very hard for the business. Commitments have often been made to customers or investors. Advertising plans, including the big Super Bowl commercial, have been timed to coincide with the release date. New personnel may have been hired to handle increased calls to sales or support. Training sessions may have been scheduled. And so on. Although changing the deadline is a wonderful, easy-to-implement option for the development team, it is not always feasible. When it is an option, though, it should be considered.

Adjust the Scope?

Finally, what about changing the scope of the release? Yes, yes, "changing scope" is a polite way of saying "dropping things." However, is dropping something always so bad? When our project was first planned we drew the line after a set of features and said, "That's what you'll get." Suppose we drew this line after the 100th feature. I'm positive that the product owner was disappointed that the team would not commit to delivering item 101 on the product backlog. That feature was dropped even before the project began.

And so the product owner is entitled now to be disappointed that we have discovered that we can finish only the first 95, not 100, items on the product backlog. However, this is not the end of the world. At least it's not if the team has been working in priority order. If the five items being dropped from the release are the five items of lowest priority, and if we assume (as we generally should) that the team did the best work it was capable of under the circumstances, then the product owner is receiving the best possible product in the amount of time provided and with the team available.

Is dropping features disappointing? Absolutely. Would it have been better if we could have better predicted how much would be completed by the target date? Definitely. Is it realistic to expect perfection in these predictions? Sadly, no.

So, then, back to our example of realizing we will not finish everything in the three months remaining on our hypothetical project. Is dropping scope a valid response in this situation? From the development team's perspective, absolutely. If it isn't going to finish all of the desired work, simply figure out what it is likely to finish and don't do the work past there. If the team is behaving agilely—in particular, driving the system to a potentially shippable state by the end of each sprint—the team will have no challenges in dropping some scope.

From the business's perspective, dropping scope is always a bad thing. But what alternatives are there? We've established that reducing quality to meet the deadline is not a good thing. We've also established that the effect of adding people is unpredictable. That leaves the business with extending the deadline or dropping scope. Because of the likely issues with changing the deadline, reducing scope is often the preferred option, again assuming that features have been worked on in priority order.

SEE ALSO
Specific advice on estimating how much functionality can be delivered and by when will be provided in the next section, "Separate Estimating from Committing."

SEE ALSO
For more on the importance of driving to a potentially shippable state at the end of each sprint, see Chapter 14, "Sprints."

Project Context Is Key

Making the appropriate trade-offs between the items on the iron triangle is all about making the appropriate decisions within the context of your project. I'm not advocating that scope always be the first thing to go. I'm certainly not advocating that reducing scope can be taken lightly. What I do want organizations to learn is that changing scope is often more feasible than we may have realized in the past, and that it is often the best side of the iron triangle to adjust.

OBJECTION

"This product is like a car; a car is no good if it has an engine but no brakes. I need it all."

True: There are a certain number of mandatory features on a car. I'll even grant that on all cars made since Fred Flintstone was driving, both an engine and brakes have been mandatory. However, there are many other features, even on a car, that are optional—sun roof, air conditioning, traction sensors, and so on. Again, remember that the team should be working in priority order. This means that the software equivalents of the engine and the brakes are done first. Then when we realize we can't deliver all desired scope, the features on the chopping block are the ones that are undeniably nice to have but are not truly fundamental. If a project is in a position where the deadline can only be met by dropping truly mandatory features (engine, brakes, and so on), then it really is time to consider other alternatives, possibly including canceling the project.

"If the product includes less than what we've planned, no one will buy it."

This is really the same situation as the car. The real problem here is that the plan was created without a sufficient margin of safety. I most commonly hear this objection when the project planning process consisted of creating the product backlog, determining the earliest possible date that all that work might be completed, and committing that date to customers or users. If the product truly needs features that cannot be delivered by the committed date, then this is one of the occasions when extending the date is necessary. The problem in this case is more that the project was improperly planned than anything else.

Separate Estimating from Committing

A fundamental and common problem in many organizations is that estimates and commitments are considered equivalent. A development team (agile or not) estimates that delivering a desired set of capabilities will take seven months with the available resources. Team members provide this estimate to their manager who passes the estimate along to a vice president who informs the client. And in some cases the estimate is cut along the way to provide the team with a "stretch goal."

The problem here is not that the team's estimate of seven months is right or wrong. The problem is that the estimate was turned into a commitment. "We estimate this will take seven months" was translated into "We commit to finishing in seven months." Estimating and committing are both important, but they should be viewed as separate activities.

I need to pick up my daughter from swim practice tonight. I asked her what time she'd be done (which we defined as finished swimming, showered, and ready to go home). She said, "I should be ready by 5:15." That was her estimate. If I had asked for a firm commitment—be outside the facility by the stated time or I'll drive away without you—she might have committed to 5:25 to allow herself time to recover from any problems, such as a slightly longer practice, the coach's watch being off by five minutes, a line at the showers, and so on. To determine a time she could commit to, my daughter would still have formed an estimate. But rather than telling me her estimate directly, she would have converted into it a deadline she could commit to.

The Right Data to Do This

A good organization learns to separate estimating from committing. We estimate first and then, based on how confident we are of the estimate, we convert it into a commitment. But without a good estimate to start with, a team's commitment will be meaningless. To come up with a good estimate, the product owner and team must be equipped with the right data. Most important, they need to know two critical things:

- The size of the work to be performed
- The team's expected rate of progress through that work

To size the user stories on the product backlog, most teams use either story points or ideal days, as described in *Agile Estimating and Planning* (Cohn 2005). The rate at which product backlog items are completed is known as velocity. Velocity is simply the sum of the story-point or ideal-day estimates of the product backlog items completed in each sprint, with most teams using a rule of no partial credit. Working with these values, the product owner is able to see how much functionality can be delivered by various dates. Let's see how the product owner can use this information to make informed scope/schedule trade-off decisions.

An Example

Consider Table 15.1, which shows the actual velocities of a team I worked with. The first thing you should notice is that velocity is volatile—it can bounce around quite a bit from sprint to sprint. This is because it is impossible to perfectly assign estimates to user stories on the product backlog; some will turn out bigger than estimated and some smaller. Similarly, teams might encounter more interruptions in some sprints or have greater focus in others. I equate a team's velocity to the number of points scored by a sports team in a sequence of games. My favorite sports team is the Los Angeles Lakers. In their last nine basketball games they scored 101, 94, 102, 102, 107, 93, 114, 117, and 97 points. Compare the volatility of those scores with the volatility shown in Table 15.1.

TABLE 15.1

The velocity of a team will vary from sprint to sprint, as this team's data shows.

Sprint Number	Velocity
1	34
2	41
3	27
4	45
5	35
6	38
7	40
8	39
9	40

Because a team's velocity will vary (perhaps somewhat dramatically) from sprint to sprint, I do not rely heavily on a single value. What I'm interested in is the likely range of future velocities, or what a statistician would call a *confidence interval*. As an example of a confidence interval, global warming between 2000 and 2030 is estimated to be between 0.1°C and 0.3°C per decade. In 2030, we'll be able to look back and calculate a precise value—say 0.21°C—but looking forward we use a range. Scientists have studied this and are 90% confident that the actual value (when we can calculate it in 2030) will fall between 0.1°C and 0.3°C per decade.

I'd like to know the same thing about a team's velocity. I'd like, for example, to say that my team is 90% likely to experience a velocity between 18 and 26 over the remaining 5 sprints of a project. Fortunately, putting a confidence interval around a team's velocity is not hard to do.

Start by gathering velocity data for as many past sprints as you can. You will need at least 5 sprints to calculate a 90% confidence interval. Throw out data from sprints that you do not think accurately represent the team as it will be going forward. For example, if new people were added to the team 8 sprints ago, I would look back at only the last 8 sprints. But, if team size has fluctuated between 5 and 7 people for the last 13 sprints and I expect it to continue to fluctuate like that, then I would include all 13 sprints. Use your judgment, but try to avoid bias in throwing out values that help you get the predicted range you want.

Once you have past velocity values, sort them from lowest to highest. Sorting the values from Table 15.1 produces the following list:

27, 34, 35, 38, 39, 40, 40, 41, 45

Next, we want to use these sorted velocities to find a range that we are 90% confident contains the velocity the team will experience going forward. To do this, we will use Table 15.2, which shows which 2 data points in our sorted set of velocities to use to determine the 90% confidence interval. For example, in Table 15.1 we had 9 observed velocities. Looking at the first column of Table 15.2, we see two choices near to 9: 8 and 11. We round down and choose 8. Looking across from 8, we find the number 2 in the second column. This means we create a confidence interval using the second observation from the bottom and the second from the top in our sorted list of velocities. These values are 34 and 41. Therefore, we are 90% confident that this team's average velocity will fall between 34 and 41.

Number of Velocity Observations	n^{th} Velocity Obsevation
5	1
8	2
11	3
13	4
16	5
18	6
21	7
23	8
26	9

TABLE 15.2

The nth lowest and n^{th} highest observation in a sorted list of velocities can be used to find a 90% confidence interval.

We can now use this confidence interval to predict how much functionality can be provided by a given date. We can then use that knowledge to decide what scope and schedule to commit to. Suppose that the team in Table 15.1 has 5 sprints remaining before a release. To see how much the team is likely to complete in that time, we can multiply the number of sprints, 5, by the values of the confidence interval (34 and 41). We then count down that many story points into the product backlog and point to the range of functionality the team is likely to deliver. This can be seen in Figure 15.4, which also shows an arrow pointing at the team's median value (39).

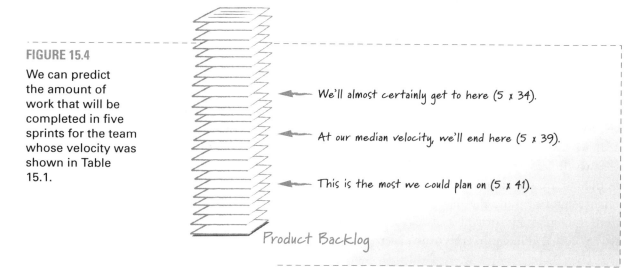

We'll almost certainly get to here (5 x 34).

At our median velocity, we'll end here (5 x 39).

This is the most we could plan on (5 x 41).

Product Backlog

Going from Estimate to Commitment

The three arrows in Figure 15.4 still show only estimates. For many projects, it will be necessary to translate those estimates into commitments. I would ideally like to convert these estimates into a commitment by saying something like, "In the next 5 sprints we believe we can commit to delivering between 170 [5 × 34] and 205 [5 × 41] story points, which means we'll deliver between here [top arrow] and there [bottom arrow] on the product backlog." This is the most realistic and accurate commitment. However, in many cases, product owners and their teams are asked to give a point estimate—"We commit to finishing exactly here." This is often the case for an organization doing outsourced, contract development work that needs to commit to a specific amount of functionality for a fixed-date contract.

When asked to turn a range like 170–205 story points into a point estimate that will be used as a commitment, it is tempting to react by saying, "Well, if you want a guarantee of what we can commit to, then it's the 170." If this is all you are willing to commit to, you will probably be able to achieve it, but you are taking on the risk right now of angering the person you are committing to. This type of decision can be viewed as trading long-term risk (there isn't much risk of delivering less than that amount of functionality) for short-term risk (your client, customer, or boss could be angry at you now if this is all you can commit to).

An alternative—committing to deliver the amount indicated by the high end of the confidence interval—makes the opposite trade-off. There is a lot of long-term risk (you might not be able to deliver that much) but very little short-term risk (everyone will think you're a superstar today for being able to commit to that much).

So, the three arrows of Figure 15.4 do not tell us what commitment to make. They tell us the likely range for our commitment. As an example, a contract development company with a lot of people on the bench might want to commit at or near the bottom arrow; the company's goal is likely to get people off the bench and back onto client engagements, even if the company takes on some risk to make that happen. Alternatively, a contract development company that has all of its developers fully engaged may commit near the top arrow for the next project.

For a fixed-scope project, similar analysis can be done to determine the likely range of how many sprints the project will take. To do this, sum the estimates of the required scope and divide that by both of the values that make up your confidence interval.

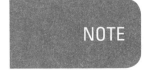

NOTE

Historical Velocity Forms the Basis for Committing

When I present information such as this to my clients, a common complaint is that they would love to do this type of analysis, but they cannot because they don't have the data. There's a very simple solution to this: Get the data. Doing so is easier than you think. Let's see how you can do this in two common problematic situations: when you have a completely new team that has never worked together and when the team size is changing or will change during the project.

The Team Has Never Worked Together

If a team has never worked together, it has no historical velocity data. The best solution in this case is to turn the team members loose on the project and let them run at least one sprint before making commitments. Running two or three sprints would be even better, of course. I understand that running one sprint before committing is not always possible, so here's an alternative approach.

Starting with a product backlog that has been estimated in story points or ideal days, pull the team together. Have members conduct a sprint planning meeting. Have them select one user story at a time from the product backlog, identify the tasks necessary to complete it, estimate each task in hours, and then decide whether they can commit to completing that user story in a sprint. They can select user stories in any order; we're not planning a real sprint but are instead trying to see how much work they can likely do in a sprint. In fact, this works best if the team grabs user stories more or less randomly from the product backlog. Encourage the team to make whatever assumptions it would like about the state of the system if they grab a user story that would be technically challenging if done in an early sprint. When team members have committed to a set of user stories and say they cannot commit to any more, add up the story-point or ideal-day estimates that were assigned earlier to the selected user stories. This becomes one estimate of the team's velocity. If you can get the team to do it, have it plan a second sprint this way and average the results. This decreases the impact of a bad estimate or two in the first sprint.

OBJECTION

"The team doesn't even exist yet. We'll hire people if it looks like we can do the project in the desired time frame."

Find others in the organization who have similar skills and experience to those you'd hire for the team. If you think you'll eventually hire two good programmers, one great programmer, two solid testers, a top-notch user experience designer, and one database engineer with five years of experience, then find a somewhat similar group of individuals. Invite them to a meeting and ask them to imagine they are the team assigned to this new project. Encourage them to take the estimating seriously—after all, maybe some of them will end up on the team.

When the meeting is over, you may want to adjust the derived velocity estimate up or down based on how you think the eventual team will compare to the estimators and based on how seriously you think the estimators performed the job.

Calculating an initial velocity this way is a first step, but we need to turn it into a range, as we did when we had historical data and created a confidence interval. One way to put a range around the estimated velocity is to use your intuition, perhaps raising and lowering the estimate by 25%, or more if you think the team took the exercise less seriously than it should have.

Another way to put a range around the estimated velocity is to adjust it based on the relative standard deviation calculated from velocities of other teams. Relative standard deviation is simply standard deviation expressed in percentage terms. Looking back at Table 15.1, we can calculate the standard deviation of those velocity values as 5.1. The average velocity of that data was 37.6. Dividing 5.1 by 37.6 and rounding the result gives 14%, which is the relative standard deviation. If you have data, like that shown in Table 15.1, for a number of teams, you can calculate the relative standard deviation for each team and then take the average of those values and apply it to the estimated velocity. This will give you a reasonable expectation of the new team's velocity as a range. Although this approach does work reasonably well, I want to reiterate that it would be better to have historical data for that team or to run a sprint or two before making a commitment. I am presenting this alternative approach for the times when neither of those is possible.

Team Size Changes Frequently

A different type of problem occurs when team size changes or is expected to change frequently. As in the previous case, my first answer is an easy one: Stop changing the team. Teams benefit tremendously from having a stable membership. Of course, team composition will change over the long term, but try not to exacerbate the problem by moving people back and forth between teams as is common in many organizations.

My second answer is again to collect data so that you are prepared and can anticipate the impact of team size changes. To do this, have someone in the organization keep track of the percentage change in velocity for the first few sprints following any change in team size. You want to track the change for a couple of sprints following a change of team size because velocity almost always drops in the first sprint, even when team size goes up. This is the result of increased communication, productive team members taking time to get a new member productive, and so on. In my experience, the long-term impact of the change is apparent by the third sprint after the change.

SEE ALSO

This type of organization-wide metric is a good thing for the Project Management Office (PMO) to collect. The PMO is discussed in Chapter 20, "Human Resources, Facilities, and the PMO."

My recommendation is to calculate the change in velocity not against the last sprint prior to the change but against the average value from the preceding five sprints. You could look back further, but often that isn't possible. Remember, we're trying to solve a problem in an environment where team sizes are changing frequently. So if we try to look back eight sprints, we might find that the team size changed over that interval.

What this leads to is something like Table 15.3. This table shows that the team in the first row went from six members to seven and experienced a 20% drop in velocity in the first sprint after the change, a 4% drop in the next sprint, followed by a 12% increase in velocity in the third sprint. The team in the last row has increased from seven to eight members but has only completed one sprint since doing so. The remaining columns of the last row will be filled in at the end of the next two sprints.

A spreadsheet like this can be kept up to date in no more than a few minutes per sprint, even when tracking dozens of teams. It is intentionally kept simple—I do not, for example, track whether it was a programmer or tester or other who moved onto or off the project. It is entirely likely that you already have a great deal of the raw data needed to create a spreadsheet like Table 15.3. If each team has been tracking its velocity and knows who was on the team during each sprint, you could re-create quite a bit of historical data.

SEE ALSO

You can download a spreadsheet for tracking this type of data from www. SucceedingWithAgile. com.

TABLE 15.3

Collecting data on the effect of changing team size.

Initial Team Size	New Team Size	Sprint +1	Sprint +2	Sprint +3
6	7	−20%	−4%	+12%
6	7	0%	−6%	+15%
7	5	−12%	−8%	−8%
8	6	−20%	−20%	−16%
7	8	−15%		

You can use data like this to answer a wide variety of questions such as these:

- What will this team's velocity be if we add two people?
- How soon could we get this project done if we added a person to each team?
- If I want this set of projects done by the end of the year, how many people would we need to add?
- What would be the impact of not approving the new employees in the budget?
- What would be the impact of a 15% layoff?

As a simple example using only the data in Table 15.3, suppose you have been asked to estimate how much more work could be completed in the next seven sprints if the team were to grow from six to seven people. By averaging the first two rows in Table 15.3,[1] you estimate that velocity will go down about 10% in the first sprint, be down about 5% in the second sprint, but then be up about 13% from then on as the new member is fully assimilated. These values are shown in Table 15.4.

TABLE 15.4

Calculating the impact of going from six to seven team members.

Sprint	Velocity Change
1	−10%
2	−5%
3–7	+13%

---

1   For simplicity, Table 15.3 has only two rows for teams increasing from six to seven people. For a real project, I would want more data than this before starting to base decisions on it.

By averaging the velocity changes, we calculate that the velocity is expected to change by just over 7% over seven sprints. You can now answer your boss by saying that going from six to seven people (a 17% increase in head count and possibly budget) will allow you to deliver approximately 7% more functionality over the planned seven sprints. The product owner should be able to use this information to determine whether the increased cost is worthwhile.

❑ Start collecting data relevant to your situation. Minimally, start a spreadsheet to capture the velocity of each team each sprint. Consider including data about team size changes or other factors if such changes are relevant in your organization.

❑ After you've gathered enough data on historical velocity, start producing a chart like Figure 15.4 so that it can be used by each project's product owner to make scope versus schedule trade-off decisions.

Summary

Becoming proficient at planning is a critical skill for any Scrum team. In this chapter we looked at ways for a team to move beyond the basics of sprint and release planning and achieve greater benefits by

- Progressively refining plans
- Working at a sustainable pace
- Looking first at changing scope when it's impossible to complete everything in the desired time frame
- Treating estimates as separate from commitments

Additional Reading

Cohn, Mike. 2005. *Agile estimating and planning*. Addison-Wesley Professional.
   The most thorough book on both estimating and planning on agile projects. It covers the advantages and disadvantages of both story points and ideal days, the two most common units for estimating by Scrum teams. It introduces the popular Planning Poker technique for estimating. Also covered in detail are prioritizing and planning in a variety of circumstances.

Moløkken-Østvold, Kjetil, and Magne Jørgensen, 2005. A comparison of software project overruns: Flexible versus sequential development methods. *IEEE Transactions on Software Engineering*, September, 754–766.

This paper was written by two respected researchers from the Simula Research Lab. It describes an in-depth survey of software development projects and concludes that agile projects have smaller effort overruns than projects using a sequential development process. A number of possible reasons are cited, including better requirements specifications (a product backlog) and improved customer communication.

Chapter 16

Quality

Early into my career as a programmer, I left my large, stable employer for an eight-person start-up. I went from a well-funded environment where we had a separate testing and quality assurance organization to a company where I was only the second programmer; there was not a tester in sight. Sometime during my first week at my new job, it hit me: I would be responsible for my own quality. There were no testers who would check my work or who would be a safety net for my meager attempts at unit testing. And then the bigger realizations hit: Without a tester, I would look like a fool to our customers (although none would know me personally), and I would also look like a fool to my boss, which could cost me my job.

I panicked. But fortunately so did another programmer who started two weeks after I did. Rather than be paralyzed by our panic, we created a wonderful suite of tools and techniques for testing our computer telephony application. Twenty years later I can look back on the systems we built at that time and continue to say they were some of the most thoroughly and amazingly tested applications I've worked on. And it was all because the company was too cash strapped at first to hire a tester, forcing us programmers to be responsible for the quality of what we were building.

By the time we did hire testers, the attitude that quality is a whole-team responsibility pervaded our growing development team. Since then, I've made an effort to instill that same mind-set in every development organization I work with. In this chapter, I describe the importance of integrating testing into the process rather than leaving it as something to be done later. I also introduce the test automation pyramid and describe how test automation efforts at most companies go awry because they fail to consider one-third of the pyramid. Finally, we look at the importance of doing acceptance test–driven development and of paying off technical debt.

Integrate Testing into the Process

I buy new cars infrequently, typically every 10 to 12 years. So when I bought a new car in 2003 I was surprised at the many advances in technology since I'd purchased my previous car, a 1993 Honda. One advance I was particularly pleased with was a sensor that automatically detects low air pressure in my tires. It is sometimes hard to tell by looking at a tire if its pressure is low, and checking tires manually is a dirty job, so I did it infrequently. A continuous test of tire pressure was, I thought, a tremendous invention.

During the same period in which car manufacturers invented ways to test tire pressure continuously, software development teams learned that testing their products continuously was also a good idea. In the early days, back when we wrote programs by rubbing sticks together, we thought of testing as something we did at the end. It wasn't quite an afterthought, but testing was intended to verify that no bugs had been introduced during the prior steps in the development process. It was kind of like making sure the oven is off, the windows are closed, and the front door is locked before heading out for a vacation. Of course, after we saw all the things that had gone wrong during the prior steps of the development process (how could they not?) testing came to be viewed not as a verification step but as a way of adding quality to a product.

It wasn't long before some teams realized that testing quality at the end was both inefficient and insufficient. Such teams typically shifted toward iterative development. In doing so, they split the lengthy, end-of-project test phase into multiple smaller test phases, each of which followed a phase of analysis-design-code. This was an improvement, but it wasn't enough.

And so with Scrum we go even further.

Scrum teams make testing a central practice and part of the development process rather than something that happens after the developers are "done." Rather than trying to test quality after a product has been built, we build quality into the process and product as it is being developed. W. Edwards Deming was an American professor and consultant best known for his work in Japan emphasizing the impact of quality on cost and productivity. He maintained that quality could not be added to a product later. He wrote that we should "cease dependence on mass inspection to achieve quality. Improve the process and build quality into the product in the first place" (2000, 23).

Why Testing at the End Doesn't Work

There are many reasons why the traditional approach of deferring testing until the end does not work:

- **It is hard to improve the quality of an existing product.** It has always seemed to me that it is easy to lower the quality of a product but that it is difficult and time consuming to improve it. Think about a time in your past when you were working on an application that had already shipped. Let's say you were asked to add a new set of features while simultaneously improving the existing application's quality. Despite lots of good work on your part, it is likely that months or even a year or more passed before quality improved enough that users could notice. Yet this is exactly what we try to do when we test quality into a product at the end.

- **Mistakes continue unnoticed.** Only after something is tested do we know that it really works. Until then you may be making the same mistake over and over again without realizing it. Let me give you an example. Geoff led the development of a website that was getting far more traffic than originally planned. He had an idea that he thought would improve the performance of every page on the site, so he implemented the change. This involved him writing some new Java code in one place and then going into the code for each page and adding one line to take advantage of the new, performance-improving code. It was tedious and time consuming. Geoff spent nearly an entire two-week sprint on these changes. After all that, Geoff tested and found that the performance gains were negligible. Geoff's mistake was in not testing the theoretical performance gains on the first few pages he modified. Testing along the way avoids unpleasant surprises like this at the end.

- **The state of the project is difficult to gauge.** Suppose I ask you to estimate two things for me: first, a handful of new features; and second, how long it will take to test and fix the bugs in a product that has been in development for six months and is now ready for its first round of testing. Most people will agree that estimating the new work is far easier and more likely to be accurate. Periodic (or better yet, continuous) testing of a product is a probe into that product that lets us know how far along we are.

- **Feedback opportunities are lost.** An obvious benefit of using Scrum is that the team can get feedback on what it's built at least at the end of every sprint. The product can be deployed onto restricted-access servers or made available for download to select customers. If the product is at a sufficient quality level for doing this only near the end of a release cycle, the team misses great opportunities to gain valuable feedback earlier.

- **Testing is more likely to be cut.** Because of deadline pressure, work that is planned to happen at the end of a project is more likely to be dropped or reduced.

OBJECTION

"It will take too much time to test continuously. We need to be realistic and acknowledge that it's better to test every fifth or sixth sprint."

When it seems better to test less often, this usually indicates that testing takes too long to do. Typically this is the case on applications that have relied on manual testing in the past and are now shifting to Scrum. If the cost of testing is so high that tests cannot be run every sprint, that cost needs to be aggressively driven down, in this case by creating automated tests to replace the manual ones. A lack of automated tests is a form of technical debt, which a later section in this chapter describes how to pay off.

"It's more efficient to have testers working one sprint behind the programmers."

If the testers work one sprint behind the programmers, who will they go to when they have questions? Will that be efficient for the programmers in that sprint? Will the testers be able to effectively take part in the sprint if the rest of the team is discussing how the next round of features should be added while they are testing the ones added already? For more on working together during a sprint, see Chapter 14, "Sprints."

What Building In Quality Looks Like

A team that has integrated testing into its day-to-day work will look and behave very differently from a team that attempts to test quality at the end. Some of the observable traits of a team that builds quality in include the following:

SEE ALSO

Test-driven development, pair programming, refactoring, and continuous integration were described in Chapter 9, "Technical Practices."

- **Most obvious will be the use of good engineering practices.** A team focused on building in quality will do whatever it can to write the highest quality code possible. This will include pair programming or thorough code inspections for at least the most complex parts of the system. There will be a strong focus on automated unit testing, if not test-driven development. Refactoring will happen continuously and as needed rather than in large, noticeable spurts. Code will be continuously integrated, and failures in the build will be treated with almost the same urgency as a customer-reported critical bug. You'll also notice that code will be owned collectively by the team rather than by individuals so that anyone noticing an opportunity to improve quality can take it.

- **The hand-offs between programmers and testers (if they exist at all) will be so small as not to be noticeable.** Chapter 11, "Teamwork," described how doing a little of everything (designing, coding, testing, and so on) all the time helps teams work together. When working that way, a programmer and tester talk about which capability (or partial capability) will be added to the product next. Then the tester creates automated tests and the programmer programs. When both are done the results are integrated. Although it may be correct to still think of there being hand-offs between the programmer and tester, in this case, the cycle should be so short that the hand-offs are of insignificant size.

- **There should be as much test activity on the first day of a sprint as on the last day.** A team that is building quality in avoids working in the miniature waterfalls that were described in Chapter 14. There are no distinct analysis, design, coding, or testing phases within a sprint. Testers (and programmers and other specialists) are as busy on the first day of a sprint as they are on the last. The type of work may differ between the first and last day of a sprint. For example, testers may be specifying test cases and preparing test data on the first day and then executing automated tests on the last, but they are equally busy throughout.

THINGS TO
TRY NOW

❑ During the next sprint, track the number of bugs reported by day. Track all of them—the ones that go into the defect system, the ones that turn into new items on your product backlog, the ones that get added into the sprint backlog, and even the ones where a tester just tells a programmer about the bug and it gets fixed immediately. If testing is built into the process, the number of bugs found per day should be fairly consistent across the sprint.

❑ Devote the next retrospective to discussing ways to improve quality.

Automate at Different Levels

Even before the ascendancy of agile methodologies like Scrum, we knew we should automate our tests. But we didn't. Automated tests were considered expensive to write and were often written months, or in some cases years, after a feature had been programmed. One reason teams found it difficult to write tests sooner was because they were automating at the wrong level. An effective test automation strategy calls for automating tests at three different levels, as shown in Figure 16.1, which depicts the *test automation pyramid*.

At the base of the test automation pyramid is unit testing. Unit testing should be the foundation of a solid test automation strategy and as such represents the largest part of the pyramid. Automated unit tests are wonderful because they give specific data to a programmer—there is a bug and it's on line 47. Programmers have learned that the bug may really be on line 51 or 42, but it's much nicer to have an automated unit test narrow it down than it is to have a tester say, "There's a bug in how you're retrieving member records from the database," which might represent 1,000 or more lines of code. Also, because unit tests are usually written in the same language as the system, programmers are often most comfortable writing them.

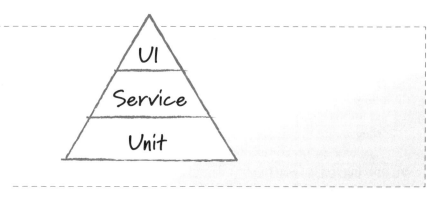

FIGURE 16.1

The test automation pyramid.

Let's skip for a moment the middle of the test automation pyramid and jump right to the top; the user interface level. Automated user interface testing is placed at the top of the test automation pyramid because we want to do as little of it as possible. We want this because user interface tests often have the following negative attributes:

- **Brittle.** A small change in the user interface can break many tests. When this is repeated many times over the course of a project, teams simply give up and stop correcting tests every time the user interface changes.
- **Expensive to write.** A quick capture-and-playback approach to recording user interface tests can work, but tests recorded this way are usually the most brittle. Writing a good user interface test that will remain useful and valid takes time.
- **Time consuming.** Tests run through the user interface often take a long time to run. I've seen numerous teams with impressive suites of automated user interface tests that take so long to run they cannot be run every night, much less multiple times per day.

Suppose we wish to test a very simple calculator that allows a user to enter two integers, click either a *multiply* or *divide* button, and then see the result of that operation. To test this through the user interface, we would script a series of tests to drive the user interface, type the appropriate values into the fields, press the multiply or divide button, and then compare expected and actual values. Testing in this manner would certainly work but would be prone to the brittleness and expense problems previously noted.

Additionally, testing an application this way is partially redundant—think about how many times a suite of tests like this will test the user interface. Each test case will invoke the code that connects the multiply or divide button to the code in the guts of the application that does the math. Each test case will also test the code that displays results. And so on. Testing through the user interface like this is expensive and should be minimized. Although there are many test cases that need to be invoked, not all need to be run through the user interface.

And this is where the *service layer* of the test automation pyramid comes in.

Although I refer to the middle layer of the test automation pyramid as the service layer, I am not restricting us to using only a service-oriented architecture. All applications are made up of various services. In the way I'm using it, a service is something the application does in response to some input or set of inputs. Our example calculator involves two services: multiply and divide.

Service-level testing is about testing the services of an application separately from its user interface. So instead of running a dozen or so multiplication test cases through the calculator's user interface, we instead perform those tests at the service level. To see how this might work, suppose we create a spreadsheet like Table 16.1, where each row represents one test case. The first two columns represent the numbers to be multiplied, the third column is the expected result, and the fourth column contains explanatory notes that will not be used by the test but that make the tests more readable.

SEE ALSO

Service-level testing was also described as a technique for specifying the behavior of a system through examples in Chapter 13, "The Product Backlog."

TABLE 16.1

A spreadsheet showing a subset of the multiplication service tests.

multiplier	multiplicand	product?	notes
5	1	5	Multiply by 1
5	2	10	
2	5	10	Swap the order of prior test
5	5	25	Multiply a number by itself
1	1	1	
5	0	0	Multiply by 0

What's needed next is a simple program that can read the rows of this spreadsheet, pass the data columns to the right service within your application, and verify that the right results occur. Despite this simplistic example where the result is simple calculation, the result could be anything—data updated in the database, an e-mail sent to a specific recipient, money transferred between bank accounts, and so on.

The Remaining Role of User Interface Tests

But don't we need to do some user interface testing? Absolutely, but far less of it than any other test type. In our calculator example, we no longer need to run all

NOTE

Although writing a tool to read a spreadsheet and pass data to specific services within your application is something the programmers on the team could easily write, there are already excellent tools to do this. FitNesse, available at www.fitnesse.org, is the most popular such tool.

multiplication tests through the user interface. Instead, we run the majority of tests (such as boundary tests) through the service layer, invoking the *multiply* and *divide* methods (services) directly to confirm that the math is working properly. At the user interface level what's left is testing to confirm that the services are hooked up to the right buttons and that the values are displaying properly in the result field. To do this we need a much smaller set of tests to run through the user interface layer.

Where many organizations have gone wrong in their test automation efforts over the years has been in ignoring this whole middle layer of service testing. Although automated unit testing is wonderful, it can cover only so much of an application's testing needs. Without service-level testing to fill the gap between unit and user interface testing, all other testing ends up being performed through the user interface, resulting in tests that are expensive to run, expensive to write, and brittle.

The Role of Manual Testing

It is impossible to fully automate all tests for all environments. Further, some tests are prohibitively expensive to automate. Many tests that we cannot or choose not to automate involve hardware or integration to external systems. A photocopier company I consulted to had a number of tests that needed human intervention before they ran. For example, making sure there were exactly five pieces of paper in the paper tray was easier to do manually than to automate.

In general, manual testing should be viewed primarily as a way of doing exploratory testing. This type of testing involves a rapid cycle through the steps of test planning, test design, and test execution. Exploratory testing should feature short, feedback-generating cycles through these steps in a manner analogous to test-driven development's short cycle of test-code-refactor.

Beyond finding bugs, exploratory testing can also identify missing test cases. These can then be added at the appropriate level of the test automation pyramid. Further, exploratory testing can uncover ideas that are missing from the user story as initially understood. It can also help a team discover things that seemed like a good idea at the time but seem like bad ideas now that the feature has been developed. These situations usually result in new items being added to the product backlog.

Automate Within the Sprint

Automation on a Scrum project is not optional. For a team to sprint effectively (and therefore deliver value quickly), it needs to rely heavily on test automation. Automated tests provide cheap insurance that what used to work correctly still does. Further, an always-growing suite of automated tests provides insight into the state of the product (and the process). If the automated test suite hasn't been run successfully for two weeks, that should be a great big warning sign. On the other hand, if the automated test suite is growing daily and has run without error every night of this sprint, the team is probably in good shape.

Scrum teams approach test automation differently than do teams using a sequential development process. A highly automated test suite is considered mandatory by Scrum teams; it is considered a luxury by traditional teams. One reason why traditional teams have struggled to see the value in automation is that they don't automate early enough. Tests are often automated months after the code was initially written. Teams new to Scrum often make the same mistake, falling into a pattern of writing code in one sprint and then automating tests of that code in a later one. When tests are automated long after the code is written, much of the value of automating is lost. Code is changing most frequently while it is being actively developed, so automated tests are most useful during that time.

SEE ALSO

If you feel like it is impossible to code, then test, and then automate all within a sprint, see "Do a Little Bit of Everything All the Time" in Chapter 11.

Figure 16.2 illustrates the value of automating early. The cost of automation resembles the familiar s curve: The cost does not rise for a couple of sprints; after that though, costs rise significantly before plateauing. Anyone who has ever tried to retrofit automated tests onto an existing application knows that it is harder to do than if the tests are added when the design of those tests could have still influenced the design of the product. When adding tests late, we are often forced to over-rely on the top level of the test automation pyramid; adding automated unit and service-level tests is too difficult until some significant refactoring of the application occurs.

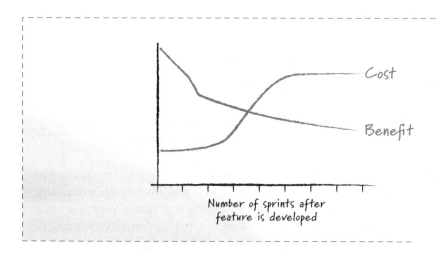

FIGURE 16.2

The costs and benefits of automating a test over time.

Although the initial flatness of the cost curve may tempt you into deferring automation for a sprint or two, don't. The steep drop-off in the benefits of automation should encourage you to automate as early as possible. Over time, the benefits of automation drop because the likelihood and frequency of changes affecting that area of the application drop. Eventually a product may be so stable and its expected remaining life so short that the cost of automating outweighs the benefits. This is the argument made by many traditional teams or by teams who put automation off entirely.

What should be clear from Figure 16.2 is that the maximum benefit can be gained by automating in the same sprint a new feature is added to the system. This provides the most value and does it at the lowest cost.

Sampling the Benefits

To see how significant the benefits can be of testing across all levels of the test automation pyramid, consider the case of Salesforce.com. Salesforce.com provides Software as a Service for customer relationship management. Nine months after adopting Scrum, Salesforce.com had achieved the following reductions:

- Reduced the number of staff involved in its nine deployments of the application by 65% (to 15 people)

- Reduced the amount of time spent on final go-live tests—two to three hours of manual effort became ten minutes of automated testing

- Reduced the amount of time on post-release sanity tests—three to four hours of manual testing became 45 minutes of running over 200 automated tests

- Reduced the number of people involved in patch releases by almost 80% (to approximately five people)

- Saved over 300 person hours per major release and hundreds more for all patch releases (Greene 2007)

These results are not unusual for an organization that takes automated testing seriously. Use them as starting goals for your own automation efforts.

OBJECTION

"While the programmers are working on a feature, things are changing much too quickly for the testers to automate tests."

To address this, let's consider the three types of test automation that were shown in the test automation pyramid and should be occurring. Clearly, the unit tests should be written during the sprint, perhaps even in a test-driven manner. Experience shows us that it is rare for a programmer to come back later into working code and add unit tests. It is usually our past history with capture-and-playback style automated testing that leads us to think that we can only automate once a feature is complete. It is true that a tester cannot finish running the automated service-level and user interface tests until the programmers finish coding, but this does not mean that development of them cannot be started in parallel. Exactly how to do so is the topic of the next section.

❑ In your next retrospective, discuss the three levels of the test automation pyramid. Where is testing happening now? What types of your current tests would be better done with a different type of automation? Try to identify two or three ways to get started with test automation in the coming sprint.

Do Acceptance Test–Driven Development

Scrum teams have learned to smooth the flow of work through a sprint by doing acceptance test–driven development (ATDD). In ATDD, work occurs in response to acceptance tests. Acceptance tests serve as a record of the decisions made about the implementation of a feature. As such they are written throughout the sprint as those conversations occur.

ATDD can be thought of as analogous to the test-driven development (TDD) of Chapter 9. Lasse Koskela, author of *Test Driven: Practical TDD and Acceptance TDD for Java Developers*, shows the relationship between ATDD and TDD, as shown in Figure 16.3. I've amended Koskela's original diagram to show only the role of the conditions of satisfaction in this cycle.

SEE ALSO

Conditions of satisfaction were described in Chapter 13.

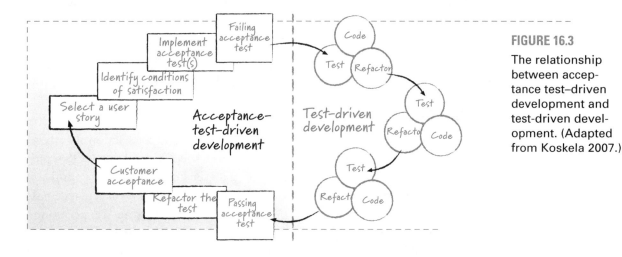

FIGURE 16.3

The relationship between acceptance test–driven development and test-driven development. (Adapted from Koskela 2007.)

As described in Chapter 13, COS are meant to convey a product owner's high-level expectations about a user story. As such, they typically reside a level above specific acceptance-test cases, which makes them ideal for driving the ATDD process itself.

The use of conditions of satisfaction in the cycle shown in Figure 16.3 frees the product owner from the need to be involved constantly throughout the ATDD cycle. A product owner can convey the COS for a user story either at the start of the sprint or when the team is ready to begin work on the story. To the extent that the subsequently identified acceptance tests are in line with the product owner's expectations, acceptance tests can be written by testers, analysts, or perhaps other team members, without involvement from the product owner.

In an ideal world, the product owner would show up at the sprint planning meeting having recently identified the conditions of satisfaction for each high-priority user story on the product backlog. Having done this, the product owner will be in a much better position to answer the usual type of questions asked during the planning meeting. So, minimally, doing ATDD and starting with the COS helps reduce the amount of time spent in planning meetings.

Unfortunately, the real world sometimes intrudes on our plans, and product owners may not always come to the sprint planning meeting with the conditions of satisfaction preidentified. For example, a crisis near the end of one sprint may prevent the product owner from preparing for the next. Or during the planning meeting the team may request to work on a user story a bit further down the product backlog and for which the product owner has not yet identified conditions of satisfaction (because they should be identified as close to implementation as possible).

Situations such as these do not preclude doing ATDD. When conditions of satisfaction do not yet exist, the product owner and team have two choices. The first is to use the sprint planning meeting to identify the COS for the product backlog items that don't have them. The second option is to identify them as one of the first activities of the new sprint. Either approach is acceptable, but the first is preferable in most cases and whenever time permits.

The Right Level of Detail

It may sound like a lot of work to identify conditions of satisfaction shortly in advance of each sprint planning meeting. However, keep in mind that COS represent the high-level things that must be true of a user story for it to be considered done at the end of the sprint. The goal is to discuss the high-level acceptance tests that provide guidance to the developers about the product owner's expectations, not to identify every small test case that will eventually be needed.

For example, a team I worked with was creating a website to be used by active stock traders. Its product included many different ways for the traders to visualize data about stocks and stock prices. One chart, called a treemap, showed companies as small rectangles placed within a larger rectangle. Each of the small rectangles was sized to reflect the total market value of the stock of the company. If a company had a market value twice that of another company, its rectangle would be twice as big. An example is shown in Figure 16.4. Users could select whether they wanted to view the entire stock market, one segment of it (such as software companies), or other comparative sets.

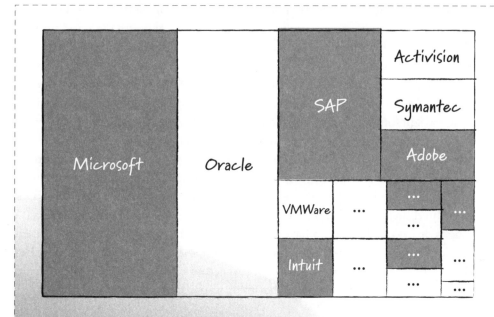

FIGURE 16.4

A treemap in which the size of each rectangle represents the market value of a company.

At first glance, placing small rectangles inside larger ones may seem like an easy problem. But, it's actually harder than it might look. Imagine one of those games where you're given a few dozen blocks of various shapes and are asked to put them together into a fixed shape with no gaps. Creating these rectangles is a bit like that but with potentially thousands of pieces. During this team's sprint planning meeting its product owner described the following conditions of satisfaction to the team:

- Rectangles should be as close to square as possible; target is an average ratio of long side to short of 1.1.
- The system must be able to generate five treemaps of a specified complexity per second on the planned hardware.
- Support up to 5,000 items in one treemap.
- Support up to 500 groups in one treemap.

You'll notice how high level these conditions of satisfaction are. That's one of the reasons why COS has caught on for describing the "tests" applied to a user story or product backlog items. Conditions of satisfaction often are one level above a true acceptance test. For example, to make a true acceptance test of "support up to 5,000 items in one treemap," we would need to know more about those items; making a treemap of 5,000 identically sized items is trivial; doing the same for 5,000 widely varying items is not.

Information about the 5,000 items will be added during the sprint. The tester will take the product owner's high-level expectations (expressed as conditions of satisfaction) and turn them into specific tests. The tester will also add all the specific tests implied but not stated by the product owner. For example, in the case of the treemap, our product owner clearly wanted a treemap to render correctly even if it had only one data point. She didn't tell the team that because it was obvious. But it was still something that needed to be coded for and tested during the sprint.

Doing acceptance test–driven development keeps a team continuously focused on the objectives of the product owner. Starting a sprint with conditions of satisfaction identified for each user story to be worked on (or identifying them as early as possible within the sprint) helps teams from going astray ("Oh, I thought you wanted such-and-such") and from being tempted to gold-plate a feature ("I thought this would be cool to have as well"). Acceptance test–driven development provides the additional benefit of stimulating additional early conversation between testers and the other developers on a team at a time when testers might otherwise be tempted to wonder what their responsibilities are.

THINGS TO TRY NOW

❑   Select a product backlog item being worked on in the current sprint. Ask each team member (including the product owner) to privately write the conditions of satisfaction for that item. Then, starting with the COS written by the product owner, share all the other items. It will be possible that the product owner failed to identify a few key conditions. (After all, we're not going to spend a lot of time on this exercise.) But it will be even more likely that there will be some conflicting conditions among team members or some surprising realizations of what is essential in the backlog item.

Pay Off Technical Debt

Technical debt, a concept originated by Ward Cunningham, referred originally to the increased cost of working on an application with "immature" or "not-quite-right" code (1992). The term is now generally used to refer to the cost of working on a system that is poorly designed, poorly written, includes unfinished work, or is deficient in any of a number of ways. Cunningham warns of the consequences of accumulating technical debt.

> Danger occurs when the debt is not repaid. Every minute spent on not-quite-right code counts as interest on that debt. Entire engineering organizations can be brought to a standstill under the debt load of an unconsolidated implementation. (1992)

Technical debt is often the result of a rushed implementation. This is not always bad. As Cunningham writes, "Shipping first-time code is like going into debt. A little debt speeds development so long as it is paid back promptly with a rewrite" (1992). The key is that the debt must be paid back quickly. This doesn't always happen, and as such many teams are left with huge accumulations of technical debt. Because Scrum teams take a long-term view of the life of their products, paying down technical debt becomes a serious consideration.

Some technical debt is obvious: Unexpected data in the database that causes the application to crash is clearly technical debt. Fragile code that is broken by any programmer who touches it is also clearly debt. But what about the case of a team that has not upgraded to last month's release of a new version of Java? This, too, is technical debt. It's probably not a problem that the team has not yet upgraded, and I certainly don't want to imply that every team should upgrade instantly to every new tool released. But, using even a slightly outdated language, library, or tool is debt. The debt will need to be paid eventually. Keep in mind Cunningham's observation: "A little debt speeds development so long as it is paid back promptly."

Paying Down Testing Debt in Three Steps

It is not necessary for a team to pay off all incurred technical debt for them to become and remain agile. Doing so would be nice, but it's not always realistic or appropriate. However, enough of the debt must be paid down that the team is not crushed under its weight. As an example of how a team can pay down its technical debt, let's consider how to handle one of the most common forms of technical debt: a critical lack of automated tests.

When a team that has relied mostly or entirely on manual testing decides to adopt Scrum, it will quickly discover how hard it is to run short sprints when there's a lot of manual testing to be done each sprint. It will also realize that unless it does something drastic, the technical debt will continue to accumulate. Teams in this situation can follow a three-step process (as shown in Figure 16.5) to extricate themselves from at least the worst of these problems:

1. Stop the bleeding.
2. Stay current.
3. Catch up.

The first priority of a team with technical debt in the form of an over-reliance on manual testing is to stop the bleeding, stop things from getting worse. The best tourniquet is to find ways to automate some of what is being tested manually. To mix metaphors, teams should find the low-hanging fruit: tests that will be easy to automate but save a lot of manual effort. Brian Marick, a leading authority on testing and coauthor of the Agile Manifesto, observes that "the real low-hanging fruit is often not automating some test execution but automating other testing tasks, like populating databases or automatic navigation to the page where you'll start manual testing. You're not reducing the number of manual tests, but you're reducing the total time it takes to run them."

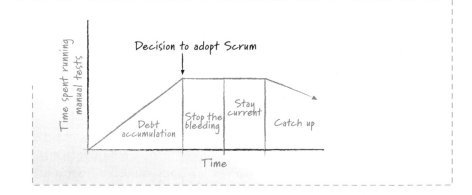

While team members are doing triage, they are also gaining proficiency with automated testing, which may be a new skill for some individuals. Test servers and test environments have to be configured and tools selected. It will take a considerable investment of time. But if it is not done, every new bit of functionality added to the system will only add to the amount of time manual testing will take, compounding the technical debt. What takes 20 hours this sprint may take 21 hours the next sprint. Eventually, the project will collapse under the burden of the technical debt from manual testing.

After the bleeding has been stopped, the situation will no longer be getting worse from sprint to sprint. Manual tests still will be added each sprint but the team is finding enough low-hanging fruit each sprint to offset the time needed to run the new manual tests. At this point, it is time to move to step two: learning to stay current. During this phase, the team focuses on learning how to write and automate tests for whatever new features are added during the sprint. While doing this, no more debt is accumulating, so the situation isn't getting any worse, but it's not yet getting any better either. Learning to add automated tests in the same sprint as the feature will be a new skill for the team. It won't be as hard to learn as the initial skills were during the first phase but will require new discipline.

Eventually the team enters the final phase, which is when it catches up on additional outstanding testing debt. This can be seen by the descending line of Figure 16.5. I generally tell teams that I coach that I don't care how rapidly that line descends as long as it is now moving in the right direction. Obviously, I would prefer the debt to come down as fast as possible. But, by stating it this way I am emphasizing that what I am most concerned with are the first two steps.

Quality Is a Team Effort

An emphasis on quality can have dramatic results. Nine months after adopting Scrum and taking the steps recommended here, Steve Greene of Salesforce.com says that his company had already achieved "over 300 person hours saved per major release, and hundreds more across the lifespan of all the patch releases. That is a lot of time we now spend on features, automation, design, basically all things good and productive" (2007).

As impressive as these results are, they are not unusual and can be matched by any committed Scrum team. Just as all customers suffer if a product is of low quality, the entire team suffers if testing is not integrated into the process or is not done at the right levels. Acquiring new testing skills, learning how to apply them within the strict timeboxes of Scrum, and paying off technical debt are the responsibility of the whole team. These are not challenges to be sloughed off onto the testers. A good Scrum team will be constantly vigilant of the state of its testing practices, always looking for ways to improve.

Additional Reading

Adzic, Gojko. 2009. *Bridging the communication gap: Specification by example and agile acceptance testing.* Neuri Limited.

> An excellent book that strives to improve communication between project stakeholders and team members through the use of specification by example and identifying conditions of satisfaction.

Crispin, Lisa, and Janet Gregory. 2009. *Agile testing: A practical guide for testers and agile teams.* Addison-Wesley Professional.

> This book is for anyone seeking to understand how to integrate testing into an agile project. Testing is split into four quadrants (somewhat similar to the layers of the test automation pyramid), and the types of testing done in each are described. The book equips agile testers with the mind-set and skills needed for their new roles.

Mugridge, Rick, and Ward Cunningham. 2005. *Fit for developing software: Framework for integrated tests.* Prentice Hall.

> This book starts out with the basics and then progresses into a case study. The first 180 pages are meant for anyone—programmers, testers, business people, etc.—and will show you how Fit can benefit your develop projects. The next 150 or so pages are meant for those with a programming background and describe how to extend Fit by writing and using custom fixtures.

Koskela, Lasse. 2007. *Test driven: TDD and acceptance TDD for Java developers.* Manning.

> Part Four of this book provides excellent coverage of acceptance test–driven development. The book covers the reasons to do ATDD, how to do it using FIT (the Framework for Integrated Test), and how to get started on your project.

PART IV

The Organization

Every organization must be prepared
to abandon everything it does
to survive in the future.

—Peter Drucker

Chapter 17

Scaling Scrum

My wife, Laura, cooks dinner nearly every night. Some nights she makes something a bit fancier; other nights, if she's more rushed, she cooks something simple. But it's always tasty, healthful, and prepared without a great deal of stress. Except for Christmas dinner. Cooking Christmas dinner is stressful. The house is full of guests—her parents, my parents, maybe an aunt and uncle, and a brother or sister or two. And yet she seems to prepare more dishes than we have guests. Christmas dinner is done at a scale unseen the rest of the year. And anything done at a larger scale than we are accustomed to—including a software development project—is more difficult.

SEE ALSO

Distributed development brings with it such unique challenges that it receives its own chapter, which follows this one.

When a software project gets large, it is complicated by more than just having more mouths to feed. Large projects are often more critical to the organization, under greater scrutiny, more time-sensitive, more prone to personality clashes, longer, and more likely to be distributed across multiple sites.

The first round of defense against large projects is to attack them not with one large team but with multiple small teams. Chapter 10, "Team Structure," introduced the idea of the two-pizza team, a team of perhaps five to nine members—small enough that it can be fed with two pizzas. When faced with a large project, we will use many of these two-pizza development teams rather than one much larger team.

In this chapter we look at ways to overcome the challenge of successfully using Scrum on a large, multiteam project. Specifically, we look at scaling the product owner role, working with a large product backlog, managing dependencies among teams, coordinating work among teams, scaling the sprint planning meeting, and the role of communities of practice on large Scrum projects.

Scaling the Product Owner

The product owner role can be one of the most challenging on a Scrum project. On all projects, the product owner is torn between competing inward-facing and outward-facing needs. Among the inward-facing tasks are participating in planning meetings, sprint reviews, sprint retrospectives, and daily scrums; managing the product backlog; answering questions from the team; and simply being available to the team during the sprint. A product owner's outward-facing tasks include talking to users about their needs, creating and interpreting user surveys, traveling to customer sites, attending industry trade shows, managing stakeholder expectations, prioritizing the product backlog, determining product pricing, developing a medium- and long-term product strategy, watching for industry and market trends, performing competitive analysis, and more. On a project with one team of developers, this is often a vast but achievable amount of work. On a large project with multiple teams, however, the product owner role is too big for one person, so we must find ways of scaling it.

As a project grows to include multiple teams, ideally a new product owner is found for each. If you cannot achieve a one-to-one correspondence between teams and product owners, try to have each product owner responsible for no more than two teams. This is usually the most that one product owner can effectively work with.

At some point as the overall size of the project grows, it makes sense to introduce a hierarchy of collaborating product owners. Figure 17.1 shows such a hierarchy, with a product owner working with each team, two product line owners each working with a cluster of teams, and a chief product owner. Naturally, layers can be added or removed as needed for the scale of the project.

FIGURE 17.1

The product owner role can scale up to include product line owners and a chief product owner.

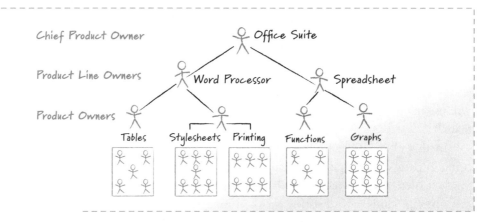

Sharing Responsibility, Dividing Functionality

The chief product owner is responsible for having an overall vision of the entire product or product suite. The chief product owner conveys this to the entire team in whole-team meetings, e-mails, team get-togethers, and through whatever other means are available. But the chief product owner is almost certainly too busy to assume hands-on responsibility for working as the actual product owner for one of the five- to nine-person teams building the product. At this level, the external-facing requirements of the role are too great. A good chief product owner will be very involved with teams—attending daily scrums occasionally, walking through team areas whenever in the office, and offering support and feedback. But the chief product owner will need to rely on the product line owners and product owners to handle the intricate details of their product segments within the overall project vision.

Suppose, for example, we decide to develop an office productivity suite that will include a word processor, spreadsheet, presentation software, and personal database. Competing with Microsoft Office, Google Apps, and other products will be daunting, but our chief product owner is fearless. Because the chief product owner will be focused on strategic issues, competitive positioning, and such, product line owners are selected to own the individual products in the suite—the word processor, spreadsheet, presentation program, and database. Each product line owner in turn identifies product owners who will be responsible for feature areas within the product. The product line owner for the word processor, for example, may work with one product owner who is responsible for tables, another responsible for stylesheets and printing, another who is responsible for the spell checker, and so on.

Although as previously mentioned, the chief product owner is too busy to be the product owner for one team, it is possible for a chief product owner to act as the product line owner for part of the product. Continuing with the preceding example, our chief product owner may choose to also be the product line owner responsible for the word processor, perhaps because of being in that role previously. Similarly, a product line owner will often want to stay involved in a more hands-on manner and will work also as one of the product owners. Perhaps our product line owner for the spreadsheet product also acts as the product owner for the team that will add charts to the spreadsheet product.

Although functionality can be divided along these lines, it is important for all product owners to feel a shared responsibility for the full product. They must also instill this feeling of shared responsibility in the teams they work with.

The labels "chief product owner" and "product line owner" are the ones I generally favor, but they are representative only; use others if you wish. In addition to these, I've seen both program owner, super product owner, area owner, and feature owner used successfully.

For consistency with the bulk of existing Scrum literature, I prefer to use "product owner" for the individual who works directly with one or two teams, prioritizing their work and doing all of the other things associated with the product owner role. In these multilayer hierarchies the product owner is often someone whose business card reads "Business Analyst."

NOTE

Working with a Large Product Backlog

Most large project teams opt to use one of the commercial agile tools that provide support for working with a large product backlog. I won't, therefore, go into all of my preferences for how to work with a single large product backlog because much of how an organization works with its product backlog will be dictated by its tool selection. There are, however, two guidelines worth pointing out that remain valid regardless of which backlog management tool is selected:

- If there's only one product, there should be only one product backlog.
- The product backlog should be kept to a reasonable size.

These topics are addressed in the sections that follow.

One Product, One Product Backlog

There's a reason it's not called a "project backlog" or a "team backlog" or any other similar but deficient term. It's called a product backlog because there should be one per product. If a team is working from more than one product backlog, the multiple backlogs must be prioritized against one another. It is not enough to prioritize each product backlog and tell the team to take the top five items off of each. The top item on one product backlog might be lower priority than the lowest item on another product backlog.

As an example, consider successful Scrum adopter Ultimate Software of Weston, Florida. Ultimate Software develops Software as a Service (SaaS) for human capital management. This includes features for human resources and payroll management. Although these features are obviously entwined (the human resources you manage need to be paid), the underlying software is modular. Within Ultimate there are teams that focus on enhancing the human resources portion of the product and other teams that focus on enhancing the payroll portion. However, even with teams focused on different areas of the system, Ultimate maintains a single product backlog for the overall product.

Having a single product backlog allows the chief product owner at Ultimate to see the relationship between the top-priority human resources features and the top-priority payroll features. Suppose that all of the items at the top of the product backlog are human resources features. This is an indicator to the chief product owner to either redirect the payroll-focused teams toward human resources features (where they'll be less productive at first because they aren't as familiar with that domain or code) or have them continue on lower-priority payroll features.

Logistical problems can arise, however, when multiple teams and multiple product owners work with a single product backlog. Although we can agree that all features should be prioritized relative to all other features, this can be extremely difficult to do on a project with numerous product owners, multiple product line owners, and a chief product owner. Rather than allowing each product owner to maintain his or her own private product backlog, a better solution is to have a single product backlog but to provide views into it for each product owner. This can be seen in Figure 17.2.

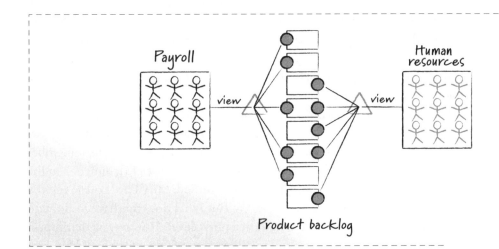

FIGURE 17.2

There should be one product backlog per product, but there can be multiple views into it.

Figure 17.2 shows two teams sharing a common product backlog. When the team on the right, which is developing the human resources features of the system, views the product backlog, it sees items that the team is or could be responsible for delivering. The payroll team on the left has a similar view of the product backlog, which shows items of interest to that team. Notice that some product backlog items may be shown in both views. This can indicate that the feature may be fully implemented by either team or that both teams will need to be involved in developing it. Suppose, for example that the word processor and spreadsheet teams of an office suite product were looking at their product backlog views. It is likely that each would see a product backlog item for enhancing the shared spell checker.

Keep the Product Backlog to a Reasonable Size

We need to balance our desire for a single product backlog with the competing desire that the product backlog not become unmanageable. In fact, from my experience, things degrade rapidly if anyone involved in the project is expected to be familiar with more than 100–150 items. I have two reasons why I think this to be a reasonable upper limit. First, by observing and working with hundreds of Scrum teams, when I hear a complaint of "our product backlog is too big," it is almost always in reference to a product backlog with 100 or more items. My second argument in support of keeping the product backlog under 100–150 has to do with a release party I went to in 2000.

As the vice president of development in this organization, I was pleased when my teams finished a particularly large project on time. We decided to have a party to congratulate the team and celebrate its success. The party was at a hotel banquet room and was attended by 160 team members and their significant others. I walked around the room with my wife, introducing her to those I worked with and meeting their guests. Until, uh-oh, I saw a couple and had no idea which of the two I worked with. This was bad—one of them reported to me or to someone who reported to me, but I couldn't remember if it was him or her. My brain failed me because of something called Dunbar's Number, which I read about for the first time shortly after this party.

Robin Dunbar was a British anthropologist who suggested that the human brain has a limit of around 150 individuals with whom one can maintain a normal social relationship. Up to approximately 150 people, and we can remember who each person is and how each relates to all others ("That's Joachim; he's in the testing group"). Beyond that number, we get confused. Aha! This explained why I couldn't remember each person at the party. But what does this have to do with product backlogs? Perhaps not much at a scientific level. However, if the human brain is wired such that we can only remember 150 people and the relationships among them, I'm willing to go along with the idea that most of us can only keep 100–150 or so product backlog items and the relationships among them straight in our brains. Combined with anecdotal evidence that teams with 100 or more items on their product backlogs complain about them to me and teams with smaller product backlogs don't, 100–150 seems like a good upper limit.

Although this may seem to be a small number of product backlog items, consider that we have two ways of keeping the number of backlog items manageable.

SEE ALSO

Epics and progressive refinement of the product backlog were introduced in Chapter 13, "The Product Backlog."

- **Make use of epics and themes.** By writing some large stories (epics) on the product backlog and by grouping small stories together into themes, even the product backlog for an immense project can be made to fit within my guideline of no more than approximately 150 product backlog items.
- **Provide views into the product backlog.** Notice that I didn't say there cannot be more than 150 items on the product backlog; I only said that no one should need to be familiar with more than that many. This can be achieved by providing multiple views into the product backlog, as shown earlier in Figure 17.2. Imagine again that you are building a competitor to Microsoft Office and Google Apps. The chief product owner of such a product would be overwhelmed if she had to be aware of and look at 500 or more product backlog items at one time. It would be more useful for a chief product owner such as this to be able to see rollups of individual product backlog items into themes while allowing the individual user stories to be visible to teams.

This can be seen in Figure 17.3, which shows a partial product backlog. The chief product owner can see themes, which are groups of related user stories. The individual teams and their product owners, however, can see individual user stories written at the level of detail they need to turn each into new capabilities in the product.

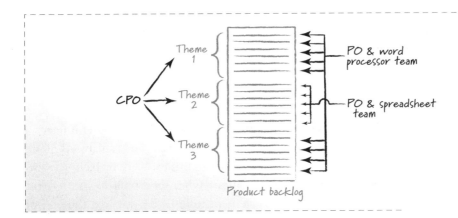

Product backlog

FIGURE 17.3

Multiple views into one product backlog.

- ❏ If your project has multiple product backlogs, offer to assist the product owner in consolidating them into one.
- ❏ If your product backlog has more than 100–150 items, group items together into themes. Write a user story or other descriptive label on the theme so that the collection of user stories can be thought of as one item.

THINGS TO TRY NOW

Proactively Manage Dependencies

For the most part, Tom's project was moving along fairly well: The teams had become accustomed to the iterative and incremental nature of Scrum and were beginning to truly embrace automated testing, test-driven development, and even pair programming. Tom had embraced his new role as ScrumMaster with only a few remaining traces of his previous life as a command-and-control project manager. After every sprint, Tom's two teams would demonstrate the new functionality in their online payment and money transfer application. The stakeholders were pleased at the progress. Usually. Every now and then, Tom's teams would complete only a small portion of what they'd committed to. The teams used their retrospectives to consider root causes each time this happened. In an e-mail to me about the situation, one of the team members, Campbell, summarized what they learned.

> Almost every time a sprint blew up on us, it was because of a dependency between our two teams. We wouldn't think about it

during sprint planning. Or we'd think about it but misjudge the effort involved.

On any multiple team project such as Tom's and Campbell's, the potential for dependencies between teams exists. Good team structure can go a long way toward reducing dependencies but will not eliminate them. Similarly, continuous integration helps point out problems caused by some dependencies. Fortunately, there are additional techniques Scrum teams can employ to further manage dependencies. These include doing rolling lookahead planning, holding release kick-off meetings, sharing team members, and even using a dedicated integration team.

SEE ALSO

Advice on structuring teams was given in Chapter 10. Continuous integration was described in Chapter 9, "Technical Practices."

Do Rolling Lookahead Planning

All too often a team finishes its sprint planning meeting only to discover it needs a small amount of work done by another team but that team is not available. Rolling lookahead planning greatly reduces the frequency of this problem by having teams spend a few minutes each sprint thinking about what they will do in the next couple of sprints. Normally the most convenient time to do this is at the end of the sprint planning meeting, as the team and product owner are already together with their minds on planning.

Depending on the team, the sprint length, and a few other factors, planning one sprint takes anywhere from an hour to a full day. Planning an additional couple of sprints in the same meeting would seem both impossible and tediously boring. Fortunately, we only need to look ahead at the subsequent two sprints using average historical velocity, with no consideration of tasks or hours. This means planning those two sprints will take about ten minutes, assuming the team knows its historical average velocity and the product owner has prioritized the product backlog.

So, a team doing rolling lookahead planning will walk out of the meeting with the coming sprint planned in detail (a selected set of product backlog items and the tasks with hours for each) and a set of product backlog items tentatively selected for the following two sprints. An example can be seen in Table 17.1, which illustrates what a rolling lookahead plan might look like after the sprint planning for sprint three. One sprint later, the team will identify tasks for the product backlog items of sprint four and will peer forward at sprints five and six, which will have rolled into view. It is worth noting that the product backlog items selected for the later sprints are subject to change when work begins on those sprints. Rolling lookahead planning should be viewed as a chance to consider what might be worked on next, not as a locked-down plan. The product owner will still be able to revise his or her opinion based on then-current information.

TABLE 17.1

Rolling lookahead plans include details for the current sprint but only the high-level items of the next two sprints.

Sprint 3	
As a site visitor, I can read current news on the home page so that I can stay current on what's happening in the Scrum and agile world.	
Code the middle tier.	12 hours
Code new user interface.	4 hours
Design and automate tests.	12 hours
Design new UI and run it by some users.	8 hours
As the site editor, I can add news items to the website so that users can stay up to date with the latest happenings.	
Identify and make database changes.	12 hours
Code Ruby on Rails code.	4 hours
Design and automate tests.	8 hours
As a site visitor, I can access old news that is no longer on the home page so that I can find old items I want to reread or missed when they were first published.	
Add code to set these and to use them.	6 hours
Design and automate tests.	8 hours

Sprint 4
As a site editor, I can set a Start Publishing Date and a Stop Publishing Date on all news items so that only timely news is shown.
As a site visitor, I can send e-mail via a form to the webmaster of the site.
As a site visitor, I can send e-mail via a form to the editor of the site.

Sprint 5
As a site visitor, I want to read a new article on the front page once a week.
As a site visitor, I can do a full-text search of article body, title, and author name.

I recommend looking two sprints ahead because doing so gives teams adequate time to respond to most newly discovered dependencies. To see why, consider what would happen if a team were to plan only one sprint ahead. If you need something from another team by the start of the next sprint, your only option is to ask that team to do it in the coming sprint. If that team were planning the coming sprint at the same time you were, it has probably fully planned its sprint by the time you ask. Looking ahead two sprints, though, allows you to go to that team with more advance notice. The other team has time to plan and perform the needed work in the next sprint and have it ready for you by the start of the following sprint, which is when you needed it. Some teams—usually those involved in hardware or embedded development—may look even further ahead with rolling lookahead planning.

OBJECTION

"We barely have time to plan one sprint. We definitely don't want to plan three at a time. And if we look ahead two sprints, sprint planning meetings will become repetitive as we'll be planning the same sprint two or three times."

Keep in mind that rolling lookahead planning does not involve breaking user stories into tasks and estimating the hours for each, as should planning the current sprint. The team simply uses its average historical velocity to take a guess at which product backlog items will be developed in the next two sprints. This can almost always be easily accomplished in ten minutes if starting with a prioritized product backlog.

During rolling lookahead planning, the team is not committing to deliver a specific set of items in the next two sprints. Rather, it is guessing at what it might work on next, so it can identify any dependencies or preparation work that should be done in the coming sprint.

Hold a Release Kickoff Meeting

Another technique for proactively managing dependencies is to bring everyone together for a release kickoff meeting. An ideal time for doing so is the start of a new project or release cycle. A kickoff meeting can mitigate one of the biggest risks on a large project: that the different teams or individuals will start pulling in wrong or different directions.

Prior to a release kickoff meeting, each two-pizza team and its product owner has created a rough plan of what will be delivered over a reasonably foreseeable period, typically around three months. At the release kickoff, these plans are shared with everyone involved in the project. Normally, the product owners for each team take turns sharing what their teams plan to work on.

Salesforce.com delivers a new release of its SaaS platform every three or four months and has found release kickoff meetings essential. Eric Babinet and Rajani Ramanathan say that "it is difficult to identify dependencies or negotiate commitments with other teams if those teams don't yet know what they're doing in the release. The Release Kickoff meeting acts as an important synchronization point for teams and helps ensure more productive discussions around inter-team dependencies" (2008, 403).

Teams at Salesforce.com have introduced a worthwhile innovation beyond a standard release kickoff meeting. Later in the same week they hold what they call a "Release Open Space." This is patterned after the Open Space Technology approach[1] that has become popular at conferences in recent years. Each team is

---

1 Open space is a self-organizing approach to meetings, conferences, and the like. It has become a staple of agile conferences. For more information see http://en.wikipedia.org/wiki/Open_Space_Technology.

asked to send at least one person to the open space. This informal meeting starts with individuals identifying topics of interest relevant to the release and writing them on large pieces of paper taped to the walls. After topics have been identified, groups form to discuss the topics of interest. Salesforce.com provides 45 minutes for discussion followed by a 30-minute debrief with everyone back together. The cycle is repeated as long as there is passionate interest in the topics remaining on the walls.

Share Team Members

Another possible approach for proactively managing dependencies is to share team members among teams. This is an effective approach when dependencies are difficult to identify in advance or when they need to be addressed quickly. This is not a very effective strategy when dependencies can occur among any number of teams and in any direction. However, it is a good strategy when dependencies are likely to exist between feature teams and component teams.

SEE ALSO

There are, of course, drawbacks to having people on more than one team. Some of these were described in "Put People on One Project," in Chapter 10.

Using this approach, the shared team member is on two teams concurrently, working on both sides of a known or likely dependency. This can be seen in Figure 17.4, which shows three feature teams, two of which share a part-time member with a component team. Additionally, two of the feature teams share a member.

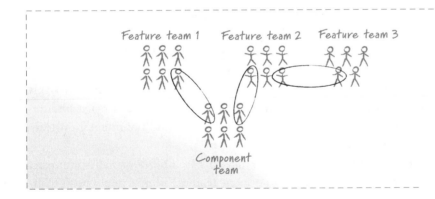

FIGURE 17.4

Sharing a few individuals be-tween teams is a good way to ensure interteam communication.

Use an Integration Team

Although sharing a part-time team member is sometimes a step in the right di-rection, it may not be a step far enough. Sometimes it is necessary to create an integration team. This is most common on projects with ten or more teams. An integration team works in the gaps that may exist between the development teams. Most of these gaps occur in the interfaces between teams (Sosa, Eppinger, and Rowles 2007). Interface problems can be broadly split into these two categories:

- **Unidentified interfaces.** An unidentified interface is one that exists but that no one has discovered yet.

- **Unattended interfaces.** An unattended interface is one that exists and that at least one team is aware of but which no one is doing anything about.

Integration teams focus directly on unattended interfaces, while being on the lookout for unidentified interfaces. After an integration team has uncovered an unattended or unidentified interface, its first strategy should be to encourage one of the development teams to assume responsibility for it. When that is impossible or impractical, the integration team takes ownership of the interface.

Normally, the first thing integration team members do each morning is check the results of the official nightly build to make sure that the system built successfully and that all tests passed. If it did not, integration team members do whatever is necessary to get all tests to pass. This will usually involve identifying the problem, finding the source of the problem, determining which team or teams are involved, and then working with those teams to resolve the issue.

On a large project, an integration team may be made up of full-time team members who work only on the integration team. In fact, on a very large project, there may be multiple integration teams, each with full-time members. Many other projects—those with perhaps a handful to a dozen teams—get along quite well with a virtual integration team, where individuals are assigned to the integration team but remain primarily on their individual development teams. Members of a virtual integration team meet each morning to assess the state of the previous night's build and agree upon who will resolve any issues. Members then spend the rest of the day working with their individual development teams.

It is also common at the start of a new project to dedicate individuals to an integration team for a few sprints. This team is tasked with getting all of the necessary servers installed and configuring project-wide software such as wikis, continuous integration servers, and so on. After these systems are in place, integration team members return to their development teams, and the integration team becomes a part-time endeavor.

As an example, consider a large San Francisco-based bioinformatics company that has a dozen feature teams, two component teams, and one integration team. Beyond monitoring the nightly build and fixing issues with it, the integration team develops automated tests to verify integration points. These are the types of tests that aren't obviously the responsibility of either team but that someone needs to be responsible for before the product can ship. Because these are often unidentified interfaces, integration team members spend a lot of effort looking for potential trouble spots. For example, there is usually one representative from an integration team at all of the standard meetings held by the feature and component teams. It is not unheard of for a member of an integration team to attend three daily scrums some days. They are at those meetings—plus sprint planning, review, and retrospective meetings—listening for unattended and unidentified interfaces.

Because being on an integration team requires good analytical skills, including the ability to connect comments made weeks apart by different teams, you should be careful not to consider an integration team as a dumping ground for poor performers. Integration teams require senior people with broad skills. That being said, an initial tour of duty on an integration team is an excellent way to provide new employees with a broad view of the overall system. It also allows new employees a very structured way to meet just about everyone else on the project and to form important connections that will serve them well later. Just make sure that your integration team isn't mostly made up of new employees.

> **"If the project were truly agile, it wouldn't need an integration team. If the team were truly producing a potentially shippable product each sprint, there would be no need for an integration team. Use of an integration team is the sign of a team that isn't really agile."**

OBJECTION

Normally when I hear this comment, it is made by someone who hasn't worked on a truly large project and the person is hypothesizing. Linda Rising, an independent consultant who has worked on a number of very large projects, including one developing software for the Boeing 777 airplane, has "never worked on a large project without an integration team," she says.

> I think it's typical that folks who have never worked on a very large project believe that it can be run as a bunch of small projects just glued together. The problem the very large projects face is that the glue can be overwhelming, especially if it's not anticipated. That glue gets worse over time.

Second, the use of an integration team should not be viewed as an inadequacy of the other teams; rather, it is an indication of a large and complex project. Consider the alternative—each team could seek out all unattended and unidentified interfaces between itself and every other team. The combined effort for each team to do this would be much greater than when done by an integration team. Each feature and component team should absolutely be held to a high standard as far as how many and what types of integration issues fall through the cracks to be caught by an integration team, but the integration team itself is not the sign of an agility deficiency.

Still, although there is nothing inherently wrong with using an integration team, you should use one only when necessary.

Coordinate Work Among Teams

Because Scrum scales by having multiple small teams rather than one large team, the problem arises of how to coordinate the work of all those teams. A ScrumMaster named Joanne told me how she learned the importance of this after running her first multiple-team project. Fresh from success on a one-team Scrum pilot, Joanne accepted the challenge of being the ScrumMaster for five teams working together to deliver a new version of her company's ambulance dispatch product. She provided short training to each team and turned them loose. Things went as well as could be expected for the first four sprints until the dependencies among teams became more critical. It then became apparent that the teams were working in isolation, each trying to go as fast as possible toward its own goals but failing to pay adequate attention to integration points. Joanne admitted to me in an e-mail that she did too little to encourage cross-team communication.

> Everyone was very good at figuring out what needed to be done on his own team. If we forgot something during sprint planning, the team would be all over it during the sprint and resolve the issue. But no one was watching for the thousand little issues that were piling up between teams. It was like two baseball players who watch the ball fall between them because each thinks the other will catch it.

There was no animosity or competitiveness among teams. It was merely that each team was so focused on what it considered its own goals that it ignored the overall goal. Chapter 11, "Teamwork," introduced the idea that Scrum teams are built on whole-team thinking and shared responsibility. On multi-team projects, the "whole team" is not just one two-pizza team along with its product owner and ScrumMaster, but all of the two-pizza teams, product owners, and ScrumMasters together.

In this section we will look at what Joanne could have done to improve the coordination of effort among her teams. Specifically we will look at look how to conduct *scrum of scrums* meetings and whether teams should synchronize sprint start and end dates.

The Scrum of Scrums Meeting

A fairly universal practice for coordinating work among several teams is the scrum of scrums meeting. These meetings allow clusters of teams to discuss their work, focusing especially on areas of overlap and integration.

Imagine a perfectly balanced project comprising seven teams each with seven team members. Each of the seven teams would independently conduct its own daily scrum. Each team would then also designate one person to attend a scrum of scrums meeting. The decision of who to send should belong to the team. Usually the person chosen should be a technical contributor on the team—a programmer, tester, database administrator, or designer, for example—rather than a ScrumMaster or product owner. Being chosen to attend the scrum of scrums meeting is not a life sentence. The attendees will change over the course of a typical project. The team should choose its representative based on who will be in the best position to understand and comment on the issues most likely to arise at that time during a project.

If the number of teams participating is small, it may be acceptable for each team to send two representatives—a technical contributor, as previously described, and the team's ScrumMaster—if the teams desire. I tend to do this only when there are four or fewer teams, which keeps the meeting size to eight or less. Most scrum of scrums groups do not designate a specific ScrumMaster for themselves. After all, the individuals who attend are accustomed to participation on self-organizing teams. In some groups, however, someone volunteers to act as the ScrumMaster or just assumes the role. It is up to the group to decide if this is acceptable.

The scrum of scrums meetings can be scaled up in a recursive manner. If a large product is being built by many teams of teams, one representative of each scrum of scrums can attend what might be called a "scrum of scrum of scrums" meeting, although this starts to sound silly, and most organizations stick to calling it a scrum of scrums meeting regardless of the level at which it is occurring. An example of this can be seen in Figure 17.5, which shows 11 individual teams. The 11 teams are part of 3 teams of teams, each of which has its own meeting. But since those 3 teams of teams combine their work into one product, there is another level of meeting, attended by one person from each of the scrum of scrums meetings.

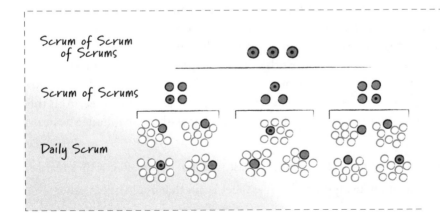

FIGURE 17.5

Scrum of scrums meetings can be applied recursively at as many layers as needed to coordinate work among clusters of teams.

Frequency

Scrum of scrums meetings differ from daily scrums in three important ways:

- They do not need to be held daily.
- They do not need to be timeboxed to 15 minutes.
- They are problem-solving meetings.

I find that holding scrum of scrums meetings two or three times a week is sufficient for most projects. This makes a Tuesday–Thursday or Monday–Wednesday–Friday schedule appropriate. Although a scrum of scrums meeting will often be completed in 15 minutes, I recommend blocking 30 or 60 minutes for them on the calendar. This is because, unlike daily scrums, these are problem-solving meetings. If an issue is brought to the attention of this group, and the right people are present to address the issue, they should do so.

Think about how many people might be waiting for a resolution. There could be close to 100 people waiting for an answer from a scrum of scrums meeting (and many more from a scrum of scrum of scrums meeting). Issues brought to this group should be resolved as quickly as possible, which means the meetings cannot be as readily timeboxed and issues cannot just be left for another day.

SEE ALSO
Certain types of issues are often resolved by communities of practice, which are a scaling mechanism described a bit later in this chapter.

Sometimes, of course, issues arise that cannot be immediately addressed. Perhaps other people are needed to address the issue or additional information is needed. When an issue cannot be resolved immediately it is placed on the group's *issues backlog*, which is a list of outstanding issues that the scrum of scrums group either plans to resolve or wants to track to make sure another group resolves them. Often a simple, low-tech tracking mechanism is adequate for this backlog. Most teams use a large piece of paper hanging in a team room, a spreadsheet, or a wiki.

Agenda

A scrum of scrums meeting will feel nothing like a daily scrum despite the similarities in names. The daily scrum is a synchronization meeting: individual team members come together to communicate about their work and synchronize their efforts. The scrum of scrums, on the other hand, is a problem-solving meeting and will not have the same quick, get-in-get-out tone of a daily scrum. The agenda for the scrum of scrums meeting is shown in Table 17.2. As you can see from this table, the scrum of scrums, like the daily scrum, starts with each attendee answering three questions:

1. What has my team done since we last met that could affect other teams?
2. What will my team do before we meet again that could affect other teams?
3. What problems is my team having with which it could use help from other teams?

Duration	Agenda Item
Timeboxed to 15 minutes	Each participant answers three questions: ● What has my team done since we last met that could affect other teams? ● What will my team do before we meet again that could affect other teams? ● What problems is my team having with which it could use help from other teams? Note: No personal names during this part of the meeting.
As needed	Resolve problems and discuss items on an issues backlog.

TABLE 17.2

An agenda for the scrum of scrums meeting includes three questions followed by a discussion of an issues backlog.

Topics raised during this discussion are added to the group's issues backlog. This part of the meeting is meant to be fast-paced and fairly short. You should timebox it to 15 minutes as you would a daily scrum. One technique for achieving this is adopting a guideline that personal names should be avoided. There are two reasons for this. First, leaving out names keeps the discussion at the appropriate level of detail. While attending the meeting, I want to hear about each team, not about each person on each team. Second, too many people equate importance with how long they talk during a meeting. Following this guideline will keep this part of the meeting moving briskly.

After everyone has answered the three questions, the meeting participants address any issues, problems, or challenges that were raised during the initial discussion or that were already on the issues backlog.

Scrum of scrum groups do not conduct formal sprint planning and sprint reviews. Participants in these meetings are first and foremost individual contributors on their teams. The higher-level scrum of scrums is a more transient group, with members changing occasionally throughout the project. The sprint planning and commitments that most drive a project forward rightly belong at the individual team level.

Synchronize Sprints

On my first Scrum project, we started with only one team. That project soon grew to three teams, with the typical dependencies between them. I quickly arrived at what I thought would be a good way to manage those dependencies. I would stagger the sprint start dates by a week, as shown in Figure 17.6. The idea was that when a team went to start its sprint it would know the stories one of the other teams had recently committed to and which stories the other team was likely to finish.

FIGURE 17.6

Overlapping sprints cause problems.

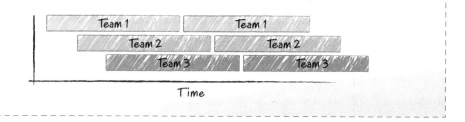

Well, that part of my plan did work out well. But, overall, staggering the sprint start dates was a horrible idea. The biggest flaw in overlapping sprints is that there is never a time (except the end of the project) when all teams are done. One or more teams are always partway into a sprint. Some are planning a new sprint, others just planned a week ago, and still more teams will plan next week. This makes it difficult to give the full system to a customer for feedback or to an operations group for deployment.

All sprints do not necessarily need to end on exactly the same day. It is acceptable on a large project to have sprints that end over a two- or three-day period. In fact, there can be advantages to doing this. Allowing sprints to end over a two- or three-day period can make it easier for someone on multiple teams to attend all the review and planning meetings expected of someone on multiple teams. Additionally, it has the advantage in many cases of better accommodating remote team members who may travel into town for these meetings. A remote team member who is on multiple teams will find it easier to justify the travel time and expense if she can participate fully in each of her teams' meetings.

Although the primary benefit of synchronized sprints is that all teams start and stop within a day or two of each other, this does not mean that all teams must work in sprints of the same length. A project with multiple teams can accommodate different sprint lengths through the use of nested sprints, as shown in Figure 17.7. The most common use of nested sprints is when the various teams on the project cannot agree on a common sprint length, with some wanting two-week sprints and others wanting four-week sprints.

FIGURE 17.7

For sprints to be synchronized, not all sprints need to be the same length.

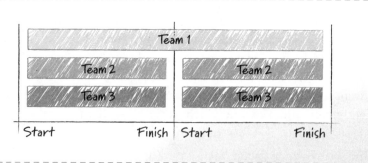

❑ Synchronize the sprints of teams that are working on the same project. Try this for two sprints, and then hold a combined retrospective and discuss whether it has helped in any ways. Seek solutions to any problems it has surfaced.

❑ Unless you are already holding productive scrum of scrums meetings, try running them as described here. Many teams who struggled with how to conduct this meeting had success after trying this approach.

THINGS TO TRY NOW

Scaling the Sprint Planning Meeting

Most of the standard meetings held by Scrum teams are deliberately unaffected as the overall project size grows and multiple teams are involved. Teams continue to hold daily scrums, sprint reviews, and sprint retrospectives just as they would if working on a project as a lone team. Sure, teams will sometimes decide to hold joint reviews when it makes more sense to view the work of multiple teams together. And teams will occasionally hold joint retrospectives both to mix things up and to perhaps focus on interteam issues. But it is the sprint planning meeting that is most severely impacted when a Scrum project grows to include multiple teams.

SEE ALSO

See Chapter 18, "Distributed Teams," for specific advice on conducting these meetings with distributed teams.

With multiple teams working on the same project, a number of problems arise during the sprint planning meeting, including the following:

● Some people are needed in multiple sprint planning meetings. With all sprints sharing a common start date, people need to be in two places at once.

● If one team discovers a dependency on another team, it may not be able to get the other team to commit to taking on a task if the other team finishes its planning first.

● If multiple teams are pulling items from the same product backlog, those items have to be preallocated to teams before sprint planning starts.

Fortunately, there are a couple of approaches to large-scale sprint planning that can reduce or eliminate these problems and others like them.

Stagger by a Day

As described in the earlier section on synchronized sprints, the benefits of synchronizing can still be had even with sprints that are offset by a day or two. We can take advantage of this, and instead of having all teams do sprint planning on exactly the same day, we can have one-third of the teams plan on, say, Tuesday, one-third on Wednesday, and the final third on Thursday. When teams do this, the issues surrounding a shared product backlog are, fortunately, mostly eliminated.

When my team plans tomorrow, we will know which product backlog items your team committed to today.

Staggering by a day also addresses the problem of requiring an in-demand product owner, architect, user interface designer, or other shared team member to be in two places at once. However, it replaces that problem with perhaps "three days of pain," as one product owner put it. The shared team member is able to help more teams, but doing so can be exhausting; no one enjoys attending planning meetings for two or three full days straight.

Despite this drawback, staggering by a day remains a valid option, usually for projects of up to nine teams, with three teams planning each day. After that, even with staggering, there are usually too many days of planning, so other approaches are needed.

The Big Room

In the big-room approach, all of the teams (or as many as will fit) are assembled into a large room. The chief product owner starts things off with any remarks he or she would like to share with the group of teams: perhaps the results of recent discussions with customers, prospects, or users; or maybe a general description of the types of things that everyone will be working on for the coming sprint or two. After the meeting is kicked off, each team (including its product owner and ScrumMaster) moves to a portion of the room where it will be able to work together for a few hours. Some teams stake out the corners, others claim the side walls, a few more pull some tables together in the middle of the room. In these locations, each team works on planning its coming sprint in the same manner it would if it were the only team on the project.

The room gets loud and cacophonous, but the energy and hopefully the passion in the air are obvious. As teams plan their sprints, it won't be long before they begin to uncover dependencies on each other. As this happens, one person jumps up, runs over to the other team's temporary camp (which is in the same room), and asks, "Can your group do such-and-such for us this sprint? We'll need it if we want to finish one of the backlog items our product owner wants us to do." The team member can either wait for a reply or return to her team and wait for an answer to be shouted or ferried across the room a few minutes later.

The big-room approach also works exceptionally well for critical, shared resources. A product owner who is working with two teams can bounce between them; the company's chief software architect, too busy to be on any one team but needed by all, can move about the room, going where called. On most projects a team usually signals its need for a product owner, architect, or other shared resource by yelling to the person. This works well, except by the time the shared resource finishes his current discussion, he forgets who called him.

A technique I've found successful is to augment yelling by using nautical signaling flags as shown in Figure 17.8. When team members need the architect, for example, they hang the appropriate 1' × 1' signal flag near their area. When the architect finishes what he's doing, he can look around the room for his flag. If team members need a product owner, they would display a different flag. A team displaying a product owner flag would be helped by either its product owner or perhaps the product line owner or even chief product owner when possible. This works well: It solves most problems of knowing who needs help next, it lets shared resources see how many teams need help, and it is fun.

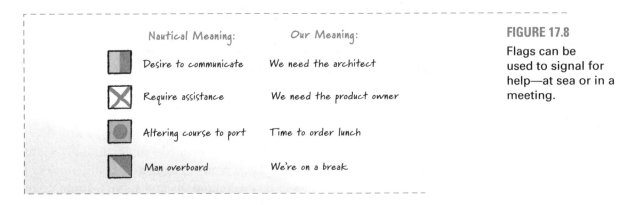

Nautical Meaning: Our Meaning:

Desire to communicate   We need the architect

Require assistance   We need the product owner

Altering course to port   Time to order lunch

Man overboard   We're on a break

FIGURE 17.8

Flags can be used to signal for help—at sea or in a meeting.

For the big-room approach to work, the product owners must be prepared prior to the meeting. This usually entails a variety of short meetings between the chief product owner and his or her staff. Each level of the product owner hierarchy needs to understand the product vision as it trickles down from the chief product owner through the various levels.

Cultivate Communities of Practice

On a multi-team project, it is possible for individuals to become isolated, speaking mostly to others on their individual teams. Good ideas are slow to propagate across the organization. Similar functionality is implemented differently by different teams. We put scrum of scrums meetings in place to reduce the impact of some of these problems, but those only go so far. An additional solution and one that is critical to the success of any large Scrum project is the cultivation of communities of practice. Like improvement communities (a special type of community of practice introduced in Chapter 4, "Iterating Toward Agility"), a community of practice is a like-minded or like-skilled group of individuals who voluntarily come together because of their passion and commitment around a technology, approach, or vision. On a large project, these communities of practice are helpful for cutting across the boundaries of and pulling together individuals from the many cross-functional teams. An example can be seen in Figure 17.9.

FIGURE 17.9

Communities of practice cut across the development teams and create additional channels of communication.

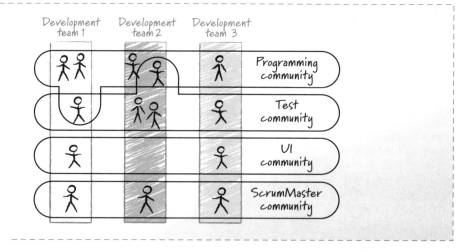

Figure 17.9 shows communities of practice formed simply around various project roles. In addition, a sufficiently large project might have communities of practice form around technologies (a Ruby community and a .NET community, for example), around interests (mock objects, artificial intelligence, test automation), or around any thread of common interest to multiple development teams.

A good example of a community of practice is the Virtual Architecture Team at Salesforce.com, as described by Eric Babinet and Rajani Ramanathan.

> The Virtual Architecture Team (VAT) is "virtual" as it is made up of developers from every Scrum team. Members work on the VAT in addition to being on a Scrum team. The VAT owns maintaining and extending our industry-leading software architecture. They do this by defining the architectural road map, by reviewing architecturally significant changes to the code, and by defining standards to ensure consistent and maintainable code. (2008, 405)

Communities of practice can span more than one project. For example, a community of practice around test automation may form and include members from multiple, completely unrelated projects. Unlike improvement communities, a general community of practice does not form around the pursuit of a single, specific goal. Instead, a community will generally have many related goals. Because of this, a community of practice can remain in existence indefinitely. A community can also dissolve after it has achieved its goals or if members lose passion.

Because they span teams, communities of practice are a primary mechanism for spreading good ideas among teams and for ensuring desirable levels of consistency or commonality across a set of development teams. A community of middle-tier programmers might, for example, discuss and decide when would be the best time to upgrade to the latest version of application server software for a family of products. Discussions among members of an orthogonal test team would ensure consistent test tool usage and the sharing of good practices.

Formal or Informal

A community of practice can be either formal or informal; most organizations will have a mix. Organizations with strong functional management in place prior to adopting Scrum usually rely on those strong functional managers to support or even establish some of the communities of practice. Etienne Wenger, who invented the term "community of practice," and his colleagues distinguish five types of communities of practice based on the degree of recognition of the community by the organization. These are shown in Table 17.3.

Type of Community	Definition	Typical Challenges
Unrecognized	Invisible to the organization and possibly even to its members.	Hard to see the value of the community to the organization or members; probably doesn't include all the right members.
Bootlegged	Visible but only to a small, select group of insiders.	Difficulty gaining resources or credibility; difficult to make an impact.
Legitimized	Officially sanctioned as a valuable entity.	Unrealistic expectations; rapid growth and assimilation of new members.
Supported	Provided with resources (time, money, facilities, people).	Accountability for return on invested resources; short-term pressure to prove value.
Institutionalized	Given an official status and responsibilities in the organization.	Overmanagement; slow moving; outlives its usefulness; permanent members become separate from actual projects.

TABLE 17.3

Communities of practice range from those no one knows exist to those given official status. (Adapted from Wenger, McDermott, and Snyder 2002.)

Table 17.3 is not meant to represent a hierarchy. No one type of community of practice is always superior to another; each has its unique strengths and weaknesses. Similarly, Table 17.3 is not meant to indicate the life cycle of a typical community of practice, even though it is easy to see how a community could move from *unrecognized* to *institutionalized* as its purpose becomes clearer to the community members and its value becomes clearer to the organization. Although communities of practice do sometimes follow this life cycle, it is not by design. Many communities will move in the opposite direction, and some will disband entirely.

Creating an Environment for Communities to Form and Flourish

The most effective type of community of practice within Scrum organizations seems to be one that forms organically rather than by management request, although both approaches can be used for different purposes. Because self-organization is critical to successful agile teamwork, the formation of self-organizing communities of practice creates a powerful synergy. In this sense it is up to the organization and its leadership to create an environment in which communities of practice can form, flourish, and then fade away as they run their course.

According to Etienne Wenger and his colleagues, "because communities of practice are organic, designing them is more a matter of shepherding their evolution than creating them from scratch" (Wenger, McDermott, and Snyder 2002, 51). They provide seven principles for creating an environment that supports this evolution:

- **Design for evolution.** Acknowledge that each community will change over time. It will rise and fall in importance, members will come and go, goals will shift. This is good as it represents the progress of each community adjusting in response to changing project, people, and organizational needs.
- **Open a dialogue between inside and outside participants.** Although communities work largely within themselves, they cannot work in isolation from the overall organization. A good community is receptive to hearing what the organization needs, is struggling with, and can provide.
- **Invite different levels of participation.** Not everyone interested in a community will have the same amount of time and energy to devote to it. Encourage individuals to participate at the level and frequency that suits them.
- **Have both public and private events.** A good community understands that sometimes the most beneficial discussions are among no one but themselves, but also understands that public events are sometimes necessary. An example might be a community focused on improving the experience across a suite of products. Members meet privately every other week to bounce ideas around but also occasionally host open sessions where anyone in the company can attend and see what they're thinking.
- **Focus on value.** The more value a community of practice provides to the organization, the more additional communities will be encouraged to

form. Also, as communities deliver value, they are given more support and leeway in how they operate.

- **Combine familiarity with excitement.** A mature community of practice often settles into a series of habits—the weekly conference calls, the monthly meeting, and the annual two-day get-together at headquarters, for example. Although there is value in this, there is also value in occasionally mixing things up, which creates a sense of vibrancy within the community. Inviting an outside speaker with a different opinion or holding an open space–style event are just two examples of how to add some excitement.

- **Create a rhythm for the community.** Communities of practice do not generally work in the same, regular sprints of Scrum development teams. Without the project-oriented deliverables of a development team, sprints are not a must. However, a community still benefits from the establishment of a regular rhythm. Accomplish this by having a regular set of activities at whatever frequency suits the community.

If you want communities of practice to form organically, you may need to provide some encouragement. Potential community members will need to know that it is OK—and in fact encouraged—for them to form communities. I've encountered a few situations where managers and executives gave their Scrum teams a great deal of leeway in self-organizing and were left wondering why no communities of practice formed. When I asked the team members about this, they told me they were under the impression that such informal groups would be frowned upon by management. Make sure your team members know that such cross-team communities are not only OK but encouraged.

Participation

Most formally recognized communities of practice benefit from designating a community coordinator. The community coordinator is not a leader of the group but does serve the community in two important ways:

- Developing the practice around which the community has formed
- Developing the community itself

The community coordinator does this by being the one to schedule meetings and other events, convincing members to attend, connecting individuals with common interests, participating in community events himself, and so on. In some respects, the role of community coordinator is similar to that of ScrumMaster. From my experience, being a community coordinator takes 5 to 20 hours per month, depending of course on the community. The community coordinator might even be a full- or nearly full-time position in a community that has been assigned formal responsibilities in the organization.

There are no rules about how many hours a community should take away from a member's project team. It can literally vary from a few hours a year to a few hours a week. Babinet and Ramanathan describe the relatively high level of commitment on Salesforce.com's Virtual Architecture Team.

> The VAT meets for two hours twice a week to review the technical implementation of products and features being built by the Scrum teams. The teams building the most complex features in the release are asked to present to the VAT. The group provides valuable feedback to the Scrum team on how their technical design will impact or be impacted by other areas. The VAT focuses primarily on the technical implementation, especially scalability and performance considerations. Teams asked to make significant changes must present again in the same release cycle [approximately three months] and provide details on how they modified their design. (2008, 405)

Communities of practice are well worth the time and investment. The service they provide in aiding communication and coordination across a large organization or a large project is invaluable. If communities of practice have not yet formed in your organization, start one around a topic that interests you or is causing your organization pain. As that community begins to contribute to the organization, other communities are likely to form as well.

Scrum Does Scale

You have to admire the intellectual honesty of the earliest agile authors. They were all very careful to say that agile methodolgies like Scrum were for small projects. This conservatism wasn't because agile or Scrum turned out to be unsuited for large projects but because they hadn't used these processes on large projects and so were reluctant to advise their readers to do so. But, in the years since the Agile Manifesto and the books that came shortly before and after it, we have learned that the principles and practices of agile development can be scaled up and applied on large projects, albeit it with a considerable amount of overhead. Fortunately, if large organizations use the techniques described regarding the role of the product owner, working with a shared product backlog, being mindful of dependencies, coordinating work among teams, and cultivating communities of practice, they can successfully scale a Scrum project.

Additional Reading

Beavers, Paul A. 2007. Managing a large "agile" software engineering organization. In *Proceedings of the Agile 2007 Conference*, ed. Jutta Eckstein, Frank Maurer, Rachel Davies, Grigori Melnik, and Gary Pollice, 296–303. IEEE Computer Society.

This experience report describes the first couple of years of BMC Software's adoption of Scrum on a 250-person project. It is an excellent first-person account of the struggles and rewards faced by the project's engineering leader. It concludes with nine guidelines for success distilled from the author's experience on the project.

Larman, Craig, and Bas Vodde. 2009. *Scaling lean & agile development: Thinking and organizational tools for large-scale Scrum*. Addison-Wesley Professional.

This book covers many topics, but in Chapter 11, Larman and Vodde focus specifically on large-scale Scrum. They present two frameworks for scaling Scrum: one for scaling up to ten teams, another for scaling beyond that.

Leffingwell, Dean. 2007. *Scaling software agility: Best practices for large enterprises*. Addison-Wesley Professional.

This book focuses on two different types of scaling: scaling agile within large organizations and scaling agile on large projects. A bit more emphasis is on the former type of scaling, but both are covered. The heart of the book, Part II, focuses on seven agile practices and how to scale them: teams, planning at two levels, iterations, small releases, concurrent testing, continuous integration, and regular reflection.

Wenger, Etienne, Richard McDermott, and William M. Snyder. 2002. *Cultivating communities of practice*. Harvard Business School Press.

This book is the authoritative source of information on communities of practice. Included is information on how to encourage them to form, how to lead them, how to measure the value they provide, and some of the downsides of using communities.

Chapter 18

Distributed Teams

A few years ago, collocated teams were the norm, and it was unusual for a team to be geographically distributed. By now, the reverse must be true. Personally, I'm now surprised when someone tells me that everyone on the team works in the same building. With the prevalence of teams that are spread across the globe, or at least across a couple of time zones, it is important to consider how well Scrum works when a team is geographically distributed.

A common misconception is that Scrum is not a good fit for a geographically distributed team. Scrum's preference for face-to-face communication, the argument goes, makes it a poor choice for distributed teams. Fortunately, this argument is false. Although it's true that a collocated team will always outperform the equivalent distributed team (Ramasubbu and Balan 2007), Scrum can actually help geographically distributed teams perform at near-collocated levels. Suppose you have made the commitment to outsource a large portion of a project to developers on another continent. Why would you not want the following benefits?

- Increased visibility from seeing demonstrable progress at the end of every sprint
- The ability to adjust priorities after each sprint
- More frequent communication
- An emphasis on quality and test automation
- Improved knowledge transfer, especially between developers doing pair programming

Clearly, the benefits of Scrum far outweigh any difficulties that its reliance on frequent communication might bring. That doesn't mean implementing Scrum on a distributed team is going to be a cake walk, though. As Michael Vax and Stephen Michaud point out, "extending agile to a distributed model is not for the faint of heart" (2008, 314).

The rest of this chapter is devoted to describing actions that a distributed team can take to move its performance as close as possible to the level it could achieve if collocated, while still capturing the benefits of being distributed, such as cost savings, the ability to recruit in multiple cities, and so on. Along the way, we consider the best approach to structuring a team across geographic boundaries, how to create a coherent distributed team, the need for team members to get together in person occasionally, the necessary changes in communication, and suitable ways to conduct meetings.

Decide How to Distribute Multiple Teams

When a project involves enough people to create more than one Scrum team, an important decision is how to organize those teams across geographic boundaries. A large project can be organized into multiple *collaborating collocated teams* or multiple *deliberately distributed teams*. These alternatives are shown in Figure 18.1, which shows a two-location situation.

FIGURE 18.1

Two different approaches to distributing teams between the United States and France.

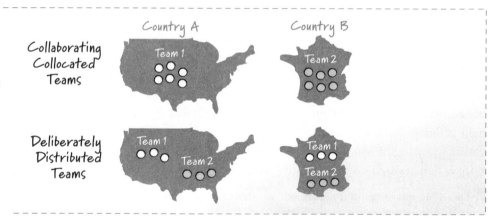

Collaborating collocated teams occur when a project has enough people in two or more cities to establish a team in each city. Each of the collocated teams contains all the skills necessary to take a product backlog item from idea to implementation. These teams are called *collaborating* collocated teams to reinforce the notion that each collocated team is working with the other remote (but themselves collocated) teams to deliver a product rather than as an entirely independent team that happens to be in the same company as other independent teams. In contrast, deliberately distributed teams occur when a project *could* use collaborating collocated teams yet makes a deliberate decision to distribute the teams.

There are, of course, advantages and disadvantages to each of these options. The primary advantage to organizing a project around collaborating collocated teams is that it simplifies the day-to-day work of most team members, largely because whole-team, globe-spanning conference calls are eliminated. After working as part of a project that had first been structured as collaborating collocated teams and was then deliberately distributed, Sharon Cichelli, a developer in Austin, Texas, found that she preferred collaborating collocated teams.

> The developers in one city worked on one feature, and likewise for the other city. The only people who really suffered here [with collaborating collocated teams] were the product owners and the ScrumMaster, who had to accommodate a ten-and-a-half-hour time difference to have sprint planning meetings. (2008)

Although the advantages of organizing around collaborating collocated teams are readily apparent, what can the advantages be to deliberately distributing a team? Why would we choose to create two distributed teams rather than a fully capable team in each location? To see why, think for a moment about the types of communication problems likely to arise on a distributed project. Your list might include some of these or other common problems:

- Developers working remotely from the product owner do not adequately understand the business or domain.
- Developers in different cities unknowingly disagree about what is being developed.
- Developers in different cities make incompatible decisions.
- An antagonistic, "us and them" relationship develops between individuals in different locations.
- Developers in one city do not know what developers in the other city are doing or why they are making the decisions they make.

Each of these problems can be severe enough to jeopardize the entire project. Fortunately, each situation is improved or made less likely to arise when the project is organized using deliberately distributed teams. Scrum coinventor Jeff Sutherland worked with Xebia, and its teams spread between the Netherlands and India, during which time they experienced the benefits of deliberately distributing teams. They concluded that while a deliberately distributed team "appears to create communication and coordination burdens, the daily scrum meetings actually help to break down cultural barriers and disparities in work styles while simultaneously enhancing customer focus and offshore understanding of customer needs" (Sutherland et al. 2008, 340).

An excellent way to minimize the communication and coordination burden that is created by deliberately distributing teams is to carefully consider who is on each of the teams. John Cornell, a development director with Kofax in California but also with team members in Vietnam, recommends that organizations "seed teams with boundary spanners. If possible seed teams with people who have worked together before or with people who are known to have contacts throughout the organization. Those who already have such contacts can be useful for remote team members who may not know who to contact."

In *The Tipping Point*, Malcolm Gladwell called these individuals "connectors." Connectors "link us up with the world…[they are] people with a special gift for bringing the world together" (2002, 38). Connectors are "people with a truly extraordinary knack…[for] making friends and acquaintances" (41). Connectors do, as Cornell and Gladwell both suggest, make excellent members of distributed teams.

Scrum consultant and trainer Kenny Rubin points out that a lack of transparency is at the root of many of the problems that occur between subgroups in different locations.

> Problems caused by a lack of transparency were abundant on a project split between New York and India. The India team was a subcontractor. Things got totally out of control in India, and the project was being reconstituted. I was involved in the reconstitution. In trying to understand why the first project failed, I asked questions. The most common response I got was, "I don't know." Like, "I don't know why they originally thought 15 people could do the job and now they are at 42 people. I don't know what those 42 people are doing." Because of this, when we reconstituted the project, we chose to deliberately distribute the teams.

As for choosing between collaborating collocated teams and deliberately distributed teams, each approach is suitable for some circumstances. The decision for me usually comes down to how fearful I am of the problems that can arise from a lack of communication or transparency between locations. If I think these are likely to occur or will be significant if they do, I deliberately distribute the team. For example, in a situation where a distributed team consists of locations put together through a merger or acquisition, I always deliberately distribute the team. These situations are always full of potential conflict between locations, and deliberately distributing the teams reduces the risk of full-scale blow-ups between locations.

THINGS TO TRY NOW

❏ If you have collaborating, collocated teams, ask whether that way of distributing the team was chosen consciously or whether it was merely the default or easiest way to split the team. If the latter, consider whether deliberately distributing the team could be better and possibly try it for two or three sprints.

Create Coherence

The English word *coherent* comes from the Latin *cohaerent*, which means "sticking together." I find "sticking together" a perfect description of what we want a team to do. We want a team stuck together in pursuit of a common goal for a project, and we want a team stuck together to overcome the challenges that face any team involved in a difficult pursuit. Many factors work against creating coherence within a distributed team: Language, culture, physical separation, and time zone differences are just a few. Because of this, it becomes particularly important for members of distributed teams to consciously strive to create coherence.

Acknowledge Significant Cultural Differences

In seeking to create coherence, we must start by acknowledging that significant cultural differences might exist between team members in different locations. One of the most comprehensive analyses of key cultural differences was done by Geert Hofstede, who surveyed IBM employees in over 50 countries. Hofstede identified five key dimensions along which cultures varied.

- **Power Distance Index (PDI).** The extent to which less powerful members of a culture accept that power is unequally distributed.
- **Individualism (IND).** The extent to which individuals prefer to function as individuals rather than as part of a group.
- **Achievement Orientation[1] (ACH).** The extent to which the culture is oriented toward achievement, such as earnings, visible signs of success, and possessions.
- **Uncertainty Avoidance Index (UAI).** The extent to which the culture is tolerant of uncertainty and ambiguity.
- **Long-Term Orientation (LTO).** The extent to which the culture favors long-term considerations over immediate physical and financial benefits.

Some results[2] from Hofstede's surveys are shown in Table 18.1. As much as I distrust sweeping cultural generalizations, I find it useful to share data like this with team members of a distributed project. This can be done as part of a project kickoff meeting or any early meeting when team members are getting to know one another.

---

1   In his original research from 1967–1973, Hofstede referred to this dimension as "Masculinity." Even with a distance of 40 years, it's hard to accept that was an appropriate label then. It's not today, so I have relabeled it as Achievement Orientation.

2   Values are from www.geert-hofstede.com/hofstede_dimensions.php, which includes many more countries.

TABLE 18.1

Cultural differences among representative countries. A blank indicates that the dimension was not measured.

Country	PDI	IDV	ACH	UAI	LTO
Brazil	69	38	49	76	65
China	80	20	66	30	118
Denmark	18	74	16	23	
Finland	33	63	26	59	
India	77	48	56	40	61
Israel	13	54	47	81	
Japan	54	46	95	92	80
Netherlands	38	80	14	53	44
Norway	31	69	8	50	20
Poland	68	60	64	93	32
Russia	93	39	36	95	
Spain	57	51	42	86	
Sweden	31	71	5	29	33
United Kingdom	35	89	66	35	25
United States	40	91	62	46	29

You can use the data in a table like this by finding the row for your country and seeing how your country compares to others on the project. For example, if I were about to start a project with team members in China, I would compare the United States and China rows. I find that China has a much higher PDI score (80 compared to 40 for the United States). This tells me that my Chinese colleagues will be less likely to challenge authority than I am used to. If I am in a role of real or perceived authority (ScrumMaster, senior developer, or so on), I will put extra effort into making sure that team members in China engage me in open discussion.

Looking next at the individualism scores (20 for China, 91 for the United States), I learn that my team members in China will be more interested in team unity than I am used to. They will be less likely to want to be singled out, even for praise.

Continuing, I would see that our countries' achievement orientation scores are about the same. A larger difference in ACH values could indicate differences in how team members would determine the success of the project. For example, consider the dramatic difference in achievement orientation between the U.S.

(62) and Norway (8). On a project developed in these two countries, Americans might view the project as an overall success if the product is a financial success, even if that comes at the cost of team morale and energy for the next project. Norwegians on the project, however, could view this as a failure and might prefer to sacrifice financial success if that is the only way to develop a team that is ready and anxious for the next version or project.

Looking again at a U.S.–China team, I would see that my Chinese teammates will probably be more comfortable with uncertainty than my fellow American teammates. I might make a mental note to take advantage of this in helping the U.S. team get comfortable with Scrum because my Chinese team members will be more accepting of uncertainty in role definitions, product specifications, schedules, and so on.

Finally, I notice a dramatic difference in long-term orientation (118 for China and 29 for the United States). From this difference, I'll know that the regular visible progress demonstrated by sprint reviews will be a strong positive motivation for the U.S. team but might not have a similar effect on the team's Chinese members, who bring a much longer time horizon to the project.

Any cultural analysis such as Hofstede's here leads to generalizations. Although generalizations might be true across a population, each individual is unique and should be treated as such. Generalizations can provide some initial insight into a culture, but personal experience is the best way to understand individuals on a team.

NOTE

Acknowledge the Small Cultural Differences

Hofstede's work focused on grand cultural differences. In addition to these significant differences, geographically distributed development projects must also deal with a plethora of minor but important cultural differences. For example, it won't surprise anyone to know that different countries, religions, and cultures have different holidays. Many distributed teams work around this by creating a page on the project's website or wiki showing the union of all holidays celebrated by team members. Some teams I've worked on spend a few extra minutes in the daily scrum before a holiday and have the local team explain the purpose and customs of the holiday. This is how I learned about the Indian holiday of Gandhi Jayanti, Canada's Victoria Day, Norway's Constitution Day, and others. It's not that knowing that many of my Indian coworkers abstain from meat and alcohol on Gandhi Jayanti or that my Canadian colleagues head to lakeside cottages for Victoria Day makes me a better team member. That they know I care enough about them to ask what they celebrate and why is what makes me a better team member.

Although different holidays were not a surprise, I was shocked to discover that the Monday through Friday workweek is not universal. Growing up and living my entire life in the U.S., where Monday through Friday is universal for essentially all office jobs, I'd never contemplated a different standard workweek could exist. "Of course, everyone around the world works Monday through Friday," I mistakenly assumed. It wasn't until I worked with teams in Israel and Egypt that I learned the typical workweek there, and in other countries in the region, was Sunday through Thursday.

Another cultural difference I've witnessed is how people use and enjoy their evenings. In the United States, a typical workday might go until 5:00 or 6:00 p.m. Work is commonly followed by a family dinner, typically between 6:00 and 7:00 p.m. I assumed this pattern of work–dinner–family–sleep was fairly universal. If I need to participate in a nightly scrum call, my preference would probably be to do it around 9:00 p.m.; my kids are in bed by then, and most nights I can fit a 15-minute call in around that time quite easily. In India, however, 9:00 p.m. is prime meal time for many families. It's likely the worst possible time for a nightly call for many team members there. Unfortunately, before I knew this, I worked on a couple of projects with team members in Bangalore and Hyderabad and suggested 9:00 p.m. phone calls for them. It was several weeks before someone spoke up and asked if we could change the meeting time because it was right in the middle of his dinner. I had tried to pick the best possible time but had inadvertently picked the worst.

Seeding visits and traveling ambassadors (both discussed later in this chapter) are excellent ways to pick up the local customs and preferences of a team in one location and return them to another location.

Strengthen Functional and Team Subcultures

As strong as our national cultures can be, it might be the case that the software development subculture is even stronger. Professor Erran Carmel, who has studied distributed teams for years, wrote about this phenomenon.

> Software professionals worldwide belong to the computer subculture. Software guru Larry Constantine argues that the computer subculture is stronger than national culture and that the programmer in Moscow is more similar to his American programming peer than to other Russians. Engineers, like software professionals, place high value on achievement and relatively low value on social relationships. The stereotype of the antisocial programmer has a kernel of truth. (1998, 73–74)

Studies have proven the strength of the computer subculture (Carmel 1998, 74), and effective teams make use of functional and team subcultures to create coherence among team members. We want individuals to think, "I am a member of the Orion project team," rather than, "I am a member of the Indian team working on the Orion project." The distinction may seem minor, but I contend that the subtle shift in mind-set it implies is important.

Many techniques for connecting individuals to their functional ("I am a programmer/tester/DBA") or team subcultures are useful, especially when a team is distributed. For example, a corporate environment that encourages the formation of communities of practice is important for distributed as well as collocated teams. There are, however, a few techniques that are especially important for strengthening functional and team subcultures within distributed teams.

Communicate and Establish a Shared Vision

Without a shared vision, it will be almost impossible for a strong team culture to develop. This makes a shared vision especially important for a distributed team. Elaine Thierren, of First American CoreLogic in Santa Ana, California, was part of a distributed team spread between her office and Bangalore. After the project she was able to look back and see that the product vision was not adequately shared and communicated.

SEE ALSO

Techniques for establishing a shared vision can be found in the section "Energize the System" in Chapter 12, "Leading a Self-Organizing Team."

> The lack of visibility into the product vision or roadmap had two major impacts. First, the product often required rework as new features were requested. In other words, the team did not have the visibility they needed into the overall direction of the product to architect the application in such a way that it would be easy to incorporate future features. Secondly, it left the team in India feeling as though there was not enough work ahead of them and that they may soon find themselves with excess capacity. (2008, 369)

As Thierren experienced, a shared vision is critical for the team to be coherent. Usually, responsibility for making sure this happens falls to the product owner. Mark Summers, an agile coach with EMC Consulting in London, was fortunate to work with a product owner who understood his role in making sure the product vision was shared by all sites involved in the project.

> At the start of each release our product owner would travel out to India to try to immerse the offshore teams in the vision for the release. Therefore, it is very important that you have a product owner who can engage with the team and take them along the journey with him. We had had many previous instances of the offshore people not understanding what the business wanted, so having this engagement upfront really started to help. (2008, 338)

Reach Agreements

Part of a team's culture derives from agreements that team members make with one another. Some agreements are explicit: Be on time for the daily scrum and don't break the build are examples. Other agreements may be left implicit: Don't needlessly copy people on e-mails, for example. A distributed team will want to make more of these agreements explicit.

For example, distributed Scrum teams often agree on an acceptable response time for e-mail, perhaps deciding that all e-mail should be replied to within one working day, even if the response is just to say, "I'm working on it and will get back to you tomorrow." Although such an agreement may exist on a collocated team, it is more likely to be an unstated expectation than an explicitly stated guideline for team behavior. If I'm slow to respond and we're collocated, you'll probably just tip your chair back and yell, "Hey, Mike, you didn't answer my e-mail from yesterday about whether we should use Groovy." Not only will I get the message that I need to answer your question, all team members within earshot will get a reinforcement that our team norm is *answer e-mail promptly*.

Beyond how quickly to respond to e-mails, many distributed teams arrive at explicit agreements on when individuals will be in the office, when individuals can be reached outside normal working hours, how promptly meetings should start, what type of communication (phone, e-mail, IM, and so on) is best for which type of discussion, what type of issues need to be discussed with the entire team rather than a relevant subset, and so on.

One thing a distributed team should definitely agree on is how it will do Scrum; not every team in every office needs to do Scrum the same way, but teams will need to agree on some core things across all teams. Because Scrum is merely a project management framework, a great deal of how it is implemented is left to each team. There is a tremendous opportunity for different locations to do Scrum in different ways. Some of these variations are good: Some will lead to improvements that can be used across all locations; others are adaptations necessary for Scrum to work in a given location. Other differences may be incompatible and need to be resolved. Jane Robarts, a project manager at ThoughtWorks, was on a project distributed between the United States and India when she encountered just such a situation.

> We had assumed that the team in India was practicing agile the same way we were planning on doing it in the U.S. It was several days into the first iteration before we realized that each location had a different version of "agile." (2008, 331)

Although it is important for teams in different locations, but on the same project, to agree on a common set of Scrum practices, this does not mean that distributed teams should stick to doing Scrum strictly "by the book." A new Scrum team should start that way but will eventually need to add and adapt project-specific practices that make Scrum its own. In fact, in comparing successful and unsuccessful distributed Scrum implementations at Yahoo!, coaches Brian Drummond and J. F. Unson found that doing Scrum solely by the book on distributed teams was a source of problems.

> Without sufficient guidance, teams fell back to following "Scrum by the book" and suffered greatly…to the point where people resented Scrum and agile. These teams did not adapt the practices to factor in the difficulties brought about by the special requirements of distributed development. (2008, 320)

As with other types of working agreements, the solution here is for the ScrumMaster to facilitate one or more sessions with team members to arrive at agreements on the parts of Scrum they wish to make uniform across locations.

Build Trust by Emphasizing Early Progress

Critical to creating a coherent team is building trust among team members. This is much more difficult on a distributed team. In *Mastering Virtual Teams*, Deborah Duarte and Nancy Snyder discuss the difficulties in trusting people whom we are unable to see physically.

> In face-to-face settings, a number of familiar clues help us determine whom we should trust and whom we should not. We are able to evaluate people's nonverbal communication and observe their interactions with other team members. Part of the way we judge trustworthiness is through our perceptions, over time, of the other person's reliability and consistency. (2006, 85)

Unable to rely on repeated, frequent face-to-face communication, distributed teams need to take other measures to build trust. Traveling ambassadors, starting meetings with casual conversations, occasional in-person meetings of the full team, working agreements, and similar activities all help. What also helps is early pressure for the team to produce working software by the end of each sprint, even the earliest ones. Unfortunately, many projects schedule too much time for team-building exercises and discussions too early in the project. This is a common and dangerous mistake, as shown by research from Professor Lynda Gratton and her coauthors, as published in the *MIT Sloan Management Review.*

> Guiding these diverse teams to success requires some counterintuitive management practices. In particular, team leaders should focus on tasks at the early stages, rather than on interpersonal relationships, and then switch to relationship building when the time is right. (Gratton, Voigt, and Erickson 2007, 22)

Though this research suggests that the early focus should be on tasks, I do not mean to suggest that product owners or ScrumMasters should be assigning tasks to developers. Rather, I mean that these leaders should emphasize the need for the team to make demonstrable progress even in the early sprints. The problem with an early emphasis on relationship building is that it encourages less-than-ideal subgroups to form. Any large group will inevitably split into subgroups. If these subgroups are allowed to form too early they will form around surface-level attributes—Americans, Swedes, C++ programmers, Java programmers, female database engineers, male programmers, and so on. As Gratton and her coauthors write, "Simply put, in a team's early going, the more people interact with one another, the more likely they are to make snap judgments and to emphasize their differences" (26).

What we'd like to do is defer relationship building until team members have learned more significant things about each other, such as specific skills, competencies, approaches to work, and so on. This is done through early emphasis on progress rather than relationship building. The subgroups that form at that time will be based on the mutual need to work together to develop the product. To develop a particular user story from the product backlog, you and I need to work together. In doing so we learn each other's skills and specific competencies. I come to know you not just as a Java programmer but as a Java programmer with a real passion and strength for automated unit testing. You find that I am not just a DBA, but one who is strong at optimizing SQL statements.

Teams with subgroups formed around compatible skills, attitudes, approaches to work, and so on are less likely to lead to a later breakdown in trust than subgroups formed on superficial attributes (such as American, Swede, programmer, tester, and so on). Think back to one or more troubled teams you were a member of. Odds are that conflict on those teams was of an us-versus-them nature based on superficial attributes: this office versus that office, programmer versus DBA, Linux fanatics versus Windows fanatics. When teams feel an immediate need to make progress, those types of subgroups do not have time to form.

After a team has worked together for a few sprints, shift the emphasis toward relationship building by incorporating more social activities and shared downtime into the sprints. A team needs to have a sufficient amount of shared experience before social activities and relationship building can be useful. But when that has been achieved, "instilling confidence in the team and creating opportunities to socialize at that point helps the development of new abilities and allows the team to grow" (Gratton et al. 2007, 29).

I want to be clear that I am not saying that no time for socialization should be included at the start of a project. Seeding visits and whole-team, in-person get-togethers at the start of a project for its initial release planning can be very useful. Three points are key here: First, the project should start with intensity and a focus on early demonstrations of progress. Second, the entire "budget" for socialization should not be spent in the first couple of sprints. Third, early social activities should tie into the work of the project, such as bringing a team together for release planning.

☐ Locate each of your project's office locations in Table 18.1. At the next sprint retrospective discuss the differences. Do the differences seem real? Are there other differences? What subtle future problems could these differences cause?

☐ During future sprint planning meetings, discuss any cultural or national celebrations that will occur during the sprint in each location. Don't just mention the holiday or celebration. Have people in the celebrating location tell others something deeper about it—how they spend the day, a folk tale about the event, any special rituals, or so on.

☐ In your next sprint retrospective, discuss and document team operating agreements. What is appropriate behavior on your team?

Get Together in Person

All of the distributed teams I've worked with report benefits from getting together occasionally. How teams do this differs tremendously—some teams collocate entirely for the first few sprints, other teams plan occasional full-team get-togethers, others rotate members between sites. Most use a combination of techniques. We will consider each in this section.

Seeding Visits

One of the most popular approaches to getting together is what Martin Fowler has termed a "seeding visit." He says these should "occur early in the project and are intended to create the relationships" (2006). A seeding visit that brings all team members together at the start of a project can be one of the best possible investments in the success of the project. This can be especially important for projects on which team members do not know each other, have minimal shared history, speak different languages, or come from different cultures. Allowing a team a short period of collocation allows team members to take huge first steps toward knowing and trusting each other. This can be started in as little as a few days or a week, but many teams find collocating for the entire first sprint very helpful. This is exactly what Jane Robarts found on a project distributed between Hong Kong and China.

> This face-to-face kickoff gave us an opportunity to meet each
> other, establish a rapport, and understand the project together.

By the time people separated to their different locations, they all knew each other, were comfortable phoning each other, and felt like part of the same team. (2008, 328)

Ade Miller, of Microsoft's patterns and practices group, says to "use these periods of working in the same place to not only build shared understanding of the problem domain but also working relationships within the team" (2008, 18).

<table>
<tr><td>**OBJECTION**</td><td>**"Flying some of the team halfway around the world and then putting them up in hotels will be very expensive. We're using a distributed team to save money, so this would defeat the whole purpose of a geographically distributed team."**</td></tr>
</table>

Refusing to bring team members (or at least some of them) together is chasing a false economy: Yes, this will save you money today, but it will cost you more through the rest of the project. Never forecast cost savings on an outsourced project by looking only at the labor cost per hour of team members. There are many hidden costs to using a distributed team. An increased travel budget should be part of any distributed project. Erran Carmel, in his book *Global Software Teams,* concurs: "Air travel from site to site is a costly yet necessary part of global teams" (1998, 157). Tom DeMarco, Tim Lister, and the other principals of the Atlantic Systems Guild agree: "To succeed at distributed development, you almost certainly will have to increase, not decrease, your travel budget" (2008, 42).

If the budget allows it, you may want to keep a team collocated even longer than one sprint. At the start of a 20-person-year project, Xebia chose to collocate Dutch and Indian developers for five two-week sprints. Jeff Sutherland, a consultant to that project, and coauthors from Xebia describe the benefits of doing this.

In the shared onsite iterations the team members forged personal relationships to last throughout the project and Indian team members acquired a good sense of customer context. It also got everyone aligned concerning practices, standards, tooling, and natural roles in the team formed. (2008, 341)

As logical as it is to get together at the start of the project, sometimes doing so is not feasible. When that's the case, get distributed team members together whenever you can. Periods of collocation do not need to be limited to the beginning of a project. Any time a team can be brought together is the right time. Microsoft's Ade Miller points out that "there's no substitute for face-to-face communication, particularly at pivotal points in the project" (2008, 10).

One of the best uses of seeding visits I've come across occurred at Oticon, the world's oldest hearing instrument manufacturer. Oticon's primary development office is in Smørum, just outside of Copenhagen in Denmark. In June 2007, the decision was made to hire a significant number of new developers, but to hire them in Poland. Oticon already had an office there but did not use that office for software development. Poland was chosen because it had become difficult to find developers in Denmark; it was not chosen primarily for the more common reason of saving money.

Oticon knew that integrating the Polish and Danish developers would be critical. Ole Andersen, a manager at Oticon, was responsible for hiring the Polish developers and for integrating them with his team in Denmark. He describes how he was able to successfully integrate them.

> We decided that every Polish developer should come to Denmark for a two-month stay and join one of our Scrum teams. We rented a nice apartment close to the office so they would feel comfortable and enjoy their time here. Some took the opportunity to invite members of their families to come and stay in the apartment for a week or so. During the two-month stay in Denmark, the Polish developers were introduced around the company by their Scrum team, and they worked as any other member in the Scrum teams. We received very positive feedback from the Danish developers about this process, and some of them became good friends with some of the developers in Poland. The Polish developers felt very welcome in Denmark, and the good apartment made a big difference instead of staying two months in a hotel.

Contact Visits

After a seeding visit (ideally at the start of the project but perhaps not) has established an initial relationship, contact visits are used to maintain those relationships. As with a seeding visit, a contact visit should be oriented around completing a task (planning, designing a solution to a problem, or so on) but, as Fowler says, "Remember that the primary purpose of the visit isn't to do the task but to build the working relationship." He suggests that one-week visits be done at least every couple of months (2006).

Some teams find that quarterly release planning is a good time to bring the whole team back together. Consider the case of a product with plans to put out a new release approximately every three months over the product's life. Or consider a large product with a schedule of a year or more. In both cases, a quarterly cycle may begin with a product owner communicating the product vision to the team. Temporarily collocating makes this easier to achieve.

Additionally, don't forget that, as in both of these cases, usually when one release cycle is beginning, the preceding one is ending. This makes it an ideal time to bring a team together. With the expense and hassle of a single trip, a team can be collocated for the vision-setting and planning of the new release and sprint as well as for the final sprint of the preceding release, including its review and retrospective. Microsoft's Miller recommends going even one step further.

> Bringing the team back together for the last couple of iterations before the final release makes the process of shipping a final deliverable much smoother. It helps the team focus on "getting things out the door." Being in the same room means that the whole team is available when key decisions have to be made. (2008, 11)

Traveling Ambassadors

The common practice of Management By Walking Around (MBWA) is replaced on distributed projects by MBFA—Management By Flying Around. Of course, on a distributed Scrum project, it needs to be more than just *managers* flying around. In many ways, individuals flying from one city to another can be thought of as ambassadors. Martin Fowler defines ambassadors as "semi-permanent people who spend several months in the 'other' location." Although spending several months in another location may be ideal, I've found that I often need to compromise, sending ambassadors more often but for shorter visits.

I'm not very familiar with the work of actual ambassadors. So I usually think of these project ambassadors in much the way that jazz great Louis Armstrong sang about himself in the 1961 song, "The Real Ambassador." In this song, Armstrong tells politically appointed ambassadors that as a jazz musician traveling around the world, he is his country's "real ambassador" even though, he says, "All I do is play the blues and meet the people face-to-face."[3] Armstrong's statement perfectly summarizes what project ambassadors are asked to do: Write some code and meet the people face-to-face. Fowler acknowledges the importance of the informal aspect of an ambassador's job.

> An important part of the ambassador's job is to communicate gossip. On any project there's a lot of informal communication. While much of this isn't important, some of it is—and the trouble is that you can't tell which is which. So part of an ambassador's

---

3 See http://www.therealambassadors.com/2.htm to hear Armstrong sing this song and to read information about his and collaborator Dave Brubeck's experience as "the real ambassadors."

job is to communicate lots of tidbits which don't seem important enough for more formal communication channels. I am referring, of course, to the types of tidbits that help us understand our coworkers ("Fernando said his baby took her first steps last night") and not malicious rumors. (2006)

I've found that the personal relationships established by ambassadors can be extremely valuable even long after the ambassador returns to native soil. Ben Hogan participated in a project distributed between Bangalore and Sydney. He comments, "We found exchanging ambassadors between our sites to be one of the most effective techniques for improving cross-team communication. It allowed us to build personal relationships and provided a mechanism to build trust and transfer knowledge. The ambassadors were able to communicate lessons learned as well as set future direction for the project" (2006, 322).

On one project I coached, I had developers in Denver and Toronto. Teams in the two cities had been thrust together on a common project because of an acquisition, which initially had led to an unfriendly relationship between the two teams. Frank, a programmer in Denver, volunteered for a couple of two-week visits to Toronto. I knew the Toronto developers very well, having already worked with them for two years. I wanted to make sure we got the most benefit from Frank's trips, so I talked with him about his hobbies and interests outside of work. When I discovered he was a rock climber, I contacted Marcel in Toronto, who was an obsessive climber. I asked Marcel to do me the favor of spending a little time with Frank, possibly setting him up with a guest pass to his indoor rock-climbing gym. Marcel very willingly did so, and the two of them became good friends and discovered they had other interests in common as well.

The budding friendship between Marcel and Frank served the project well right from the start. But it really paid dividends a few months later when a potential conflict started to emerge between departments on the periphery of our two-city project. The IT staff in Denver had named a server "Pandora" that would be used by the Toronto team. The Toronto team was furious over this and assumed the name had been intended as an insult because of the mythological story of Pandora's box containing all the evils of mankind. I was in Toronto when the trouble started, so I asked Marcel to get Frank on the phone and to ask him if he would discreetly find out if the name had been intended as an insult. Two hours later Frank informed us that the employee who selected the name pulled it from a previously generated list of server names and had no idea who Pandora was. Because of the trust built between Marcel and Frank, we were able to quickly defuse the situation.

Jane Robarts has also found that the benefits of ambassador visits go well beyond achieving whatever formal goals are associated with a visit.

Throughout the release, we scheduled visits for our U.S. product managers and team leads to the Indian office. The idea of this was to provide easy transfer of domain knowledge to business analysts, developers, and quality analysts in India. An amazing byproduct was that visitors to the Indian office invariably came away with a better understanding of the environment. After visiting the office, they often started scheduling calls at different times, found ways to limit the number of calls and, most significantly, changed their tone of communication. Their awareness of the commitment and dedication of the Indian team increased, and they understood the personal sacrifices everyone was making for the project. A reciprocal understanding also developed from the Indian team members towards the U.S. team, having now met some of them in person. (2008, 328)

THINGS TO TRY NOW

- ❑ Buy a plane ticket. Occasional face-to-face interaction is important. If it's been awhile since you've visited one or more of the other locations on your project, plan a visit.
- ❑ If a project has just begun or is early enough to still benefit, identify ambassadors and have them schedule their initial visits.

Change How You Communicate

As Robarts' ambassadors discovered, one of the most profound impacts of distributing a team will be the changes to how they communicate. Collocated Scrum teams rely heavily on face-to-face communication. Swiveling your chair around and asking, "Hey, Chris, what do you know about this encryption algorithm?" is very different from making a phone call to Chris in the office four time zones away. And it's even more different from sending an e-mail to Chris and waiting until tomorrow for a response.

Adding Back Some Documentation

There is no way around it: A distributed team will need to write more than a collocated team. There may be more reliance on written status reports to supplement sprint reviews for attendees who cannot attend. Prospective designs may be sketched and written and then sent between distributed team members, especially team members with limited overlapping work hours. Hallway conversations will be replaced with e-mails. There will undoubtedly be more writing.

Fortunately, more written communication does not need to mean the death of agility on a project, but team members do need to be aware of how easy it is to miscommunicate. I've been involved in a few projects where team members in different cities were highly distrustful of each other. Usually these were teams that were put together through an acquisition. Because of the distrust and how easily e-mail could be misinterpreted, these teams chose to temporarily ban e-mail and resolve to pick up the phone each time they needed to communicate.

Not all of the effects of writing more need to be negative. Jane Robarts, for example, tells an interesting story of a coworker of hers who used written communication to successfully augment verbal messages.

> He always ensured that when delivering a message verbally he also included a written version of the message, usually as a PowerPoint. Often we would not even use the PowerPoint during the conference call, but it was an artifact that could later be read to clarify the message with team members who could not hear the call clearly, were not present at the time, or required clarification on the exact messaging. (2008, 329)

This can be a particularly helpful technique when team members speak multiple languages. Non-native speakers can read the document at their leisure, aiding comprehension.

Adding Detail to the Product Backlog

Chapter 13, "The Product Backlog," stressed the importance of shifting from writing about requirements to talking about them. Many teams have found, however, that when distributed, they cannot shift as far away from requirements documents as they would like. Martin Fowler has said that "with greater distance, you need to put more ceremony into communicating requirements" (2006). Summarizing her experiences with a distributed project's product backlog, Elaine Therrien of First American Corelogic says that "supplementing the high-level user stories with more detailed specifications helps to empower offshore resources. More detailed requirements enable the team to gain insight into the feature and the end user objectives at times when the product owner is not accessible" (2008, 371).

Fowler's experience, as well as Therrien's with her teams in California and Bangalore, is similar to my own with highly distributed teams. With time differences, such as the 12.5-hour one between Bangalore and California, teams that are very widely distributed will face significant challenges simply due to the complete lack of an overlap during a normal workday. Often in situations like this, the product owner and team are located in vastly different time zones. With teams such as these I advocate a technique I call "send along a test." The idea is that when a user story on the product backlog is sent from the product owner to the team, it needs to be accompanied by the high-level test cases that will indicate whether the user story is complete.

SEE ALSO

These test cases are the "conditions of satisfaction" that were introduced in Chapter 13.

Encourage Lateral Communication

On a typical project using a sequential development process, most communication between subteams in different sites occurs through a designated team leader. On a Scrum project we want to avoid this and encourage lateral communication—anyone in one city can speak with anyone in another city. This isn't just allowed; it is encouraged. As Ade Miller of Microsoft points out, "A coach should help the team remember the value of intensive communication even when distribution makes this harder" (2008, 13).

One significant benefit of lateral communication is that it helps counter the "mum effect" (Ramingwong and Sajeev 2007). The mum effect occurs when a project participant fails to share bad news with others. By failing to share bad news, this person puts the project at risk, because without knowledge of a problem it cannot be addressed. It is well known and easily accepted that individuals from different cultures share bad news in different ways and have different levels of willingness to do so. This makes the mum effect more prevalent, and potentially more devastating, on widely distributed projects. Ramingwong and Sajeev identified three reasons why a team member might not share bad news:

- The fear of being punished, including being fired
- A desire to maintain team solidarity
- No clear channel through which to communicate the problem

A project that enjoys free and frequent lateral communication will be less likely to suffer from the mum effect. It's difficult to establish a project culture where everyone is willing to share everything with everybody else. Fortunately, lateral communication makes that goal less necessary. I may be unwilling to take some bad news directly to the product owner, but I am willing to casually mention it to you while we pair on some task. And I know you're willing to take it to our product owner. This type of lateral communication is especially important on projects involving team members whose cultures or individual personalities make them less willing to share bad news or more intimidated by those in leadership roles.

THINGS TO TRY NOW

- During the next sprint planning meeting, discuss whether enough detail is provided with each product backlog item being planned into the new sprint. If not, either add more detail during that meeting or consider adding detail to upcoming product backlog items during the sprint.
- In the next sprint retrospective, discuss the mum effect. Discuss the possible effect of a team member remaining silent about bad news. Brainstorm ways to help each other avoid these problems.

Meetings

When I was 10, I spent the summer with my grandmother who lived near New Orleans in the hot, sticky, southern part of the United States. Having grown up in southern California with its near-perfect weather, I complained (more than once, I'm sure) about how hot it was in New Orleans. My grandmother's reply was always the same: "It's not the heat, it's the humidity." Analogously, for a distributed team, it's not the distance, it's the time difference.

A time zone difference has a far greater impact on how a team works together than does the geographic distance separating a team. I once worked on a project with team members in California, London, and South Africa. Figure 18.2 shows the distances between these three locations in kilometers, miles, and number of time zones. The physical distance between San Francisco and London (8,600 kilometers) is not too different from the distance between London and Cape Town (9,700 kilometers). However, San Francisco and London are eight hours apart, while London and Cape Town are only two hours apart. As you would imagine, team members in San Francisco faced far greater challenges than those in London and Cape Town because there was an extensive workday overlap between London and Cape Town, which made a huge difference in how those teams worked together.

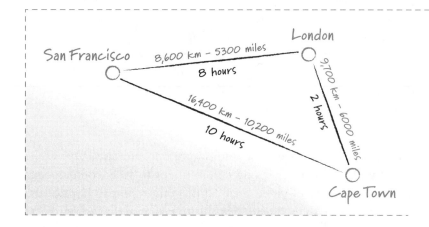

FIGURE 18.2

Achieving a balance between anticipation and adaptation involves balancing the influence of the activities and artifacts on each side.

Of course, this is not to imply that distance itself does not cause problems. A team distributed between Oslo and Frankfurt, which are in the same time zone, will still face challenges it would not face if the whole team were in one of those cities. But, at least it will share a common workday during which it can address those problems.

General Advice

Throughout this section we will consider how the twin problems of time and distance affect the four common meetings of a Scrum project—daily scrums, sprint planning, sprint retrospectives, and sprint reviews—and the scrum of scrums meeting used on multi-team projects. First, though, we'll begin with some general advice applicable to all meetings.

Include Time for Small Talk

Collocated teams have many opportunities for informal, getting-to-know-you conversations. They can afford to let some slip by. Distributed teams need to deliberately take advantage of whatever opportunities for small talk arise. Martin Fowler has observed that "it's a good habit to start conference calls with chit chat on local news. Recent odd bits of local color—politics, sport, weather—help each side get a sense of the broader life context on the other side of the wire" (2006). Recalling their experiences with a project distributed between San Francisco, Boston, and Toronto, Cynick Young and Hiroki Terashima concur.

> When the developers first began technical discussions, we found that some members were being too professional and tense. It was hard to discuss anything except work, and every meeting resulted in information overload. Realizing that this was not a healthy way to collaborate, we began incorporating a short greeting period at the beginning of each meeting. We discussed ordinary subjects such as the weather, each person's wellness, and anything else that came to mind. This way of starting each meeting allowed everyone to relax and get a feel for how the other members were doing that day, which contributed to a more pleasant meeting. (2008, 306)

Technology can also help replace these impromptu opportunities. One company that I worked with had made a strong commitment to videoconferencing, which meant there were plenty of video-enabled meeting rooms in both of the offices involved in the project, so each team was able to take one over as a dedicated team room. As strongly as I could, I encouraged team members to eat lunches, take breaks, and so on in these always-on video rooms. With teams located three time zones apart, this worked well. Team members on the west coast of the United States might take a short morning break around the time those on the east coast (three hours later) were eating lunch; team members on the east coast would take an afternoon break in their videoconference room at the same time that west coast team members were eating lunch. The informal chats that naturally took place helped people in both offices feel more like one team.

Share the Pain

If your project is distributed such that meetings will occur well before or after the usual workday, be sure to share the pain. Do not schedule the meeting such that it permanently favors people in one location. For example, for a team split between California and Bangalore, with a 12.5-hour time difference, do not schedule a phone call for 8:00 a.m. California time and 8:30 p.m. in India. Whereas most team members in California would find this a bit earlier than normal working hours but not unduly unreasonable, team members in India would consider this a horrible time to meet regularly.

So, do like Matt Truxaw did when he was an application development manager at First American CoreLogic in California. Matt encouraged the California/India teams he coached to share the pain by alternating when the calls would be held, so that one month the calls were in the evening and the next month they were in the morning.

> This helped both teams connect on a regular basis without either group feeling like it was expected to take on more burden than the others. This also helped the teams in India feel that they were part of the process—not just hired guns, but true team members.

Alternating call times in this way helps ensure an appropriate balance of power between the two locations. There is a tendency for power to accumulate where the company headquarters is, where the product owner is, or where a majority of developers are. Allowing power to build in one location can lead to feelings of resentment in the other. Simple actions like alternating call times help prevent this.

Participating in a meeting by phone can be particularly painful if most of the other attendees are participating in person. This happens often when most of the team is collocated, with only two or three members elsewhere. The problem is especially prevalent if those two or three members work from home offices. An easy way to share this pain is to get everyone on the phone occasionally so that we're all reminded how hard it is to be fully engaged by phone.

Tell Everyone Who Is Speaking

An obvious challenge of using the phone for meetings is recognizing the voices of all the different speakers. Some people are good at this and quickly learn to distinguish among the various voices at a remote location. I've never been one of them, so I appreciate teams that use the time-tested technique of always stating your name before making any comment whatsoever. Although this works well, unfortunately calls seem to take longer with all the "This is Mike…" prefacing that occurs. Also, during a rapid or heated discussion, it is very hard to remember to start each statement that way.

One team I worked with found an interesting nuance that improved upon this speak-your-name-before-you-speak approach. Team members called the technique "low fidelity videoconferencing" and often preferred it to regular videoconferencing because of the inevitable problems and delays with that equipment. Low-fidelity videoconferencing involved one person in each city who had a good ear for different voices holding up a photo of whoever was speaking at the remote location. When Sonali starts talking, someone holds up her photo. When she finishes and Manish starts talking, his picture is held up instead. Photos of each person had been taken in advance and were taped to rulers, making it easy to quickly hold up the right picture.

I realize that this technique may sound silly when you are only reading about it, rather than witnessing it. However, I observed two interesting things while watching teams at this company do a few phone calls this way. First, while some teams let the same person always hold up the photos, on other teams, anyone would hold up the photo. It became a bit of a contest to see who could recognize the voice and hold the picture up first, which seemed to make everyone pay more attention. Second, people didn't just glance at the photo to see, "Oh, it's Ranjeet speaking." Instead, they continued to look at the photo as though Ranjeet's lips were magically going to start moving.

Sprint Planning Meeting

In this section we will look at two common strategies for conducting a distributed sprint planning meeting. The strategies are referred to by their descriptive names: the long phone call and two calls. I will point out the strengths and weaknesses of each approach.

The Long Phone Call

The default approach taken by most teams is to have everyone dial into a conference call but otherwise conduct the sprint planning meeting as normal. The call attempts to mimic the format and interaction of an in-person sprint planning meeting. All of the work of a regular sprint planning meeting is done during this phone call. When the call ends, the sprint is as fully planned as it would be if the team were collocated.

This is a perfect example of how time separation is worse than physical separation on its own. Clearly, this approach to distributed sprint planning is only feasible when there is significant overlap in the regular working hours of all team members. No team should be routinely asked to plan a sprint from 7:00 p.m. to midnight, for example.

In general, I like the long phone call approach. The practicality of this approach, however, is usually determined by how widely distributed the team is. If team members work in the same time zone, can work a slightly extended day, or can shift their hours a bit, the long phone call approach has much to recommend it. The pros and cons of the approach are summarized in Table 18.2.

Pros	Cons
Can lead to good discussion as long as participants remain engaged.	Participants may mentally disengage from such a long phone call.
Sprint planning can be finished in one day.	Only works when there is significant overlap of the workday.
Is consistent with the approach used by collocated teams.	May involve extending the workday in one or more locations.

TABLE 18.2

The pros and cons of doing sprint planning with a single long phone call.

Two Calls

For some teams, it is simply impractical to plan on completing sprint planning in a single phone call—the time zone separation is too great to provide sufficient overlap in the work days. The next approach to sprint planning, two calls, addresses this by splitting the meeting across two phone calls held on consecutive days. Roger Nessier, a vice president at Symphony Services, points out how his team segmented the call.

> Replacing the initial eight-hour session with two separate four-hour sessions conducted over consecutive days is more practical. For example, the first session focuses on identifying major tasks, deliverables, and high-level dependencies. During the second session, each team member defines activities and provides estimates for each task he accepted. (2007, 8–9)

Some teams prefer to do no planning work outside the phone calls; others prefer to use the gap for individual preparation for the second part of the meeting. This was the approach taken by the Yahoo! Vespa News Search team, which had product managers in two California locations and developers in Norway, nine hours away. Because they were working in two-week sprints, team members decided to timebox the initial call to two hours. They decided to run it from 4:00 to 6:00 p.m. in Norway and 7:00 to 9:00 a.m. in California. They also agreed to stick strictly to that timebox. Team members Brian Drummond and J. F. Unson describe the meeting.

> Team members would pore over each product backlog item, probing the product manager with questions regarding acceptance criteria, scope boundaries of each feature, business constraints, and the like. Once the discussions ended, then the team

would go their separate ways—with the Norway team going home for the evening, and the California team continuing onward with their earlier-than-normal start. (2008, 317)

The first meeting focuses on discussing the product owner's highest-priority features and expectations. As pointed out by Drummond and Unson, this meeting is characterized by lots of discussion between the development team and the product owner. Once this first meeting is over, location-based subteams continue with meetings to plan their own portions of the coming sprint. These meetings may occur the same day or the following morning, depending on where teams are located. During these second meetings, subteams identify the tasks needed to complete the features that were discussed during the initial, whole-team call.

Sprint planning is then concluded with a second phone call, usually on the second day at about the same time as the call on the first day. The purpose of this call is to synchronize the commitments each subteam is willing to make. For example, suppose that four features are discussed during an initial call. After that call, the subteam in Norway decides it can commit to only three of them, whereas the team in California can commit to all four. During the second phone call, the whole team would explore ways to fully commit to the fourth item or perhaps find a smaller item that both subteams could commit to. Drummond and Unson of Yahoo! found that this approach worked well.

The team was able to minimize and equally spread the pain of having an inconvenient meeting across different time zones. They kept the fidelity of information high by keeping the meetings focused on the topic, allowing the team to meet the strict time box rule. Any discussions that didn't affect the other party were tabled to a more locally convenient time. (2008, 318)

The pros and cons of this approach are summarized in Table 18.3.

TABLE 18.3

The pros and cons of spreading sprint planning across two phone calls.

Pros	Cons
Can be a more efficient use of time.	Usefulness can vary greatly based on how the team is distributed.
Can be used even if work hours only overlap slightly (or can be made to overlap slightly).	Because many discussions happen within subteams, not all knowledge is shared with the full team, possibly leading to later misunderstandings and miscommunications.
	Cannot be completed in one day.

NOTE

A third approach that is sometimes used is to have technical leads in each location do all the planning. Although this does minimize time zone challenges, I cannot recommend this approach due to three main drawbacks:

● Not everyone is involved in the planning, so there is less buy-in and less understanding of the work being committed to.

● Without everyone involved, tasks are more likely to be forgotten or misestimated.

● This approach hampers self-organization and prevents the team from feeling ownership of the challenge given it.

Daily Scrum

The daily scrum presents an entirely different set of challenges than does the sprint planning meeting. Whereas sprint planning requires long but somewhat infrequent meetings, the daily scrum is a short but daily meeting. Because the daily scrum is timeboxed to 15 minutes, conducting this meeting does not present a problem for teams with overlapping workdays. Daily scrums are a problem, however, for widely distributed teams with no overlap in their workdays. To be asked to call in each and every day at a time when you wouldn't normally be working is not sustainable long term. There are three primary strategies such teams use: single call, writing the meeting, and regional meetings.

Single Call

Perhaps the most common approach and the one tried first by most distributed teams is to get everyone together on a single phone call. For teams within a few time zones of each other, this is an excellent approach. Unfortunately, the approach breaks down quickly as the number of time zones increases. Eventually, most widely distributed teams find they must find a different strategy for their daily calls.

Some widely distributed teams attempt to overcome the inconvenience and unsustainability of the single call by holding scrums less frequently, perhaps every two or three days. I can totally sympathize with and relate to the inconvenience of a daily call held outside of common work hours. However, whenever I am tempted to reduce the frequency of a project's daily meetings, I recall Fred Brooks in *The Mythical Man-Month*: "How does a project get to be a year late?…One day at a time" (1995, 153). My recommendation is to keep *daily* scrums *daily*. If you choose not to, at least replace the skipped meetings with written versions of the meeting or with a call with one person from each location participating. Each of these approaches is described in the next two strategies for handling the daily scrum.

Teams that choose to use the single call approach should consider alternating the time of the call as described in the "Share the Pain" section earlier in this chapter. The pros and cons of the single-call approach are summarized in Table 18.4.

Pros	Cons
Similar to the approach used with col-located teams, so nothing new needs to be learned.	Can be very inconvenient for team members.
Discussions are held with the entire team present.	Not sustainable if people are forced to make calls far outside of normal work hours.
Everyone learns of all issues, leading to greater team learning and commitment to a shared purpose.	

Writing the Meeting

To alleviate the pain of off-hours phone calls for at least one location, some teams abandon daily scrums altogether. Not wanting to give up the value of daily communication entirely, such teams usually replace daily scrums with a written form of the meeting. Team members agree to send an e-mail, update a wiki page, or make an entry in another asynchronous collaboration tool providing the same information they would share in a phone call.

A variation of this approach is to hold a phone call at a time that is convenient for the largest number of team members and have other team members "participate" by submitting a written report. This is particularly common when most of the team is collocated with only a couple of remote members.

I usually do not advocate this approach as a primary technique. It can be used to supplement daily calls if the team decides that daily calls are too much and needs to reduce their frequency. There are important side effects to a daily phone call that are lost when the call is turned into a daily written update. For example, the commitment to complete a piece of work seems stronger when a team member says, "I will do this today," than when the same words are written. Perhaps this is because the spoken message is a commitment made in front of one's coworkers; the written message is a commitment made in private and perhaps read only by one's coworkers. This and other pros and cons of this approach are summarized in Table 18.5.

Pros	Cons
Can be sustained over the long term.	Issues are not discussed and so may lay dormant for days.
Helps overcome language problems, including thick accents.	Fails to take advantage of a great opportunity to foster improved relationships and knowledge sharing among team members through daily interaction.
	No guarantee that written updates will be read.
	Team members will be less likely to hold each other accountable for prior day's commitments.

TABLE 18.5

The pros and cons of replacing the daily scrum with equivalent written information.

Regional Meetings

The third and final approach to the daily scrum meeting is to have a set of regional meetings followed by some effort to share key issues from the meetings. If a team is split across two fairly distant cities, each city may have its own daily scrum. This would be the case, for example, for a team with members in the company's San Francisco and London offices, which are eight hours apart.

Sometimes a distributed team has a few offices with overlapping work hours, plus one office that is more remote. In these cases, those locations with overlapping hours might have one regional daily scrum. The more remote location, though, would have its own meeting. If, for example, our San Francisco and London teams were joined by a team in Los Angeles, one likely arrangement might be to hold a daily scrum by phone for the two California teams but have a separate, in-person meeting in London.

A common approach is to have separate phone calls for the western and eastern hemispheres. The western-hemisphere phone call can easily accommodate everyone in North and South America, with an eastern-hemisphere call taking care of the rest of the world (with the possible exception of Australia and New Zealand). If an individual team is truly so widely distributed that it has members in, let's say, San Francisco, Seattle, Toronto, London, Prague, Stockholm, Beijing, and Melbourne, it may want to have three calls at different times rather than two. But, keep in mind we are discussing the daily scrum here, not the scrum of scrums (which we'll get to next). Most individual teams can get along fine with two calls scheduled at different times.

These regional meetings (whether everyone is present in one office or dialing into a multi-city call) are then usually followed by additional communication, so that each subteam is aware of the work of the other subteams. One way to conduct this follow-up communication is a phone call with at least one representative from each subteam. This is the approach used by Martin Fowler who says, "We do standups with a shore's team, but not between the different shores. We do however do daily cross-shore meetings, but these don't involve the entire team" (2006).

Another approach to ensure communication across the subteams is for the team to designate one or more team members who will participate in all scrums. The designated team member participates in the normal subteam scrum but then also participates in one or two other scrums, which usually occur outside of that individual's normal working hours.

Whichever of these approaches to sharing information between and coordinating the work of subteams is used, the pain of off-hours phone calls is greatly reduced. It is not, however, eliminated as at least one person is participating in an off-hours call each day. The inconvenience of this can be further reduced by rotating who is assigned this responsibility.

I find that holding regional meetings is suitable for most widely distributed teams. As much as I'd prefer everyone on a single call every day, that is not always a valid long-term option. Although this approach has its weaknesses, they are outweighed (though not outnumbered) by its strengths, both of which are summarized in Table 18.6.

TABLE 18.6

The pros and cons of using regional meetings to conduct the daily scrum.

Pros	Cons
Pain of off-hours calls is greatly reduced.	Information relayed from one meeting to the next may be incorrect or incomplete.
Allows local subteams to share information most important to them.	Can lead to a feeling of "us" and "them" between different subteams.
	Not everyone is present for all discussions.
	Information may not be shared between subteams in a timely manner.

SEE ALSO

The scrum of scrums meetings was described in Chapter 17, "Scaling Scrum."

Scrum of Scrums

The scrum of scrums is used by multiple teams to coordinate their work. It involves one representative of each team participating in a meeting, usually two or three times a week. The reduced frequency of this meeting makes it less troublesome to replicate with a distributed team. This meeting is almost always an hour or less; therefore, a distributed team with any overlap to its workday at all will be able to easily schedule a scrum of scrums meeting.

The challenges arise, of course, when the team is so widely distributed as to share no common working hours. In these cases, successful teams use one of the better strategies for the daily scrum—either single call or regional meetings. When only a handful of teams is involved, a single call usually works, as the meeting participants can find some time that will be minimally inconvenient for enough people. This is easier to do than it is for the daily scrum for two reasons: First, most scrum of scrums calls are not daily and second, most teams occasionally change who participates in those calls. Having to be on a 7:00 p.m. phone call for the next four Tuesdays and Thursdays may be inconvenient, but it pales in comparison to being on a phone call at 7:00 p.m. five nights a week until you retire.

Larger teams, or those with more difficult time zone challenges, often opt to hold regional meetings. A project with four teams in Toronto, three teams in Bangalore, and two in Beijing, for example, may opt to hold a face-to-face scrum of scrums in Toronto for those four teams. This meeting would be at an inconvenient time for participants in Bangalore and Beijing, so individuals there may schedule a conference call at a better time in their day. Information is shared between these two groups either through a person or two who participate in both meetings or through a phone call including a representative from each meeting.

Sprint Reviews and Retrospectives

Sprint reviews and retrospectives share attributes of both the daily scrum and the sprint planning meeting. Like sprint planning meetings, these meetings are not held every day, so team members are more able to participate outside of normal work hours. Like daily scrums, though, reviews and retrospectives are a bit easier to plan because they are shorter than a sprint planning meeting. This makes finding a suitable time for a sprint review or retrospective relatively easy.

Teams with overlapping work hours will naturally schedule these meetings during the overlapped portion of their days. Teams whose work hours nearly overlap usually schedule these meetings at the end of one work day and the start of another. For example, a team split across Denver and Helsinki is nine hours apart. It may schedule a review for 8:00 a.m. in Denver and 5:00 p.m. in Helsinki. The Denver team members will need to arrive for work a little earlier than some would like, and Helsinki team members will need to stay a little later than some would like; but, overall, this type of approach works well considering that the meetings happen only once every few weeks.

Teams more widely distributed need to find a time that is minimally intrusive in the personal lives of members in one or more locations. A team spread between London and New Zealand, 12 hours apart, may decide to hold the meeting at 8:00 a.m. in one location and 8:00 p.m. in the other. As with all such off-hours meetings, you should vary which location gets the early shift and which gets the late shift.

If both the review and retrospective tend to be short, some teams prefer to schedule the review and retrospective back-to-back. Other teams prefer scheduling them on consecutive days. The trade-off is between two days with shorter off-hours phone calls and one day but with a longer call.

Participation Is Not Optional

A challenge with sprint reviews and retrospectives is that some team members will be tempted to consider participation optional. It's not. But, while I don't consider participation optional, I do consider it unrealistic to expect a team member be available off-hours every time the team has a meeting. I like to set the expectation that team members are expected to be at each review and retrospective, but that I know they will sometimes miss one. I set the expectation that if you are going to miss one of these meetings, call someone on the team or e-mail the rest of us so that we know you won't attend.

I equate participation in off-hours reviews and retrospectives to my daughters' swim team practices. Practices are not optional; my daughters cannot skip practice and then show up at a swim meet anxious to compete. To compete, they need to show up at practice. But their coach knows these are school-age kids who may miss an occasional practice for many reasons: doctor appointments, a sick sibling, no way to get to practice, a school field trip, and so on. Miss a few, not a problem. Miss too many, and the coach will demand an explanation. The same is true on a Scrum team.

Hold Occasional One-City Retrospectives

I'm not generally a fan of leaving a person or group out of the retrospective. I would never advise a team to leave the testers out of the meeting one time so we could talk without them. Similarly, I wouldn't want a team to leave the product owner out of a retrospective. However, telephones can introduce strange behavior into meetings, so I do want a team to occasionally leave the telephone out of the meeting, meaning that each location should periodically have its own local retrospective. Any topic is fair game for a one-city retrospective, but I would particularly encourage the subgroup in a given city to focus on two things: issues unique to its location and anything it can do to help interactions with other locations.

Proceed with Caution

No one chooses to distribute a team for the benefit of the team. The decision to distribute team members geographically is made for some other reason—to save money, to recruit in multiple locations, to gain expertise in a new region, because of an acquisition, or some similar reason. Distributing a team creates additional work and stress for the individuals involved and creates substantially more risk for the organization.

The advice in this chapter has been drawn both from my experience and from the experiences of those I've spoken with. Distributed development can be made to work, but a distributed team will never perform as well as a collocated team. Yet, because collocation is not always an option, organizations are forced to find ways, such as the techniques described in this chapter, to help distributed teams work as well as they can. Still, we would be wise to consider the conclusion of Emmeline de Pillis and Kimberly Furumo in an article published in the *Communications of the ACM*. After conducting experiments comparing the performance, satisfaction, and group dynamics of distributed and collocated teams, they concluded that "virtual teams yield significantly lower performance, lower satisfaction, and a lower results-to-effort ratio. Virtual teams appear to excel only at lowering commitment, morale, and performance" (2007, 95).

SEE ALSO

Iacovou and Nakatsu present a compendium of risks facing distributed projects (2008).

Additional Reading

Carmel, Erran. 1998. *Global software teams: Collaborating across borders and time zones.* Prentice Hall.

Dr. Carmel is a professor at American University and is a recognized expert on technology globalization. This book nicely complements Duarte's and Snyder's in that it covers software development and IT projects specifically. An earlier book, *Global Software Teams*, focused specifically on software development, but I prefer this newer book.

Duarte, Deborah L., and Nancy Tennant Snyder. 2006. *Mastering virtual teams: Strategies, tools, and techniques that succeed.* 3rd ed. Jossey-Bass.

The best general book on working with distributed (or "virtual") teams. Provides useful information on group dynamics, culture, meetings, and more. Although the book does not have a Scrum or even software development perspective, much of it is applicable.

Fowler, Martin. 2006. Using an agile software process with offshore development. Martin Fowler's personal website, July 18. http://martinfowler.com/articles/agileOffshore.html.

This web page summarizes the thoughts on offshore agile development from ThoughtWorks chief scientist, Martin Fowler. It includes lessons learned, comments on the costs and benefits of offshore development, and predictions about the future of offshore and agile.

Miller, Ade. 2008. *Distributed agile development at Microsoft patterns & practices.* Microsoft. Download from the publisher's website. http://www.pnpguidance.net/Post/Distributed-AgileDevelopmentMicrosoftPatternsPractices.aspx.

Ade Miller of Microsoft's patterns & practices groups summarizes challenges faced by that distributed group and how it addressed them.

Sutherland, Jeff, Anton Viktorov, and Jack Blount. 2006. Adaptive engineering of large software projects with distributed/outsourced teams. In *Proceedings of the Sixth International Conference on Complex Systems*, ed. Ali Minai, Dan Braha, and Yaneer Bar-Yam. New England Complex Systems Institute.

Sutherland, Viktorov, and Blount present a case study of a particularly successful Scrum project that was distributed across three sites on two continents.

Chapter 19

Coexisting with Other Approaches

It's one thing to look at agile software development in a test tube; it's another to experience it in the real world. In the test tube, agile methodologies like Scrum are easily adopted by all members, and the nasty realities of corporate politics, economics, and such cannot intrude. In the real world, though, all of these unpleasant issues do exist. It is rarely as simple as deciding to use Scrum and then being able to do so with no other constraints. One project might be allowed to try Scrum as long as it doesn't interfere with the organization's CMMI Level 3 certification. Another project might be allowed to try it as long as it passes the preliminary architecture review and then has a successful meeting at the design complete checkpoint.

There might be valid reasons for an organization to put these constraints on projects, but they are constraints nonetheless. I'm not using "constraint" here in any significantly pejorative manner; I'm using it to indicate that a degree of freedom has been taken away from the team and how it does its work. Not all constraints are bad things—in the United States (as in much of the world) I am constrained to driving on the right side of the road. I'm happy to do so because I know all the other drivers here are similarly constrained and are therefore much less likely to run into me. Similarly, many Scrum teams must work inside, within, and around the rules and norms of their organization, at least at first.

In this chapter we look at how a Scrum project is affected when it intersects with a sequential (waterfall) process. We next consider the impact of project governance and how Scrum projects can successfully coexist with non-agile governance approaches. Finally, we explore ways Scrum projects can comply with standards such as ISO 9001 or CMMI.

Mixing Scrum and Sequential Development

Few large organizations will enjoy the luxury of doing all of their projects with Scrum. Most will be forced to endure a period in which some projects have moved to Scrum while others have not. This might be because it would be too disruptive to transition the entire company at once, because it would be disruptive to make a mid-course process change to a particular project, or any number of other reasons. Because many organizations will face problems of mixing Scrum and sequential development at some point, we turn our attention to that topic in this section.

Three Scenarios of Interaction

Not every intersection of Scrum and sequential development will be the same. And the problems faced by a project will depend on the points at which Scrum and sequential development meet. Scrum trainer Michele Sliger describes three different scenarios in which Scrum and sequential development might interact (2006).

Waterfall-up-front. The confluence of Scrum and sequential development at the start of the project usually occurs when an organization has project approval hurdles. Clearing these hurdles usually requires the Scrum team to set aside any distaste it has for documents and create a specification, project plan, or other artifact that is required for approval. After a waterfall-up-front project is approved, it runs as a normal Scrum project. Sliger recommends following Alistair Cockburn's advice and producing documentation that is "barely sufficient" (2000). Sliger describes a team that wrote a barely sufficient specification to gain approval for the project.

> They set aside the specification and rarely referenced it during the course of the release. The creation of this specification was not, however, viewed as a waste of time. Rather, team members felt they had benefitted from the shared product vision created from the exercise of compiling the specification. And, of course, the financial managers on the project approval board got the information they needed as well. (2006, 29)

Waterfall-at-end. When Scrum and sequential development meet at the end of the project, it is usually for a testing phase. Sometimes waterfall-at-end occurs because the organization has only tentatively embraced Scrum and has left the testers or quality assurance people as a separate group who swoop in at the end to verify and validate the product. Other times, waterfall-at-end occurs when there is an external group—operations for example requires that some testing to occur at the end. The usual response to a waterfall-at-end requirement is to dedicate one or more sprints to completing this work. By the end of the project, the team has become accustomed to its new agile way of working, so it continues to use as much of Scrum as possible even at the end. In other words, it continues to work in sprints, will hold sprint planning meetings, have daily scrums, and so on.

Waterfall-in-tandem. Perhaps the most difficult way in which Scrum and sequential development interact is waterfall-in-tandem. A common example of this is when two or more teams must work together to create a single product and at least one team is using Scrum and at least one team is using a sequential approach. Coordinating work and communicating frequently are usually the chief sources of problems when waterfall-in-tandem is required. The sequential team will prefer to communicate through meetings and documents that lock down interfaces; the Scrum team will prefer to leave interfaces vague and communicate informally but frequently as interfaces and commitments are progressively defined.

The Scrum team that finds itself in this situation usually finds it helpful to entice the managers of the waterfall projects to attend sprint planning meetings or daily scrums. Sliger wrote about her experience getting sequential team managers to attend sprint planning meetings.

> Initially, the waterfall managers grumbled that all these planning sessions were wreaking havoc on their calendars. However, once they had attended a few sessions, the managers began to realize the value of the shared information and the improved ease and coordination of the work. (2006, 30)

Three Areas of Conflict

Sliger describes the intersections between Scrum and sequential development in terms of how to approach the specific instances where two unlike methodologies converge. Barry Boehm and Richard Turner, on the other hand, write more in terms of how to avoid the three types of conflicts that arise when Scrum and a sequential process coexist:

- **Development process.** A development process conflict originates from the differences between the Scrum and sequential processes.
- **Business process.** A business process conflict is one created by the different ways in which Scrum and sequential teams interact with the business. An organization used to the plans created by a sequential team will be unfamiliar with the type of planning done by a Scrum team.
- **People.** Conflicts around people arise from the different and changed roles when using Scrum and from Scrum's emphasis on self-organization, teamwork, and communication (Boehm and Turner 2005).

Some of these conflicts will occur within a single team—for example, Scrum expects lightweight requirements in the form of user stories or something similar, whereas a sequential process expects more thoroughly documented up-front requirements. Problems can result when an up-front agile activity feeds a downstream sequential activity but does so with less detail than expected.

The remainder of the conflicts are those that arise between two teams that are using different types of processes. We see this, for example, in the need to synchronize work between teams. Boehm and Turner write about the challenge of a Scrum team and a sequential team who must combine their work.

> If the Scrum team evolves its own interfaces, it might leave other parts of the team at risk for developing against a changing standard. However, the traditional [sequential] approach of locking the interface specification early could encumber the Scrum team's need to refactor some part of their design. (2005, 31)

As remedies for these problems, Boehm and Turner offer the following suggestions:

- **Do more analysis than Scrum would usually call for.** If a Scrum team is to work successfully with a sequential team, one compromise it will need to make will be to do more up-front analysis than it would usually prefer. This is necessary so that work can be partitioned among the teams involved and the large interfaces can ideally be identified.

- **Build up a process that is barely sufficient rather than strip a large process down.** Experience shows that when a large process is stripped down, it is rarely stripped far enough. The problems this causes are best avoided by starting with an empty process and then adding only that which is necessary.

- **Define an architecture that compartmentalizes Scrum and sequential approaches.** During project initiation and the first few sprints, focus on identifying areas of the system most suited for Scrum and sequential approaches. Those areas with stable, well-known requirements can be built by the sequential teams; those areas with uncertain requirements or where multiple design approaches are valid should be built by the Scrum teams.

- **Adopt the agile practices that work well regardless of the process.** Some of the agile practices are good ideas no matter what process is used. Continuous integration, heavy reliance on automated testing, pair programming, and refactoring are practices that can be as at home on a sequential project as they are on a Scrum project.

- **Educate stakeholders.** Because some stakeholders will interact with both Scrum and sequential teams, educating them is critical. These stakeholders will need to understand enough about each process to participate in it or understand it as their roles dictate.

❑ Encourage the sequential teams to work on smaller batches of work. Rather than turn something over to, or integrate with, a Scrum team every few months, we'd like the sequential team to do it every few weeks.

❑ Experiment with having a rule that a Scrum team does not pull a product backlog item into a sprint if completing that item requires the sequential team to complete unfinished work during the sprint. Only bring a product backlog item into a sprint if the sequential team has already finished its work on the item.

❑ Request that a member of the sequential team also be assigned to the Scrum team. Have that person attend planning, reviews, retrospectives, and daily scrums.

THINGS TO TRY NOW

Can Scrum and Sequential Coexist Forever?

Opinions are split on whether Scrum and sequential development approaches can coexist forever. Certainly there are organizations doing this today, and organizations have successfully supported multiple, non-agile development processes in the past. But is there something fundamentally different about Scrum that would prevent it from coexisting forever with a sequential process? Michele Sliger believes there is.

> I used to say that companies could mix agile and traditional approaches indefinitely, as they might not wish to move every project to an agile environment. But after what I've seen in the past year, I no longer believe that to be true. I think that companies must eventually make a choice to go one way or the other, and I've been calling this tipping point "high-centering." High-centering is a term used in four-wheeling. It happens when your Jeep climbs over a rock or pile of dirt only to end up balancing on its chassis, with none of its wheels able to make any purchase to move either forward or backward. When these companies get to a certain point of driving their Jeep up that agile mountain, they have to make a conscious and public decision to push forward when they get stuck—otherwise their teams will slide back down into the waterfall at the bottom.

I am inclined to agree with Sliger. Having Scrum temporarily coexist with a sequential process is often necessary in a large organization. But it is important to remember that agile is not a destination; being agile involves continuous improvement. As an organization attempts to become more and more agile, the conflicts between Scrum and sequential development will become more painful. If the sources of these conflicts are not removed, organizational gravity will pull the organization back to whatever software development process was in place before adopting Scrum. A few nonthreatening agile practices such as daily scrums or continuous integration might remain, but the organization will have been unable to achieve the compelling benefits of becoming agile.

Governance

One of the reasons why many organizations adopt a sequential approach to software development is the natural fit between a defined sequence of development phases and the need for project oversight. The purpose of project oversight, commonly called governance, is to make sure that a project does not go astray. Effective project governance can, for example, identify a project that will exceed its budget, leading to conversations about whether the project should be canceled. Governance can also identify a product that is drifting too far from its original goals, a project that is deviating from an architectural standard, or any number of similar high-level considerations important to the organization.

Project governance is not a new concept, but it finds its most natural home in the stage-gate process invented by Dr. Robert Cooper and shown in Figure 19.1. The central idea is that after each stage of a development process, the project is forced through a gate. Each gate acts as a formal review checkpoint on the project; the project might be approved to move forward, sent back for rework in the previous stage, or canceled (2001).

FIGURE 19.1

Stage-gate approaches are the source of many challenges. Stage-Gate® is a registered trademark of the Product Development Institute.

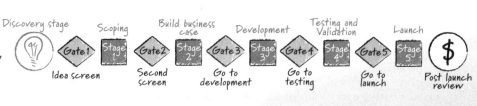

A software team might encounter gates or governance checkpoints at a variety of times: an early review of their plans for scope, budget, and schedule; a review of architectural and design decisions; a review that the application is ready for system or customer acceptance testing; a review that the product can be handed off to a support organization; and so on. These checkpoints often wreak havoc on a software team's desire to use Scrum as they are not suitable to work done in an iterative manner. For example, a Scrum team that allows the design of the system to emerge will have a difficult time clearing an early checkpoint that considers the appropriateness and correctness of the system's architecture.

The first step in reconciling the need for project governance and the desire to use Scrum is to realize that project governance and project management are not the same thing. It is OK to separate project governance from project management. But in separating them we would like to achieve the ability to have high-level checkpoints to provide the necessary oversight, while still allowing the team the freedom of managing itself and the project in an agile manner.

As evidence that governance is not inherently evil, suppose that you are suddenly promoted to president or CEO of your company. As the new boss, you are going to want some visibility into the company's major projects. Maybe you establish a rule that you personally need to approve the start of any project expected to cost over a certain amount. And, while you plan to attend as many sprint reviews as you can, you want any project that lasts over three months to give you a two-page summary of key information every three months. This would be a lightweight governance model and a reasonable one to put in place. So it is not the existence of governance that is objectionable; it is when governance starts to affect how we run the projects that we object.

Running Scrum Projects with Non-Agile Governance

Because few organizations will go so far initially as to completely revamp their current approaches to governance, teams will need ways to work with their organization's non-agile governance. Taking the following actions should help.

Negotiate and set expectations up front. Undoubtedly, the first Scrum project to go through the governance process in your company will have challenges. There will almost certainly be some things they cannot do; for example, a Scrum team cannot provide a thorough design before getting permission to start coding, because design and coding will be done concurrently. The only solution to this is for the team to negotiate with the necessary governance groups in advance. The more support a team has for this and the higher up in the organization that this support reaches, the better. The team does not need to solicit a permanent change in governance policies. The change can be pitched as a one-time experiment.

Fit your reporting to current expectations. The project review boards or oversight committees that provide project governance have existing expectations for what information each project is to provide at each checkpoint. Don't fight these expectations. If they expect a Gantt chart, provide a Gantt chart. When you can, however, try to slowly shift expectations by providing additional, more agile-friendly information. If burndown charts are suitable to show, do so. Or perhaps you want to include a report showing the number of times the build server kicked off continuously integrated builds and the thousands (or perhaps tens or hundreds of thousands) of test runs that were executed.

Invite them into your process. Scrum teams can supplement less-detailed formal governance checkpoints by inviting governance committee members to participate in the regular meetings they will hold. Teams at Yahoo! undergo a review by an architectural review committee. Gabrielle Benefield, former director of agile product development at Yahoo!, recalls how its early agile teams handled this.

> Agile teams…invited people from the architectural review committee to their sprint reviews early on. They then still had one formal checkpoint, but by then most major questions had been resolved. This was a lot less painful, and trust and collaboration [were] built earlier.

I like to extend the well-known technique of management by walking around into management by standing around. Encourage managers and executives involved in the governance of a project to attend the daily scrums, where they can stand and listen to what is occurring on the project. The same shift from documents to discussions that is created by working with user stories needs to occur with project reporting. Encourage people to visit the team or join its meetings to see for themselves what is being built.

Reference a success. Nothing convinces like success. Do whatever you can to get a first project or two through lightened or reduced governance checkpoints. Then point to the success of those projects as evidence that future projects should also be allowed through. Gabrielle Benefield points out that "once you get a few agile teams showing favorable results, you build trust. And you can then work on the larger overall governance process."

The concepts of agility and project governance are not fundamentally opposed. Each is an attempt to improve the finished product. Scrum strives to do this through close collaboration and the short inspect-and-adapt cycles of the time-boxed sprints. Project governance strives to do it by what we might call inspect-and-approve (or reject) checkpoints in which the product or project is compared to a set of desirable attributes. However, while pursuing similar goals, Scrum and project governance take entirely different routes to achieving those goals. It is in these different routes where problems will arise in mixing the two. Fortunately, a few compromises on each side, combined with the advice in this section, can lead to a successful combination of agility and oversight.

Compliance

Not every team or even software development department has the luxury of having complete control over its development process. For example, in outsourced, contract development, customers often mandate that suppliers be CMMI Level 5 certified, which requires those software developers to follow certain established best practices. Additionally, some software-intensive products are delivered into regulated industries and must comply with standards such as ISO 9001. Companies producing medically regulated devices must comply with ISO 13458. Publicly traded companies in the United States must comply with Sarbanes-Oxley. The list goes on.

None of these standards prescribes a life cycle that is completely at odds with Scrum. Some of them, however, come close, as they assume that a sequential process will be used. Because complying with standards such as these is rarely optional, Scrum teams must concern themselves with how best to comply, starting in some cases with the question of whether doing so will even be possible with a Scrum process. In this section we will look at how Scrum teams comply with ISO 9001 and CMMI, two of the more common standards with which Scrum teams have learned to coexist. From examining ISO 9001 and the CMMI, we can generalize some coping strategies useful in other compliance situations.

ISO 9001

The International Organization for Standardization (ISO) maintains standard 9001, which is usually fully designated as ISO 9001:2000 or ISO 9001:2008, both of which indicate the year of a specific version of the standard. ISO 9001 certification is not intended to guarantee that an organization's products achieve a specific quality level. Rather, ISO 9001 certification indicates that the organization follows a set of formal practices in developing its products. A large part of the effort in complying with ISO 9001 is the creation of a *quality management system*, which is usually a lengthy document or set of web pages that describes the quality practices followed by the organization.

Primavera Systems, developer of project and portfolio management systems, created its quality management system over a ten-month period. The company conducted 30 workshops to document its existing processes, and each workshop included a cross-functional representation of developers.

Primavera already had substantial experience with agile practices at the time it initiated its ISO 9001 effort. In such an environment it would be natural for employees to be concerned about a loss of agility with the introduction of ISO 9001. Bill McMichael, of Primavera, and Marc Lombardi, a consultant with expertise in ISO 9001, worked together on the initiative and found that the documentation did not diminish their agility.

> There were concerns about violating the principle of "working software over comprehensive documentation." Our mantra was to provide just enough documentation to be a useful reference and to help with enforcement of existing processes. (2007, 264)

Corroborating Primavera's experience of taking nearly a year to get to the point where it could pass an ISO 9001 certification audit is Graham Wright. A coach at Workshare in London, Wright was involved in his organization's successful ISO 9001 certification, which took a little over a year and began 13 months after Workshare adopted Extreme Programming. Wright reports that "in achieving certification no changes were made to our existing XP practices" (2003, 47).

My Experience with ISO 9001

These experiences with ISO 9001 match my own. In 2002 I managed a team of developers whose organization had decided to become ISO 9001 certified. Because my team was newer to Scrum than Primavera was at the time of its effort, I took a different approach and wrote the majority of our quality management system myself.

A few months before the official audit, we met with our auditor to familiarize him with how we built software and to learn his specific expectations of us. This being early 2002, he had never heard of Scrum, and none of us had prior experience with ISO 9001. As a result of that meeting we made a few process changes. The first was that he was adamant that he would not let us pass an audit with user stories written on index cards. The user story format was fine, but he insisted we produce a "document." We agreed to photocopy the user stories onto notebook-sized paper and store them in a binder with a sequence number on each user story. The second change was that while our informal design processes were fine, we would need to produce more design documentation. Our auditor suggested we take photos of the whiteboard after every design discussion and file these along with copies of any handwritten notes anyone had taken. We put a locking file cabinet in the team room and stored all design documentation there.

When our auditor returned, we passed his audit. What was most interesting about that visit was how impressed he was with our automated test processes. In addition to a build server doing continuous integration, we did an official nightly build that included thousands of tests, mostly written in JUnit. We showed the results of the last month of nightly builds; every night the build and all tests had completed successfully. As great as this team was, it was a bit fortunate to have not had a single failed test during that period. The auditor took one look at all those claims of successful tests and asked, "How do you know the tests aren't broken? Maybe they aren't running at all and your test harness just reports success." Well, we knew because inevitably there were test failures during the day. There just had not been any failures at night. But that wasn't good enough for our auditor, who insisted we include a failing test in every night's build. We added

```
assertTrue(false);
```

That test fails because false isn't true. Once we added our failing test we passed our ISO 9001 audit.

Although I don't think any of these steps helped us produce better software, they did not add significant ongoing overhead. Documenting everything about our process took time, but that was a one-time effort (with planned annual updates), and I bore the brunt of that for the team. Juan Gabardini, who has worked with Scrum in two ISO 9001-certified companies, concurs.

> There was overhead for the company, but for the team it wasn't so bad. I don't say it is painless! And you will need the help of an open-minded ISO consultant to help you keep everything as lean as possible but no leaner. (2008)

Capability Maturity Model Integration (CMMI)

Almost since the first agile project emerged from the primordial ooze, companies have been asking whether agile methodologies are compatible with the Software Engineering Institute's Capability Maturity Model Integration (CMMI). As a measure in some ways of how much process an organization has (or at least how much of it has been defined), the CMMI and its predecessor, the Software Capability Maturity Model (SW-CMM), are often viewed as heavyweight ways of developing software and the antithesis of agile development. Richard Turner, who was on the original team that wrote the CMMI, and professor Apurva Jain have said that "while there are significant differences, the 'oil and water' description of CMMI and agile approaches is somewhat overstated" (2002).

Turner is not the only one of the CMM authors to have considered its applicability on agile projects. Mark Paulk, lead author of the initial SW-CMM, assessed Extreme Programming against the 18 key process areas of the original SW-CMM. Paulk's opinion was that XP partially or largely addressed 10 of the 13 areas necessary to reach Level 3 and was not an obstacle to the other three.

> We can thus consider CMM and XP complementary. The SW-CMM tells organizations what to do in general terms but does not say how to do it. XP is a set of best practices that contains fairly specific how-to information—an implementation model—for a particular type of environment. XP practices can be compatible with CMM practices (goals or KPAs), even if they do not completely address them. (2001, 26)

Experience combining agile practices with CMMI is not only theoretical though. There are now many companies who have successfully combined agile development with the SW-CMM or the CMMI. Erik Bos and Christ Vriens of Philips Research led one of the first agile projects to be documented as undergoing a CMM audit. They say that their "assessors were especially impressed with the transparent, easily accessible, and uniform project information" (2004).

Joe Fecarotta, whose agile project was assessed as CMMI Level 3, also found CMMI and agile compatible. He says that "CMMI and the associated audits were not forcing a particular methodology but attempting to help the group follow best practices" (2008).

Agile methodologies like Scrum have also been introduced into organizations already assessed as CMMI Level 5. Systematic, an independent software developer in Denmark and the UK, employs over 400 people and develops software in the defense, healthcare, manufacturing, and services industries. After approximately two years at Level 5, it decided to also adopt Scrum. It reports that the two complemented each other well.

> Scrum now reduces every category of work (defects, rework, total work required, and process overhead) by almost 50% compared to our previous CMMI Level 5 implementation while maintaining the same level of process discipline. (Sutherland, Jakobsen, and Johnson 2007, 273)

The incorporation of Scrum into Systematic's CMMI Level 5 process shows a solution to a common problem with CMMI implementations. In pursuing a particular CMMI level, many organizations forget that the ultimate goal is to improve how they build software (and presumably, therefore, the products they deliver). They instead become focused on filling in supposed deficiencies according to CMMI documentation without concern for whether the changes will improve the process or its products. This problem can be eliminated when CMMI goals are combined with the value-focused, "what-have-you-done-for-me-lately" mindset inherent in Scrum. Jeff Sutherland, Carsten Jakobsen, and Kent Johnson, who were all involved in Systematics' adoption of Scrum, refer to the combination of Scrum and CMMI as a "magic potion."

> When mixing the two, a magic potion emerges, where...Scrum ensures that the processes are implemented efficiently while embracing change, and CMMI ensures that all relevant processes are considered. (2007, 272)

Achieving Compliance

We've firmly established that Scrum is compatible with at least ISO 9001 and CMMI, on both theoretical and empirical grounds. Let's turn our attention to specific things that you can do to successfully combine them with Scrum in your organization:

- **Put enough effort into your product backlog.** A common thread running through projects with compliance requirements is that they all benefitted from putting effort into their product backlogs. They didn't feel the need to fully elaborate all product requirements up front, but teams that invested in a well-formed product backlog that could be progressively refined with more detail, as described in Chapter 13, "The Product Backlog," found that doing so contributed to meeting their compliance goals.

- **Put compliance work on the product backlog.** If a document or other artifact needs to be produced to achieve compliance, put the work to produce it on the product backlog. Not only does this ensure the work isn't forgotten, but it also keeps the cost of compliance visible.

- **Consider the use of checklists.** A number of projects reported that the use of checklists was helpful. It is important that checklists not introduce new mandatory steps. Instead, checklists should include steps the team already does and should exist only to prove to an auditor or appraiser that the activities are being performed. As an example, Systematic, the CMMI Level 5 company mentioned earlier, used a one-page story completion checklist that started with whether the story had been estimated and ended with the story being integrated into the system. A team's definition of done, as described in Chapter 14, "Sprints," could easily be turned into a checklist.

- **Automate.** Build and test automation are important to the success of any Scrum project. They are doubly so for projects with compliance requirements.

- **Use an agile project management tool.** Traceability is an important consideration for most compliance standards. As much as I prefer tangible artifacts—handwritten index cards and big, visible charts hanging on walls—an agile project management tool should at least be considered by teams with compliance requirements.

- **Move slowly but steadily.** You probably cannot overhaul a significant process element, such as an ISO 9001 quality systems manual, overnight. So, do what Scrum teams do best: Do it incrementally. Gradually revise the quality systems manual to be more agile. Because much of ISO 9001 is about making sure a company follows its own quality system, the company can revise its quality system to support Scrum.

- **Work with your auditor.** Whenever possible, meet your auditor in advance. Have an informal discussion about how you develop software, and ask the auditor to point out any red flags. When possible, work with experienced auditors who understand that just because the process might be strikingly different does not mean it cannot achieve the goals of the standard.

- **Bring in outside help.** If you have not been through a certification attempt of the type you are after, bring in an outside consultant who has. If you are not yet adept at Scrum, bring in an experienced ScrumMaster. Having or bringing in expertise on both fronts is critical.

SEE ALSO

The website www.userstories.com offers reviews of agile project management tools.

Onward

Scrum will rarely be implemented in a pristine environment with no intrusions from the outside real world. In this chapter we looked at three different types of intrusions: the need to work with another sequentially managed project (or to run part of the Scrum project in a sequential manner); the need to work within a corporate governance system; and the need to comply with laws, regulations, or standards. In the next chapter, we continue looking at challenges to succeeding with Scrum. We look at some of the ways Scrum teams and projects can be affected by other groups or departments in the organization, including facilities, human resources, and the project management office.

Additional Reading

Boehm, Barry, and Richard Turner. 2005. Management challenges to implementing agile processes in traditional development organizations. *IEEE Software*, September/October, 30–39.

> In 1988, Boehm presented the spiral model, one of the first valid alternatives to a waterfall process. In this book, along with coauthor Turner, he presents the view that agile and "disciplined" processes exist along a continuum and may be mixed as needed based on the specific risk factors of a project.

Glazer, Hillel, Jeff Dalton, David Anderson, Mike Konrad, and Sandy Shrum. 2008. *CMMI or agile: Why not embrace both!* Software Engineering Institute at Carnegie Mellon, November. http://www.sei.cmu.edu/pub/documents/08.reports/08tn003.pdf.

> This white paper presents the opinion that CMMI best practices and agile methodologies are not at odds with one another and that the approaches can be successfully combined.

McMichael, Bill, and Marc Lombardi. 2007. ISO 9001 and agile development. In *Proceedings of the Agile 2007 Conference*, ed. Jutta Eckstein, Frank Maurer, Rachel Davies, Grigori Melnik, and Gary Pollice, 262–265. IEEE Computer Society.

> This short experience report provides specific advice on how Primavera added ISO 9001 to its existing Scrum process.

Paulk, Mark. 2001. Extreme programming from a CMM perspective. *IEEE Software*, November, 19–26.

> This 2001 article is a bit dated, as it compares Extreme Programming to the now-replaced CMM. However, as it is by the lead author of the CMM, his opinions are still well worth reading.

Sliger, Michele. 2006. Bridging the gap: Agile projects in the waterfall enterprise. *Better Software*, July/August, 26–31.

> This article presents the view that agile and waterfall processes can coexist in organizations. It provides specific advice for doing waterfall up front, at the end, or concurrent with an agile process.

Sutherland, Jeff, Carsten Ruseng Jakobsen, and Kent Johnson. 2007. Scrum and CMMI level 5: The magic potion for code warriors. In *Proceedings of the Agile 2007 Conference*, ed. Jutta Eckstein, Frank Maurer, Rachel Davies, Grigori Melnik, and Gary Pollice, 272–278. IEEE Computer Society.

> This report about a highly productive project presents the claim that the combination of Scrum and CMMI is more powerful than either is alone, and includes guidelines for mixing Scrum and CMMI.

Chapter 20

Human Resources, Facilities, and the PMO

To achieve long-term success with Scrum, the implications of becoming agile must be transferred into other parts of the organization. When this is not done, organizational gravity—those influences that formed the organization into whatever shape it existed in before the start of the transition—will kick in. I have seen Scrum transitions stalled or completely stopped because they ignored the impact of becoming agile on groups outside development. Doing so results in situations like these:

- **Human resources.** Scrum teams start out doing extremely well until annual review time comes around. Suddenly, everyone realizes they will again be assessed, and receive raises, based entirely on individual performance. The annual review might have one field for assessing whether an individual plays well with others, but at the end of the day individual contributions and heroics bring home the raises and promotions.

- **The facilities group.** It's much easier to be agile when the whole team sits together. But when a facilities group makes that difficult, or when it prevents teams from using wall space for burndown charts and other important project data, teams become demoralized. It becomes harder to continue the push toward becoming better at Scrum when it feels like everyone is against you.

- **The project management office (PMO).** Without thinking about how its project relates to an existing PMO, a Scrum team kicks off with a "damn the paperwork and process" attitude. This creates an enemy out of the PMO, a group that was already uneasy about the organization's initial, tentative experiments with Scrum. The PMO responds by convincing departmental management that Scrum is OK as long as it is supplemented by a crushing set of documents and practices.

When Scrum is mistakenly viewed solely as a change within the development group, the organizational gravity created by the departments outside of IT can pull the development group right back where it started. In this chapter we look at things you can do to help your organization's transition effort achieve sufficient escape velocity to break free. In particular, we look at the impact of Scrum on the three groups mentioned—human resources, facilities, and the project management office.

Human Resources

Many of the issues involving the HR group are the result of a change to shared accountability. In *The Wisdom of Teams*, Katzenbach and Smith describe why this is difficult.

> Most organizations intrinsically prefer individual over group (team) accountability. Job descriptions, compensation schemes, career paths, and performance evaluations focus on individuals.... Our culture emphasizes individual accomplishments and makes us uncomfortable trusting our career aspirations to outcomes dependent on the performance of others.... Even the thought of shifting emphasis from individual accountability to team accountability makes us uneasy. (1993, 3–4)

As an example, consider the case of Chuck. When I told Chuck and his teammates that I wanted them to try pair programming for a few sprints, Chuck stood up, said, "I'm going to HR about this," and left the sprint retrospective. What was he going to do? Have me fired? I wasn't even an employee, so I was totally confused. The looks on the faces of the rest of the team showed they were equally perplexed, but we continued the meeting.

Later that morning, and before I had a chance to talk to Chuck so I could understand his perspective, I got a call from Ursula, the company's human resources director, asking me to come by her office. Our discussion was the first of a handful of nearly identical discussions I've had since then at other companies. Chuck had gone to Ursula complaining that if the team instituted pair programming, he would be unfairly penalized. Chuck, who was one of the better and more quality-conscious programmers, explained to Ursula that his annual pay raises historically had been above average because he had consistently written the best code in the group. If pair programming were introduced, he said, his manager would be unable to adequately review him because it would be impossible to know which code was Chuck's and which code was someone else's. As a result, Chuck argued, his raises would be unfairly dragged down. Ursula bought the argument and told me that I would not be allowed to have developers write code in pairs because it would hide performance problems and result in unfair reviews.

Because of situations like this one and employees like Chuck, some of the thorniest issues you'll encounter will be those related to human resources policies. Employees in that department can be either a significant help or a hindrance with these problems. In this section we look at human resources issues you might encounter involving reporting structures, periodic performance reviews, handling performance problems, and determining career paths.

Reporting Structures

There is no one reporting structure that must be used to be successful with Scrum. I have seen functional, project-oriented, and matrixed organizations each be successful. A matrixed organization will be prone to more challenges, but that should not be surprising to an organization that has chosen that structure for its other benefits. So, although I won't argue strongly in favor of a specific type of organizational structure, I will say that the organization should be as flat as possible. The more layers there are between team members and the top of the company, the more opportunities there are for dysfunctionality to creep in.

Reporting to the ScrumMaster

When discussing management layers, questions often arise about whether team members can report to their ScrumMaster. Common advice is that this is a bad idea. I'm going to deviate from this common advice and say that I am not strongly opposed to having team members report to their ScrumMaster. My view might come from having been both a ScrumMaster and boss for years in small organizations in which we couldn't afford to separate those roles. Or it might be a result of my hiring exceptional individuals who could fill both roles.

The usual objection is that a team member who reports to the ScrumMaster will not speak freely during daily scrums. A developer will not, for example, mention an impediment out of fear that the impediment will later be mentioned in a performance review. Of course this is a risk. But it is easily mitigated by having ScrumMasters who understand the implications of using voiced impediments as ammunition. Further, there are some benefits to a team whose ScrumMaster is also their boss, including that such a person is sometimes better able to remove some types of impediments.

Are there some ScrumMasters to whom I would not want team members to report? Absolutely. In fact, I prefer that team members report to functional managers rather than to their ScrumMaster. However, in the pantheon of agile sins, having team members report to their ScrumMaster is a minor one—if the right ScrumMaster is in place.

Reporting to the Product Owner

Considering my willingness to allow the team members to report to their Scrum-Master, you might be surprised to learn that I strongly advise against them reporting to their product owner. The difference is that in healthy teams there is a natural tension between the product owner and the team. It is part of a product owner's job to push for more features and faster delivery. A good team would always love to deliver more faster. But it also needs to sometimes push back against a product owner's demands if it feels that doing so would harm the internal quality of the product. I find that when the team reports to their product owner, the natural tension that should exist evaporates. It's one thing for team members to sometimes resist a product owner's pressure for more; it's another for them to do so when the product owner is also their boss.

For the same reasons, it would be unwise to have the ScrumMaster report to the product owner. The ScrumMaster and product owner do not need to be peers on the company's org chart, but they should treat each other as peers and partners on the project.

Periodic Performance Reviews

Many people have called for organizations to abolish the annual merit rating system. I've argued for this with various human resources groups but have only won the argument in very small organizations, where the human resources director was probably too busy to institute annual reviews anyway. So, rather than just advise you to rail against a practice you probably can't eliminate, let's look at the impact of periodic performance reviews on your Scrum teams and explore ways you can minimize the negative impact and accentuate the positive.

Try to eliminate most individual factors from assessments. It is no surprise that individuals will behave in accordance with what is valued during their performance reviews. I'm looking at an old review form right now. It asks me to rate the employee on "the degree to which the individual effectively manages tasks within budget and timeline." How would you anticipate someone to behave in regard to this factor if it were something he was rated poorly on the last time? Would the person be responsive to coworker requests for assistance? Probably not. Individual assessment factors lead to individual-focused behavior. We want instead to encourage people to do what is most beneficial for the team and product. In many western cultures, eliminating all individual performance factors from reviews will also meet resistance from many team members. In such situations, try instead perhaps for a 50/50 split between individual and team factors.

Include teamwork factors. Most performance reviews have a section for the manager to indicate whether the employee plays well with others. A useful review needs to go beyond that to establish the teamwork focus we want. Consider the case in which employees are assessed on whether each "effectively manages tasks within budget and timeline." An initial improvement might be to change that to "helps the team finish tasks within budget and timeline." But even this does not go far enough because "helps the team finish" is still an individual measure. The factor here should be "the team effectively manages its work within budget and timeline," and everyone on the team should get the same rating.

"Teams might function as a unit, but they are made up of individuals. When we ask one of the individuals on my team to help, she always says, 'Tough luck. I'm done with my stuff,'" and goes back to surfing the web. Someone else usually steps up and does whatever needs to be done. But it would be demotivating to get the same rating as she gets."

I'm sure that would be demotivating. Someone needs to talk to this person about the effect her attitude is having on the team. Ideally, the full team has the courage to do this in a sprint retrospective. If not, the Scrum-Master should coach her about how her attitude is affecting others. Additionally, since part of the review will almost certainly be based on individual performance factors, there should be ample opportunity to include this performance problem in the review.

Review performance much more often than annually. Employees and their managers should meet as often as they can, of course, for informal discussions about performance, expectations, and objectives. But, if you're going to do formal performance appraisals at all, you need to do them much more often than once a year. Although this is true even for non-agile organizations, it becomes critical when using Scrum because Scrum projects move more quickly, and employees are learning new skills and ways of working, especially in the first year or two.

Solicit input into the review from a broad set of people. When you sit down to write a periodic performance review, it is extremely unlikely that you know all there is to know about the person's performance. So, solicit feedback from others, and do so broadly. A functional manager should ask for comments from the employee's ScrumMaster, product owner, some team members, some peers in the functional group, and some users or customers the person has worked with. I usually select a handful of contributors for each review and e-mail them asking that they tell me what the employee could start doing, stop doing, or continue doing that would improve his performance. I then look for common threads through the responses and from them try to formulate actionable suggestions.

Educate and engage the human resources group. Many of the changes we've discussed require the participation or approval of your HR group. But, beyond that, actively seek to educate them about what changes are afoot in the development organization. If you're doing a half-day training session on Scrum, ask someone from HR to attend. Gabrielle Benefield did this while director of agile product development at Yahoo!. The senior HR representative who attended her training was so intrigued that the HR department began using Scrum to manage its own project of updating the annual review process. Benefield describes the results.

> Using Scrum, they completed the project on time, and it was successful. They loved the rhythm of the iterations and meeting frequently to keep up to date on progress as the team was distributed and interrupt-driven.

Removing Team Members

When I saw Derek walking toward me at the conference, I was thrilled. I had first met him a year earlier when I taught a class at his company. I had been back a handful of times, and I always enjoyed talking to him, but we hadn't talked in three months. I thought this would be a good chance to catch up. As we said hello, I could tell something was really bothering him, so we sat down to talk. Derek told me that at his team's sprint review the week before, the team members had decided to ask him to resign as their ScrumMaster and to leave the team. He had done so and was looking around within his company to find another Scrum team to join. But the shock of being asked to leave had not yet worn off.

Although rare, Derek's situation is not unheard of. The question of whether the team has the authority to remove someone from the team is a common topic. Commonly referred to as "voting someone off the island," removing a team member is not an action to be considered lightly. Before such measures are taken, efforts should be made to address problems that lead some or all team members to feel that they might be better off without one of their members.

A team alone should not have the right to remove someone from the team. If we think back to Chapter 12, "Leading a Self-Organizing Team," you will recall that self-organization does not occur in a vacuum. The right preconditions must be in place for self-organization to occur. Individuals then self-organize within boundaries established by the organization. This was referred to as the CDE model, which says that for self-organization to occur there must be a container that bounds the individuals, some differences among them, and transforming exchanges. Chapter 12 also made the point that leaders within the organization exert influence on the self-organizing team by adjusting its containers, differences, and exchanges. For example, over time and through attrition a team might have become too homogeneous. An astute product owner, functional manager, or even ScrumMaster might counter that by adding two new team members with radically different backgrounds, skills, decision-making styles, or so on.

Doesn't it seem possible—likely even, in this example—that a team might have a knee-jerk reaction and vote the new, nonconforming individuals off the team, negating the work of the leader who deliberately added them? Ultimate authority for team composition, therefore, must reside with the leadership of the organization. Those leaders should listen, of course, when team members say they think they'd be more productive without a member. But, team members should not be allowed on their own to remove someone from the team.

Career Paths

Although some employees might be worried about being voted off the team, others will be more worried about the next step in their careers. In most organizations, it has historically been easy to see one's career path. You developed a reasonable level of technical proficiency, became a team leader over a small group of similarly skilled individuals, then a manager, a senior manager, and so on. At each level up that ladder, you lost a little technical proficiency but had more names under yours on the org chart. The number of people reporting to you could be directly correlated to your importance in the organization.

With the flattening of the organizational chart brought about by Scrum and the elimination of some roles or titles, many employees will wonder what their new career path will be. They will want to know what type of work they'll be doing down the road and how they (and everyone else) will know that their work has become more valuable. After an organization adopts Scrum, a person's success can no longer be measured by how many people report to him. It can, however, be measured by how much responsibility the person is given. A new ScrumMaster might, for example, be given responsibility for one small, perhaps mature, team. After successfully handling that situation, this ScrumMaster might work with a different team that has no Scrum experience and is on a more important project. This might continue until our ScrumMaster is working with multiple teams, leading a ScrumMaster community of practice, and so on.

This same career path (success on one project leads to increased responsibility on the next) applies to all roles on a Scrum team, including programmers, testers, designers, and so on. Early in her career, a programmer might be assigned to a team to do little more than code. Later, that programmer might be assigned to another team because we want others to learn from her experience with high-availability websites. Later again, she might be put on a particular team because her problem-solving and interpersonal skills will be needed. Success leads to increased responsibility.

This attitude is prevalent at SAS, a privately owned software development company with over 4,000 employees. SAS has been in the top 20 of *Fortune* magazine's Best Companies to Work For list every year the list has been published. An article in the *Harvard Business Review* describes the motivational culture at SAS.

SAS operates on the belief that invigorating mental work leads to superior performance and, ultimately, better products. It does not try to bribe workers with stock options; it has never offered them. At SAS, the most fitting thanks for a job well done is an even more challenging project. (Florida and Goodnight 2005, 126)

OBJECTION

"But wait, if teams are self-organizing, how is responsibility for problem solving or designing a system for high availability given to one person?"

Responsibility isn't given to one person; it remains with the team. But leaders can communicate their increased expectations of one team member: "We need you on this team because of your interpersonal skills. We remember how you defused that issue between Francois and James a year ago, and we might have similar conflicts on this team." There is nothing that implies that a leader's expectations of someone or reasons for putting someone on a team must remain a secret. They might in an example such as this one. But when someone is put on a team because of a particular technical skill, there is no reason not to share that with the full team.

With People Involved, There Will Always Be People Issues

Because software development is an inherently human-intensive activity, there will be people problems. It's impossible to identify all of them in advance. Those covered here are the ones you are most likely to encounter. Other personnel problems that arise can hopefully be tackled by adhering to the same principles underlying the actions proposed for the obstacles in this section.

THINGS TO TRY NOW

❑ Meet with someone in your human resources or personnel department. Briefly explain what Scrum is and why your department or team is adopting it. Explain the conflicts you foresee with existing personnel policies. Ask if this person can anticipate any others. Ask for help in mitigating these situations.

Facilities

Any team that has tried to do Scrum in an inappropriate workspace knows how difficult it can be. An ideal workspace will support team members as they learn to work in an agile manner. Unfortunately, there are many less-than-ideal workspaces that actually impede a team's efforts. In fact, a team's physical workspace can have so much influence on how it works that Gerald Weinberg has asked, "Who is the most important process person? The one who arranges the furniture" (Dinwiddie 2007, 208).

A team's physical environment can have so much influence on how agile the team can become that in the second edition of *Extreme Programming Explained*, Kent Beck and Cynthia Andres elevated an "Informative Workspace" to the level of a primary practice (2004). Given the influence that a team's physical environment can have on its ability to be agile, in this section we will consider two aspects of that environment: the physical space and the furniture in the space.

The Space

The traditional high-tech office with six-foot (nearly two meter) high cubicle walls is a definite impediment to collaboration. The most common replacement for it among teams that have had input into designing their workspaces is what commercial interior designers call "caves and commons." This approach combines small, quiet places (caves) with common areas.

A typical pre-Scrum caves-and-commons approach might have included a dedicated cubicle for each employee and a central area containing perhaps a pair of couches, a white board, and a bookshelf. The idea was that employees would meet in the commons area for spontaneous discussions. When given the chance, Scrum teams take this idea but shift the ratio of caves to common space far in favor of common space. A Scrum caves-and-commons workspace will typically forgo the cubicles altogether and feature a large common work area surrounded by a couple of small offices or meeting rooms that can be used by anyone.

The Scrum teams at 3M had this to say about their switch to an open work environment: "We have found an open area wonderful in encouraging impromptu collaboration. Team members can quickly see if other team members are available." The collaborative spirit and energy inherent in an open area, they say, has energized the team. They conclude: "Designing a team room focused on collaboration has been beneficial to implementing a Scrum work environment and has improved the focus and cohesiveness of the team" (Moore et al. 2007, 176).

A further benefit to this type of open work environment is the ease with which the layout of the area can be changed. As the people on the team are learning how best to work with one another, they often experiment with different arrangements in the space. Additionally, as teams change size, it is beneficial to have the flexibility to reconfigure an open workspace to better accommodate the needs of the team.

OBJECTION	**"I don't want to work in a shared space. It's too noisy; I need quiet to concentrate."**

There are indeed times on a software project where absolute quiet and pure concentration is needed. There are more times where collaboration, discussion, and shared knowledge and understanding are crucial. When someone really does need quiet, retreating into a cave should be an option respected by the team. Alternatively, although headphones should generally be frowned upon, they can be an acceptable option if used sparingly and only when absolute concentration is needed.

Fortunately, most people find that the benefits of more frequent interaction with their teammates outweighs an increase in noise. This was the experience of Syed Rayhan and Nimat Haque.

> Surprisingly, the team liked the open space concept from the beginning. We did not have any [trouble] convincing them. Some of them though were apprehensive whether they would be able to concentrate on their tasks due to close proximity and overcommunication. However, they found that the interaction actually helped them resolve issues faster and allowed them to learn from each other. Now they agree that the cubicles are counterproductive and they would not want to have it any other way. (2008, 354)

The War Room Becomes the Whole Space

Before adopting Scrum, many teams used to lust after a "war room," which was a conference room the team was given permission to occupy and use for all of its meetings. A dedicated war room becomes less necessary for a Scrum team because its entire open workspace becomes the war room. Daily scrums and other meetings are often held in the openness of the team's space rather than in a conference room.

One benefit of the traditional war room was that it provided a convenient place for unscheduled meetings to occur. Four team members who suddenly decide to have an extended discussion about an issue could simply walk into the war room without scheduling a meeting on a shared calendar. Because the room belonged to the team, it would almost certainly be available when needed. Scrum teams still require a place for spontaneous meetings. But while this is sometimes still a small conference room dedicated to a team (or shared among a small number of Scrum teams), it is just as often a small table situated in the middle of the team's open workspace. Whether impromptu meeting space is behind a door or in the shared space depends largely on the team's preference for hearing all discussions (and being able to opt into or out of them) versus moving lengthy discussions behind a door to keep the space a bit more quiet.

If you are going to take on the work of reconfiguring space to create a large, open area, make sure to include enough room for everyone on the team, including the ScrumMaster and ideally even the product owner. There is nothing worse than collocating all but a handful of team members. Having the designers, for example, sit apart from others will cause resentment. Worse, while team members sitting together bond because of their proximity, those sitting apart will begin to feel like outsiders on their own project.

This is not to say that an entire 100-person project, comprising perhaps a dozen teams, must sit in one extremely large open space. For large projects, the most common, successful approach is to create multiple open areas that can each comfortably house 20 or so people. Three or four teams who are working together can then share such an area. When doing this, be careful to have people sit with their Scrum development teams rather than with their functional teams. Avoid, for example, having all the programmers in the company sit together in a different part of the building than the testers.

Executive Sponsorship Is Helpful

It is, of course, the ScrumMaster's job to remove any impediments to productivity. And a workspace that hinders communication and teamwork is a definite impediment. However, a ScrumMaster will often need help from the Enterprise Transition Community or an executive in making improvements to the workspace. Scrum trainer Gabrielle Benefield found this to be the case when she led Yahoo!'s transition to Scrum.

> An executive sponsor is pretty critical in working with Facilities, as they tend to be very set in their own process and bureaucracy and have a lot of power. You get told no a lot; you just need to keep chipping away and seeing what you can get away with. Some teams were more proactive and simply removed furniture themselves (against company policy) and sometimes got away with it, sometimes not. This is where you need an upper manager to help remove these impediments, as it can be difficult for team members to do this and not jeopardize their jobs. When you get told no you need to find out the real reason behind the answer. Sometimes it's financial, in which case, see if there's a cheaper approach or if you can secure funding some other way. If it's a fire policy, this is pretty much impossible to change. If it's time or resources, see if you can do it yourselves.

"I don't want to give up my cubicle, especially now that I've been here long enough to have a premium spot with a window."

A common challenge when transitioning to Scrum is that those who have benefitted from doing traditional software development often have to give up the most. Those who have earned nice big titles become simply "team members." Those with cubicles—or worse yet, offices—with nice big windows have to move into a shared, common workspace. In many cases, fancy titles and more desirable cubicles have become status symbols within the organization. And those with them are understandably reluctant to give them up.

Sometimes an appeal that "we're doing this for the common good" will work. Other times, a better approach is to agree that life isn't fair, but that if the transition to Scrum is successful, the organization will be more successful, which will provide everyone with better opportunities, such as more challenging and interesting projects.

The Furniture

Some teams get very creative with their furniture and are fortunate to be given the budget to go with big ideas. A common approach for teams in this situation is to combine movable desks with a large open workspace. This allows teams to form workspaces in whatever arrangements they see fit. Some teams will prefer to sit facing each other across two-deep desks. Other teams find it unsettling to look at someone else's face all day and prefer to arrange desks with team members' backs to one another. Beyond providing the ultimate in ad hoc reconfigurability, movable desks send a powerful message to the team: it literally reinforces the idea that they are to organize themselves—and their workspace—to best develop the product or system they have been asked to produce.

Probably more important than movable desks is the shape and width of the work surfaces. Most good Scrum teams will eventually incorporate some amount of pair programming (or, more generally, pairing of any two team members). Even if they choose to pair on only the most critical tasks, the process can be made much more feasible with an appropriate work surface. Small or curved work surfaces make it difficult for two people to work side-by-side at the same monitor. The problem is made worse when only one person can put his or her legs under the desk.

Sweating the Small Stuff

Attention must be paid even to items much smaller than desks. Phones are a common source of problems. Although it might be easy for a team member to roll a desk from one location to another or to pack and unpack a desk, changing where the phone rings always seems far harder than it should be. Some companies try to get around this with VoIP phones. But the teams that I've talked to that have tried this generally report having many of the same problems.

John Cornell, director of agile development at Kofax, experienced an entirely different problem with phones when introducing an open workspace.

> The initial plans for the first open space called for office phones that would be shared amongst team members, replacing the individual phones that each person previously had in their cubes. Management did not think this would be an issue as everyone has mobile phone these days and the vast majority of technical staff do not receive business-related calls. The staff strongly felt otherwise. They saw the office phones as critical. Once again, the team members felt that management was inhibiting their ability to be productive.

I'm confident that some of those developers did not have landlines at home and relied entirely on their mobile phones from there. But, I also suspect that some of the team members would have felt like second-class citizens without their phones. Although this was certainly not the message that management intended to send the team, it is easy to see how it would be interpreted that way.

Where Everyone Sits

Where people sit within a shared, open workspace is usually less critical than it is when everyone works in a cubicle. With fewer cubicle walls, everyone can enjoy the view. Frequent pairing keeps people from sitting in the same place all day. And the ability to move from one part of the open space to another (even without movable desks) decreases the sense of permanence.

As the protector of the team, the ScrumMaster often sits closest to the main entry into the team area. Agile coach George Dinwiddie recalls one team where the team's manager/ScrumMaster acted as a watchdog for the team. One of the developers referred to it as the manager's "Doberman impression," so called "because he'd abruptly interrupt his work to halt and interrogate anyone entering the room" (2007, 208). If the manager could provide the needed information, he did so, and the team was protected from an interruption. If not, and the need was genuine, the visitor was granted access to the team's area.

Items That Should Be Visible in Your Workspace

Now that we've considered both the space and furniture of a good Scrum workspace, this section contains a checklist of things that should be visible within the ideal agile workspace.

- **Big, Visible Charts.** A good Scrum team will fill its workspace with a variety of big, visible charts. One of the most common is the sprint burndown chart, showing the number of hours remaining as of each day of the current sprint. Charts like these provide a strong visual reminder of the current state of the project. What is shown on these charts will get the attention of team members, so consider varying the information to showcase what is most important for that sprint. Ron Jeffries suggests a variety of charts, including ones that show the number of passing customer acceptance tests, the pass/fail status of tests by day, sprint and release burndown charts, number of new stories introduced to the product backlog per sprint, and more (2004a).

- **Additional feedback devices.** In addition to big, visible charts, it is common for a Scrum team to use additional visual feedback devices in their workspace. One of the most common is a lava lamp that is turned on whenever the automated build is broken. I've also worked with teams that use flashing red traffic lights to indicate exceptional conditions, such as an issue on a production server. LED signs can be programmed to display messages from Twitter. Also popular are ambient orbs and Nabaztag rabbits, which are wireless programmable devices that can also be configured to change colors, speak messages, or wiggle their ears as a team desires. Software architect Johannes Brodwall exhibits the agile preference for simple solutions and recommends using USB-connected devices, such as those from Delcom, which he has used to monitor testing, staging, and production servers (2008). Devices like these make a workspace more lively, unobtrusively bringing into it information the team might find helpful.

- **Everyone on your team.** Each person on the team should ideally be able to see every other person on the team. This absolutely includes the ScrumMaster and ideally includes the product owner. I do understand, however, that product owners often have responsibilities to other groups outside the development team and so might sit near them instead. Still, in an ideal world the product owner would be visible to everyone in the team workspace.

- **The sprint backlog.** One of the best ways to ensure that everything necessary is completed in the sprint is to make the sprint backlog visible. The best way to do that is by displaying the sprint backlog on a wall, ideally in the form of a task board. A task board is usually oriented in rows and columns, with each row containing a particular user story and one index card or sticky note for each task involved in that story. An example can be seen in Figure 20.1. Task cards are organized in columns, minimally including *To Do*, *In Process*, and *Done*.[1] Task boards allow team members to see at a glance how work is progressing and all the work left to be done.

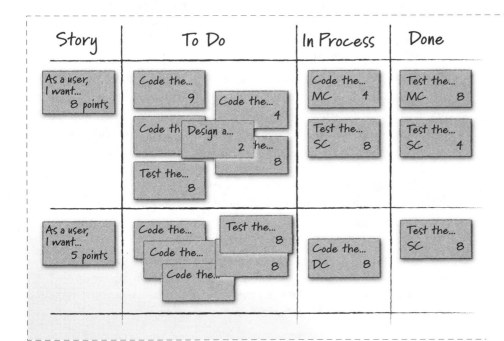

FIGURE 20.1

A task board makes the sprint backlog highly visible.

- **The product backlog.** One problem with running an endless series of sprints is that each can feel disconnected or isolated from the whole of a planned released or related set of new capabilities. A good way to reduce the impact of this problem is by displaying the product backlog somewhere clearly visible. This can be as simple as keeping the shoebox full of user-story index cards on a table in the middle of the team's space. Even better, tack the index cards of upcoming user stories on a wall where all can see them. This allows team members to see how the user stories they are working on in the current sprint relate to others that are coming soon.

- **At least one big whiteboard.** Every team needs at least one big whiteboard. Locating this in the team's common workspace encourages spontaneous meetings. One developer might start using the board to think through a problem; others might notice and offer to help.

- **Someplace quiet and private.** As important as open communication is, there are times when someone needs some peace and quiet. Sometimes this is for something as simple as a private phone call. Other times it can be to think through a particularly challenging problem without being interrupted.

---

1   For photos of various task boards, see http://www.succeedingwithagile.com.

- **Food and drink.** It's always a good idea to have food and drink available. These don't need to be fancy, and they don't even need to be provided by the organization. I've worked with plenty of teams that buy a small under-desk refrigerator and share the expense of buying water bottles or soda for it. Other teams buy a coffee machine. Some teams rotate bringing in snacks, both healthful and not.

- **A window.** Windows are often a scarce commodity and are doled out to an organization's favored employees. One of the nice things about an open workspace is that windows are shared. Even if the view is of the parking lot and can only be seen across three messy desks, it's nice to be able to see the window and some natural light.

THINGS TO TRY NOW

❑ Make a prioritized list of things about the team's physical workspace that could be affecting its productivity. Solicit support from your Enterprise Transition Community. See if someone from that group will go talk to the facilities group with you.

❑ If there are things you can do to improve your team's workspace without seeking permission first, do them. Be careful to avoid blocking fire lanes or violating other laws, but often an act-then-ask approach results in at least a few improvements.

The Project Management Office

A project management office (PMO) that is engaged in and supportive of transitioning to Scrum can be a tremendous boon. Members of the PMO often view themselves as protectors and supporters of a practice, so a PMO can help implement and spread agile practices across the organization. However, when the PMO is not properly involved, it can be a source of resistance as it tries to defend the current process, rather than improve it.

One of the reasons why the natural response of most people in the PMO is to resist the change to Scrum is that much of it is personally and professionally frightening. Scrum scatters traditional project management responsibilities among the ScrumMaster, product owner, and the team, leaving project managers to wonder what their role is. The absence of the PMO in most Scrum and agile literature adds to the natural concerns of PMO members.

SEE ALSO

The role of the project manager was addressed in Chapter 8, "Changed Roles."

In this section, we will ease those fears by looking at the type of work performed by PMOs in organizations that have successfully transitioned to Scrum. We will look at the contributions and work of the PMO in three areas: people, projects, and process.

People

Although it's called the *Project* Management Office, the PMO has tremendous influence on the people involved in a Scrum transition. An agile PMO should do the following:

- **Develop a training program.** There is much to adopting Scrum that will be new and unfamiliar to many team members. The PMO can be a tremendous aid in putting together a training program, selecting outside trainers to deliver the training, or delivering the training themselves.
- **Provide coaching.** Beyond training people, individual and small-group coaching is incredibly helpful. In a training class, the instructor says, "Here's how to do a sprint planning meeting," for example, and perhaps runs the class through an exercise to practice it. With coaching, someone with deep experience sits with the team and helps them through their own real sprint planning meeting (or whatever skill is being coached). Early on, members of the PMO might not have these skills themselves, but they should focus on acquiring them from outside coaches and then do the hands-on coaching themselves.
- **Select and train coaches.** A successful Scrum initiative will eventually lead to more coaching needs than the PMO can fill on its own. The PMO should identify and develop coaches by watching the teams they help and then providing training or assistance to help selected individuals become skilled coaches. These coaches usually retain their current jobs but are given additional responsibilities, such as spending up to five hours per week helping a specific team.
- **Challenge existing behaviors.** When the organization begins to adopt Scrum, the members of the PMO look for teams who are falling back into old habits or whose old habits are preventing them from becoming agile. Later, members of the PMO can remind teams that Scrum is about continuous improvement and can help prevent the onset of complacency.

SEE ALSO

Coaches, such as described here, can play a vital role in spreading Scrum. For one way to use them, see "Internal Coaching" in Chapter 3, "Patterns for Adopting Scrum."

Projects

Although some project-oriented responsibilities go away with the change to an agile PMO, some responsibilities remain, including the following:

- **Assist with reporting.** In most organizations large enough to have a PMO, there is usually something like a weekly report or meeting on the status of each project with the department head. If this is a meeting, it should be attended by appropriate project personnel, such as the product owner or ScrumMaster. But if it is a weekly standardized status report, the PMO can assist in preparing the report.

SEE ALSO

Compliance was discussed in Chapter 19, "Coexisting with Other Approaches."

- **Assist with compliance needs.** Many projects need to comply with standards (ISO 9001, Sarbanes-Oxley, and so on) or with organization-specific rules, such as those for data security. An agile PMO can assist teams by making them aware of such needs, advising them on how to comply, and serving as a central clearinghouse for tips and shared knowledge on compliance and similar matters.
- **Manage the inflow of new projects.** One of the most important things an agile PMO can do is assist in managing the rate at which new projects flow into the development organization. As described in Chapter 10, "Team Structure," it is important to limit work to capacity. Otherwise work piles up, leading to a litany of problems. For each project completed, a new project of the same size can be started. The agile PMO can serve as gatekeeper and help the organization resist the temptation to start projects too quickly.

Process

As keepers of the process, members of the PMO will find themselves working closely with the organization's ScrumMasters to make sure Scrum is implemented as well as it can be. These process-related activities include the following:

- **Provide and maintain tools.** In general, tool decisions should be left to individual teams whenever possible. When not, a community of practice might decide that there are sufficient benefits to choosing one tool for all projects. As a last resort, tool decisions might sometimes be made by the PMO, although this should be extremely rare. But the agile PMO can assist teams by acquiring the appropriate tools and performing any configuration or customization necessary.

SEE ALSO

A variety of metrics and approaches for assessing progress toward becoming agile are discussed in Chapter 21, "Seeing How Far You've Come."

- **Assist in establishing and collecting metrics.** As it did before becoming agile, the PMO can identify and collect metrics. Scrum teams are even more leery of metrics programs than traditional teams, so this is an area where the PMO should proceed cautiously. One thing an agile PMO should collect is information on how well teams are doing at delivering value.
- **Reduce waste.** The PMO should aggressively help the team eliminate all wasteful activities and artifacts from its process. An agile PMO should avoid introducing documents, meetings, approvals, and so on unless absolutely necessary. It should also help teams look for things that they are doing that might not be adding value.
- **Help establish and support communities of practice.** One of the most important things an agile PMO can do is to help encourage the formation of communities of practice and then support them after they begin. Not

only do communities of practice help Scrum spread through the organization, they also help spread any good idea from one team to another.

- **Create an appropriate amount of consistency across teams.** Most teams, especially Scrum ones, bristle at the thought of consistency enforced through dictate. The best type of consistency across teams comes from most or all teams agreeing that a particular practice is a good idea. The agile PMO facilitates this by making sure good ideas spread rapidly among teams. Two practices they can use for this are communities of practice and shared coaches.
- **Coordinate teams.** Because they work with individuals from many different teams, PMO members are vital in coordinating the work of separate teams. Someone from the PMO will often be the first to notice when the work of two teams starts to diverge or overlap. PMO members can provide value to teams by alerting teams to these situations when they occur.
- **Model the use of Scrum.** Through their intensive exposure to Scrum, most agile PMOs quickly realize its usefulness as a general-purpose project management framework. At that point, many choose to use Scrum itself to run the PMO. They plan monthly sprints, conduct daily scrums, and so on just like any other team.
- **Work with other groups.** The PMO can be a great assistance to teams in working with other groups, especially human resources and facilities, as already described in this chapter.

Renaming the PMO

Many PMOs choose to rename themselves to better match their revised role. There is no one standard name, but I've heard these most frequently:

- Scrum Center of Excellence
- Scrum Competence Center
- Scrum Office
- Development Support

In Chapter 2, "ADAPTing to Scrum," I cautioned against naming the effort to adopt Scrum. Many people have become cynical and suspicious of name changes and of well-crafted names. That cynicism will be directed at the PMO if it is renamed but remains otherwise unchanged. So, whatever it's called—PMO, Scrum Center of Excellence, or so on—to succeed with Scrum, the PMO that supported the organization's sequential development process will need to change more than just its name. But as this section has pointed out, there is a great deal an agile PMO can bring to the organization.

The Bottom Line

You can ignore the implications of Scrum on these groups and be successful—for awhile. Eventually, though, you will need to engage with these groups to create a successful, long-term transition. It is almost farcical to think of adopting a process founded on a preference for "individuals and interactions over process and tools" without engaging the human resources department. In the typical organization, this group might have even more influence on how people perceive their jobs and act in them than do those individuals' functional managers.

Similarly, the physical environment in which we work has a direct influence on us. Consider the conflicting messages sent when a company proclaims "people are our greatest asset" while the facilities group prohibits hanging burndown charts on the walls. The real message is loud and clear: "The walls are a greater asset."

A PMO often has tremendous political clout and project experience. By getting this part of the organization on board with Scrum, not only do you avoid a possible source of resistance, you also benefit from their experience. Members of the PMO become guardians of self-organization, continuous improvement, ownership, communication, experimentation, collaboration, and other values.

It's easy to view human resources, facilities, and the project management office as obstacles to be overcome. A more productive approach is to view each as an ally to be enlisted. Though an adversarial relationship might work for a while, long-term success requires the support of the entire organization. The road to becoming agile can be a long one; when you can, choose to make friends, rather than enemies.

Additional Reading

Cockburn, Alistair. 2006. *Agile software development: The cooperative game*. 2nd ed. Addison-Wesley Professional.

> In this Jolt Award-winning book, Cockburn covers a wide variety of topics, but Chapter 3, "Communicating, Cooperating Teams," is essential reading. This chapter includes wonderful information on the impact of the physical environment on the project team. This chapter from the first edition is available online at www.informit.com/articles/article.aspx?p=24486. Do yourself a favor, though, and pick up the entire book.

Jeffries, Ron. 2004. Big visible charts. *XP*, October 20. http://www.xprogramming.com/xpmag/BigVisibleCharts.htm.

> An excellent description of some of the big, visible charts that should be found in an agile team's workspace.

Nickols, Fred. 1997. Don't redesign your company's performance appraisal system, scrap it! *Corporate University Review*, May–June.

> There are many great references about the evils of periodic performance reviews. This is a good starting point because of its brevity and the strength of the arguments.

Seffernick, Thomas R. 2007. Enabling agile in a large organization: Our journey down the yellow brick road. In *Proceedings of the Agile 2007 Conference*, ed. Jutta Eckstein, Frank Maurer, Rachel Davies, Grigori Melnik, and Gary Pollice, 200–206. IEEE Computer Society.

> Seffernick describes the successful transition to an agile PMO at KeyCorp, a large financial institution with 1,500 people in its development organization. Included is how the pre-agile PMO was stripped to a core set of members, with others returning to the development teams, and how the PMO reinvented itself as the Software Development Support Center.

Tengshe, Ash, and Scott Noble. 2007. Establishing the agile PMO: Managing variability across projects and portfolios. In *Proceedings of the Agile 2007 Conference*, ed. Jutta Eckstein, Frank Maurer, Rachel Davies, Grigori Melnik, and Gary Pollice, 188–193. IEEE Computer Society.

> Tengshe and Noble established the agile project management office at Capital One Auto Finance. This paper describes their experience doing so and provides good advice for transitioning a PMO from traditional to agile.

PART V

Next Steps

When you have completed 95 percent of your journey,
you are only halfway there.

—Japanese proverb

Chapter 21

Seeing How Far You've Come

Soon after beginning your effort to adopt Scrum, someone will ask, "How are we doing?" This is not a question with a simple answer like, "We're doing great." Similarly and fortunately, you cannot distill your answer down to, "We're Scrum level three." Adopting Scrum is a complex process, and answering how you're doing at it will require a complex answer. Fortunately, many early-adopter companies have experimented with ways of doing this, and a handful of suitable approaches have been documented and are available.

In the following sections, we look at various ways of measuring how far you've come. We start by looking at three general-purpose agility assessments that have been used by multiple companies. Next we look at how you might tailor one of these assessments. We wrap up with a look at the importance of viewing a Scrum adoption from a balanced perspective and show a scorecard for doing just that.

The Purpose of Measuring

Before diving into the topic of what to measure, let's consider why we measure something. Ask most people what the purpose of measuring is, and they will probably say that it is to determine how big, how heavy, how long, or how much of something there is. This is an overly ambitious definition of *measuring*. The real purpose of measuring is to reduce uncertainty. A measurement does not need to be exact for it to help in reducing uncertainty. As an example, consider the soup I had for lunch today. I was at an unfamiliar restaurant, and the tomato basil soup was appealing. I asked the waitress how big the cup and bowl were so I could decide between them. Rather than say something like "five ounces and eight ounces," she used her hands to show me the approximate size of each. That reduced enough of my uncertainty, and I ordered the bowl.

This is an important point because discussions of software metrics often bog down in pursuit of perfection. We don't need perfect measurements. We need measurements that help us answer questions. The most common questions around the success of a Scrum adoption are ones like these:

- Has our investment in adopting Scrum been worthwhile?

- What should we focus on improving next?

- Should we continue with Scrum?

- Are we better at software development than we were a year ago?

- Are we producing better products?

- Do our products have fewer defects?

- Are we faster than we used to be?

THINGS TO TRY NOW

❑ Talk to teams that have already started adopting Scrum and find out what metrics they have collected. Also, ask them which metrics they wish they'd collected.

❑ Before initiating your own metrics program, make a list of the questions you are trying to answer.

General-Purpose Agility Assessments

Many of these questions can be answered directly. For example, to determine whether our products have fewer defects after adopting Scrum, you could compare the number of customer-reported defects reported in the first 90 days after release to data collected on past, pre-Scrum projects. You might even normalize the data for number of lines of code, person-months invested in the project, or number of users. Sometimes, though, what we're interested in is the more esoteric question: How agile are we?

SEE ALSO

We will see some examples of measuring things such as Scrum impact on quality in the section "A Balanced Scorecard for Scrum Teams" later in this chapter.

I understand the arguments that say we shouldn't care how agile we are; we should care only if we are producing better products more quickly and at a lower cost, so what we should really measure is how well the development organization achieves those goals. At one level, I'd like to say that the best way to see if the development organization did a better job this year than last is to see if products it developed accounted for more revenue. There are many problems with this approach, however. For example, there can be a long lag between when the development organization improves and when revenue increases as a result. Additionally, external factors, such as a recession or shift in demand for the company's products, can overwhelm the effect of improvements by the developers. Or changes in how the organization's sales staff are compensated could shift their attention toward other products.

Clearly, looking at metrics such as the revenue generated for a product tells us something about the overall product development process, but it is ultimately unsatisfying at answering questions about how well a software development team did. To address this we can use proxy metrics, which are generally leading indicators that stand in for other measures that are too expensive to collect, jumble too many factors together, or can only be collected too late to be of use. How agile a team or organization has become is a useful proxy metric.

To see why, suppose we looked at your project team last year and are looking at it again now. Through some form of assessment, we find that the team has become better at working within sprints. Perhaps it is better able to plan how much work fits within a sprint. Perhaps team members work more closely with one another during the sprint. Perhaps sprints more consistently produce potentially shippable product increments. Whatever it is, your team is better at sprinting than it was a year ago. Does this mean your team is producing better products more quickly and cheaply? No. But it is indicative that it might be. When we measure to see how agile a team is, we are looking to see if the team is improving in ways that we can predict should lead to improvements in what we truly desire—better business results. But we use the proxy measure of "how agile is the team" because it can be measured well in advance of business results and because it allows us to focus on just one factor of business success—the development team.

Let's take a look at three general-purpose approaches to measuring how agile a team is.

Shodan Adherence Survey

One of the earliest assessment approaches and one that continues to have merit is Bill Krebs' Shodan[1] Adherence Survey (Williams, Layman, and Krebs 2004). Krebs' approach is a self-administered survey of 15 questions, which cover the spectrum of the Extreme Programming practices. An example question is shown in Table 21.1. As you can see, each question includes a brief description and a list of facts that would be true of a team fully following the practice. Questions were answered on a scale from 0 ("disagree with using this practice") to 10 ("fanatical about this practice").

The Shodan Adherence Survey results in a number from 0 to 100% that indicates how strongly the 15 practices are followed. This final score is determined by combining the respondents' answers with Krebs' fixed weighting of the importance of each practice area. Daily scrums contribute the least to the final score (less than 1%), while pair programming contributes the most (at 12.5%).

Using the Shodan Adherence Survey

This 15-question survey is short enough that it could be completed at the conclusion of every sprint. My opinion is that this is too frequent. We want to use the survey to look for trends and to find areas in which we need to improve. These become harder to detect when the survey is given too frequently. Another

---

1 *Shodan* is Japanese for "first degree." It is commonly used in martial arts to refer to someone who has earned the lowest black belt and by Go players to refer to a strong amateur.

problem I've seen is teams who incorporate this survey into their sprint retrospectives in place of the more open-ended discussion that should be part of a retrospective.

In my view, the correct use of a Shodan Adherence Survey involves having all team members answer all questions perhaps every six months and certainly no more often than every three months. This will allow meaningful comparisons to be made between results from different times.

By periodically administering the Shodan Assessment Survey, an organization can spot trends; for example, how well are we doing with customer acceptance tests? A company-specific variation could be made that incorporates additional important agile practices or that changes the weights Krebs assigned to the practices.

TABLE 21.1

A sample question from the Shodan Adherence Survey.

Customer Acceptance Tests
Customer acceptance tests exist to ensure both the developers and customer know what they want. All acceptance tests must be passed before the product can be delivered to the customer. *How important are customer acceptance tests to the development of your product?*   • Acceptance tests are used to verify system functionality and customer requirements. • A customer provides acceptance criteria. • A customer uses acceptance tests to determine what has been accomplished at the end of an iteration. • Acceptance testing is automated. • A user story is not finished until its acceptance tests pass. Acceptance tests are run automatically every night.

Strengths and Weaknesses

The survey has the advantage of having only 15 questions, although that number is deceptive due to the compound nature of each question. A disadvantage of the Shodan approach is that its results are not directly actionable. A low score in a practice could be the result of low adherence to any one of the bullet point statements comprising the question. Further investigation would be needed before a coach or consultant would know how to help the team improve at the practice.

Agile: EF

Krebs, the originator of the Shodan Adherence Survey, and his colleagues at IBM have also introduced additional approaches to assessing how well agile teams are doing. Most notable among these is the Agile Evaluation Framework, or Agile:EF (Krebs and Kroll 2008). The Agile:EF takes to heart the agile advice to keep things simple and is therefore less of an actual framework than a process for assessing teams.

In this approach, Krebs and coauthor Per Kroll suggest having team members complete a very short questionnaire, perhaps as often as the end of every sprint. Questions are kept shorter than in the Shodan survey. But, as in that approach, each question concerns one agile practice. Each question is answered with a score from 1–10, with 10 indicating the practice is done 100% of the time, 1 indicating it is never done, and 5 indicating the practice is done 50% of the time. Agile:EF does not provide a recommended set of questions. The authors instead recommend that existing sets of questions be used. The Shodan Assessment Survey questions could, for example, be used.

Figure 21.1 illustrates how the results of an Agile:EF assessment might be reported. In this figure the solid bar indicates the team's mean result. The darker, thinner line indicates how widely opinions vary. If you are assessing a sufficiently large group, calculate the standard deviation and indicate it with these lines. If you are assessing just one team, use the thin line to indicate the lowest and highest responses.

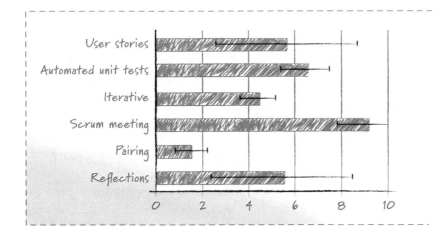

FIGURE 21.1
Sample results from an Agile:EF survey showing the mean result and one standard deviation around it.

Strengths and Weaknesses

As a general approach, Agile:EF has much to recommend it. Periodic, quick, unobtrusive assessments are likely to have a higher response rate than longer, more detailed assessments. Although the ability to use any set of questions with Agile:EF is a strength, it is also a drawback that limits Agile:EF from realistically living up to its name as a framework.

Although I like Agile:EF's focus on simplicity and quick surveys, my experience is that you will not get useful results by asking the team the same 15 or so questions at the end of every sprint. Instead I recommend having multiple sets of questions, each focusing on a different aspect of the software development process. Cycle through the sets of questions by asking a different set after each sprint or once a month. By the time you are ready to repeat a set of questions, enough time should have elapsed for the team to have made meaningful improvements in the areas asked about by the survey.

Comparative Agility Assessment

A handful of years ago, some of my clients began to ask me, "How are we doing?" My replies were always something like, "You're doing pretty well at pair program-ming, and I like how teams have shifted from writing requirements documents to talking about user stories. But teams really haven't embraced the idea of au-tomated testing yet, and that's where we need to focus most." But this wasn't the type of answer they wanted; they wanted to know, "How are we doing *compared to our competition?*"

At first this question bothered me. It doesn't matter how your competitors are doing at agile, I reasoned. If you're not perfect yet, keep improving. It took me awhile, but I eventually realized the flaws in my thinking. A business does not need to be perfect; it needs only to be better than (and stay ahead of) its com-petition. Google is the dominant search engine today not because the results it shows are perfect but because its results are usually better than those shown by its competition.

This means that agile does not need a five-level maturity model similar to CMMI. Organizations are not striving for perfection against some idealized list of agile principles and practices. Rather, they are trying to be more agile than their competitors. This does not mean that becoming agile is itself the goal. Producing better products than the competition remains the goal. But being more agile than one's competitors is indicative of the organization's ability to deliver better prod-ucts more quickly and cheaply.

With this in mind, Kenny Rubin and I created the Comparative Agility as-sessment (CA), which is available for free online. Like the Shodan Adherence Survey and Agile:EF, a CA assessment can be based on individual responses to survey questions. However, it was also designed to be completed by an experi-enced ScrumMaster, coach, or consultant on behalf of a team or company based on interviews or observation.

Survey responses for the organization are aggregated and may then be com-pared against the entire CA database. Responses can also be compared to a subset of the database. You can, for example, choose to compare your team to all other companies doing web development, all companies that are about six months into their agile adoption efforts, all companies in a specific industry, or a combination

SEE ALSO

For an example of a five-level agile maturity model model, see the description of the Sidky Agile Maturity Index at http://www.agilejournal .com/content/view/ 411/33/.

NOTE

The CA assessment can be taken online at www.Comparative Agility.com.

of such factors. You can also compare your team against its own data from a prior period, showing you what improvements have been made since then.

At the highest level, the CA approach assesses agility on seven dimensions: teamwork, requirements, planning, technical practices, quality, culture, and knowledge creation. Partial results showing a team assessed on three dimensions are shown in Figure 21.2. This figure shows how one particular team compared to a population of other teams pulled from the CA database (in this case, other teams doing web development). Zero represents the mean value of all matching teams in the database. The vertical lines labeled from −2 to 2 each represent one standard deviation from the mean. From Figure 21.2 we can see that this team is doing much better than average at Planning, a little better than average at Requirements, and significantly worse than average at Quality.

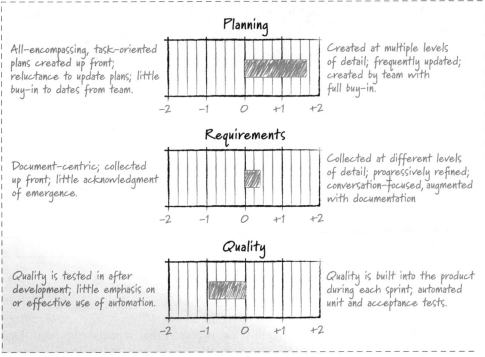

FIGURE 21.2

The results of a Comparative Agility assessment show that this team is better than average at planning and requirements but worse at quality.

Each of the three dimensions shown in Figure 21.2 is composed of from three to six characteristics. A set of questions is asked to assess a team's score on each characteristic. For example, characteristics of the planning dimension include

- When planning occurs
- Who is involved
- Whether both release and sprint planning occur

- Whether critical variables (such as scope, schedule and resources) are locked
- How progress is tracked

The questions for the "when does planning occur" characteristic are shown in Table 21.2. As can be seen in that figure, questions are answered on a scale including *true*, *more true than false*, *neither true nor false*, *more false than true*, *false*, and *not applicable*.

TABLE 21.2

One of the characteristics considered by the Comparative Agility assessment is when a team plans.

	True	More True than False	Neither True nor False	More False than True	False	Not Applicable
Up-front planning is helpful without being excessive.						
Team members leave planning meetings knowing what needs to be done and have confidence they can meet their commitments.						
Teams communicate the need to change release date or scope as soon as the need is discovered.						
Effort spent on planning is spread approximately evenly throughout the project.						

Strengths and Weaknesses

A strength of the Comparative Agility assessment is that it was designed to lead more easily to actionable results. Like the other assessments, the results point first to a shortcoming in one of the seven dimensions, but unlike the other assessments, drilling into that dimension reveals the specific characteristic the organization is struggling with. This should help the team or its ScrumMaster more easily identify actions to take. For example, if we were to look into the low score for quality in Figure 21.2, we would see that there are three characteristics to the quality dimension: automated unit testing, customer acceptance tests, and timing. Because the CA approach assesses each characteristic individually, it is possible to see which of these characteristics is dragging down the organization's overall quality score.

The comparative nature of the CA assessment was intended to be its biggest strength. By seeing how your organization compares with other organizations, improvement efforts can be focused on the most promising areas.

The most significant weakness of CA is the breadth of the survey. The survey includes nearly 125 questions about the development process. There are two common solutions:

- Perform a full assessment only once or twice a year. (Quarterly might be acceptable and relevant in some organizations.)

- Assess only one of the seven dimensions per month.

THINGS TO TRY NOW

- ❏ If you have never surveyed any of your agile teams, do so now. Don't wait six weeks while you create the perfect survey. Review the questions on the Comparative Agility assessment or the Shodan Adherence Survey, and select 15 that you think will give you useful or interesting information and start.

- ❏ While waiting for results to come in from that first set of survey questions, think about your long-term strategy and create or select the approach you'll use routinely.

Creating Your Own Assessment

Some organizations choose to create their own assessments. Doing so requires more work, of course, but it brings the advantage of being able to fully tailor the assessment. Organizations with large Scrum initiatives such as Ultimate Software, JDA Software, Yahoo!, and Salesforce.com have pursued this approach. If you take this route, by all means start by looking at the questions in approaches such as the Shodan Adherence Survey and the Comparative Agility assessment. Discard any questions that are irrelevant in your organization or that will not provide interesting results. If, for example, automated testing is an established practice and one that all teams already do well, you can save time by dropping those questions.

Most of the company-specific assessments I've seen include a fair number of questions aimed at employee opinions about the change. Yahoo!, for example, asked questions similar to these about its transition to Scrum:

- Since adopting Scrum, how productive do you think your team is?

- Since adopting Scrum, how has morale changed?

- Since adopting Scrum, how has your sense of accountability and feeling of ownership in the project changed?

- Since adopting Scrum, has the degree of collaboration and cooperation in the team changed?

- What do you think of the overall quality of what has been developed since adopting Scrum?

Questions were answered with *Scrum is much worse, Scrum is worse, Scrum is about the same, Scrum is better,* or *Scrum is much better.*

Salesforce.com asked similar questions during its transition to Scrum:

- Do you think Scrum is an effective approach?
- What has been the impact of Scrum on the quality of our products?
- Would you recommend Scrum to your colleagues inside or outside the company?

Beyond these qualitative metrics, Salesforce.com also collected some effective, but simple, quantitative metrics. This allowed the company to look at its Scrum transition from multiple perspectives, which is the topic of the next section.

OBJECTION

"I don't like questions like these. Who cares what employees think about how productive they are or whether quality has improved?"

Those involved in developing the software are in an excellent position to assess changes in how they work. Certainly, they will exhibit biases if someone has previously announced that bonuses will be given if Scrum doubles productivity. But I haven't suggested doing that. Neither did the companies that used these questions. Without an incentive to mislead, most employees will answer truthfully. And their answers to questions such as these can be as useful as customers' answers to similarly subjective questions.

A Balanced Scorecard for Scrum Teams

It's well known that if we introduce a new metric and tell teams that they will be evaluated against that metric, they will alter their behavior to optimize that metric. Tell a team that it will be measured on the number of defects in the defect tracking system and that number will go down—perhaps because of good, honest improvements, but perhaps also because team members will find ways to more informally communicate about some bugs, thereby bypassing the defect tracking system. Even if we could devise a metric that couldn't be gamed, one number does not present a complete view. Maybe the team decreased the number of defects by dramatically cutting back on productivity. It delivered 90% less functionality than before because every line of code is so heavily scrutinized. We need a more *balanced* view than can be provided by any one number.

The idea of providing a balanced view into an organization led Robert Kaplan and David Norton to create what they call a *balanced scorecard*. Their idea is that to fully understand the performance of a business, it is necessary to look beyond the income statement and balance sheet, which are merely two measures of how the business is doing. The view presented by looking only at financial statements is no more complete than the view of a development organization given only by the number of defects in the bug database. Kaplan and Norton suggest that a business should be looked at from four perspectives: financial, customer, business processes, and learning and growth. These different perspectives make up the balanced scorecard (1992).

Since 2000, I've used balanced scorecards as a way for software development groups to assess themselves from multiple perspectives. The initial four perspectives suggested by Kaplan and Norton are not necessarily the best fit when applied directly to a software development department, IT group, or especially an individual team. I've experimented with a variety of different perspectives over the years, but I think the best I've found are the four listed here, suggested by Liz Barnett for Forrester Research.

- **Operational excellence.** Teams strive to produce high-quality products with high rates of productivity while meeting target costs and dates.
- **User orientation.** Teams focus on delivering features desired by users and customers.
- **Business value.** Teams deliver value to the business in the form of cost savings, increased revenue, or other similar ways.
- **Future orientation.** While delivering products and new features today, teams build skills and capabilities for the future (Barnett, Schwaber, and Hogan 2005).

If a balanced scorecard is created near the time you start adopting Scrum, and the team, department, or organization is then periodically evaluated against it, progress should be visible. A team that is doing well at Scrum should be able to improve simultaneously in each of these perspectives. Even better, a balanced scorecard takes the focus off strictly becoming agile and places it on achieving whatever goals have led the organization to try to become agile by adopting Scrum.

Constructing the Balanced Scorecard

Each perspective on a balanced scorecard is augmented by typically one to four strategic objectives. Progress toward each objective is measured by both leading and lagging indicators, for which target values are preidentified. If we consider the operational excellence perspective, for example, we might identify objectives such as improving productivity, increasing quality, producing better estimates, lowering total development cost, and so on. The set of objectives you choose should not be a laundry list of admirable goals; instead, choose only those objectives you can focus on.

For each objective, it is important to identify metrics that will tell us if we are achieving (or have achieved) the goal. Although you must identify at least one metric for each objective, it will usually be beneficial to identify at least one leading indicator and one lagging indicator. A leading indicator is a metric that you expect to see change in advance of achieving the objective. For the objective of improving quality, for example, a leading indicator would be the number of test cases written. Having more test cases does not guarantee that the product is of higher quality, but it might be a good indicator that it is.

A lagging indicator, by contrast, is a metric that changes after the objective is achieved or that can only be measured at that time. Continuing with the example of improving quality, a lagging indicator might be the number of post-release defects reported by customers. Lagging indicators are usually the metrics used to ascertain whether an objective has truly been met. But they suffer, of course, from not being measurable until afterward. This is why a combination of leading and lagging indicators is often best. Table 21.3 shows examples of objectives, leading indicators, and lagging indicators for the operational excellence perspective.

TABLE 21.3

A balanced scorecard provides multiple perspectives on performance.

Perspective	Objective	Leading Indicators	Lagging Indicators
Operational excellence	Improve productivity	Percentage of product backlog items dropped per sprint (target = 5–15%)	Number of features delivered per developer (target = 20% increase)
		Percentage of source control check-ins occurring on weekends (target = less than 5%)	
	Schedule predictability		Number of projects completed within –1 to +2 sprints as predicted at project midpoint (target = 95%)
	Higher quality	Percentage of tests passing in continuous builds (target = 95%)	Number of defects reported in first 30 days post-release (target = 50% reduction)

TABLE 21.3
Continued

Perspective	Objective	Leading Indicators	Lagging Indicators
User orientation	Improve uptime		Server downtime (planned + unplanned) is less than 120 minutes per year.
	Increased user satisfaction	Increased responses from customer focus group (target = improve e-mail responses by 20%)	Net promoter score (target = improve by 25%)
			Better scores on quarterly customer survey (target = 80% say "exceeds" or "far exceeds expectations")
Business value	More frequent major releases	Release burndown charts produced and displayed for all projects (target = 100%)	At least one major release every quarter (target = no more than 90 days between)
	More features in releases		Number of user-visible product backlog items per release (target = 300)
Future orientation	Improve employee satisfaction	Number of complaints to human resources (target = 1 per month)	Number of employees saying they are having a great or the best time working here (target = 80%)
	Improve our under-standing of Scrum and agile prac-tices	Attendance at various agile conferences (target = send at least 40 people this year to conferences with agile content)	Number of employees who would recommend Scrum to a friend at another company (target = 80%)

Favor Simple Metrics

From reading Table 21.3 you might have noticed that some of the metrics are quite simple. Surely, you might be thinking, the number of features delivered per developer (the first lagging indicator shown in Table 21.3) is too simple to be helpful. What constitutes a feature? Is it really appropriate for small features to count the same as big features? In general, simple metrics such as this can be helpful, especially when compared over longer periods of time and considered in combination with other simple metrics.

The number of features delivered per developer is one of the simple metrics that I referred to earlier that Salesforce.com used to assess the benefits of its Scrum adoption. Twelve months after initiating the transition, the company measured a 38% increase in the number of features delivered per developer over the preceding year. Was it possible that one of the reasons for this increase was that the features were smaller? Of course. But a simple metric such as this one helped them quantify the general feeling of being more productive than they had been. Consider this metric in relation to the purpose of measuring given at the start of this chapter: reducing uncertainty. Prior to taking this measurement, those in Salesforce.com's Enterprise Transition Community might have been uncertain if Scrum had been helping teams be more productive. After measuring, they had their answer.

Another simple metric Salesforce.com used showed the improved flow of features to customers. The *cumulative value* chart created by Steve Greene and Chris Fry is shown in Figure 21.3, which we also saw in Chapter 1, "Why Becoming Agile Is Hard (But Worth It)." Again counting each feature the same regardless of its size or importance, this chart shows both how many new features were delivered and when they were delivered. The general idea is that the area under the curves represents the overall value of the features to users—a feature delivered sooner is more valuable than one delivered later. In 2006, before adopting Scrum, Salesforce.com delivered no new features to users until January 2007. Compare the total area under the 2006 line with the total area under the 2007 line, during which time Salesforce.com's use of Scrum led to more frequent releases and more total features delivered.

FIGURE 21.3

A year after beginning its transition to Scrum, Salesforce.com used this powerful chart to illustrate a 568% improvement in the simple metric the company called cumulative value delivered.

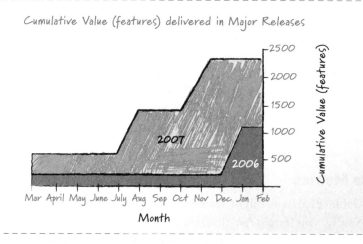

It would be easy to poke holes in simple metrics like this one: Not all features are the same size, not all features are equally important to all customers, there were more developers in 2007 than in 2006, and so on. Although each of these criticisms could be valid, none do anything to seriously cripple the impact of a chart such as Figure 21.3 in helping everyone see the benefits brought by Scrum to Salesforce.com.

THINGS TO TRY NOW

- ❑ Make a list of simple metrics you can easily collect that will answer some of the open questions about your Scrum adoption. Start collecting them.
- ❑ Create a balanced scorecard. It can be for a project, the department, or even for the Scrum transition. Begin by identifying objectives—what would you like to achieve? Then identify one or more leading indicators for each that can be used to gauge whether you are on track to achieving the goal. Finally, identify at least one lagging indicator for each objective that can be used to determine whether the objective was met.

Should We Really Bother with This?

Collecting metrics, even simple ones, takes effort and is not something that we in the software industry have a stellar record of doing. With so much else that demands our time and attention, should we really bother collecting data on how well we're doing at becoming agile? Yes, we should. I can point to three major benefits:

- **Metrics help fight the pull of organizational gravity.** As pointed out way back in Chapter 2, "ADAPTing to Scrum," there are reasons why the status quo existed before you began to adopt Scrum. Organizational gravity seeks to pull us back to that status quo. Periodic assessments and metrics showing the benefits of Scrum will be one of the best ways to fight the pull of organizational gravity.
- **Metrics help us promote the transition effort.** Not only does a good assessment program help fight organizational gravity, but it can also help get other groups interested in adopting Scrum. Think again about the ADAPT model of Chapter 2 and recall the importance of the promotion step. To get others interested in also adopting Scrum, it is important to promote your team's early successes. Metrics help quantify these successes.
- **Metrics help us know where to focus further improvement efforts.** Metrics should lead to action. If you are collecting data that never leads to action, stop collecting that data and instead collect some different data. A good assessment program will help you identify areas for improvement (and for praise). If you find teams are doing less of a valuable practice than

they used to, investigate why. If you find that some teams have adopted a new practice and are outperforming other teams, seek ways to spread the use of that practice.

As much as I know it is helpful and important to collect metrics on how well a team is doing at adopting Scrum and becoming agile, I want to end this chapter with a cautionary note. Whenever numbers are collected, there is usually someone in the organization who becomes too attached to them and gives them undue significance. The metrics are then used to beat up teams. I'm not going to go so far as to say that metrics should never be used as a stick—my boss at the auto repair center where I worked during college was probably right to yell at me when I didn't meet my monthly quota. But the metrics described in this chapter are very different. As such, they should be used to focus effort and aid understanding, not to place blame or enforce compliance.

Additional Reading

Gilb, Tom. 2005. *Competitive Engineering: A handbook for systems engineering, requirements engineering, and software engineering using planguage.* Butterworth-Heinemann.

Gilb, the originator of the Evo process, takes a rigorous approach to measurement. His book shows numerous examples of quantifying and measuring what you might think unmeasurable. Gilb's approach is particularly useful when used to define the leading and lagging indicators of a balanced scorecard.

Hubbard, Douglas W. 2007. *How to measure anything: Finding the value of "intangibles" in business.* Wiley.

A wonderful book that really does live up to its name. It offers many different ways of measuring things and makes the underlying math relatively easily to follow. If you are struggling with how to measure something, this book will probably give you some ideas.

Kaplan, Robert S., and David P. Norton. 1992. The balanced scorecard: Measures that drive performance. *Harvard Business Review*, January-February, 71–79.

This was the article that started the balanced scorecard movement. It was followed by a book by the same authors, but this short article remains the best quick introduction to the subject.

Krebs, William, and Per Kroll, 2008. Using evaluation frameworks for quick reflections. *Agile Journal*, February 9. http://www.agilejournal.com/articles/columns/column-articles/750-using-evaluation-frameworks-for-quick-reflections.

This article is the best introduction to the Agile:EF approach to assessing a team's progress.

Leffingwell, Dean. 2007. *Scaling software agility: Best practices for large enterprises.* Addison-Wesley Professional.

> Chapter 22 of this book includes additional information on using balanced scorecards. The same chapter also includes a team-oriented agile assessment survey similar to the ones presented in this chapter. The assessment is available online at scalingsoftware agility.files.wordpress.com/2008/01/team-agility-assessment-in-pdf.

Mair, Steven. 2002. A balanced scorecard for a small software group. *IEEE Software,* November/December, 21–27.

> This article provides background on the balanced scorecard approach and shows how to create one for a small department using Kaplan and Norton's original four perspectives.

Williams, Laurie, Lucas Layman, and William Krebs. 2004. Extreme programming evaluation framework for object-oriented languages, version 1.4. North Carolina State University Department of Computer Science, TR-2004-18.

> This technical report describes the Extreme Programming: Evaluation Framework (XP:EF), which builds on the Shodan Adherence Survey to include project context and outcome metrics. The additional data collected might be of interest to researchers or even Project Management Offices looking for additional rigor. However, a team simply looking to improve can stick with just the Shodan survey, which is also the heart of XP:EF and is described fully in an appendix.

Chapter 22

You're Not Done Yet

We've come a long way together. My hope is that you have been implementing many of the recommended practices and "things to try" throughout the book. If so, you've hopefully made a lot of progress. You've established an Enterprise Transition Community (ETC) to introduce Scrum into your organization. The ETC, in turn, has created an environment that encourages improvement communities to form and flourish. Some of these improvement communities have disbanded already, after accomplishing what they sought to improve; other improvement communities have expanded their focus or are still hard at work at more persistent improvement opportunities.

By now Scrum has become the default way of working for at least some teams in your organization. It started with individuals on those teams becoming aware of the need to change how they developed software. As the awareness grew, it turned into a desire to develop software differently. In response, individuals acquired the ability to work in an agile manner. This led to early success with Scrum, which was promoted to others so that they could begin their own cycles of awareness, desire, and ability. Finally, the implications of doing Scrum were transferred to other parts of the organization so that organizational gravity did not pull everyone and every team back to where it started.

Along the way you have changed not only people's job descriptions but also how they view their roles on the team. Teams are now structured around the delivery of features rather than around the technologies or layers of the architecture. And although given the opportunity to self-organize, teams are subtly influenced by leaders who have themselves learned how to work on self-organizing teams. Team members have incorporated new technical practices that help them write higher-quality code. The team understands the importance of its product backlog, how to work effectivity within Scrum's strictly timeboxed sprints, and how to plan with incomplete information. Quality has probably improved—not only are testers integrated into the development process, but programmers are helping with automated tests as well.

By now, you might also have scaled Scrum onto larger projects or projects spread across multiple cities or continents. You've learned how to overcome some of the bigger challenges created by those projects. Scrum is now more deeply integrated into the organization and might even coexist with other corporate mandates, such as CMMI or ISO 9001 compliance. Employees in human resources, facilities, and the project management office are now your allies in creating sustainable change. The organization has made tremendous progress.

Don't stop.

I don't care how agile you have become or how well you do Scrum. It doesn't matter how good you are today; if you're not better next month, you're no longer agile. You must always, always, always try to improve.

Wait, you say, I have a final objection. Being agile isn't my goal, delivering great products is. If I'm good enough, why can't I stop? To that I say, of course being agile is not your goal. Your primary goal is to develop amazing products, quickly and cheaply, that thrill your customers and users. To do that, though, I believe you will need to be agile. And to be agile, you must continuously improve.

Continuous improvement is easier than it might sound. You've planted all the seeds already. Your improvement communities will play a key role inside the risk-tolerant, idea-generating, nurturing culture fostered by the ETC. Through trial-and-error experimentation, these communities will lead the organization toward better and better ways of working. Beyond that, though, they will engage employees' passion. The organization will shift from seeing problems to seeing possibilities.

And with that, you are on your way to succeeding with agile.

Reference List

Adler, Paul S., Avi Mandelbaum, Vien Nguyen, and Elizabeth Schwerer. 1996. Getting the most out of your product development process. *Harvard Business Review*, March–April, 13–151.

Adzic, Gojko. 2009. *Bridging the communication gap: Specification by example and agile acceptance testing.* Neuri Limited.

Allen-Meyer, Glenn. 2000a. *Nameless organizational change: No-hype, low-resistance corporate transformation.* Syracuse University Press.

Allen-Meyer, Glenn. 2000b. *Overview: Nameless organizational change; No-hype, low-resistance corporate transformation.* Previously available at http://www.nameless.org.

Allen-Meyer, Glenn. 2000c. 21st century schizoid change. *OD Practitioner* 32 (3): 22–26.

Ambler, Scott. 2008a. Agile adoption rate survey, February. http://www.ambysoft.com/surveys/agileFebruary2008.html.

———. 2008b. Scott Ambler on agile's present and future. Interview by Floyd Marinescu. InfoQ website, December 1. http://www.infoq.com/interviews/Agile-Scott-Ambler.

———. n.d. Agile Data Home Page. http://www.agiledata.org.

Ambler, Scott W., and Pramod J. Sadalage. 2006. *Refactoring databases: Evolutionary database design.* Addison-Wesley.

Anderson, Philip. 1999. Seven levers for guiding the evolving enterprise. In *The biology of business: Decoding the natural laws of enterprise*, ed. John Henry Clippinger III, 113–152. Jossey-Bass.

Appelo, Jurgen. 2008. We increment to adapt, we iterate to improve. *Methods & Tools*, Summer, 9–22.

Armour, Phillip G. 2006. Software: Hard data. *Communications of the ACM*, September, 15–17.

Avery, Christopher M. 2005. Responsible change. *Cutter Consortium Agile Project Management Executive Report* 6 (10): 1–28.

Avery, Christoper M., Meri Aaron Walker, and Erin O'Toole. 2001. *Teamwork is an individual skill: Getting your work done when sharing responsibility.* Berrett-Koehler Publishers.

Babinet, Eric, and Rajani Ramanathan. 2008. Dependency management in a large agile environment. In *Proceedings of the Agile 2008 Conference*, ed. Grigori Melnik, Philippe Kruchten, and Mary Poppendieck, 401–406. IEEE Computer Society.

Bain, Scott L. 2008. *Emergent design: The evolutionary nature of professional software development.* Addison-Wesley Professional.

Barnett, Liz. 2005. Metrics for agile development projects: Emphasize value and customer satisfaction. With Carey Schwaber and Lindsay Hogan. Forrester. http://www.forrester. com/Research/Document/Excerpt/0,7211,37380,00.html.

———. 2008. Incremental agile adoption. *Agile Journal*, February 11. http:// agilejournal.com/articles/columns/from-the-editor-mainmenu-45/755-incremental-agile-adoption.

Beavers, Paul A. 2007. Managing a large "agile" software engineering organization. In *Proceedings of the Agile 2007 Conference*, ed. Jutta Eckstein, Frank Maurer, Rachel Davies, Grigori Melnik, and Gary Pollice, 296–303. IEEE Computer Society.

Beck, Kent. 2002. *Test-driven development: By example.* Addison-Wesley Professional.

Beck, Kent, and Cynthia Andres. 2004. *Extreme programming explained.* 2nd ed. Addison-Wesley Professional.

———. 2005. Getting started with XP: Toe dipping, racing dives, and cannonballs. PDF file at Three Rivers Institute website. www.threeriversinstitute.org/Toe%20Dipping. pdf.

Beck, Kent, Mike Beedle, Arie van Bennekum, Alistair Cockburn, Ward Cunningham, Martin Fowler, James Grenning, Jim Highsmith, Andrew Hunt, Ron Jeffries, Jon Kern, Brian Marick, Robert C. Martin, Steve Mellor, Ken Schwaber, Jeff Sutherland, and Dave Thomas. 2001. Manifesto for agile software development. http://www. agilemanifesto.org/.

Benefield, Gabrielle. 2008. Rolling out agile in a large enterprise. In *Proceedings of the 41st Annual Hawaii International Conference on System Sciences*, 461–470. IEEE Computer Society.

Boehm, Barry W. 1981. *Software engineering economics.* Prentice Hall.

Boehm, Barry, and Richard Turner. 2005. Management challenges to implementing agile processes in traditional development organizations. *IEEE Software*, September/October, 30–39.

Bos, Erik, and Christ Vriens. 2004. An agile CMM. In *Extreme Programming and Agile Methods: XP/Agile Universe 2004*, ed. C. Zannier, H. Erdogmus, and L. Lindstrom, 129–138. Springer.

Bradner, E., G. Mark, and T.D. Hertel. 2003. Effects of team size on participation, awareness, and technology choice in geographically distributed teams. In *Proceedings of the 36th Annual Hawaii International Conference on System Sciences*, 271a. IEEE Computer Society.

Bridges, William. 2003. *Managing transitions: Making the most of change.* 2nd ed. Da Capo Press.

Brodwall, Johannes. 2008. An informative workplace. *Thinking inside a bigger box*, November 23. http://brodwall.com/johannes/blog/2008/11/23/an-informative-workplace/.

Brooks, Frederick P. 1995. *The mythical man-month: Essays on software engineering.* 2nd ed. Addison-Wesley Professional. (Orig. pub. 1975.)

Campbell, Donald T. 1965. Variation and selective retention in socio-cultural evolution. In *Social change in developing areas: A reinterpretation of evolutionary theory*, ed. Herbert R. Barringer, George I. Blanksten, and Raymond W. Mack, 19–49. Schenkman.

Cao, Lan, and Balasubramaniam Ramesh. 2008. Agile requirements engineering practices: An empirical study. *IEEE Software*, January/February, 60–67.

Carmel, Erran. 1998. *Global software teams: Collaborating across borders and time zones.* Prentice Hall.

Carr, David K., Kelvin J. Hard, and William J. Trahant. 1996. *Managing the change process: A field book for change agents, team leaders, and reengineering managers.* McGraw-Hill.

Catmull, Ed. 2008. How Pixar fosters collective creativity. *Harvard Business Review*, September, 65–72.

Cichelli, Sharon. 2008. Globally distributed Scrum. *Girl Writes Code* blog entry, May 9. http://www.invisible-city.com/sharon/2008/05/globally-distributed-scrum.html.

Cirillo, Francesco. 2007. The pomodoro technique. PDF from website of same name. http://www.pomodorotechnique.com/resources/cirillo/ThePomodoroTechnique_v1-3.pdf.

Clark, Kim B., and Steven C. Wheelwright. 1992. *Managing new product and process development: Text and cases.* The Free Press.

Cockburn, Alistair. 2000. Balancing lightness with sufficiency. *Cutter IT Journal*, November.

———. 2006. *Agile software development: The cooperative game.* 2nd ed. Addison-Wesley Professional.

———. 2008. Using both incremental and iterative development. *Crosstalk*, May, 27–30.

Cohn, Mike. 2004. *User stories applied: For agile software development.* Addison-Wesley Professional.

———. 2005. *Agile estimating and planning.* Addison-Wesley Professional.

Conner, Daryl R. 1993. *Managing at the speed of change: How resilient managers succeed and prosper where others fail.* Random House.

Conway, Melvin E. 1968. How do committees invent? Originally published in *Datamation*, April 1968. Currently published on author's website. http://www.melconway.com/research/committees.html.

Cooper, Robert G. 2001. *Winning at new products: Accelerating the process from idea to launch.* 3rd ed. Basic Books.

Coyne, Kevin P., Patricia Gorman Clifford, and Renée Dye. 2007. Breakthrough thinking from inside the box. *Harvard Business Review,* December, 71–78.

Creasey, Tim, and Jeff Hiatt, eds. 2007. *Best practices in change management.* Prosci.

Crispin, Lisa, and Janet Gregory. 2009. *Agile testing: A practical guide for testers and agile teams.* Addison-Wesley Professional.

Crosby, Philip. 1979. *Quality is free: The art of making quality certain.* McGraw-Hill.

Cunningham, Ward. 1992. The WyCash portfolio management system. In *Addendum to the Proceedings on Object-Oriented Programming Systems, Languages, and Applications,* 29–30. ACM. Also at http://c2.com/doc/oopsla92.html.

Davies, Rachel, and Liz Sedley. 2009. *Agile coaching.* The Pragmatic Bookshelf.

Deemer, Pete, Gabrielle Benefield, Craig Larman, and Bas Vodde. 2008. *The Scrum primer.* Scrum Training Institute.

DeGrace, Peter, and Leslie Hulet Stahl. 1990. *Wicked problems, righteous solutions: A catalogue of modern software engineering paradigms.* Prentice Hall.

DeMarco, Tom, Peter Hruschka, Tim Lister, Suzanne Robertson, James Roberts, and Steve McMenamin. 2008. *Adrenaline junkies and template zombies: Understanding patterns of project behavior.* Dorset House.

DeMarco, Tom, and Timothy Lister. 1999. *Peopleware: Productive projects and teams.* 2nd ed. Dorset House.

Deming, W. Edwards. 2000. *Out of the crisis.* MIT Press.

de Pillis, Emmeline, and Kimberly Furumo. 2007. Counting the cost of virtual teams. *Communications of the ACM,* December, 93–95.

Derby, Esther. 2006. A manager's guide to supporting organizational change. *Crosstalk,* January, 17–19.

Derby, Esther, and Diana Larsen. 2006. *Agile retrospectives: Making good teams great.* Pragmatic Bookshelf.

Deutschman, Alan. 2007. Inside the mind of Jeff Bezos. *Fast Company,* December 19. http://www.fastcompany.com/magazine/85/bezos_1.html.

Dinwiddie, George. 2007. Common areas at the heart. In *Proceedings of the Agile 2007 Conference,* ed. Jutta Eckstein, Frank Maurer, Rachel Davies, Grigori Melnik, and Gary Pollice, 207–211. IEEE Computer Society.

Drummond, Brian Scott, and John Francis "JF" Unson. 2008. Yahoo! distributed agile: Notes from the world over. In *Proceedings of the Agile 2008 Conference,* ed. Grigori Melnik, Philippe Kruchten, and Mary Poppendieck, 315–321. IEEE Computer Society.

Duarte, Deborah L., and Nancy Tennant Snyder. 2006. *Mastering virtual teams: Strategies, tools, and techniques that succeed.* 3rd ed. Jossey-Bass.

Duck, Jeanie Daniel. 1993. Managing change: The art of balancing. *Harvard Business Review*, November–December, 109–119.

Duvall, Paul, Steve Matyas, and Andrew Glover. 2007. *Continuous integration: Improving software quality and reducing risk.* Addison-Wesley Professional.

Dybå, Tore, Erik Arisholm, Dag I. K. Sjøberg, Jo Erskine Hannay, and Forrest Shull. 2007. Are two heads better than one? On the effectiveness of pair programming. *IEEE Software*, June, 12–15.

Edmondson, Amy, Richard Bohmer, and Gary Pisano. 2001. Speeding up team learning. *Harvard Business Review*, October, 125–132.

Elssamadisy, Amr. 2007. *Patterns of agile practice adoption: The technical cluster.* C4Media.

Emery, Dale H. 2001. Resistance as a resource. *Cutter IT Journal*, October.

Eoyang, Glenda Holladay. 2001. Conditions for self-organizing in human systems. PhD diss., The Union Institute and University.

Feathers, Michael. 2004. *Working effectively with legacy code.* Prentice Hall PTR.

Fecarotta, Joseph. 2008. MyBoeingFleet and agile software development. In *Proceedings of the Agile 2008 Conference*, ed. Grigori Melnik, Philippe Kruchten, and Mary Poppendieck, 135–139. IEEE Computer Society.

Feynman, Richard P. 1997. *Surely you're joking, Mr. Feynman! Adventures of a curious character.* W. W. Norton & Co.

Fisher, Kimball. 1999. *Leading self-directed work teams.* McGraw-Hill.

Florida, Richard, and James Goodnight. 2005. Managing for creativity. *Harvard Business Review*, July, 125–131.

Fowler, Martin. 1999. *Refactoring: Improving the design of existing code.* With contributions by Kent Beck, John Brant, William Opdyke, and Don Roberts. Addison-Wesley Professional.

———. 2006. Using an agile software process with offshore development. Martin Fowler's personal website, July 18. http://martinfowler.com/articles/agileOffshore.html.

Fry, Chris, and Steve Greene. 2007. Large-scale agile transformation in an on-demand world. In *Proceedings of the Agile 2007 Conference*, ed. Jutta Eckstein, Frank Maurer, Rachel Davies, Grigori Melnik, and Gary Pollice, 136–142. IEEE Computer Society.

Gabardini, Juan. 2008. E-mail to Scrum Development mailing list, February 23. http://groups.yahoo.com/group/scrumdevelopment/message/25071.

Gates, Bill. 1995. E-mail to Microsoft executive staff and his direct reports, May 26. Downloaded from the U.S. Department of Justice online case files. http://www.usdoj.gov/atr/cases/exhibits/20.pdf.

George, Boby, and Laurie Williams. 2003. An initial investigation of test-driven development in industry. In *SAC '03: Proceedings of the 2003 ACM symposium on applied computing*, 1135–1139. ACM.

Gilb, Tom. 1988. *Principles of software engineering management*. Addison-Wesley Professional.

———. 2005. *Competitive Engineering: A handbook for systems engineering, requirements engineering, and software engineering using planguage*. Butterworth-Heinemann.

Gladwell, Malcolm. 2002. *The tipping point: How little things can make a big difference*. Back Bay Books.

Glazer, Hillel, Jeff Dalton, David Anderson, Mike Konrad, and Sandy Shrum. 2008. *CMMI or agile: Why not embrace both!* Software Engineering Institute at Carnegie Mellon, November. http://www.sei.cmu.edu/pub/documents/08.reports/08tn003.pdf.

Goldberg, Adele, and Kenneth S. Rubin. 1995. *Succeeding with objects: Decision frameworks for project management*. Addison-Wesley Professional.

Goldstein, Jeffrey. 1994. *The unshackled organization: Facing the challenge of unpredictability through spontaneous reorganization*. Productivity Press.

Gonzales, Victor M., and Gloria Mark. 2004. Constant, constant, multi-tasking craziness: Managing multiple working spheres. In *Proceedings of the CHI 2004 Connect Conference*, 113–120. ACM.

Gratton, Lynda. 2007. *Hot spots: Why some teams, workplaces, and organizations buzz with energy—and others don't*. Berrett-Koehler Publishers.

Gratton, Lynda, Andreas Voigt, and Tamara J. Erickson. 2007. Bridging faultlines in diverse teams. *MIT Sloan Management Review*, Summer, 22–29.

Greene, Steve. 2007. Wall posting on the Facebook page of Adaptive Development Methodology (ADM), October 27. http://www.facebook.com/wall.php?id=4791857957.

———. 2008. Unleashing the fossa: Scaling agile in an ambitious culture. Session presented at Agile Leadership Summit, Orlando. http://www.slideshare.net/sgreene/unleashing-the-fossa-scaling-agile-in-an-ambitious-culture-presentation.

Greene, Steve, and Chris Fry. 2008. Year of living dangerously: How Salesforce.com delivered extraordinary results through a "big bang" enterprise agile revolution. Session presented at Scrum Gathering, Stockholm. http://www.slideshare.net/sgreene/scrum-gathering-2008-stockholm-salesforcecom-presentation.

Griskevicius, V., R. B. Cialdini, and N. J. Goldstein. 2008. Applying (and resisting) peer influence. *MIT Sloan Management Review*, Winter, 84–88.

Grossman, Lev. 2005. How Apple does it. *Time*, October 24, 66–70.

Hackman, J. Richard. 2002. *Leading Teams: Setting the stage for great performances*. Harvard Business School Press.

Hackman, J. Richard, and Diane Coutu. 2009. Why teams don't work. *Harvard Business Review*, May, 98–105.

Hiatt, Jeffrey. 2006. *ADKAR: A model for change in business, government and our community*. Prosci Research.

Highsmith, Jim. 2002. *Agile software development ecosystems*. Addison-Wesley.

———. 2005. Managing change: Three readiness tests. *E-Mail Advisor*, July 14. Cutter Consortium.

———. 2009. *Agile project management: Creating innovative products*. 2nd ed. Addison-Wesley Professional.

Hodgetts, Paul. 2004. Refactoring the development process: Experiences with the incremental adoption of agile practices. In *Proceedings of the Agile Development Conference*, 106–113. IEEE Computer Society.

Hofstede, Geert, and Gert-Jan Hofstede. 2005. *Cultures and organizations: Software of the mind*. 2nd ed. McGraw-Hill.

Hogan, Ben. 2006. Lessons learned from an extremely distributed project. In *Proceedings of the Agile 2006 conference*, ed. Joseph Chao, Mike Cohn, Frank Maurer, Helen Sharp, and James Shore, 321–326. IEEE Computer Society.

Honious, Jeff, and Jonathan Clark. 2006. Something to believe in. In *Proceedings of the Agile 2006 conference*, ed. Joseph Chao, Mike Cohn, Frank Maurer, Helen Sharp, and James Shore, 203–212. IEEE Computer Society.

Hubbard, Douglas W. 2007. *How to measure anything: Finding the value of "intangibles" in business*. Wiley.

Iacovou, Charalambos L., and Robbie Nakatsu. 2008. A risk profile of offshore-outsourced development projects. *Communications of the ACM*, June, 89–94.

James, Michael. 2007. A ScrumMaster's checklist, August 13. Michael James' blog on Danube's website. http://danube.com/blog/michaeljames/a_scrummasters_checklist.

Jeffries, Ron. 2004a. Big visible charts. *XP*, October 20. http://www.xprogramming.com/xpmag/BigVisibleCharts.htm.

———. 2004b. *Extreme programming adventures in C#*. Microsoft Press.

Johnston, Andrew. 2009. The role of the agile architect, June 20. Content from Agile Architect website. http://www.agilearchitect.org/agile/role.htm.

Jones, Do-While. 1990. The breakfast food cooker. http://www.ridgecrest.ca.us/~do_while/toaster.htm.

Kaplan, Robert S., and David P. Norton. 1992. The balanced scorecard: Measures that drive performance. *Harvard Business Review*, January-February, 71–79.

Karten, Naomi. 1994. *Managing expectations*. Dorset House.

Katzenbach, Jon. R. 1997. *Real change leaders: How you can create growth and high performance at your company*. Three Rivers Press.

Katzenbach, Jon R., and Douglas K. Smith. 1993. *The wisdom of teams: Creating the high-performance organization*. Collins Business.

Keith, Clinton. 2006. Agile methodology in game development: Year 3. Session presented at Game Developers Conference, San Jose.

Kelly, James, and Scott Nadler. 2007. Leading from below. *MIT Sloan Management Review*, March 3. http://sloanreview.mit.edu/business-insight/articles/2007/1/4917/leading-from-below.

Kerievsky, Joshua. 2005. Industrial XP: Making XP work in large organizations. *Cutter Consortium Agile Project Management Executive Report* 6 (2).

Koskela, Lasse. 2007. *Test driven: TDD and acceptance TDD for Java developers*. Manning.

Kotter, John P. 1995. Leading change: Why transformation efforts fail. *Harvard Business Review*, March–April, 59–67.

———. 1996. *Leading change*. Harvard Business School Press.

Krebs, William, and Per Kroll, 2008. Using evaluation frameworks for quick reflections. *Agile Journal*, February 9. http://www.agilejournal.com/articles/columns/column-articles/750-using-evaluation-frameworks-for-quick-reflections.

Krug, Steve. 2005. *Don't make me think: A common sense approach to web usability*. 2nd ed. New Riders Press.

LaFasto, Frank M. J., and Carl E. Larson. 2001. *When teams work best: 6,000 team members and leaders tell what it takes to succeed*. Sage Publications, Inc.

Larman, Craig, and Victor R. Basili. 2003. Iterative and incremental development: A brief history. *IEEE Computer*, June, 47–56.

Larman, Craig, and Bas Vodde. 2009. *Scaling lean & agile development: Thinking and organizational tools for large-scale Scrum*. Addison-Wesley Professional.

Larson, Carl E., and Frank M. J. LaFasto. 1989. *Teamwork: What must go right/what can go wrong*. SAGE Publications.

Lawrence, Paul R. 1969. How to deal with resistance to change. *Harvard Business Review*, January–February, 4–11.

Leffingwell, Dean. 2007. *Scaling software agility: Best practices for large enterprises*. Addison-Wesley Professional.

Liker, Jeffrey K. 2003. *The Toyota way*. McGraw-Hill.

Little, Todd. 2005. Context-adaptive agility: Managing complexity and uncertainty. *IEEE Software*, May–June, 28–35.

Luecke, Richard. 2003. *Managing change and transition*. Harvard Business School Press.

MacDonald, John D. 1968. *The girl in the plain brown wrapper*. Fawcett.

Machiavelli, Nicollò. 2005. *The prince*. trans. Peter Bondanella. Oxford University Press.

Mah, Michael. 2008. How agile projects measure up, and what this means to you. *Cutter Consortium Agile Product & Project Management Executive Report* 9 (9).

Mair, Steven. 2002. A balanced scorecard for a small software group. *IEEE Software*, November/December, 21–27.

Mangurian, Glenn, and Keith Lockhart. 2006. Responsibility junkie: Conductor Keith Lockhart on tradition and leadership. *Harvard Business Review*, October.

Mann, Chris, and Frank Maurer. 2005. A case study on the impact of Scrum on overtime and customer satisfaction. In *Proceedings of the Agile Development Conference*, 70–79. IEEE Computer Society.

Manns, Mary Lynn, and Linda Rising. 2004. *Fearless change: Patterns for introducing new ideas*. Addison-Wesley.

Marick, Brian. 2007. *Everyday scripting with Ruby: For teams, testers, and you*. Pragmatic Bookshelf.

Marsh, Stephen, and Stelios Pantazopoulos. 2008. Automated functional testing on the TransCanada Alberta gas accounting replacement project. In *Proceedings of the Agile 2008 Conference*, ed. Grigori Melnik, Philippe Kruchten, and Mary Poppendieck, 239–244. IEEE Computer Society.

Martin, Angela, Robert Biddle, and James Noble. 2004. The XP customer role in practice: Three studies. In *Proceedings of the Agile Development Conference*, 42–54. IEEE Computer Society.

Martin, Robert C. 2008. *Clean code: A handbook of agile software craftsmanship*. Prentice Hall.

McCarthy, Jim. 2004. Twenty-one rules of thumb for shipping great software on time. Posted as part of a David Gristwood blog entry. http://blogs.msdn.com/David_Gristwood/archive/2004/06/24/164849.aspx.

McCarthy, Jim, and Michele McCarthy. 2006. *Dynamics of software development*. Microsoft Press.

McFarland, Keith R. 2008. Should you build strategy like you build software? *MIT Sloan Management Review*, Spring, 69–74.

McKinsey & Company. 2008. Creating organizational transformations: McKinsey global survey results. *McKinsey Quarterly*, August. http://www.mckinseyquarterly.com/Creating_organizational_transformations_McKinsey_Global_Survey_results_2195.

McMichael, Bill, and Marc Lombardi. 2007. ISO 9001 and agile development. In *Proceedings of the Agile 2007 Conference*, ed. Jutta Eckstein, Frank Maurer, Rachel Davies, Grigori Melnik, and Gary Pollice, 262–265. IEEE Computer Society.

Mediratta, Bharat. 2007. The Google way: Give engineers room. As told to Julie Bick. *The New York Times*, October 21. http://www.nytimes.com/2007/10/21/jobs/21pre.html.

Mello, Antonio S., and Martin E. Ruckes. 2006. Team composition. *The Journal of Business* 79 (3): 1019–1039.

Meszaros, Gerard. 2007. *xUnit test patterns: Refactoring test code.* Addison-Wesley.

Miller, Ade. 2008. *Distributed agile development at Microsoft patterns & practices.* Microsoft. Download from the publisher's website. http://www.pnpguidance.net/Post/DistributedAgileDevelopmentMicrosoftPatternsPractices.aspx.

Miller, Lynn. 2005. Case study of customer input for a successful product. In *Proceedings of the Agile Development Conference*, 225–234. IEEE Computer Society.

Mintzberg, Henry. 2009. Rebuilding companies as communities. *Harvard Business Review*, July–August, 140–143.

Moløkken-Østvold, Kjetil, and Magne Jørgensen, 2005. A comparison of software project overruns: Flexible versus sequential development methods. *IEEE Transactions on Software Engineering*, September, 754–766.

Moore, Pete. 2005. *E=mc²: The great ideas that shaped our world.* Friedman.

Moore, Richard, Kelly Reff, James Graham, and Brian Hackerson. 2007. Scrum at a Fortune 500 manufacturing company. In *Proceedings of the Agile 2007 Conference*, ed. Jutta Eckstein, Frank Maurer, Rachel Davies, Grigori Melnik, and Gary Pollice, 175–180. IEEE Computer Society.

Mugridge, Rick, and Ward Cunningham. 2005. *Fit for developing software: Framework for integrated tests.* Prentice Hall.

Nicholson, Nigel. 2003. How to motivate your problem people. *Harvard Business Review*, January, 56–65.

Nickols, Fred. 1997. Don't redesign your company's performance appraisal system, scrap it! *Corporate University Review*, May–June.

Nielsen, Jakob. 2008. Agile development projects and usability. Alertbox, the author's online column, November 17. http://www.useit.com/alertbox/agile-methods.html.

Nonaka, Ikujiro, and Hirotaka Takeuchi. 1995. *The knowledge-creating company: How Japanese companies create the dynamics of innovation.* Oxford University Press.

Ohno, Taiichi. 1982. *Workplace management.* trans. Jon Miller. Gemba Press. Quoted in Poppendieck 2007.

Olson, Edwin E., and Glenda H. Eoyang. 2001. *Facilitating organization change: Lessons from complexity science.* Pfeiffer.

Paulk, Mark. 2001. Extreme programming from a CMM perspective. *IEEE Software*, November, 19–26.

Pichler, Roman. Forthcoming. *Agile product management with Scrum: Creating products that customers love*. Addison-Wesley Professional.

Poppendieck, Mary. 2007. E-mail to Lean Development mailing list, October 6. http://tech.groups.yahoo.com/group/leandevelopment/message/2111.

Poppendieck, Mary, and Tom Poppendieck. 2006. *Implementing lean software development: From concept to cash*. Addison-Wesley Professional.

Porter, Joshua. 2006. The freedom of fast iterations: How Netflix designs a winning web site. *User Interface Engineering*, November 14. http://www.uie.com/articles/fast_iterations/.

Putnam, Doug. Team size can be the key to a successful project. An article in QSM's Process Improvement Series. http://www.qsm.com/process_01.html.

Ramasubbu, Narayan, and Rajesh Krishna Balan. 2007. Globally distributed software development project performance: An empirical analysis. In *Proceedings of the 6th Joint Meeting of the European Software Engineering Conference and the ACM SIGSOFT Symposium on the Foundations of Software Engineering*, 125–134. ACM.

Ramingwong, Sakgasit, and A. S. M. Sajeev. 2007. Offshore outsourcing: The risk of keeping mum. *Communications of the ACM*, August, 101–3.

Rayhan, Syed H., and Nimat Haque. 2008. Incremental adoption of Scrum for successful delivery of an IT project in a remote setup. In *Proceedings of the Agile 2008 Conference*, ed. Grigori Melnik, Philippe Kruchten, and Mary Poppendieck, 351–355. IEEE Computer Society.

Reale, Richard C. 2005. *Making change stick: Twelve principles for transforming organizations*. Positive Impact Associates, Inc.

Rico, David F. 2008. What is the ROI of agile vs. traditional methods? An analysis of extreme programming, test-driven development, pair programming, and Scrum (using real options). A downloadable spreadsheet from David Rico's personal website. http://davidfrico.com/agile-benefits.xls.

Robarts, Jane M. 2008. Practical considerations for distributed agile projects. In *Proceedings of the Agile 2008 Conference*, ed. Grigori Melnik, Philippe Kruchten, and Mary Poppendieck, 327–332. IEEE Computer Society.

Robbins, Stephen P. 2005. *Essentials of organizational behavior*. Prentice Hall.

Rossi, Ernest Lawrence. 2002. The 20-minute ultradian healing response: An interview with Ernest Lawrence Rossi. Posted in the Interviews section of the author's personal website, June 11. http://ernestrossi.com/interviews/ultradia.htm.

Sanchez, Julio Cesar, Laurie Williams, and E. Michael Maximilien. 2007. On the sustained use of a test-driven development practice at IBM. 2007. In *Proceedings of the Agile 2007 Conference*, ed. Jutta Eckstein, Frank Maurer, Rachel Davies, Grigori Melnik, and Gary Pollice, 5–14. IEEE Computer Society.

Schatz, Bob, and Ibrahim Abdelshafi. 2005. Primavera gets agile: A successful transition to agile development. *IEEE Software*, May/June, 36–42.

———. 2006. The agile marathon. In *Proceedings of the Agile 2006 conference*, ed. Joseph Chao, Mike Cohn, Frank Maurer, Helen Sharp, and James Shore, 139–146. IEEE Computer Society.

Schubring, Lori. 2006. Through the looking glass: Our long day's journey into agile. *Agile Development*, Spring, 26–28. http://www.agilealliance.org/agile_magazine.

Schwaber, Ken. 2004. *Agile project management with Scrum*. Microsoft Press.

———. 2006. The canary in the coal mine. Recorded video of session at Agile 2006 Conference, 1 hour, 9 min., 14 sec.; embedded on InfoQ website, November 13. http://www.infoq.com/presentations/agile-quality-canary-coalmine.

———. 2007. *The enterprise and Scrum*. Microsoft Press.

———. 2009. *Scrum guide*, March. Posted as a downloadable PDF resource on the Scrum Alliance website. http://www.scrumalliance.org/resources/598.

Schwaber, Ken, and Mike Beedle. 2001. *Agile software development with Scrum*. Prentice-Hall.

Schwartz, Tony, and Catherine McCarthy. 2007. Manage your energy, not your time. *Harvard Business Review*, October, 63–73.

Seffernick, Thomas R. 2007. Enabling agile in a large organization: Our journey down the yellow brick road. In *Proceedings of the Agile 2007 Conference*, ed. Jutta Eckstein, Frank Maurer, Rachel Davies, Grigori Melnik, and Gary Pollice, 200–206. IEEE Computer Society.

Shaw, D. M. 1960. Size of share in task and motivation in work groups. *Sociometry* 23: 203–208.

Sliger, Michele. 2006. Bridging the gap: Agile projects in the waterfall enterprise. *Better Software*, July/August, 26–31.

Sliger, Michele, and Stacia Broderick. 2008. *The software project manager's bridge to agility*. Addison-Wesley Professional.

Sosa, Manuel E., Steven D. Eppinger, and Craig M. Rowles. 2007. Are your engineers talking to one another when they should? *Harvard Business Review*, January, 133–142.

Spann, David. 2006. Agile manager behaviors: What to look for and develop. *Cutter Consortium Executive Report*, September.

Stangor, Charles. 2004. *Social groups in action and interaction*. Psychology Press.

Steiner, I. D. 1972. *Group process and productivity*. Academic Press Inc.

Striebeck, Mark. 2006. Ssh! We are adding a process…. In *Proceedings of the Agile 2006 conference*, ed. Joseph Chao, Mike Cohn, Frank Maurer, Helen Sharp, and James Shore, 185–193. IEEE Computer Society.

———. 2007. Agile adoption at Google: Potential and challenges of a true bottom-up organization. Session presented at Agile 2007 conference, Washington, DC.

Subramaniam, Venkat, and Andy Hunt. 2006. *Practices of an agile developer: Working in the real world.* Pragmatic Bookshelf.

Summers, Mark. 2008. Insights into an agile adventure with offshore partners. In *Proceedings of the Agile 2008 Conference*, ed. Grigori Melnik, Philippe Kruchten, and Mary Poppendieck, 333–339. IEEE Computer Society.

Sutherland, Jeff, Carsten Ruseng Jakobsen, and Kent Johnson. 2007. Scrum and CMMI level 5: The magic potion for code warriors. In *Proceedings of the Agile 2007 Conference*, ed. Jutta Eckstein, Frank Maurer, Rachel Davies, Grigori Melnik, and Gary Pollice, 272–278. IEEE Computer Society.

Sutherland, Jeff, Guido Schoonheim, Eelco Rustenburg, and Mauritz Rijk. 2008. Fully distributed Scrum: The secret sauce for hyperproductive offshore development teams. In *Proceedings of the Agile 2008 Conference*, ed. Grigori Melnik, Philippe Kruchten, and Mary Poppendieck, 339–344. IEEE Computer Society.

Sutherland, Jeff, Anton Viktorov, and Jack Blount. 2006. Adaptive engineering of large software projects with distributed/outsourced teams. In *Proceedings of the Sixth International Conference on Complex Systems*, ed. Ali Minai, Dan Braha, and Yaneer Bar-Yam. New England Complex Systems Institute.

Sutherland, Jeff, Anton Viktorov, Jack Blount, and Nikolai Puntikov. 2007. Distributed Scrum: Agile project management with outsourced development teams. In *Proceedings of the 40th Annual Hawaii International Conference on System Sciences*, 274a. IEEE Computer Society.

Sy, Desirée. 2007. Adapting usability investigations for agile user-centered design. *Journal of Usability Studies* 2 (3): 112–132.

Tabaka, Jean. 2006. *Collaboration explained: Facilitation skills for software project leaders.* Addison-Wesley Professional.

———. 2007. Twelve ways agile adoptions fail. *Better Software*, November, 7.

Takeuchi, Hirotaka, and Ikujiro Nonaka. 1986. The new new product development game. *Harvard Business Review*, January, 137–146.

Tengshe, Ash, and Scott Noble. 2007. Establishing the agile PMO: Managing variability across projects and portfolios. In *Proceedings of the Agile 2007 Conference*, ed. Jutta Eckstein, Frank Maurer, Rachel Davies, Grigori Melnik, and Gary Pollice, 188–193. IEEE Computer Society.

Thaler, Richard H., and Cass R. Sunstein. 2009. *Nudge: Improving decisions about health, wealth, and happiness.* Updated ed. Penguin.

Therrien, Elaine. 2008. Overcoming the challenges of building a distributed agile organization. In *Proceedings of the Agile 2008 Conference*, ed. Grigori Melnik, Philippe Kruchten, and Mary Poppendieck, 368–372. IEEE Computer Society.

Thomas, Dave. 2005. Agile programming: Design to accommodate change. *IEEE Software*, May/June, 14–16.

Toffler, Alvin. 1970. *Future shock*. Random House.

Tubbs, Stewart L. 2004. *A systems approach to small group interaction*. 8th ed. McGraw-Hill.

Turner, Richard, and Apurva Jain. 2002. Agile meets CMMI: Culture clash or common cause? In *Extreme Programming and Agile Methods: XP/Agile Universe 2002*, ed. D. Wells and L. A. Williams, 153–165. Springer.

Unson, J. F. 2008. E-mail to Scrum Development mailing list, May 26. http://groups.yahoo.com/group/scrumdevelopment/message/29481.

Vax, Michael, and Stephen Michaud. 2008. Distributed agile: Growing a practice together. In *Proceedings of the Agile 2008 Conference*, ed. Grigori Melnik, Philippe Kruchten, and Mary Poppendieck, 310–314. IEEE Computer Society.

Venners, Bill. 2003. Tracer bullets and prototypes: A conversation with Andy Hunt and Dave Thomas, part VIII. *Artima Developer*, April 21. http://www.artima.com/intv/tracer.html.

VersionOne. 2008. The state of agile development: Third annual survey. Posted as a downloadable PDF in the Library of White Papers on the VersionOne website. http://www.versionone.com/pdf/3rdAnnualStateOfAgile_FullDataReport.pdf.

Wake, William C. 2003. *Refactoring workbook*. Addison-Wesley Professional.

Ward, Allen C. 2007. *Lean product and process development*. Lean Enterprise Institute.

Wenger, Etienne, Richard McDermott, and William M. Snyder. 2002. *Cultivating communities of practice*. Harvard Business School Press.

Williams, Laurie, Lucas Layman, and William Krebs. 2004. Extreme programming evaluation framework for object-oriented languages, version 1.4. North Carolina State University Department of Computer Science, TR-2004-18.

Williams, Laurie, Anuja Shukla, and Annie I. Anton. 2004. An initial exploration of the relationship between pair programming and Brooks' law. In *Proceedings of the Agile Development Conference*, 11–20. IEEE Computer Society.

Williams, Wes, and Mike Stout. 2008. Colossal, scattered, and chaotic: Planning with a large distributed team. In *Proceedings of the Agile 2008 Conference*, ed. Grigori Melnik, Philippe Kruchten, and Mary Poppendieck, 356–361. IEEE Computer Society.

Woodward, E. V., R. Bowers, V. Thio, K. Johnson, M. Srihari, and C. J. Bracht. Forthcoming. Agile methods for software practice transformation. *IBM Journal of Research and Development* 54 (2).

Wright, Graham. 2003. Achieving ISO 9001 certification for an XP company. In *Extreme Programming and Agile Methods: XP/Agile Universe 2003*, ed. F. Maurer and D. Wells, 43–50. Springer.

Yegge, Steve. 2006. Good agile, bad agile. *Stevey's Blog Rants*, September 27. http://steve-yegge.blogspot.com/2006/09/good-agile-bad-agile_27.html.

Young, Cynick, and Hiroki Terashima. 2008. How did we adapt agile processes to our distributed development? Overcoming the challenges of building a distributed agile organization. In *Proceedings of the Agile 2008 Conference*, ed. Grigori Melnik, Philippe Kruchten, and Mary Poppendieck, 304–309. IEEE Computer Society.

Index

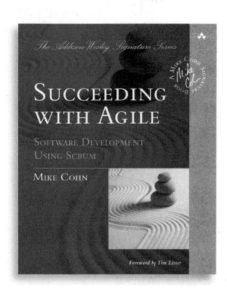

FREE Online Edition

Your purchase of **Succeeding with Agile** includes access to a free online edition for 45 days through the Safari Books Online subscription service. Nearly every Addison-Wesley Professional book is available online through Safari Books Online, along with more than 5,000 other technical books and videos from publishers such as Cisco Press, Exam Cram, IBM Press, O'Reilly, Prentice Hall, Que, and Sams.

SAFARI BOOKS ONLINE allows you to search for a specific answer, cut and paste code, download chapters, and stay current with emerging technologies.

Activate your FREE Online Edition at www.informit.com/safarifree

> **STEP 1:** Enter the coupon code: AVFWXFA.

> **STEP 2:** New Safari users, complete the brief registration form.
> Safari subscribers, just log in.

If you have difficulty registering on Safari or accessing the online edition, please e-mail customer-service@safaribooksonline.com